HOW MUCH
MONEY
CAN I MAKE?

HOW MUCH
MONEY
CAN I MAKE?

**Proven Strategies for Starting,
Managing and Exiting a Canadian
Small Business**

TIM YOUNG

Library and Archives Canada Cataloguing in Publication

Young, Tim, 1957-, author
    How much money can I make? : proven strategies for starting, managing and exiting a Canadian small business / Tim Young.

Issued in print and electronic formats.
ISBN 978-0-9939822-0-0 (paperback).--ISBN 978-0-9939822-1-7 (ebook)

1. Small business--Canada. 2. Small business--Canada--Management.
3. Small business--Purchasing--Canada. 4. Sale of small businesses--Canada.
5. New business enterprises--Canada. I. Title.

HD2346.C2Y59 2015   658.02'2   C2015-902126-X
                                                 C2015-902127-8

Published by Y2 Innovations
Edited by James Osborne and JoAnn Young
Cover by Ares Jun and Y2 Innovations

Disclaimer: The following information is intended as a general reference guide for the start-up, purchase, sale or operation of small businesses. The opinions expressed herein are solely those of the author unless cited otherwise. The author and publisher are not engaged in offering legal, accounting, tax, insurance, or other professional advice in this publication. Readers are cautioned to seek the advice of a professional advisor before implementing any of the suggestions in this book. The strategies mentioned in this book may not apply to all business situations and the author and publisher offer no guarantee or warranty as to the outcome the implementation of any suggestions in this book. All examples, samples, advertisements and forms are intended as illustrations only.
The author, publisher and their agents assume no responsibility for any liability, loss, or risk incurred as a direct or indirect consequence of the use or application of any of the contents of this book.

All inquiries should be directed to:
Y2 Innovations
c/o: www.howmuchmoneycanimake.com
Substantial discounts are offered on bulk orders of *How Much Money Can I Make?* Please request details via our website.

CONTENTS

PART TWO

Before You Start or Buy a Business!

PART THREE

Buying a Going Concern

PART FOUR

Selling Your Baby!

PART FIVE
How to Get in the Top 25% of Your Industry and Stay There!

PART SIX
How Much Money do Small Businesses Actually Make?

DEDICATION

As one matures, the meaning and value of family becomes clearer by the day. I am extremely fortunate to have been raised in a family of love and laughter.

I dedicate this book to my late parents, Mary and Nick Young, and to my sister, Kathy.

Mom and Dad never let me down.
Kathy left me much too soon, and I miss her dearly.

As the youngest in our family, I had the privilege of learning from my siblings Bud, Susan, Kathy, Bill, Bob, and Nicky.

ACKNOWLEDGEMENTS

I T IS DIFFICULT TO imagine a scenario where I could have had better support than that offered by my wife, business partner and best friend, JoAnn. She has worked tirelessly helping me create this collection of words. Her many talents shined through in editing, proofreading, formatting and designing this book from cover to cover. Jo's attention to detail and passion for creating nothing less than professional results was a huge benefit to the entire process. Lastly, Jo provided unwavering and positive support in her typically unselfish way. I cannot thank her enough.

I must also thank my friend and colleague, James Osborne, for the many hours he spent editing my manuscript. Perhaps just as important was Jim's encouragement which started twenty-two years ago when I first conceived the basic premise of this book. Thank you Jim, you're a great mentor!

INTRODUCTION

L EARNING HOW TO SUCCESSFULLY start and manage a small business in Canada has been a process of trial and error for far too long, and for far too many Canadian entrepreneurs. No wonder only half of Canadian start-ups make it past year five. *How Much Money Can I Make?* is a proven guide, filled with practical strategies on how to not only survive, but how to become a leader in your chosen industry.

I have a passion and it's called Small Business! For more than thirty-five years my wife and partner, JoAnn, and I have owned and operated more than twelve vastly different business ventures. Eight of the twelve ventures have been successful. From these experiences, what we have learned about business and ourselves is invaluable. Over this time period, I noticed that small business owners (SBOs) lacked many resources enjoyed by larger organizations. When it's only yourself and a handful of employees, I understand how difficult it can be to work "on" your business, rather than "in" your business.

Don't let the title to this book fool you. There is much more included than just numbers! Yes, you will learn how much money you can realistically earn being self-employed in Canada. However, you will also learn many tried and true management techniques that will help you achieve better than the average results presented.

Having managed very small enterprises, as well as a $19 million Corporation with over 100 employees, I noticed a serious lack of much-needed resources for the SBO. No wonder only half of small businesses make it past year five!

Fundamental business concepts such as Key Performance Indicators, EBITDA multiples and Benchmarking are often a mystery for many small business people. This lack of knowledge is the main reason why I decided to write this book. My goal is two-fold. First, I want to help existing small business owners in becoming more productive, competitive and profitable. Second, I want to assist those considering a new business venture to make the best decisions possible.

Readers will find this publication quite unique in the genre of business books because it is a hybrid between a "how to" book and a "reference manual". Not only will people learn some useful business lessons, but they can also review the profitability of many different business types . . . powerful and highly useful information, indeed!

Who Should Read This Book? If you own a business in Canada and your total revenues are less than about $5,000,000 per year, there is something in these pages of significant value to you.

If you are considering starting or buying a business, you are also part of my target market. After all, isn't it a good idea to get a realistic estimate of how much money you can make (and the effort that takes) before you make such an important decision?

Until now, the SBO, and those thinking of becoming an SBO, have had few "Canadian" resources available to answer such critically important questions as:

- ***How Much Money Can I Make?*** It is surprising how many people start a business without even knowing how much money they can "realistically" expect to earn. Most other business publications deal with much more subjective matter and fail to address the numbers that people should know. This book will answer this question using the most factual data available for national averages, and 100 specific business categories.

- ***How is my Business Doing and What Can I do to Make it More Profitable?*** Using Key Performance Indicator (KPI) metrics can really help SBOs become far more profitable. Believe me, it works! If you could only find it! I believe this book is the first publication ever to offer factual and up-to-date data that will help Canadian SBOs formulate their own KPIs.

- **What is my Business Really Worth?** Having bought and sold many businesses and helped many more do the same, I am amazed at the lack of understanding on this subject. This book will show SBOs what they can expect in return for all their hard work. Many SBOs don't understand how their EBITDA is the critical metric in determining what their business will sell for. In fact many don't even know what EBITDA stands for . . . down-right shocking, I know.

- **What's it Like Owning a Small Business?** Based on over thirty-five years of experience, I will try to point out the highs and lows of being self-employed in Canada. We have laughed and cried. We have been confident and scared. We have been excited and bored. We have been exhilarated and dog-tired. In the end, we can say that being self-employed is . . . well, I guess you'll just have to read on.

Even though I have a Bachelor's Degree in Business Administration, I felt somewhat unprepared for street-smart business competition. So perhaps even well-educated readers will benefit from the real life schooling we received over all these years. Those who might benefit the most are people without a formal business education and those who wish to learn how to succeed from a practical perspective rather than an academic one.

In terms of structure, when I started writing this book I had no intention of including Part One which describes our personal journey in the world of small business. I was so focused on providing facts and proven management methods that it didn't occur to me that there would be value in sharing our wins and losses. Even though describing our losses can be uncomfortable on a personal level, my hope is that you will benefit from learning about the mistakes we made so that you are better able to avoid them.

Part Two describes many of the thought processes that one might undertake before risking time, capital, and relationships on an existing or new business venture. This series of chapters is designed to assist in the decision-making process where the answers to the questions are a function of one's personality and life experiences. There are no wrong or right answers here.

Parts Three and Four offer much more specific information in order to answer questions regarding the "how to" of buying or selling a small business in Canada. Having a better understanding of these two processes can improve one's financial position a great deal.

Part Five describes more "how to" information and focuses on achieving better-than-average results from your venture. If you wish to be a top performer in your particular industry, these chapters should help you do just that.

Last, but certainly not least, is Part Six, the reference section. It provides up-to-date financial data on different types of Canadian small businesses. These numbers can be extremely valuable in providing a basis for SBOs to build key performance metrics and financial goals, a practice used by the most successful small business operators. This process is often referred to as "benchmarking one's business" and it is a key management tool in delivering above-average growth in productivity and profitability.

These 100 examples are certainly not an exhaustive list; however, information is provided on where to find 1,000 more reports so you can directly compare your particular enterprise.

Perhaps you may have noticed by now that I have yet to use the descriptive "entrepreneur". It's not that I have anything against its use or meaning, it's more about a theory I have. I definitely see the similarities between an entrepreneur and a small business owner; however, I suggest there are some noteworthy differences, as well. Chapter 16 covers my theory and I welcome all feedback on this topic. In fact, I welcome feedback on all the topics discussed in this book. You can contact me at *howmuchmoneycanimake.com*.

Earlier I introduced you to my wife and partner, JoAnn. As mentioned, we have worked on many ventures together, and so I often interchange the words "I" and "we". In fact, both words always mean "we". As for using gender descriptive terms, my goal is to be gender neutral.

LIES, DAMNED LIES AND STATISTICS

"LIES, DAMNED LIES, AND STATISTICS" is a phrase popularized by Mark Twain to describe how numbers can be used to prove or disprove a point. Often it comes down to one's interpretation, and sometimes manipulation, of the numbers being discussed.

My premise is that small business in Canada is vitally important to the overall health and growth of our economy. I don't expect there are too many people who would argue with this statement but, in case there are, I offer some lies . . . 'er . . . I mean statistics to support my case.

Before we look at any stats, it is important to first define what small business is. This book deals primarily with small business as defined by total annual revenue. These include those incorporated and unincorporated businesses with revenues between $30,000 and $5,000,000.

Industry Canada, on the other hand, defines business size by the number of employees. They define a small business as one having 1 to 99 paid employees. We will use Industry Canada's definition for now in order to determine how significant small business is to the Canadian economy.

The source of the data below is Industry Canada, Small Business Branch, Key Small Business Statistics, July 2012 and August 2013.

1. **98% of Businesses in Canada are Small Businesses:** As of 2012, there were just over 1.08 million small businesses in Canada. 55.1% of these have only 1 to 4 employees and 87.4% have 1 to 19 employees.

2. **69.7% of the Total Private Sector is Employed by Small Business:** As of 2012, small businesses employed over 7.7 million people.

3. **2.67 Million Canadians Were Self-Employed in 2011:** This represented approximately 15.4% of the workforce. The self-employed workers range from working owners of large, incorporated businesses to part-time service providers.

4. **77.7% of all Private Sector Jobs are Created by Small Businesses:** From 2002 to 2012, over 100,000 jobs were created by small business per year, on average.

5. **Small Business Contributes 30% to Canada's Gross Domestic Product (GDP):** In 2012 this represented approximately $545 billion. Small business accounts for about 41% of the private sector GDP.

6. **Only 51% of Small Businesses Survive Five Years:** Approximately 80% survive one year and 70% survive two years.

7. **In 2012 Approximately 35% of the Self-Employed Were Women:** The share of female self-employment rose steadily from 1976 to 1998, from 26% to 36%, and has remained around 35% since 1999.

8. **The Majority of Small Business Owners Have a College or Trade School Education:** This includes general and vocational colleges.

9. **Small Business Employees Earn About 10.5% Less Than the National Average:** In 2011 these employees earned around $763/week or $39,676/year versus the national average of $852/week or $44,304/year.

Statistics can be interesting; however, unless they are helpful, what's the point? What do you conclude from the stats above? Have you learned anything you didn't know before? I believe I have: it has confirmed my belief that small business is critically important to the Canadian economy, and ultimately our entire population.

Chapter Takeaway

There is no more important segment of the Canadian economy than small business, no matter how it is defined, measured, or contemplated.

PART ONE

8 OUT OF 12 AIN'T BAD . . . OUR LIVES AS SMALL BUSINESS OWNERS

B EFORE I BEGIN THIS section, I should explain a bit about how atypical I am as a small business owner. I don't think you will run into many SBOs who have owned quite as many ventures as we have. It took many years for me to understand why this is.

It started near the end of my third year of university. I led quite a boring life in that I went to classes during the day, worked part-time at the Sears warehouse at night, and studied the rest of the time. In hindsight, I took university way too seriously which may be one reason why I wanted to leave school after my third year.

I think the tipping point was when I took a class in entrepreneurship. This was one of the first classes of its type at our business school. It was started by a professor from the University of Western Ontario who had just moved into town. One of our projects included going out into the business community and interviewing an entrepreneur. How novel, I remember thinking to myself (yes, with tons of sarcasm intended)! I interviewed a local sporting goods store owner who was also an ex-NHL player from the Montreal

Canadians. His name was Bill Hicke and he was quite a colorful character.

I left that interview feeling exhilarated, but when I went to my classes the next day, I felt down. I wanted to quit school and be like Bill. After thinking it through, however, I decided it would be wiser to finish school, considering I had only one more year to go. Yep, get your degree first and then consider your options. In addition, my goal was to climb the corporate ladder like my older brothers. This entrepreneur thing was not only new to me, but risky too!

So why am I telling you all this? I want you to understand why I made so many changes in my business life as an SBO and why such activity may not pertain to you at all! You see, as I look back, there is a pattern that developed which I call my "three-year itch". It seemed that even in the corporate world, I made a major change at least every three years. I was always promoted to a higher management position in a different department, sometimes even a couple of times within that three year period. In the small business world, I often became bored or, more precisely, developed an attitude of "been there done that . . . what's next?"

I also learned something from my accountant at the time, which didn't sink in right away, but it became a significant factor in my future decisions about exiting a small business. For years, I assumed that every SBO knew about the tax benefits of an exit from a profitable business. In fact, I found the opposite was true, and most SBOs haven't even thought about an exit plan! This was shocking to me. In fact, after selling my first business I always looked at new opportunities with an exit plan in mind. We will discuss this much more later on.

Hopefully, the above dissertation will help you better understand that my business path is not a suggested SBO career plan. It's just how it played out for me.

CHAPTER 1

Our Very First Business – Wholesale Toys

"I wanted to punch him right in the face!"

S HORTLY AFTER GRADUATING FROM the University of Regina in 1979 armed with a business degree, I quickly and easily got a great job at Sears Canada. Okay, maybe it wasn't my cleverly crafted resume that landed me this peach of a job . . . it may have helped that my older brother Bob was a senior executive at Sears and that my cousin was in charge of human resources. I still think I nailed that interview, though.

Anyway, I loved it at Sears and, while in their management trainee program, I got wind of a great little part-time business opportunity via an ad in the *The Globe and Mail* newspaper. I think the heading was something like . . . "Bonafide Business Opportunity - Distribute Disney Licensed Toys". There was going to be a company representative from Toronto in our city soon, so I called and set up a meeting.

When I arrived at the Hotel Saskatchewan I was greeted by a well-dressed and distinguished looking man of about 55-60 years. He was graying and looked like he could have been a Grandpa to just about anyone.

He showed me to his well-appointed room where I first saw a complete display of the product rack. It looked fantastic! Okay, I thought, where do I sign? I held off my enthusiasm long enough to calmly peruse the products, ask a few questions, and then I was ready to sign.

I was sure I could make a go of it. I would work at Sears full-time and do this business at nights and on weekends. Of course, I was going to do a little checking around, and seek JoAnn's approval before any money changed hands, but I must say, I was sold!

You see, the concept (nowadays they call it the business model) was to take beautiful medium-sized stuffed animals in the form of the Disney characters (Mickey Mouse, Donald Duck, Tweety Bird, etc.) display them on a gilded spinning rack with great signage, and place them on consignment in high traffic retail outlets, as close to the cash register as possible. In essence, taking a higher priced item and offering it as an impulse purchase.

Each plush toy was about twelve inches tall, well made, very eye-catching, and all had the Disney trade mark prominently displayed on each item as well as on the overhead signage. I thought I could move this product and immediately started thinking of locations like the airport gift shop where "no parent entering the gift shop could possibly leave without buying one of these". At least that is what I would tell the shop owner!

I would say that sometimes the happiest times in owning your own business is when you first start it up (or buy it) and then when you sell it; however, the part in between can be a real challenge! This can be particularly true if you choose an area of business that you don't enjoy. Anyway, I was happy, happy, happy, right then!

That night, I sat down with JoAnn and she said something to the effect of "go for it", and that is precisely what I proceeded to do.

The only problem was that we had no money. It was 1979 and we had only been married a short time. JoAnn was completing the last year of her education degree, we were renting an apartment, we had no debt and we drove an older model car sold to us at a great price by my Dad. We were just starting out and now I have caught this small business bug! Where to get the money? I'm not sure why, but I don't believe I ever considered going to our family or friends for help. I guess I was too proud?

So after some deliberation, we decided to go to the bank and borrow the $8,400 we needed to get started and purchase our opening inventory. I do want to mention this was a great deal of money for us to risk as we had so many things we could have used this money for, like a home, for example. Anyway, even though we had no credit rating we did have one fulltime job and that helped convince the bank manager to take a chance on us.

As part of my research on this Toronto company, I asked our bank manager to check them out, given both parties were using the Royal Bank at the time. The response we received was that they found no issues.

So I wrote a cheque, signed the paperwork, and sent it off to Toronto. I was expecting we would need to wait a couple of weeks to receive our goods. In the mean time, I made a list in priority order of who I was going to sell my products to. I prepared a pitch nobody could refuse and practiced it over and over while we waited and waited for our shipment to arrive. After a few weeks, I started calling the Toronto office. "Not to worry Tim, everything is fine". They explained that the demand had been so huge that it's taking longer to manufacture the product and that those who paid up first were given priority status. We just had to wait our turn. This made sense, so I anxiously waited and waited, and kept calling and calling until finally, after about a month or so we received notice that our shipment was in! Hooray, I said, and I was about as excited as a twenty-one year old could be.

Most of my friends were more interested in sports or climbing the corporate ladder than getting into a business, but I had one friend I could ask to help me. His name was Rod. We went to university together and he was the best man at our wedding. So Rod and I carried the eight huge boxes up three flights of stairs to our warehouse . . . 'er . . . I mean apartment. I told you JoAnn was supportive.

So while JoAnn was studying and attending classes, I worked at Sears during the day and called on retailers at night and on weekends. I was able to place all our racks pretty quickly . . . remember, they just couldn't say no to my sales pitch! The product was selling, the retailers were happy and both of these facts made me very happy, indeed!

It was time to reorder and fill up those shiny gold racks. You likely know from the title of this section that this business endeavor does not end well.

In order to make a long story short, I was never able to receive additional product to sell. All of a sudden the company in Toronto was gone and all the contacts I had ever spoken to were also gone. It was just a con and quite a clever one at that. The company supplied just enough of the product to keep things rolling along and then vanished when they felt the jig might be up. Too bad, both the concept and the product were good, but not good enough for those greedy SOBs at the top of this scam!

I went to work on damage control as fast as I could, trying to recoup as much of our money as possible. The retailer was never in danger as the goods were consigned, but they wanted product I couldn't supply, and they didn't like their racks looking empty. I was able to sell almost all the product we received by consolidating to a few choice locations. Our gross margins were thin at only 30%, which isn't too bad on a wholesale basis with low overhead, but the initial order pricing turned out to be too high to get the planned margin and still have acceptable retail pricing. This was supposed to improve as volumes increased but, of course, that never happened. The company made their money on both the full margin of the goods they charged (assuming they paid their manufacturer) and they made money from all the wholesalers they ripped off since many never received their merchandise.

Well, we lost what for us was an awful lot of money; however, we made every payment due the bank. Our home purchase plans were sunk and it took many years before we ever travelled or bought a new car. I felt absolutely terrible! JoAnn just said we have our health and each other and that was all that mattered. She said to look at it as a learning experience. I guess she was right, but I couldn't shake that sour feeling in my gut . . . a feeling that, unfortunately, would return from time to time over my business career.

I did learn a few important lessons that may benefit readers. First, you can never do too much due diligence when buying a business, or making any kind of investment for that matter. Never shy away from asking the tough questions. I have made this mistake too often over the years.

Second, this experience changed me somewhat from a trusting and possibly naive individual to a more wary and questioning business person. This wouldn't happen again, I vowed!

Lastly, don't rely too much on banks as a source of information for due diligence. Don't get me wrong, I'm not blaming anyone but myself for my predicament, but a person must always think about who works for whom in any business arrangement.

You may be interested in learning how this story re-emerged a few years later. I was reading a local newspaper one day and noticed an advertisement with a uniquely familiar word in its header. The word was "bonafide" and it described a business opportunity! It couldn't be, I thought. Nobody could be brazen enough to try this again? I called the number, and sure enough it sounded like another scam. The only way I could determine if it was the same fraud was to set up another meeting. And so I did.

Now I should mention that I was not the only one in my city who'd been ripped off. I discovered that two fellows who had graduated university with me, even one from the same business program, had also been conned. I recall them contacting me when this thing started to unravel.

They were a bit frustrated in securing locations as they kept running into my business cards when they approached potential retailers. So much for protected territories! Thank goodness I hit the street running or I would have been running into their business cards!

After seeing the advertisement and setting up this meeting, I called these two guys to see if they wanted to join me. It turned out that they were eager to come along.

The three of us met in the lobby of the Hotel Saskatchewan (yes, the same hotel) before going up to see who we would be meeting to sell us a toy distributorship, again!!! Surely, it wouldn't be the same company or the same representative?

I sensed from my two associates that they lost more money than I had; however, they partnered together so perhaps they fared about the same. The three of us were equally angry. However, I recall that we had no plan as to what we would do if it was indeed another scam. I guess we'd deal with that in a moment or two.

We knocked on the door. A few seconds later it was opened by a well dressed and distinguished looking man of about fifty eight to sixty three years of age. Yep, believe it or not, it was the very same guy! I was shocked, to say the least, however we remained calm so we might hear if he was going to try and scam us again all these years later.

It appeared he did not recognize us so we sat down and listened. Sure enough he was selling the same "bone fide" business opportunity! His props and paperwork were sloppily altered, but it was clear what his intentions were, and "I wanted to punch him right in the face!" The three of us challenged him very angrily, yelling at him that we wanted our money back, right then and there. He cowered in fear but denied he ever saw us before and that he didn't know what we were talking about. He threatened that he was going to call the police and we told him to go ahead as we had a complaint to file against him. He put the phone down; we'd called his bluff. He sat there in silence, sweating profusely. As angry and fired up as we were, it soon became apparent that we didn't have the desire to beat up an old man, so we all left a short time later with nothing.

I did call the RCMP fraud division and told them what had transpired at the hotel. They confirmed that they had heard of this scam; however, they were not aware it was back in town. I suggested they could probably catch the perpetrator on route to the airport and they said they would follow-up. I never heard about this scheme again.

CHAPTER 2

Went to a Party – Came Home With a Business

SHORTLY AFTER WE WERE married, I was in training to become a catalogue merchandiser at Sears Canada. Do you remember that big thick Sears catalogue that was delivered to your home? Well I used to buy sporting goods for Western Canada and I loved the job . . . at least I did at first.

A big part of what I loved about this job was the people. They treated me well and they even invited JoAnn and I to a get together one evening after work. We were nervous, but pleased to be included. The get together was at the home of a couple who would later become good friends. We arrived promptly as requested by our hosts, and were met by about four or five other couples who, like us, were curious about why we had gathered together that evening. We were led to believe it was of a business nature, as well as an opportunity to get to know each other better.

It didn't take long for the host to call us to attention and request we grab a comfortable seat. It seems we were about to be an audience for a presentation of some type? "Oh, oh, what is going on?" The presenter was introduced and the show began faster than you could say multi-level-marketing!

In those days, the presenter wouldn't tell you the name of the business opportunity until well into or at the end of the presentation. This really annoyed me, to tell you the truth, so I won't do the same . . . it was Amway!

After a good job of getting people excited about this great business opportunity, we were asked to sign up right then and there! Given that we were looking at a group of more experienced and mature peers, what could we say but, "sure sign us up!" So we left that party owning a multi-level-marketing (MLM) business.

Now don't get me wrong, in case you are sensing a little negativity, I have nothing against MLM. In fact, I was impressed with the presentation and the quality of much of the marketing materials. Remember those cassette tapes you had to buy to help keep you motivated. I have to admit that they were well done.

So, we gave it a go. We bought our start-up package; we used some of the products; we listened to tapes; we practiced our presentation for our own party. Soon it was time to call our own friends and family and stuff them into our basement suite for a show that would surely lead to business success. The rub for us was the part about calling all our friends and family. We just couldn't get past the feeling we got when we picked up that phone. As a result, it was only a few months later that we eased ourselves out of the MLM business with only a few regrets for having tried.

This experience taught me that the most important requirement for success in the MLM business is having a great product which sells on a repeat basis. I have heard people try to suggest that it's not the product in MLM; it's more about how many people you can sign up. Not completely true in my opinion. If the product doesn't sell continuously, the model will eventually fail. It's as simple as that.

Assuming you are selling a good product, the MLM model can be effective for the right kind of people. If you are a confident extrovert who is comfortable making presentations to groups and don't mind calling on your circle of contacts, then by all means take a look. So if you are invited to this kind of "party", I would suggest you accept the invitation . . . you're bound to learn something, especially about yourself.

CHAPTER 3

Let's Flip Some Real Estate

NOW ALMOST EVERYONE HAS at least thought about flipping properties, especially on a part-time basis. In my opinion, it's a great way to invest your time and resources in a relatively low risk manner. This is particularly true if you happen to be a handy person and possess some basic construction knowledge.

While I liked to think I was handy with a hammer and saw, my older brothers would beg to differ. In fact, they might just plain laugh out loud, especially my carpenter brother Bud! In order to compensate for my weakness in this regard, I decided to partner with two guys I was working with at Sears.

First there was Willard, the seasoned veteran who could fix just about anything, and he already owned a few rental properties. Next there was Les who was a little older than I and grew up on a farm . . . think handy and hard-working. Then there was me, young, enthusiastic, and that's about it! I was, however, willing to do almost anything. We all three got along quite well. What a team, we couldn't miss . . . at least that's what "I" thought.

As it turns out, I was right. To make a long story short, we bought two fixer-uppers, renovated them on a tight budget, and flipped them for a tidy profit indeed. I make it sound so easy, don't I? In fact, it wasn't too bad, as I recall. Yes, we had to work all day at the office then again at nights and on weekends, and we had some setbacks. One of these setbacks was when Les got sick and had to leave the partnership early on. Another was when we determined that one of the foundations was much worse than we anticipated and it had to be raised. Thank goodness Willard had the wherewithal, since I had no idea how to tackle that one. All in all, it was a successful venture and after my toy failure, this twenty-two year old needed a win!

I learned two important lessons from this venture. First, I discovered that the value of being handy cannot be overstated, especially for a small part-time operation. If you have to call in a plumber or electrician to do the work, then you will quickly chew up your profits. Thankfully, my partners were knowledgeable in most trades. I was the labourer, and could do a pretty good job of painting and staining, and I always showed up for work.

Second, I learned that you make money in this type of business when you "buy" a property, not when you sell! If you don't get a property at a better than market price when you buy it, your chances of turning a profit (after counting for your labour) are greatly diminished. So be patient when you buy!

CHAPTER 4

A Home-Based Winner – Supreme Secretarial Services

BY 1986 JOANN AND I had been married for seven years and were very much enjoying life and raising our two young boys, Josh and Matt. Jo had graduated with a degree from the University of Regina with a double major in Business Education and Guidance Counseling. Her goal was to teach high school students accounting/bookkeeping, keyboarding, and English composition, as well as do some part-time counselling. She taught for 6 years, but once Matt was born she chose to stay home to focus on raising the boys and managing the household.

One of Jo's biggest attributes is her ability to multi-task and I mean big-time multi-task. Even though Jo was already managing a stellar household, she wanted to do something more to contribute to the financial end of things.

Jo decided that she needed to come up with something flexible that worked within her lifestyle and skill set. So, in 1986, she started Supreme Secretarial Services in Regina, and it grew every year for six years until it was sold.

Jo accepted work at our home during limited times of the day, and completed it during the evenings. The use of a second hand IBM Selectric soon transformed into our very first PC, which cost her about $3,000. A higher end dot matrix printer could produce a quality resume or complete overflow work from business offices throughout the city.

Jo was great at what she did because her attention to detail was second to none, and she was extremely fast at 110 wpm. Soon word spread through referrals; however, things really took off once the new Yellow Pages book hit the street. Jo took a chance and placed a rather large advertisement where competition was quite sparse. This advertisement sure paid off, and the phone began to ring regularly. Jo was able to be quite selective in terms of whom she accepted as new clients.

Early on, Jo developed an 'edge' which improved profit margins quite a bit. Having just spent four years at the University of Regina, we were both familiar with the large foreign student population on campus. And what do most foreign students need help with? Yep, they need help with their English, and more specifically, writing and typing English research papers which were required in almost all non-finance university classes.

So we headed to the Campus once a week to post our flyers which included "Editing" in the header.

Jo's business model began to change from a typing service charging by the page, to a 'word processing and editing service' charging by the hour. Her competition continued to type exactly what they were given, and ended up competing on price alone.

Jo took extra time reading, correcting, moving paragraphs, spell checking, grammar checks, etc. She also offered other value-added items including fine paper, colored paper, report covers, storage discs, and graphics. These types of value-added products and services, along with her professional nature, were also welcomed by business customers who couldn't afford a full-time administrative person.

Now can you imagine the kind of multitasking prowess it takes to successfully manage a household of two very active young boys along with a thriving business? And don't you even think for a second that our home wasn't well kept or that the boys ate their meals at McDonald's . . . no way! There were always fresh, healthy meals and you could eat them off the floor.

I even recall Jo hand-sewing Halloween costumes for the boys . . . can you imagine?? Oh, and another thing, she had to prepare each week to sing and play her guitar at our church! Boy, do I know how to pick 'em.

Yes, Jo was a great success and her business was booming. It was at just about this time that the Young family decided to make a significant lifestyle change and move the family out West.

Now we had to think about what to do with the business? Supreme was humming along. It would be a shame to shut it down.

Our plan was that we would put the house and business up for sale at the same time. If the business didn't sell by the time we were ready to leave, we would deal with it at that time. I was, however, confident I could sell it.

Keep in mind this is one of the most difficult types of small businesses to sell as it could be argued that the proprietor, Jo, 'is' the business. Yes, she had some part-time help, but everything went through her before a client received it. Also, I had never before sold a business and there were no business brokers around and, even if there were, this deal was likely too small.

At this time I had no clue how to value a business. Depreciated asset values, earnings multiples, and the like were not something I had ever dealt with before.

I prepared a package which included standard financial statements and a list of the hard assets. I also listed every cost we had incurred to get Supreme to where it was. Potential buyers would then be able to compare what it would cost to start their own, versus what we were asking.

Then there were the soft assets or 'goodwill', and Jo had two great ones! First, there was her customer list which she never even had to market to because customers just kept returning on their own.

Second, and perhaps just as important, was the fact that the Yellow Pages deadline had just passed and a new competitor would have to wait an entire year for the next book to hit the streets. Jo was paying for the largest advertisement because in those days the Yellow Pages were the best and most cost-effective way for small businesses to advertise. The telephone number tied to that advertisement was quite valuable, indeed.

I don't recall how long it took, but Supreme Secretarial Services was sold before we left Regina. I believe Jo got about $10,000 which was approximately three times her cost of start-up.

There is a point I would like to make that could benefit readers who might operate a small business out of their home, where they individually "are" the business. If you make a change or move locations, don't automatically assume you must just shut the business down and get nothing for it.

If you have positive cash flow (revenues greater than all expenses) in your single-person business, you still may have something to sell even though you personally are leaving. If you can't sell the business as a going concern (a fully operational business) perhaps you can sell the pieces.

Start with the hard assets which are easiest to price. Intangible things such as telephone numbers, domain names, logos, trademarks, catchy or well-known business names, pre-paid advertising campaigns, etc. all have varying degrees of value and can be sold. For example, I have seen pizza businesses buy a competitor's telephone number just before it closes, in an attempt to capture more customers.

You may be surprised by what is being sold on sites like Kijiji and Craigslist.

The key to selling a single-person going-concern is to find someone just like yourself who has similar skills and personality to continue to take care of your client list. In Jo's case we found a capable young mother, just like Jo, who wanted to work from home while taking care of her children.

This person could have started her own service, but she realized the cost to do so wasn't too far off what we were asking. Further, it was worth it for her to pay a little extra given the existing customer base (instant cash flow) and the instant Yellow Pages exposure. Yes, it can be done.

CHAPTER 5

Number Five is a Big One - Advertising and Publishing

T HIS SECTION DEALS WITH a part of my business life that is a little more complex than other areas. I have tried to get to the key points as quickly as possible which pertain to those who may be looking for an ownership opportunity from **within** their current employment situation. Don't we all want a piece of the action?

It was about 1981 when Sears Canada initiated a plan to centralize all merchandising departments to the head office in Toronto. This could greatly affect my future with the company as only a few merchandisers would be selected to go to the big city. The opportunities left for those not chosen would be in question, to say the least.

It was a Friday when I was called in to discuss my future, and I didn't know what to expect. More interestingly, I didn't know what I wanted to happen. I guess from an ego standpoint, I wanted to be selected, but did we really want to move to Toronto? Well, I guess I must have done something right because they offered me a pretty good job in Toronto with a pay increase, travel expenses, and housing differential assistance. The average house in the Mississauga area was $100,000 more than or almost double the value of our home in Regina at the time.

JoAnn and I had the weekend to make a decision. We decided with all due respect . . . no thanks! Shortly thereafter, I was transferred to the Sears retail division . . . which was quite a downer for me. I learned quickly that if you turn down a big company promotion, your upward career path can be easily derailed. So be it, I thought, and immediately started to search for a new job.

Soon thereafter, I was able to find an administrative position with the provincial telecommunications company, SaskTel. I was excited to land a job with another large organization; however, there were two problems. One, it was a union position, and all I ever wanted to be was a Manager! Two, it was in the "Directory Division". What the heck is that? This is a telecommunications company . . . I want to help market telecommunication services!

Oh well, the pay was good and I wouldn't tell any of my management friends that I had to join the union. As for the "Directory" division, I quickly found out it was the armpit of the "telecommunications" industry. We weren't even located in the head office building. Oh dear me what will I tell my older siblings? Even though all telephone customers "needed" a telephone book, it was looked down upon by the rest of the organization, especially all those pinkie-ring wearing engineer types.

There were three levels of management in this division, and there I was, not even at the lowest level, yet! The good news was that this position reported directly to the General Manager . . . thank goodness! The other good news was that the people were great to work with and the division was able to operate autonomously (think . . . faster decision making and less head office or political interference).

I have never worked for a boss I didn't like or couldn't get along with, and this was no exception. Gerry (the General Manager) was a lot older than I, and nearing retirement. However, he had something he wanted to do (prove) and I was just the guy to help him do it. Perhaps he will help me get into management, I thought to myself?

Our mandate was to turn this unprofitable division of about 125 employees (that nobody cared about) into an efficient money-making machine! Okay, where do we start?

I suggested to my new boss that we needed a marketing department. We had a sales group and a production group, but no marketing . . . shocking, I know! So Gerry agreed, and I became the Marketing "Manager". Hooray!

I am trying to keep in mind that this book is about you as a potential or existing SBO, and not about me. My point in sharing this part of my business career is to alert you to the fact that many a good opportunity to start a business venture can come from within the organization where you are employed. The key is to keep your eyes and ears open!

We soon stopped referring to our division as Directory and started calling ourselves the "Yellow Pages People". We were not in the publishing business, we were in the advertising business!! Our real competitors were radio, television, and newspapers, not other directories.

During this transformation, I noticed that something interesting was going on. We had no accounting department, so it fell upon my small group of two; remember I am now a Manager, and I have my own staff to keep track of all the numbers. We were marketers not accountants, but we had to track sales revenue to see if and where we were growing.

I started to get calls from much larger privately owned Yellow Pages companies in Toronto and Vancouver. They were so nice and sweet. They wanted me to give them our numbers. But why, I thought? As part of a national Yellow Pages Trade Mark agreement, each Yellow Pages company had the right to use and market this brand within their territories; thus, we were not competing with each other. Sharing the numbers was, therefore, no big deal, however

I couldn't help but wonder why all the interest in little old us? More on why these big guys were calling, a little later.

We slowly but surely transformed our little division into a dynamic group of individuals with some impressive operating results. I believe these results went a long way in helping me secure my next promotion (this would be management level two in case you are keeping track).

This promotion required that I leave the directory division and go to "Head Office" to manage a group of engineers. Why me, I exclaimed? What do I know about engineering? I'm a marketer of things, not a builder of things! My new boss explained that he wanted my private sector kind of thinking to spread into the mainstream of SaskTel and that I was to do what I did with the directory division. Mmmm, I thought. I was not too sure about this move but I've always had the notion that a good manager can manage just about anything. I was about to test this theory.

Things went pretty well as I explained my management style to my rather large group of first-line managers and their staffs. I told them that my job was to do my best to remove any barriers they had to attaining company goals. I didn't need to be an engineer to do that I explained, and they seemed receptive to their newfound autonomy and support that I offered.

I was only in my new job a matter of months when I received a call from my new boss's boss to meet with him. This fellow was the new Vice President of Marketing. I had never before spoken to him one on one, so I was quite curious about what he wanted to speak to me about?

I had visited the executive suite at SaskTel's Head Office on occasion. They had a grand water fountain in the waiting area, their own bathrooms, and their own kitchen, all surrounding a huge circular Board Room with high back leather chairs. Yes, that is why I spent four boring years in university . . . the executive suite was what I wanted! Or so I thought.

It turns out that my old directory division was becoming quite a thorn in this executive's side as telephone books were being printed with either errors or missing entire sections of the Yellow Pages. Please understand the severity of this situation. If you, as a publisher, print an advertisement with an error, especially if it involves the telephone number or address of the business, it will have huge negative implications for the small business owner who's counting on that advertisement to direct business to his or her establishment. Telephone books are printed by the thousands, only once per year! If an ad is incorrect or missed, it can have devastating financial implications for the small business owner.

This new VP was clearly feeling the heat from many SBOs demanding restitution for all the errors his directory division was creating. He wanted me to leave my new head office job, where I had been for only a few months, and go back to the directory division and fix things. In return, he would appoint me as General Manager (management level three . . . cool) with a promise that he would get me back to head office ASAP, if I succeeded, that is.

Since head office was "the" place to be if you wanted to move up the management ranks (which is what I wanted at the time), I accepted the promotion and moved back to a now very, very troubled directory division.

Because I knew the business pretty well and, more importantly, the people, we were able to correct the systems that were causing all the problems. Don't get me wrong, it wasn't a quick or easy fix but we made it happen and I was enjoying my new role as General Manager. We were quite autonomous and my new boss didn't want to hear from me unless it was good news. So we made our own decisions and acted like we "owned" this business. I had great people and together we turned that ship around!

Now it was around this time that there was renewed discussion about where and how this little directory division fit into the telecommunications business. Did it really need to be part of the publicly owned telephone company? Certainly not, in my opinion, but to be taken over by a private Yellow Pages company from outside the province didn't sit well with me either.

I was told my career was safe and that if there was a privatization of this division that I would be welcome back at head office. But what about the employees, I thought? A new private company would surely replace many of the current staff with their own. That's just the way it goes in business. However, what if someone organized the current staff and management and put in their own bid to buy this thing called Yellow Pages.

I must say that I loved my role as General Manager of this division. I was able to operate with almost complete autonomy and thoughts of returning to head office and climbing that corporate ladder were beginning to diminish. Life was good. The only thing missing was to own a piece of the action, and I knew better than anyone how much action there was!

We had the knowledge; we had the people; an opportunity was forming; we just needed some money!

While I was searching for a suitable partner with sufficient financial support, I spread the word to my management and staff that a potential opportunity was unfolding. These were just regular folks who came to work largely for the security, and now I was going to ask them to put that security at risk, and throw in some of their own money to boot!

As a person who paid money for this book, I assume you have an interest in getting involved in some sort of business venture where you "own" all or at least part of that venture? I strongly suggest that if you do aspire to owning a piece of the action, make it known to your employer. You may be surprised to learn that such an opportunity exists more often than you think.

I approached a few local business owners who I thought may have some synergies with our advertising and publishing opportunity. Okay, I lie; I was primarily looking for the money; synergies were quite secondary. I had no luck on the first couple of tries, but then I received a tip from a contact suggesting I meet with a successful gentleman in the printing business. Interesting, I thought. At least there was some synergy in that our company bought a lot of printing . . . almost a million telephone books every year, in fact!

Shortly thereafter I am sitting in the office of Keith Critchley, the owner of Brigden's Printing & Publishing. I made my pitch to Keith and was pleasantly surprised at how intently he listened. He could have taken the approach that I was just a young whippersnapper (I was twenty-eight at the time), and he was the one who had all the experience, not to mention the money. It should have been me doing the listening. He did not take that approach, and that may have been part of the reason why this meeting was just one of many more such meetings to come.

I could write an entire book on what transpired over the next few months and years, but my purpose is to advise employees and business owners that collaboration under strong leadership can and does result in highly successful enterprises. In fact, over the next three years, the following results were attained:

- Succeeded over three competing bids for the right to sell advertising and publish Saskatchewan's telephone books;

- Formed a new Corporation called DirectWest Publishers Ltd. with 46% of the shares owned by the employees, 44% owned by Brigden's, and 10% retained by SaskTel;

- Formed a LSVCC (Labour Sponsored Venture Capital Corporation) which was the largest of its kind in the province's history at that time, with two seats on the Board of Directors of DirectWest;

- Oversubscribed the amount of shares sold to employees by 10%;

- All but a few employees decided to risk it and leave the employment of SaskTel to join DirectWest (no jobs were lost);

- Almost doubled revenues to approximately $19 million in the first three years of operation;

- Returned more profit to SaskTel than had ever been achieved while it was a division of the Telco;

- Attained better than average Key Business Indicator Results as compared to peer organizations across the country;

- Significant appreciation in the value of the shares. This would prove to be one of my two best investments.

A lot can be achieved when people come together with the common goal of becoming independent and empowered to be the best they can be. Keep your eyes and ears open for the opportunity, and if it isn't offered, ask for it anyway!

It was 1989 and our still new Yellow Pages company, DirectWest, was running like a well-oiled machine. I was the Vice President and General Manager (now referred to as the Chief Executive Officer) and Keith Critchley was President and Chairman of our Board. Keith and I got along very well.

I was very proud of my management team and the results achieved by the employees who trusted in my leadership enough to risk their livelihoods and follow a dream.

Yes, life was good once again. I worked long hours; however, I was fairly compensated with a competitive executive salary plus annual performance bonuses. My family was covered by a comprehensive benefits package and I enjoyed modest, yet pleasant, executive perks. I drove a very comfortable company car. I had a beautiful new corner office with matching desk, book shelves, conference table, couch and comfortable seating. I had original artwork on the wall (well maybe only one piece, but it was quite impressive). I travelled regularly to attend meetings and conferences in many of the major cities in Canada and the United States. I even had a personal secretary who insisted on bringing me fresh coffee every morning. Who could ask for anything more? Yet, I felt that something was still missing.

I was once again feeling that three-year itch where I was destined to make a move of some sort. I was fortunate to have been a minority shareholder in DirectWest; however, I kept wondering what it would be like to start something new where I owned 100%, perhaps in a new market as well . . . hey, JoAnn, what do you think of moving to Kelowna, BC?

CHAPTER 6

Our First Franchise, and in a New Market Too!

W E ARRIVED IN KELOWNA on April 22, 1992. Family and friends were curious as to why we chose to make a move to Kelowna. In fact, many wondered why we chose to leave Saskatchewan at all.

The way Jo and I looked at it was that if we were ever going to make a move, it was now or never. Our reasoning was that our two young boys, Matt aged 7 and Josh 10, were at a perfect age for a move and that the longer we waited, the more entrenched they would become, and the more difficult it would be to move in the future. Secondly, the winter weather in Saskatchewan sucked big-time! The people are definitely warm and friendly, but the winters were becoming unbearable for both of us.

When we began our search our three main criteria were:

1. It had to have significantly better weather conditions, meaning the location could be almost anywhere else;

2. It had to be in a growing economy;

3. It had to be family-friendly.

My statistical research into the area showed that A and B were both satisfied. We had to then do some travelling in order to satisfy the last criteria. Jo had never been to Kelowna, but I had made a brief visit many years prior. Our plan was to visit the Okanagan during the worst weather in Saskatchewan.

We arrived in Kelowna on New Year's Day 1992 dressed in our puffy, down-filled parkas and high-top boots. Talk about feeling out of place. At the restaurant we left our toques, mitts, and parkas in the car, but still felt uncomfortable wearing our boots, as there was no snow on the ground. Imagine that! No snow in January yet the mountains were only minutes away packed with sufficient snow to please all types of skiers. Now that was cool!

We spent a few days driving the area to see what the boys thought and quickly fell in love with everything. One more house hunting trip and we were on our way. So what are we going to do for a living you might be thinking? That is a good question, and one we had been asked many times. Honestly, we had no answer. Looking back, I'm surprised my in-laws didn't question where I was taking their daughter and grandchildren. I was the youngest in my family so I guess my parents were about done worrying about such things. At any rate, having no plan is so unlike me, so I guess we looked at it as an adventure of sorts.

After a few months of getting settled in, it was time to get to work and pay some bills. I don't believe I had any intention of working for someone else at this time. If I had, Kelowna was not a market comprised of big business with corporate ladders to climb. It was a place you go to enjoy the lifestyle and hopefully start a new business.

It was once suggested to me that a network was a very important asset for an SBO, and not an easy one to build. I didn't quite understand the importance of a network until we moved away from the one I was starting to build in Regina. Networking can be an important edge for SBOs, so I have dedicated an entire chapter to the topic. Please don't skip it.

We had finally settled in Kelowna and we knew absolutely no one! Without a network of business contacts to tap for leads on potential business opportunities, we were left to our own devices as our search unfolded. We felt that since we lacked connections and didn't know the market very well, perhaps we could reduce our risk a little if we tried something already proven.

I began researching franchises that I thought would grow in a market comprised mainly of small businesses with an entrepreneurial spirit. The success rate of franchises is much higher than that of independents (or so I thought at the time), so we would go the franchise route in order to reduce our risk.

I finally discovered a possible opportunity that seemed to fit nicely with the new market we now called home. It was a small and growing franchise out of the US, slowing moving across Canada, east to west. It was a small Business Service Center called Mail Boxes Etc. (MBE). The concept was indeed new, which was appealing to me, and it fit our skill sets, particularly that of JoAnn.

It catered to small businesses in need of office support of all types, including photocopies, faxing, printing, mailing services, shipping, word processing, and desk-top publishing. In addition, and what made it unique, was that one of the services offered was the rental of mail boxes. This service was primarily for small operators who worked from home and required a business mailing address. We offered suite numbers which certainly sounded a lot more professional than P.O. boxes. We also provided shipping and receiving services through a number of private carriers, in addition to Canada Post.

I quickly calculated how many mail boxes would have to be rented in order to pay the lease on a typical 1,000 square foot store. It was about 170 boxes. Renting more than this would go to the bottom line, I concluded. This sounded like a promising business model, so I dug a little deeper.

Franchisors are usually very accommodating in offering basic information to potential franchisees, but always remember they are in the business of "selling franchises", and some may not be too concerned about your long-term success. Be careful of franchises with few or nebulous criteria for franchisee selection. If they are only interested in whether you have the money to buy a franchise and not about your ability to profitably run one, then I would suggest you take a pass.

I missed this warning flag when we purchased this franchise and wished I hadn't. You see, a strong franchise network is only as good as the ability of the franchisees to profitably implement the operating systems set up by the franchisor. If weak (but cashed up) players are welcomed, that does not bode well for the success of the entire organization. Strong franchises don't take just anybody, no matter how much cash they may have. McDonald's and Dairy Queen are just two examples where you will have to prove yourself as a successful manager before they consider you as a franchisee.

The closest MBE franchise was in Vancouver, so I went for a visit. I did call a few franchise owners and talked to them on the phone, but I strongly recommend that your research include at least a few in-person discussions with existing franchisees. I did this, but the franchisees were so new that it was difficult to get the numbers needed for a proper evaluation. Also, I recommend you contact franchisees that are not on a list given to you by the franchisor. The ones you find may include radicals and complainers, which every franchise company has, but some thoughtful questioning should separate the facts from the fiction.

I did notice some weaknesses in this franchise, but I was confident in our abilities to overcome them through some hard work and ingenuity. Also, the franchise was still in its infancy and, thus, the cost of entry was more reasonable than more established brands. In hindsight, underestimating these weaknesses resulted in us having to work much harder than I anticipated, and it took longer to create positive cash flow.

At that time, these weaknesses included poor franchisor support in Western Canada, acceptance of some franchisees who lacked management experience, and lack of brand name development as it was difficult, costly, and time consuming to educate our target market about this new business model. For the longest time, people thought we were simply a post office.

We opened our new Mail Boxes Etc. franchise in Kelowna in 1992. We were basically on our own, with the closest other franchise and the regional office four hours west. The first year was very slow, with Jo and I sharing the hours six days per week. Thankfully, there wasn't much we couldn't do, especially JoAnn, who as a high school teacher back home, specialized in many of the services offered in our store. She also taught accounting, so the bookkeeping was done internally . . . in the evening, of course. What a great partner she was, to be sure!

Our mistake early on was waiting for the customers to come to us instead of going out after them. I thought our location was decent enough to give us sufficient exposure, but that wasn't the case. The real hurdle was educating our target market about who we were and what we did! As with many new franchises, regional and certainly national advertising was non-existent! The royalty payment apportioned to such advertising would take years to build, as I later learned. We had to do something, we had to do it soon, and we had to do it ourselves!

You hear many a business guru or academic say that to be successful in business you must provide superior customer service, you must offer competitive pricing and blah, blah, blah! Well I have some news for those of you thinking of starting a business and listening to such experts. Yes, you do have to provide these things, but a whole lot more, as well! Great customer service and good prices are expected, but in and of themselves are not enough to succeed long-term. You must be innovative and, if possible, find an "edge" you can capitalize on to help propel yourself into profitability.

Our edge at Mail Boxes originated in our shipping and packaging profit center. We boasted in our literature that we could ship and package just about anything to just about anywhere in the world, so I got to thinking . . . "what about wine?" The Okanagan was starting to increase the number of acres devoted to growing grapes for local wine production. Wine makers were looking for new markets, Kelowna was the center of tourism for the area, and we were in the center of Kelowna. Putting all these factors together smelled of opportunity, so I put a plan together to present to a few local wineries.

During my pitch, I asked the winery owners why they didn't sell their wine by the case rather than by the bottle. Unsurprisingly they scoffed at me and said if they could do that they would be richer than they were. I suggested that the reason tourists often only buy one bottle is because they are travelling (usually on to Vancouver or back to Calgary), and they have no room for more than a bottle or two. What if they had a way to buy a whole case of their favorites, and have it packed and shipped safely to their home so it was there when they returned from their trip? Yep, I had their attention.

Then I pulled out my laminated pricing sheet which had the prices the wineries would charge per case to anywhere in Canada! They were impressed. All their sales staff had to do was add this amount to the price of the wine and the customer would be amazed at the great customer service. It was a go and I started with two wineries.

We even went so far as to pick up the cases each day from each winery. Everybody was happy! The winery sold more wine and increased their service level, the customers were enamored with the convenience, and we were pleased with the margin we made on both the packaging and the shipping.

This edge helped us immensely. During our first Christmas season there were days when the cases were stacked almost to the ceiling . . . people were sending Okanagan wine as gifts to family and friends all across the country. I'm not sure who raised this issue, but someone (likely from the winery) asked . . . what happens if the wine freezes while en route? I determined that most wine freezes at about -6 degrees Celsius. Uh, oh, I thought to myself . . . it sure gets a lot colder than that going over the mountain passes, and what about crossing the Prairies in December?

I was determined to keep the program going, so I told the wineries that I would personally guarantee all shipments against loss or breakage for up to $100, which I figured was about what it cost to produce a dozen bottles of average wine. I knew the carriers would not cover such losses, but I calculated it was worth the risk . . . after all, how many cases would actually freeze? To tell you the truth, I really had no idea. The wineries agreed and we moved forward, although I must admit I was quite anxious for about three weeks, especially over the Christmas holidays.

It turned out we lost only two cases and I quickly replaced them. Thankfully, these two cases were not gifts, and the customers were not upset by the delay.

This edge pushed us into positive cash flow territory, and soon we were in the top 10% of approximately 180 Canadian stores in terms of operating results. Not surprisingly, we excelled in the packing & shipping profit center category and other franchisees called to see how we accomplished this. We had no problem sharing our "edge", and we recommend to all those considering a business venture to develop their own edge as soon as humanly possible. Great customer service and good prices are often not enough to be successful in the real business world.

We are going to discuss more about the pros and cons of buying a franchise versus going independent in Chapter 26, but if you do choose to take this route I should mention a few more things we learned from owning this particular franchise:

1. ***Open with a Bang:*** We were advised by the franchisor to do a great big Grand Opening with a ton of advertising. Due to cost concerns I didn't listen, and this turned out to be a mistake. As a result, it took much longer for people to understand what we offered and where we were. This is especially true for franchises new to a market.

2. ***Participate in all Promotions:*** As a franchisee you pay for marketing support from head office. Some of that support will be good and some not so good, but I recommend trying them all as one good promotion can make all the difference. For example, at first I couldn't wrap my head around selling one cent photocopies for an entire month, but it worked big time!

3. ***Network, Network, Network!*** This type of franchise (business to business) responded very nicely to all our networking initiatives. There will be more on this to come.

4. ***Collaborate with Fellow Franchisees:*** Always keep in touch with your fellow franchisees, especially the high performers. Find out why they are doing well, and do the same. I suggest you should be talking to your peers weekly. You should also attend formal franchise meetings. These gatherings will not only help motivate you, but you may pick up an idea or two that can improve your bottom line when you return home.

5. ***Can be Similar to "Buying a Job":*** Given we owned this business for only three years, it showed little return on investment after we paid ourselves market salaries. Our return came when we sold.

By our third year, things were clicking along pretty well. Our staff was well-trained. We were beating up on our competition. All of our key business indicators were improving and in line with, or better than, our peers across the country. We also won a few national sales awards in a few product/service categories.

Unfortunately, my interest in retail was starting to wane. I was becoming pretty cranky with customers at times to the point where JoAnn had to call me aside for some "tough love"! It was evident I wasn't enjoying myself and I was feeling that three-year itch once again. It was time to move on, and so we decided to sell.

This would be our second attempt at selling a business. I cover much more on this topic in Part Four; however, I will mention a few points that pertain to this particular type of business.

I really didn't know how to go about this process, and since the internet was just starting to develop, I couldn't Google the topic. Back then, it seemed SBOs used realtors to market their enterprises, but I just couldn't see how a realtor could do a better job than I could do on my own. After all, who knew my business better than me? Also, confidentiality was important to me. I didn't want all my financial information getting into the hands of my competitors.

As for setting an asking price, the process was quite unsophisticated as I had no experience in valuing a business such as this. I determined the price based on the current cost to set up a new franchise, plus a premium for the goodwill we had created. I was not familiar with EBITDA (Earnings Before Interest, Taxes, Depreciation, and Amortization) multiples at the time.

You may be wondering if I asked my accountant to do a valuation, and the answer is no. I'm not exactly sure why I didn't, other than I do recall from my experience at DirectWest that such a process can be extremely costly. Since I was selling assets and not shares, it seemed appropriate to do it myself.

I learned from our customers at MailBoxes that Kelowna was becoming a sought-after destination for people looking for a lifestyle change. The problem for many was that Kelowna lacked high paying jobs and if you wanted the opportunity to earn a good living, you had to create it or buy it. This was positive for us because we had something good to sell. But how would we come in contact with these potential buyers?

After doing some research I decided to go with "blind" advertisements in national newspapers. Blind means the business name was not disclosed in the advertisement. I chose the business opportunities section of *The Globe and Mail* and an ad in *The Western Investor.* On-line advertising is the primary way to go nowadays, and I will discuss that later.

You may think selling a business is a lot like selling real estate. Perhaps that is why some SBOs use realtors, but this is not the case at all. It is a far more complex process. A business is a living, breathing "going concern" with many, many variables. In real estate it is relatively easy to compare properties whereas few business entities share the same attributes and risks.

It turned out that my plan to advertise in a national newspaper was successful, and we were able to sell our first franchise to Mark and Deb, a great couple who recently celebrated their twenty year anniversary.

You may find it interesting that in 2001 United Parcel Service of North America, Inc. acquired Mail Boxes Etc. The MBE franchise was eventually re-branded, and is now called The UPS Store.

CHAPTER 7

How About a Lakefront Property Reno – Cool!

OKAY, HERE WE ARE again, unemployed and no idea what we are going to do next. We took a little time off and travelled to Disneyland for our first holiday in three years. We also went to visit my sister's family in Dallas, Texas, all the while keeping an eye out for our next venture.

I researched businesses for sale; however, nothing was meeting our purchase criteria at the time. We were convinced that the Okanagan, and Kelowna in particular, would continue to be a sought-after destination for baby boomers across Canada. We always liked real estate as an investment, so we thought why not give it a go . . . what could we lose?

We found a property not far from our home and it was right on the shores of Lake Okanagan. It included 91 feet of pristine and private shoreline, and the lot was about half an acre in size. The home was twenty-nine years old and in need of some serious updating, but the "bones" were in pretty good shape.

There was one thing that made this property particularly interesting. You see, the home was located a little high up from the beach. In fact, it was exactly 77 stairs up from the beach. I remember how many stairs because it was a big job to repair and paint each and every step! There were so many stairs that the previous owners had installed an elevator system from the home to the beach. It had steel rails with a passenger car pulled by an electric winch.

The view from this home was breathtaking, or at least we thought it would be after we removed those sixty foot pine trees! What a job that was, and nobody got injured . . . amazing.

I did up a rough one page budget on what we thought it would cost to gut the interior and spruce up the exterior. Our manpower component included JoAnn, myself, and our two young boys, Josh who was thirteen and Matt who was ten, and reluctantly, our dog, Storm.

After months of working six days per week, things were starting to take shape and we could see the end in sight. What wasn't taking shape was the real estate market in general. I will take responsibility for not keeping an eye on the market and having a plan in place for a possible price decline.

I wrongly assumed that demand would continue to increase; after all, they weren't making any more waterfront properties! What I didn't realize was that when real estate markets correct, it often hits the highest priced properties the hardest, regardless of where they are located, even those on the water. The correction for standard homes over this time period was about 1% while water-front residences dropped 24% . . . ouch! Our target profit margin was 15% to 20% which obviously vanished as the market corrected.

We ended up selling the property after about three months or so on the market and, after all costs were included, we about broke even. We were able to pay the boys a pittance, but not ourselves. You may be wondering why we just didn't sell the lower priced home we were in and move into the water-front house. After all, the gain we would have made would have been tax free. I guess the answer is that we mixed personal feelings (we loved our current home) with business.

Renting the property wasn't really an option since we were pretty stretched financially, and mortgage rates at the time were about 9.25% on a principle residence, and much higher for an income property. We couldn't judge how far down prices might go, and for how long, so we decided to exit and see if we could use the funds for something that might have a better return. Okay, I'll say it. I panicked under the heavy debt load. Man, I hate having too much debt!

Lakefront property values eventually turned around, but it would have taken seven years to surpass the level we needed in order to meet our target. If you take the opportunity cost of money into account, we didn't do too badly after all.

What did we learn from this experience?

- As mentioned earlier, you definitely make money when you "buy" a renovation project, not when you "sell" it.
- Paying others to do too much of the work cuts very deeply into profit margins. We were not skilled enough in plumbing, electrical, and flooring. Doing only the "grunt" work, plus painting and decorating, is not always enough.
- When real estate markets turn down, the highest end (yes, even waterfront) gets hit the hardest as the target market for such properties is so much smaller.
- Have a contingency plan in place, in case things go against you.
- It is an awful lot of physical work!
- Would I do it again? Probably not on my own as my skill set is not appropriate to maximize profits.

CHAPTER 8

Franchise Number Two
Made Us Secure

I T WAS 1995, AND after selling our lakefront investment property, I ran into an old customer from our retail days. His name was Dennis, and "boy did he have a deal for us"! You see Dennis was going to retire and he wanted to sell his security business. I found it curious that he had owned the business for only a few years, but he said he wanted to take it easy and travel . . . yada, yada, yada! Naturally, I was interested since we just happened to be looking for our next venture.

This business was intriguing to us for a number of reasons. The three most important factors were that it was in a growing industry, it was flexible (home-based & could eventually be worked part-time), and it created "recurring revenue".

A business model with recurring revenue was new to us; however, the more we learned, the more we liked. The thought of having positive cash flow coming in every month, whether or not you got out of bed in the morning, had a certain appeal. This was especially true considering we just endured three years of retail hours and a period of time doing heavy physical labour on our property renovation.

Most people would say we sold home and business security systems. I quickly realized we were in the "monitoring" business and most often we "rented" the equipment to customers for free! We received a portion of the $25.00 per month monitoring fee over the three-year life of a contract. The competition was still "selling" the equipment and charging the same monthly fees. Can you imagine that? The franchisor supplied the equipment and charged no royalty. All we had to do was install the equipment. Sounds pretty simple right? Of course nothing is ever that simple.

This innovative business model was developed by AlarmForce Industries Inc. and was the brainchild of founder Joel Matlin of Toronto. Joel and I got along pretty well, and I liked the model so much I bought some shares in the company for about a buck each. I later sold these shares (at a small loss) and I see they recently traded on the Toronto Stock Exchange for over $12.00! Needless to say, Joel has done pretty well.

So how did we do? In the first nine months we worked full-time and were able to double gross revenues from the previous twelve month period. During our second year, we ranked as the third highest revenue grower out of thirty-seven offices across Canada. In years two and three, before paying ourselves, we achieved a net profit of 31% and 43% respectfully. We were able to build a nice and steady (recurring) income from this venture.

How did we do it? In every business, it's always about marketing, marketing, and marketing! We had two key "edges" over our competition. One was developed by Joel, the franchisor, and is most simply described as the "free equipment and installation offer". Yes, it was a powerful business model, however in some ways it stretched the franchisees a great deal. Basically, we franchisees were left to our own devices to market the contracts locally, and produce positive cash flow at the same time. I will tell you, JoAnn and I had to hustle big-time in the first year to make this a success.

I went out on the street, and Jo handled the phones selling to new customer prospects at every opportunity. Trade shows became a big marketing initiative in year one and I hit everyone of them in our exclusive territory. At that time only a few competitors attended the shows. I'm not sure why that was, but it sure worked for us.

Our second "edge" became very important because not only did it increase sales, it did so at a very low cost. This idea came to me as I was sitting with an insurance broker and he happened to mention how his business was valued by the "quality of his customer base". This meant that the fewer claims made by his customers for stolen goods from a break-in, for example, the higher the value of his business when he went to sell it. Boy, the light went on in my head and I couldn't wait to get started on our new "edge".

My plan was to visit as many insurance brokers in our market as possible, and explain to them how I could increase the value of their business so that they would maximize their returns when they sold. I would explain that increasing the number of monitored security systems in their client base would decrease the claims those clients made, and I had plenty of third party statistics to prove my point.

It turned out I didn't even need those stats. Many of these business owners saw the value in what I was saying almost immediately. The industry knew that alarm systems decreased break-ins and, therefore, claims. They just didn't know how to convince their customers to install a system. They weren't in that business, but we were!

I suggested to my first broker (who had about 2,000 clients) that he mail out one of my promotional pieces offering a "free" system to his client list. They could just add my piece to their monthly mail-out so there was no added cost to them. I saved on the postage and added thousands of targeted new exposures to our business without having to buy a mailing list. We did very little marketing after discovering this edge, and we even stopped attending trade shows.

It was a win/win/win situation. The consumer received a free alarm system and a 10% to 25% discount on their home or business insurance premiums (not to mention peace of mind). The brokers increased the value of their businesses. We grew our recurring revenue substantially.

When the broker mail-outs began, our phone started to ring. It was a great edge over our competition and so cost effective . . . a beautiful thing, for sure!

Do you see why I keep harping on developing an "edge" for your business? You must add value to your business by constantly seeking ways to take market share from your competitors. Such an advantage will pay handsome dividends, especially when you decide to sell your business.

It was sometime during our third year with AlarmForce that JoAnn came to me, sat me down, and said something close to, "I love you, dear, but we can't work together anymore."

It turns out that being cooped up at home answering phones and dealing with customer concerns was starting to lose its appeal. I'm sure working so closely with me for so long may also have had something to do with her decision . . . ya' think? I think so too, as I can get a bit "cranky" at times.

I immediately understood her need to take a break from working and living with me 24/7 for the past six years. She is truly a saint for enduring my ups and downs as a small business owner, and she will always be my biggest hero and best business partner.

This turn of events, along with the relocation of our key installer, and my "three year itch for change", got me to thinking about another exit plan. Thus began the process of finding a buyer for our little recurring revenue business.

It was another advertisement in the business opportunities section of *The Globe and Mail* newspaper that led to this, our fourth business sale. We were able to sell this franchise for about 60% more than we paid. I realize this isn't a great ROI over three years but it's within the realm of decent.

In hindsight we should have kept this business. Yes, we weren't enjoying it much anymore, but we had just built it up so nicely that it seemed a shame to let it go. I tried to find a partner to operate it, but was not successful. Admittedly, I was a little hasty in making this decision as this was a "keeper". I should have worked "on" this business and had someone else work "in" it!

By the way, I trust readers are not offended by how I chose to name this chapter? I realize it implies that this business made us "financially" secure as opposed to "physically" secure. In actual fact, no one venture made us financially secure (whatever financially secure means). It was the net cumulative total of all twelve that resulted in where we are today. Call it diversification on steroids if you will.

What did we learn from this venture?

- Don't try to kill the goose that lays the golden eggs. I learned this lesson from a fellow SBO who owned three Tim Horton's franchises. I mention it here because quite a large complement of AlarmForce franchisees kept trying to kill the goose instead of stroking it. I had my issues with AlarmForce but found little sense in fighting a proven system. Please don't go the franchise route if your goals are total freedom, flexibility, and independence. You will become frustrated, and success may elude you.

- Don't pay more than the current market multiple for any business unless there are clear and quantifiable reasons for doing so. This topic is covered in more detail in Chapter 31; however, suffice it to say, I paid more for this particular business than I should have . . . simple as that. I didn't have the knowledge required to properly value this type of operation and failed to seek professional advice. As my son, Matt, would say . . . definitely my bad!

- If you happen to suffer from the "three year itch syndrome", as I do, then look for different structuring opportunities before you decide to sell a profitable business! For example, consider selling up to 49% or 50% to a working partner or employee group, or hire a General Manager and let him or her manage day-to-day operations.

CHAPTER 9

Let's Take a New Product to Market . . . Not!

I T WAS 1998, JUST after we sold AlarmForce, and JoAnn was working in the advertising department at Shaw Communications. I was once again "between opportunities", as it were.

For as long as I can remember I have always wanted to take a new product to market. The world is so huge; surely I could come up with something that would sell to even a small sliver of consumers. Many a night I dreamed of selling enough of my widgets in order to set us up in style for life.

As it turns out, JoAnn met an interesting couple at her new job who were trying to do just that, and they were looking for a partner. Enter me.

My potential new partners were a proper middle-aged English couple who were trying to market a unique reusable bag called the "UniBag". It was a very functional product, primarily designed to replace plastic grocery bags in supermarkets. It appealed to environmentally conscious people; however, it was so versatile and strong that it could be used for toting or storing almost anything; thus, the market potential was huge.

During our first meeting, I learned that the UniBag was selling in two local Canadian Tire stores, and about twenty or so other retail outlets. These stores were re-ordering but, at the time, I wasn't exactly sure by how much.

The process was underway to obtain a utility patent and the name was trademarked. In addition, manufacturing was organized offshore in order to achieve the lowest production cost possible. The principals had previous small business experience and were working the bag business part-time while working their day jobs. They wanted to go fulltime into this business and were seeking a partner with business experience and capital to help them take this to the next level.

I went to our local Canadian Tire store the next Saturday morning to watch a product demonstration and see how customers responded. Well, I was certainly impressed with both the product and the customer reactions. Most importantly, I witnessed people actually buying the product, and I admit I was hooked, and excited! I immediately began dreaming about . . . er, I mean thoughtfully analyzing the future potential of this great product.

It wasn't long before we negotiated a deal whereby I would receive 49% of the company and would be named as equal owner of the utility patent if, and when, it was issued. We signed the necessary legal documents. I handed over my hundred thousand dollars and the three of us shook hands. Each party then contributed $50,000 for working capital, therefore, I had $150,000 at risk in this venture, plus my time.

Boy, was I pumped and ready to go to work, and work we did! I was in charge of marketing. My two partners would handle finance and manufacturing. We all contributed to sales. We put in many hours, knocked on many doors, and introduced UniBags to hundreds of vendors in both Canada and the US.

Some of the highlights of our progress over the first six months of this partnership included:

- Gross sales of $97,000;
- More than 150 retail outlets: 73 Overwaitea/Save-On Foods, 44 London Drugs, 15 IGA, 6 Canadian Tire, and miscellaneous independent outlets;

- Approximately 11,000 packs/units sold;

- Aired on The Shopping Channel;

- Wal-Mart Canada: An order for a 10 store test in Ontario was received. Total potential number of stores was 3,600 at this time;

- Canadian Tire: Approved as a national supplier to 426 stores;

- Shoppers Drug Mart and Home Hardware: Approved as a national supplier;

- Secured QVC, the world's leading television retailer: They suggested we ship 1,550 packs and that they would sell in about twelve minutes.

I was beginning to see my dream becoming a reality, especially after returning from Toronto with orders in hand from Wal-Mart Canada and Canadian Tire, along with serious interest from Zellers and mild interest from Sears.

There was only one problem, and I would be curious to learn how many readers have figured out what that problem was?

We had a good product, although we may have been slightly ahead of the market in terms of demand for environmentally friendly products. Our price was acceptable but it could have been much better with larger volume orders to our manufacturer. Our promotion to consumers was non-existent given our budget constraints. Our packaging was acceptable but challenging as we had to do it all by hand for custom type orders such as those we received from Wal-Mart and QVC.

No, what we lacked most was operating capital, or in layman's terms . . . cash! It doesn't take long to blow through $100,000 even when you try to watch every penny. In order to keep our manufacturing cost per unit at a reasonable level, we had to order full container loads which set us back about $20,000 each. Add in legal costs for the patent process, advertising and promotion, office expenses, warehouse costs, travel, and, well, you get the picture.

Unbeknown to me at the time, my partners had no money and no source of income. In fact they would soon need to find jobs if things didn't improve quickly. I guess that shiny black Jaguar they kept in a storage unit, and drove only on special occasions, was just for show? I also later learned that the beautifully furnished townhome they lived in was just a rental.

I was shocked and disappointed, to say the least, as I discovered more and more about my "glam couple" partners as they once described themselves. I tried to be positive which can be difficult for me at times, especially when trust is broken.

The positives were that we had a good product and we all wanted to succeed. We just needed more cash; however, I was not willing to risk anymore of our savings, particularly since my partners were unable to contribute anything past part-time work.

It became clear that I would have to set my marketing initiatives aside and try to raise capital ASAP. It was sometime in the fall of 1999, and after exhausting all efforts to raise funds locally, I put a presentation together and set off to a major Angel Investor Forum in Vancouver. Such forums are commonplace today; however, they were fairly new in Canada at the time. Even though we weren't yet profitable, I was confident I could raise some capital, given we had sales along with more and larger orders in hand. Today this is referred to as "proof of concept".

The room was completely packed with investors who paid to attend. If I recall correctly, there were about 200 "angels" and about twenty or so presenters. As I sat watching and listening to the presentations before me, my confidence began to grow. Almost none of these entrepreneurs had any sales and only a few had a proprietary product or service offering. Sure I was biased, but I could read their numbers. These were mostly unproven ideas with huge projections. Where I showed projected revenue in our third year of $4.2 million, they showed projections in year one of $10 million! I was only looking to raise $750,000 for a 49% stake (somewhat negotiable), while they were seeking much more for much less equity.

I was next and I stepped up to the podium with confidence. I gave what I thought was a decent pitch, and then prepared myself for a barrage of tough questions. Interestingly, there were no questions, or none that I recall, anyway. Perhaps the moderator was trying to move things along and suggested holding questions for the networking session to follow. No problem, I thought, that is where the deals are done anyway. Over a beer, one on one, face to face, I was ready!

I carried my product sample proudly into the networking session so I could be easily identified as "that guy with actual sales". What happened next surprised me more than a little.

The "Angels" stayed away by the hundreds, as though I was the Devil himself. I quickly checked myself over for anything hanging from my nose or some other unsightly or smelly networking impediment. Everything checked out fine.

My attempts to join conversations in progress were met with disinterest and an elbow or two. What the heck is going on, I wondered?

Behind me I heard a gravelly voice say, "That's a neat product you've got there", and I turned to see a well dressed, mature gentleman standing and gesturing to look at my sample. I immediately greeted him and began outlining the benefits of the UniBag. He quickly stopped me by saying that he wasn't interested in investing. He was just curious about the quality because he was interested in buying a set for his spouse.

I inquired as to why he wouldn't be interested in investing in a product that has proven sales? He replied, "The market is not looking for products like this right now . . . ecommerce is what is hot these days". He went on to explain that investors like him were looking for fast growing opportunities with huge upside potential that only technology businesses can provide. He said most investors would rather take a much larger risk than my UniBag in exchange for a possible 1,000% return on their investment. That was just the way it was those days. The money was chasing technology, not consumer goods.

Even after follow-up calls to investors on my attendee list, I did not receive one inquiry. Yep, I was down, to say the least.

Sometime after the Angel presentation, my partners called to say they may have found an answer to our cash flow concerns. They had talked to a fellow who had recently raised a ton of capital and would show us how to do the same. So we met this fellow who we'll call the consultant, for lunch.

The consultant suggested we set up a shell company on the Vancouver Venture Stock Exchange. I'll never forget when he said, "Tim, you have to stop selling bags and put all your effort into selling shares in a new public company." When I inquired as to whom we should sell these shares, he replied, "To anyone you might know, mostly family and friends." I responded with, "I see," as the hair on the back of my neck began to stand straight up.

So as not to bore you with details, suffice it to say, I couldn't agree with the consultant's plan. I did some research on Mr. Consultant and discovered that, yes, he had made millions on a cellular phone safety accessory; however, no product was ever sold while he ran the Company. Only a prototype was produced. I spoke to people to whom he sold his company, and I discovered serious discontent.

I just wasn't prepared to go to my family and friends on what appeared to be, in my opinion, a "pump and dump" type scheme.

Also, my partners had already tapped their friends for about $85,000 before I arrived on the scene, so they didn't have any friends left to approach.

It seemed to me that considering I didn't have control of the company (with only 49% ownership), the only course of action I had was to cut my losses and move on. It was a difficult and traumatic decision. About $150,000 in cash, plus my time down the drain . . . ouch!!!!

Do I blame my partners? Mostly, I blame myself because I knew better, but I know one thing for sure . . . I never would have done this deal had I known the true financial position and business background of my partners beforehand. Presenting oneself as an "engineer" when in reality one is a "plumber" is a stretch that didn't sit too well with me.

The only upside to this experience is that I learned a lot of important and painful lessons. Here are some things I knew before I got into this venture, yet I still seemed able to ignore.

1. ***Dig Deep When Doing Your Due Diligence***: Ask the tough questions like, "How much money do you have and will you contribute more funds if needed?" or "How long can you survive without being paid?" If there is hesitation in answering, I suggest you walk away. There will always be another opportunity.

2. ***Don't Let Emotions Cloud Your Judgement #1***: I got excited about this product and skipped parts of point number one. Definitely my bad.

3. ***Don't Let Emotions Cloud Your Judgement #2***: I had a rule for investing whereby I promised myself that I would never get into a deal unless I had at least 50% ownership (preferably 51%). Obviously, I broke this rule and cannot offer a rational excuse, and being enthused about a product is not a rational excuse.

Here are a few things I learned from this experience which may have helped us succeed had I known about them at the time. Perhaps they will help you should you decide to market your own product or service.

1. *Use the USA "Patent Pending" Status or Other Methods to Protect Your Idea*: Filing for a full utility patent may be unnecessary and too costly (think $30,000). Also, doing your own initial patent search could easily save you $1,000 right out of the gate.

2. *Seriously Consider Licensing Your Product*: Unless you have tons of cash ($300,000 plus), consider accepting a smaller piece (through a royalty) of what might become a big pie. I have learned how to protect and bring products to market for as little as $300-$500 each.

3. *Don't be Overly Worried About Getting Ripped Off*: I was guilty of this for a long time. This type of thinking can create a paralysis which might prevent you from taking action, only to see your product on store shelves a few years later. You also might spend a truckload of money trying to protect a bad idea. Yes, you may eventually need to protect your concept, but realize that very few people or businesses have the inclination or ambition to steal your idea. What is more likely is that your concept is already in the marketplace somewhere on this planet, which is why proper research is so important.

This venture was definitely the biggest failure of my business career. If you are wondering if I would do it again, the answer is absolutely . . . but quite differently. In fact, as I write this, JoAnn and I have started a brand new business which focuses primarily on new product development. I have always wanted to succeed at introducing a new product to the market, and hopefully it will happen one day soon.

CHAPTER 10

What's It Like to be a Realtor?

A FTER LOSING MY PROVERBIAL shirt in the bag business, I think it's safe to say I was a little gun shy as it relates to starting or buying a new business. I did look for awhile, but nothing I could find made economic sense. I was getting bored and anxious about not creating any cash flow. Thank goodness JoAnn was still working at Shaw.

I honestly don't know what prompted me to consider becoming a real estate agent, but I do remember thinking that being a realtor is one of the purest forms of capitalism there is. If you don't produce, you don't get paid . . . simple as that. This worked for me, and I liked that I didn't have to buy any inventory to resell, especially after losing all that money on the UniBag project. Inventory was everywhere, and I could sell anything I wanted. I just needed to match a willing buyer with a willing seller.

Further, a real estate agent is not usually an employee. He or she is typically a self-employed business person with much of the flexibility and autonomy of an SBO. In addition, I liked the industry from an investment perspective, as I had some success in flipping properties in the past. Yes, this might be something that could grow on me.

I passed the real estate and mortgage broker's exam about mid-2000. The study process consisted of a rather large reference book and some online testing. It was fairly easy to understand and well organized. I would estimate that 75% of the course material dealt with the legal aspects of real estate, and the remainder dealt with mortgages and interest rates. There is nothing in this course that deals with how to sell real estate or even how to write up a deal. I'm just saying.

Soon after receiving my license, I started with Re/Max Kelowna. This was the largest office in the region as measured by both dollar volume and by the number of realtors. I believe there were 105 agents in this office when I joined. I recall this number because all of the offices were occupied at the time, and I had to wait a while to even share an office with another realtor.

Why Re/Max? Well, they seemed to dominate our market and I figured it would be good to learn from the best. The brand recognition all across Canada was huge, and it afforded some credibility which I felt was especially important for a newbie agent like me. Also, I was familiar with the Broker/Owner of this office and had some other contacts in the organization. In addition, I liked that they were a 100% organization, meaning that Re/Max realtors keep 100% of the commissions they earned. This was minus expenses, of course. They charge you for everything including office supplies, photocopies, office space, transaction fees, etc. Renting space and selling services to realtors is the business Re/Max brokers are in.

If you can envision two floors of office space filled with about seventy-five people rushing about as though late for a meeting, that was this Re/Max office on the morning of my first day. It was the day for their weekly meeting and "tour". I remember wondering, "What's a tour?"

During the ten minute "stand up" meeting, myself and another fellow were introduced to the crowd; then suddenly we were off to drive around the city for a quick view of about fifteen new homes for sale, and I mean quick. Seriously, it looked, sounded and felt like a fire bell had rung as people literally raced to their cars. I felt the buzz and it felt great! This is why I joined Re/Max!

One of the few agents who introduced himself to me on the way down to our cars was a very well known veteran who seemed shocked to learn that I, and the other newbie, had never sold real estate before coming to Re/Max. He said in all his years he had never seen such a thing. I didn't have a clue what he meant at the time, but I was soon to find out.

Upon returning from the tour, we were given an orientation by the Office Manager which lasted about an hour or so. It basically consisted of how the paperwork flows and, most importantly, how the money flows. By money I mean commissions and expenses, the two most critical considerations for any realtor.

By lunch time of my first day, my introduction, orientation and training were complete . . . yes, finito! Ah, the private sector is so efficient, I thought to myself. I was now ready to go out and do deals worth hundreds of thousands, perhaps millions of dollars. Somehow I didn't feel quite ready.

That afternoon I met with the Broker/Owner to inquire as to when my "deal" training (for lack of a better word) would begin. You know, that training which actually explains how to put real estate deals together like offers, counter-offers, financing, conditions, inspections, etc. He replied that most people who come to Re/Max are experienced realtors who have done hundreds of deals and don't require such training (a point he failed to mention during my initial interview). He told me not to worry because the Real Estate Board would be offering such a course in a few weeks.

Well, I attended that course and, frankly, I was no further ahead. They did cover which forms needed to be completed, but very little about how to go about that task.

I now realized what that prominent realtor I mentioned earlier was talking about. You see, up until about this time it was indeed rare for a person to come off the street and start at Re/Max.

Typically, people would start at a real estate company where commissions were shared, i.e., 70% to the Agent and 30% to the broker. In return for the 30%, the broker would provide training, office space and support. Once that agent became experienced, he or she would likely negotiate to keep more of the commission or perhaps move to an organization, like Re/Max, where the agents keep 100% of their commissions, partly because no training is required.

In my case, I can only surmise that the broker who hired me felt my business background would suffice and that I would eventually figure things out. I will say I was a bit shocked, but not alarmed, to learn that there would be no assistance putting together my first few deals. What if I screw things up? "Don't worry," they said, "That's why you're paying for insurance." Obviously such a response is silly and irresponsible. I wanted to be professional and offer the best service available to my clients.

If and when I need help, I'll just ask my associates for assistance. It only took a few days to realize that this plan wasn't going to fly. While most were friendly and polite on the surface, it became abundantly clear that the people with whom I shared an office were, above all else, my competitors. Yes, these were smart, savvy, experienced competitors, and here I was with not one deal under my belt! This would be interesting.

Now don't get me wrong. One can build friendships, working relationships, and eventually partnerships with fellow realtors, but it does take time. For example, shortly after starting out at Re/Max, I met Lewis who was a ten-year veteran realtor who had relocated to Kelowna from Richmond, BC. Lewis is a great marketer, and I learned a lot from him about this industry.

Being on my own is not a foreign feeling to me and, therefore, I wasn't overly concerned with most of what I faced. My only hesitation was my complete lack of experience in writing up deals. I wondered at the time whether or not I should be allowed to do this without some type of supervision.

I wanted, and needed, clean tight deals that would close properly right through the lawyer's office, through the Land Titles Office and back to the lawyer's office. Short of paying another realtor to come along on every offer, all I could do was study for every contingency I could think of, and take my time to be sure my clients were protected. After all, this business is all about one's reputation, and I couldn't afford to start out by tarnishing mine.

It took a few months or so to get my first sale, and longer to get my first listing. After significant marketing efforts, the opportunities started to come. I was able to build some humble confidence in writing and negotiating offers and closing deals. The sink or swim school of real estate can be starkly motivating.

For those of you who think that being a real estate agent is an easy profession, you may wish to reconsider. It's not that I found it particularly difficult in terms of the many other hats I have worn, but it certainly does have its own unique set of challenges. For example, you don't get paid unless you sell something, or something of yours is sold. In the mean time, one must self-fund all operating expenses. Now that's accountability!

Let me tell you a quick story to help illustrate one of the challenges facing all realtors and that is "cyclicality", or what is referred to as the ups and downs of the economy.

At one point I rented a tiny office at Re/Max, and right across the hall from me were two realtors sharing a larger outside office. These two guys were seasoned veterans, in their forties, with recognizable names in the community. I noticed that they often had their door closed for hours on end. I, on the other hand, rarely closed my door as I would have likely suffocated.

One day I was headed to my office and noticed their door slightly ajar, and I heard some talking. Now please know that our offices were so tightly nestled together that I could easily throw a crumpled piece of paper into their waste basket from where I sat at my desk.

I couldn't help but notice both men sitting at their desks with telephone books open in front of them. They were busy "cold-calling" prospective customers. I was shocked, to say the least. Here were two experienced and respected realtors going one by one through the White Pages calling people they didn't know to see if they needed the services of a realtor.

I believe these two guys were dealing with the cyclicality of the market. The local market was a bit soft, so they decided they were going to survive this downturn by working their tails off and doing one of the most hated jobs any sales person can dream of . . . cold calling!

I know I couldn't do it, but I truly respected them for doing whatever it took to survive. Personally, I would rather say, "Welcome to Wal-Mart" or "Do you want fries with that?" than do cold calling, but hey, to each, his own. The point I am trying to make is that the cyclicality of the real estate market can make this occupation very challenging. Hard work and persistence is the only solution to long-term survival.

Another example of cyclicality may help to better illustrate this point. In our local market, it is not uncommon for the number of realtors to go from a high of about 1,000 agents (which was the number when I joined) to about 600 agents a short time later.

I left the real estate business after eighteen months. Now I know what you're thinking, "Tim, what a wimp? . . . you couldn't even last through one cycle . . . this is your second failure in a row . . . go and get a government job, you coward" (ouch, that hurts).

Although some of these thoughts may be true, in my defense, I don't think I stunk too, too badly. The market conditions at that time were about balanced, not too hot, nor too cold, so I can't blame the market, darn! However, the amount of competition (number of realtors) in Kelowna was huge at the time I joined.

I didn't win any sales awards, but I did manage to bring in $121,000 in commissions over those eighteen months. I was able to cover all my expenses, and produce a very modest income which covered a good portion of our basic living expenses.

From a strictly return on investment point of view, yes, I failed because, after paying myself, there was nothing left. On the other hand, most small businesses take this long or longer to produce a net income, after salaries are paid. I really don't know if I won or lost this battle. I'll let you be the judge, but I feel confident in saying that, given more time, I would have won. My confidence and momentum were building, no doubt about it.

So why didn't I hang in there? Frankly, because I hated it! I believe this career is a great opportunity for the right person. It just wasn't right for me. I discovered about a third of the way through that I didn't have the right personality. I am a good manager of people and I have some marketing skills. That's who I am. I learned that I am not a true sales person. I simply don't have the patience required to build relationships with strangers.

No, I don't think your child is cute. No, I don't want her to wear her muddy shoes in my car. No, I don't want to meet for drinks or go to a ball game. I've shown you five houses, now it's time to buy one . . . right now! These were some of my thoughts at the time, and they didn't bode well for a successful career in this people business. No, it was time to move on.

In hindsight, I got into this business for all the wrong reasons. I was bored. I didn't want to risk too much capital after my previous loss in the bag business. I couldn't find anything else to do at the time, outside of working for somebody else, and, oh yes, I was bored! Definitely my bad once again.

Below are some things I learned during my time as a realtor.

1. ***You Need to be a People Person in Order to Succeed Long-term***: This may seem obvious by now, but, in case you were napping, I will stress this point again. In my opinion, a great realtor builds long-term relationships, and unless you truly enjoy doing the same, you may find your enthusiasm waning over time. If you're not sure if you are suited for this business, please ask people who know you well for some honest and frank feedback.

2. ***You Need to be a Bit Shameless***: The most successful realtors I have met are great at, and comfortable with, exuberant self promotion. This occupation is definitely not for shy, introverted types.

3. ***You Absolutely Must be a Self-Starter***: If you are the type who needs to be pushed or prodded along in any way, I suggest you consider a different opportunity.

4. ***You Should be Comfortable With Personal Time Interruptions***: Even when you are out of town, your personal time can be at risk of interruption. Deals are generally not done during regular nine to five business hours. This can certainly be managed, but be aware, especially if you have young children.

5. ***Managing the Ups and Downs of the Market is Key to Survival***: The more mature realtors I was acquainted with saved money during the good times because they knew markets changed repeatedly. This is tough for true-blue sales people who generally aren't the best savers. One needs to develop some discipline here.

6. ***It's all About Marketing***: Well thought-out and well-executed marketing plans are a basic necessity these days.

Being comfortable with the latest social media technologies is a must.

7. ***Advertising and Rent Can Kill You if not Properly Managed:*** I spent 22% ($26,700) of my commission income on Re/Max rent and 15% ($18,300) on advertising. Being new to the industry may have caused these numbers to be a little higher than the average.

Aside from the few thousand that one needs to get a license, and for other start-up costs, I suggest one have $20,000 - $25,000 in cash available to fund the first few years of marketing and office costs.

As shown on page 402, the 2011 average net income for an unincorporated real estate agent in Canada was $54,600.

8. ***Referred and Repeat Clients Can Take Five Years to Develop:*** These types of clients have a low cost of acquisition which is why they are so valuable. Don't bank on them too soon, however, because it takes years before they start to trickle in. I can only recall one such sale during my eighteen months.

CHAPTER 11

Always Wanted a Swimming Pool

I T'S SO MUCH MORE pleasurable discussing a positive experience, don't you think? Yes, sometimes things can go right and, with enough hard work and perseverance, sometimes you can actually make some money!

During my last six months at Re/Max I started looking for my next opportunity and discovered something one doesn't come across every day . . . a swimming pool company. The industry piqued my interest and, upon examining the books, it looked reasonably priced. The asking price may have been rational given the fact that the owners of this business were both accountants. After all, who should know better than accountants how to properly value a business?

This was to be one of our larger non-real estate acquisitions. I was going to be on my own again as JoAnn was happy as a lark working for the City of Kelowna.

I was able to negotiate the price to what I thought was a reasonable earnings multiple (much more on this later), and we closed the deal in the spring of 2002, just as the pool season was about to begin.

This business was about eighteen years old with retail space of about 2,500 square feet. The two owners, along with four full-time and a few part-time employees, made up the staff complement. There were three main competitors with bricks and mortar retail locations in our market, as well as numerous operators working out of their trucks.

The primary profit centers included in-ground pool construction (45% of sales); retail chemicals and pool parts (33%); and the balance (22%) in service and repairs, hot tub sales, and miscellaneous.

I will be discussing my personal business search criteria in Chapter 27 but, suffice it to say, this opportunity ticked off many of my boxes. I was particularly keen to get back to managing people, and the long term growth and profit potential looked pretty good.

During my due diligence process, I discovered that Kelowna had one of the highest concentrations of swimming pools per capita, in all of North America! I reasoned that even if pool installations weakened, someone still had to service all those existing pools.

The name of this business was, and continues to be, Sunshine Pools & Spas. The husband and wife team from whom I purchased this business were good people, and the sale and transition went smoothly, well, except for one thing, that is.

About a month after I bought Sunshine, I learned that a serious disagreement had occurred between my Sales Manager and our sub-contracted pool building company. It turns out this builder no longer wished to do business with Sunshine, ever again! We were now a pool company with no one to build our pools!

I was told this issue transpired near the end of the previous season. I don't think the previous owners were aware of this situation. It wasn't brought up during the purchase negotiations.

Had I known that there was no supplier of our largest product offering, I may not have bought this business, or I would have certainly negotiated a better price. At any rate, there are always surprises when you buy an existing business. I get that, but I didn't anticipate it would be one with such a potentially negative impact on both our sales and profitability.

In-ground pool installations represented almost half of total sales. The busiest time of the year for selling and building pools was just starting, and my company had nobody to build them, and I mean no one!

It was time for damage control and an action plan. These two functions are always up to the business owner; however, I had no idea how to build a swimming pool; in fact, I had never even cleaned one.

My Sales Manager (the guy who admitted to being responsible for this mess) was on a base salary plus commission, with the latter being the much larger portion. He was very motivated to help me solve this problem, or risk reducing his income, or losing his job entirely.

The closest pool building sub-contractors were four hours away in Vancouver, which was not a cost effective solution, so he suggested we build our own pools. Interesting, but with whom (we had no staff) and with what (we had no equipment). Oh right, that part was up to me! He assured me he had the know-how to build pools, if I invested in the manpower and equipment.

"Oh great," I thought, I just spent a very large sum (at least for me, low six figures was large) to buy what was supposed to be a "turn-key" or fully operational business. Now I'd have to hire additional staff and buy equipment that I hadn't budgeted for. Pass me the Alka-Seltzer, please!

I will admit that I liked the idea of having better control of our largest profit center, especially in terms of quality control. I would also be remiss if I didn't mention that the profit margin earned by the sub-contractor would now be ours, if we were successful. So, there were some positives about this plan.

I just had to come up with more money and everything would be fine. If there is one thing I have learned in business, and in life, it is that money is not the key to success or to happiness. Money is just a tool that needs to be properly managed. No, it would take more than money to turn this roadblock into an overpass.

Our average selling price for an in-ground pool at the time was about $50,000. This is where I started to analyze how to manage this part of the business. I got Ron, my newly-titled Sales & Construction Manager, to list each item, task, and sequence that goes into building a pool. I then priced every last item. Slowly I was able to formulate in my mind, and on paper, what was needed to build swimming pools at a profit. I then set out to hire people and purchase (or rent) the required equipment.

Over the next four years, my people built many pools, and thus created many more recurring revenue customers. These customers required parts, chemicals, and service on an ongoing basis in order to maintain their pools. Although not under contract per se, these types of customers tend to be quite loyal and add great value to the business.

We grew to a total of twelve full-time people during peak season. Our sales grew at an average of about 10% per year due to improved marketing initiatives. It was our net income, however, which showed the most improvement. After salaries, including my own, we saw an average increase of 132% each year. The reason for such a sharp increase in the bottom line was due to improved cost controls, increased gross margins, and improved staff efficiencies.

Yes, we were able to create a real bottom line with a nice return on investment. Our ROI ran an average of 33.6% per year after taking into account a market-rate salary for me to manage the business.

So how'd we do it? Well aside from the typical hard work required for any small business, I would have to say it started with organization and accountability (marketing came a little later).

I was surprised to learn that such a mature industry had no key performance indicators, so we had nothing to compare against. For example, in Canada the closest financial comparison available for this industry today is titled, "All Other Specialty Trade Contractors."

This category includes pool installation businesses, as well as thirty-five other business types. We were not very comparable to brick pavers, cable splicers, fence erectors, sand blasters, asphalt surfacing, crane rentals, house movers, and so on.

Beyond standard monthly financial statements, there were no performance measurement systems in place, so we slowly began to track, measure, and set goals. We were forced to create our own indicators and try to improve upon them each year. Some of these included:

- *Gross Margin Analysis and Targets by Profit Center:* Where was the profit coming from?

- *Revenue per Employee:* Did we have enough people? Too many?

- *Pool Construction Costing:* Down to the penny, how much do these babies cost and how do we track them?

- *Average Revenue per Retail Customer per Visit:* Are free water tests still viable?

- *Number of Service Calls and Pool Cleanings per Hour/Day.*

- *Cost per Service Call:* Including wages, equipment, gas, and all other vehicle costs.

- *Average Revenue per Service Call:* Is this department making any money?

- *Accounts Receivable Aging:* Are we getting paid on time?

- *Accounts Payable:* Are we paying too soon? Are we getting early payment discounts?

- *Annual Sales and Expense Budgets set up and Reviewed Monthly.*

- *Weekly Management Meetings:* Standard business practice, but still new to my team.

- *Daily Pool Sales and Construction Meetings:* Posted our first pool construction schedule for all staff to see.

Interestingly, we were able to accomplish the financial results referenced above while increasing wages to the highest level, ever. Our benefits cost were also higher than our competitors as we were the only pool company to offer any employee benefits at all. Add increased staff bonuses and company-provided uniforms, and I think you will get the picture. My people were paid more and were expected to work a little harder and, as a result, we increased our profit by improving margins, not from cutting wages and salaries.

I owe a lot to my staff at Sunshine for their dedication and hard work, particularly my protégé Terri who learned quickly to solve problems. Terri was great with customers and usually did the work of two people. We built a well-organized business led by a great and loyal team of people, and I was quite proud of them all. I also wish to say that I am quite proud of my sons, Matt and Josh who worked very hard (without complaint) for me when I owned Sunshine.

Below are some lessons I learned (or relearned) as a result of owning this business:

1. *Seasonal Businesses Which Require Skilled Labour Can be Quite Challenging*: I didn't anticipate building our own pools so this was a bigger challenge than it should have been. Laying off valuable staff over the winter and hoping they return was a risky proposition. Every spring we had to hire new, and often inexperienced, people to work in pool construction, our most important profit center. Definitely stressful!

2. *Selling Products Which Require Regular Maintenance is a Beautiful Thing*: It's not quite like razors and razor blades, but you get my point. If you sell a sofa at a 45% gross margin, you may never see that customer for years, if at all. If you install a pool or hot tub, even at a lower profit margin, that customer will very likely be back to your store the following week to buy higher margin chemicals, pool toys, or service.

This type of business model, although much more stressful and challenging than a furniture store (in my opinion anyway), provides a higher degree of security for the owners. Because the customer base can be loyal and recurring, the business as a whole has more value which is welcome news when one goes to sell.

3. ***Staff Turnover is a Reality for New Owners***: Anyone taking over an existing business must anticipate, and plan for, some changes to personnel. It's just inevitable. The new owner must slowly and thoughtfully build his or her own team which can take a year or two depending on the business type and skill levels involved.

4. ***Larger Barriers to Entry Adds Value***: The barriers to entry for this specialty construction/retail business are significant. First, a bricks and mortar location is necessary in order to satisfy customer needs and build long-term customer loyalty. A new storefront isn't cheap to build out, and the rent is still due during the winter months, so a new entrant will need substantial capital to start.

   Second, you absolutely must have skilled staff in water chemistry, pool construction, plumbing, electrical, and landscaping. Building such a broad team is crucial and takes a relatively long time to create; however, once established, the SBO can demand more money when the decision to sell is made.

5. ***Talk to Major Suppliers Before You Buy a Business***: I neglected to do this in regard to the pool construction sub-contractor, and it cost me in terms of increased stress, loss of valuable time and increased expenses.

6. ***Don't Underestimate the Risk of Legal Issues***: I must say I didn't do much research into the potential liability issues that can plague a business like this. The pool construction

task was to be completed by a sub-contractor so the liability concern seemed manageable at that time. Even though we were a limited liability company, once we moved pool construction in-house, we opened ourselves up to potential legal risks I didn't anticipate. Please understand that if you, or your people, screw up due to poor workmanship, you are most likely not covered by insurance. You are only covered by your ability to fix the problem at your own expense. If you are looking at getting into a business like Sunshine, I recommend discussing this topic with your lawyer and insurance broker long before you start up or buy.

Things were moving along pretty smoothly during my fourth year as owner of Sunshine Pools. I could have easily left town without worrying if I would have a business to come back to, and that was always a great feeling of satisfaction. Everyone seemed to know what they were doing and what was expected of them. So what's next? I once again had that itchy feeling which seemed to foretell of another career change. In addition, I also developed a health issue which required a lifestyle change.

Sunshine was now well-organized, growing, profitable, and had a great team. What more could a potential new owner desire? "Absolutely nothing," I thought, so now may be a good time to sell. I must admit I was ready for a long break as this was one of my more challenging ventures, as well as one of my most lucrative.

It took less than a year to sell Sunshine, and, except for the legal part, I did it totally on my own. I was able to sell this business for much more than I paid because it was worth much more. In fact, in terms of capital appreciation, this business vied for top spot out of all our ventures. The best part was that much of those gains came to us tax free! There will be more on this topic in Chapter 33.

The buyer was a fellow named Ken who moved his family from Calgary to Kelowna to take over Sunshine in the spring of 2006. I am very pleased that Ken and I are still friends, and that he continues to successfully own and operate Sunshine Pools. In fact, Ken recently moved to a newer and much larger location, and I wish him well.

CHAPTER 12

Early Retirement

HONESTLY, I REALLY DIDN'T have a "life plan", when I sold Sunshine. I just knew that I needed a break from my six days a week schedule, and that the timing was right for a sale. I was forty-nine and a bit drained, but not out. I was confident I would find something to do. I just didn't know what or when that would be.

I did the very typical things like taking a year to totally remodel our twenty-five year old home. I tried to take up golf, but I don't think I was ready for that, despite JoAnn's passion for the game.

After the house was done, JoAnn would often loudly proclaim, "Go get a freaking hobby, why don't you?" I didn't take this too personally, but jeepers she can be quite direct at times. I'm just not a hobby doing kind of guy.

No, I am a task-driven kind of guy. Completing a task makes me happy, and doing nothing (hobbies, in my opinion) makes Tim sad. By the way, my list of tasks does not include cooking or housework . . . sorry, Jo.

It was late 2006, and I started to take a greater interest in our investments, while keeping a vigilant eye open for business opportunities. All the while I couldn't help but feel a gentle, yet persistent nudge. Well, it started as a nudge, and then morphed into a firm push from JoAnn guiding me closer and closer to the door. She still loved me, to be sure; she just felt I needed to get out of the house more . . . go figure?

My point in sharing this rather personal information is to alert SBOs that while planning your business exit, it is a good idea to plan for what you will do after that exit. My attitude was, "Ah, what a nice problem to have; I'll deal with that once it happens". Well, it happened to me, and I had no plan. This may not be a problem for more laid back types of people, but it requires constant management for a task-driven guy like me. So be forewarned!

CHAPTER 13

Let's Get into the Markets, Baby!

I N LATE 2007, I was hearing a lot of conflicting viewpoints about the US mortgage market and how there may be a financial crisis looming. I was just starting to take a more active interest in our investments when I heard a fellow by the name of Peter Schiff of Euro Pacific Capital Inc. make a speech to a large group of American mortgage brokers. I couldn't help but think this guy was quite courageous telling this particular audience that their industry was going to sink big time, and soon.

I started to listen more and more to Peter and the very few other financial people that agreed with him, and they began to make a lot of sense to me. Someday soon, the US mortgage bubble would burst and take the stock markets down with it. I decided at that time to get out of the markets, in general, and move to the sidelines for awhile. I have never made such a big decision regarding our investments in my life. I certainly never contemplated that I would continue to make such decisions over the years to come.

As you know, Peter's prediction came true. The financial crisis began, and 2008 was the start of the Great Recession.

I am telling you this in order to explain how I started my trading and investing journey. I didn't have a plan to get into this as a "business"; it just kind of evolved out of necessity. Yes, it was a great move to exit the markets in 2007. But now what would I do?

My goal at the time was capital preservation, not growth. I was only going to do this investing thing for a limited time, depending upon how the crisis panned out.

In fact, I didn't, and still don't, believe anyone can consistently beat the markets for a long period. My research confirmed this thesis as study after study proved that fund managers produced no better results than mimicking the market itself.

Nonetheless, I left my confirmed thesis behind and started to read investment books and the latest online material. I discovered that the "experts" say it takes about six or seven years to develop a successful trading/investing system that suits one's personality. Yes, that surprised me too.

I must clarify that I am not talking about day trading here, which by definition means you close out or sell all of what you bought before the end of each day. I may have done this once in a while, but it was a rare occurrence for me. I didn't have the stomach, nor do I have the proper system, to trade this way.

I am more of a "momentum" trader/investor. I may hold a stock for weeks or months, and even a few for more than a year. I try to "buy what's going up and sell what isn't" which sounds so easy to do, yet for me has been extremely difficult.

If I had to define my investing style, it would have to be a combination of a value investor and a speculator. This may be an oxymoron in the investment world, but I enjoy finding good safe companies at a great price, as well as swinging for the fences with some high risk commodity or technology plays.

This journey continues for me, and I estimate I will be forever on the learning curve. No doubt I could write a book on this roller coaster experience alone; however, it wouldn't be relevant to SBOs unless they were planning to treat their trading as their business, which is what I was attempting to do.

For those SBOs who are planning to trade or invest for a living, I don't yet feel that I can offer much guidance without getting into a ton of detail, which again is not the purpose of this book.

I will, however, recommend that if you are looking to earn your living by trading stocks, you must read and study as much as you can before you begin. I highly recommend a book called *Trade Your Way To Financial Freedom* by Van K. Tharp. This is an excellent reference book to add to your library.

CHAPTER 14

I Wanted to Write This Book 22 Years Ago

A S MENTIONED IN MY introduction, I have had this project on my mind for a very long time; twenty-two years, in fact. Two catalysts prompted me to finally begin.

First, the data in the reference section became available at a price I was willing to pay, which was nothing. I really shouldn't say it was nothing as Jo and I have put in a great many hours reviewing thousands of pages of financial information and refining how it is presented. To be sure, we have not altered any numbers from our source. We just changed how those numbers are presented to be more reader-friendly in a book format. Previously, the cost to obtain this data was in the low thousands of dollars.

Second, the timing was right. I was looking for something to keep me occupied while I developed more patience in my trading/investing activity. My plan was to do both at the same time, thus working about the equivalent of a standard work week. Nights and weekends would be for relaxing and working on one other new sideline . . . a little product-scouting and licensing business.

I wanted my book project to be a "labour of love". I would work on it only when I truly had the desire, and would not pressure myself with a deadline (although how long it would take was something I thought about often). Perhaps this was to be my hobby? I really don't know for sure if it is or it isn't. What I do know is that for the most part, I do enjoy it!

Make no mistake, I "want" to make money by selling this book; however, I don't really "expect" to make much money. I am told that very, very few books of this type in Canada sell more than a few hundred copies; so, I know what you're thinking . . . "why go to all the trouble and expense?"

Well, if I sell enough to cover my costs and I help a few people along the way, I would count such a result as quite satisfying. Now there are varying degrees of satisfaction and the higher up that scale I can achieve (in terms of number of books sold), the greater the satisfaction.

In case you're wondering, no, I didn't know anything about writing a book when I began and, after reading this far, perhaps you still think I don't know anything about writing. In reality, the longest thing I have ever written were those annoying university papers. Nevertheless, I do have considerable experience being an SBO, and it is my hope that this experience may benefit current and future SBOs.

My planning and implementation process included the following steps:

1. *General Research*: I read a few books and talked to a few industry people on the subject of authoring a non-fiction business book.

2. *Created Synopsis*: I wrote a nine page synopsis including a sample cover, the purpose and goals of this book, as well as who might benefit from reading it (the target market). It also included some specific questions that I would try to answer. Lastly, it contained a draft table of contents and a sample of the reference material.

3. *Created Business Plan and Budget:* Okay, I must admit I didn't do quite as much work on this as would be warranted

for a standard business investment; however, in my defense this was to be my quasi hobby.

I based my largest expense item (print costs) on nine quotes I received before I wrote a word beyond the synopsis. You can see my original budget in Appendix 1. Please note that I really had no idea how many pages there were going to be, especially given that it was to include a reference section. I requested printers to quote on 256 pages as it seemed like the size of most business books I owned at the time. Obviously this estimate was way off the mark as you can see from the actual number of pages you are reading.

I then used the print costs as a basis for estimating my break-even at various sales volumes and retail price points. I will say that it is with great anxiety that I share these numbers with you. I was obviously way off with my original budget; however, it provided the guidance I needed to get started.

While we're at it, my start-up cost estimates are outlined in Appendix 2.

4. ***Conducted Market Research:*** I did the standard online searches including Amazon.com and Barnesandnoble.com to see if there was anything like my concept on the market. I couldn't find anything even remotely similar, especially in Canada. A trip to our local Chapter's store revealed a serious lack of any kind of Canadian-focused business books.

I then used my synopsis as a research tool by sending it to people whose opinions I respect. I tried to choose people who I thought would be honest and not try to falsely encourage me. I tried to ask specific questions like, "Do you think this book would sell and, if so, for how much?" and "Would you buy such a book?"

The feedback was encouraging from non-business people to very encouraging from small business types.

5. ***Began Researching Material and Writing April 2013:*** As mentioned above, I have included the original Revenue/Expense Budget that I produced for this book in Appendix 1. Once available, I plan to publish some actual profit/loss results on howmuchmoneycanimake.com.

I don't know why exactly, but I called David Chilton to whom I had never spoken before, and I was pleasantly surprised when he called me back within half an hour.

Now, I can't believe that anyone reading this book would not know the name David Chilton; but just in case, I'll provide an introduction. Dave (as I now call him) is the author of *The Wealthy Barber*, a wildly successful bestselling personal finance book published in 1989. This book has sold an astounding two million plus copies! Twenty-two years later, Dave released a sequel called, *The Wealthy Barber Returns*.

Dave is also one of the Dragons on CBC Televisions *Dragons' Den*. This is one of my favorite shows; I even watch the odd rerun. Dave adds a lot to the Den with his clever sense of humor and the very thoughtful advice he gives to presenters.

As mentioned earlier, I wasn't quite sure what I wanted from David when I first called him. I suppose I wanted to hear something like, "Tim, that's a great concept you have. Perhaps we can work on it together?" Well, I can dream can't I?

Shortly after I left that telephone message for Dave, JoAnn shouted to me that David Chilton was on the phone. As I walked quickly to my home office, the yogurt I was eating for lunch dripped from my chin. A quick wipe and I took the handset from JoAnn. "Hello", I say. "Hi Tim, this is Dave Chilton calling you back. What can I do for you?" I thanked him for getting back to me and immediately went into my pitch which culminated with, "I am going to write a book that will do for the Canadian small business owner, what *The Wealthy Barber* did for the Canadian investor." I know it was a bit cheeky and overzealous to make such a claim, but I needed to get his attention.

David was polite and professional when he shut me down. Well maybe 'shut down' is a little strong. What he did say was that he gets about forty book proposals every week and he was done with publishing ventures. He is simply too busy with Dragons' Den and other projects.

I interacted with Dave for about a year and a half, mostly via email and the odd telephone conversation. When I was about half way through my manuscript, I contacted Dave to update him. Within minutes he emailed me back saying, "Keep going!" I will always be grateful to Dave for his responsiveness and encouragement. He is definitely a class act.

CHAPTER 15

Y2 Innovations is Born

I T WAS EARLY 2013 when Jo and I decided to take another crack at introducing a new product to the market. It's been about fourteen years since I lost all that money in the bag business. Now that wound has healed, leaving a scar of experience we can hopefully use to our advantage.

Our objective is to find one simple idea with large market potential, with the emphasis on simple.

In a nutshell, our plan is to come up with new product ideas that we will research, protect, prototype, and introduce to manufacturers. We do not wish to produce anything beyond a prototype. We plan to accept a fair royalty through a licensing agreement. The size of the world's consumer product market is almost beyond comprehension; we only want a tiny slice.

We began this venture just prior to my decision to write this book, so little has yet been accomplished with Y2. As Jo would attest, I generally can't do two things at one time, so I felt compelled to focus primarily on writing. I am, however, very anxious to spend more time on product development once this book is ready to go to market.

In terms of status thus far, we have generated eighteen new product concepts which are ready to begin the research stage of the eight-step review process we have developed.

We have filed for US patent-pending status on two products. One is a yard tool called the BagHolderPro and the other is an eyeglass adornment designed by JoAnn called EyeWearBling™. We were granted a US trademark in August of 2013. We are utilizing a third party to land a licensing agreement for EyeWearBling™, until we get more time to devote to this very exciting product.

We will likely go to our graves trying to bring new products to market.

PART TWO

BEFORE YOU START OR BUY A BUSINESS!

CHAPTER 16

Are You a Small Business Owner or an Entrepreneur?

I REALLY HAD TO SCRATCH my head and think about how to write this section. I want to explain what I think the difference is between a small business owner and an entrepreneur. Perhaps there is no difference, however, as you will see in subsequent chapters, it is important for one to understand oneself as much as possible before risking capital on a new business venture. I believe this chapter will help facilitate that understanding.

I see a small business owner, myself included, as an individual who:

- prefers to be independent and master of their own destiny
- is self-driven and takes full responsibility for their actions
- is a moderate risk-taker
- has a healthy compliment of common-sense
- has the capability to lead and manage people
- looks to be prudent and create security
- is task-driven
- is okay with copying an existing business model
- is a generalist in terms of education and training

I see the entrepreneur as one who may possess the above SBO characteristics but may differ in the following ways:

- prefers to innovate, not copy
- possesses a very high level of self-confidence and has a healthy ego
- is much more creative than pragmatic
- looks to go big or go home
- is vision-driven
- may not be as good a manager as he is a leader and inspiration to others
- is a specialist (and often highly trained) in terms of capability

For example, an SBO might aspire to open a car wash or two in order to gain independence and provide a good living for his family. An entrepreneur might aspire to have a national chain of car washes, while creating a completely new washing system in the process. Can a person be both? Certainly, as they are not mutually exclusive.

Since I would classify myself more as an SBO type who has less experience in innovating and more experience in managing, my focus is on SBOs, and those aspiring to become SBOs.

Chapter Takeaway

The more you realistically know about yourself, the better your chances of success in the business world . . . and in life in general.

CHAPTER 17

Key Personality Traits of Successful Small Business Owners

I WROTE THIS CHAPTER ABOUT eight months after writing the previous chapter which compares a small business owner to an entrepreneur. I am including it now because of the feedback I received suggesting that this book wouldn't be complete without describing personality traits that may be required to become a successful small business owner.

As you have discovered, I believe SBOs and entrepreneurs share many of the same traits; however, there are also differences. In keeping with my goal of focusing on small business owners, I began by preparing a list of attributes which I personally feel people need in order to become successful SBOs. My plan for this chapter was to then compare my list with that of some of the latest studies on this subject.

My list is based solely on my first thirty-five years of business experience. All people and businesses are different. However, if you possess most of these attributes, your chances of success in the small business world should be much improved.

1. ***Massive Desire for Independence:*** If you don't constantly dream of being on your own, then maybe you shouldn't. Perhaps you lack the self-confidence required to overcome the adversities faced by all business owners. If your need for autonomy is tenuous, you will likely soon be back in the employ of others.

2. ***Common Sense:*** You don't need to be Einstein to become a successful SBO; however, one needs to be able to reason between alternative courses of action, and quickly decide which option is in line with enterprise goals. In other words, this is no place for indecisive procrastinators.

3. ***Self Confidence / Healthy Ego:*** Let's face it. Most people who own their own businesses or lead large corporations have large egos. Not only do I believe this to be true, but I also believe that a larger ego is an important characteristic of a successful business person. I don't necessarily mean a monstrous ego where people get turned off, but a "healthy" level of self-confidence necessary to succeed in the business world. After all, what makes a person think that he or she can start something from nothing, make money at it, and get people to follow them while they do it?

4. ***Strong People / Management Skills:*** Do you have experience managing people? Do you enjoy it? Are you good at it? This skill is a definite requirement if you want your business to grow. You can't do it all yourself, so the ability to lead and delegate are of major importance.

5. ***Self Responsibility:*** You strive to be in control of your own destiny, and you are comfortable taking full responsibility for your actions and decisions. If you have a tendency to blame others for your misfortunes, perhaps being on your own is not for you.

6. ***Disciplined and Persistent Self-Starter:*** Perhaps this is too obvious to mention. Everyone is aware of the personal sacrifices a small business owner makes. Staying a step ahead of customers, staff, competitors, shareholders, creditors, and suppliers requires an internal fortitude supported by a strong work ethic and persistence.

7. *A Flare for Marketing and Sales:* Something always has to sell in order to become successful in business. Are you comfortable engaging people and convincing them to buy from you? Skill in this area can make you a market leader over those who possess only the first six traits.

8. *Miscellaneous:* The first seven attributes are required no matter the business one is in. However, there are additional attributes which may be of more or less importance, depending upon the strengths and weaknesses of the owner, or even the industry he or she is operating in. Things like organizational skills, attention to detail, and above-average risk tolerance are all very important, yet they may vary from essential, to good-to-have. For example, I have seen situations where great selling skills have compensated for lack of organizational skills and attention to detail. In addition, a strong desire to be independent usually makes taking higher risk more palatable.

After completing my list, I spent many hours "researching the research" on this topic. Firstly, I should mention that, for the most part, recent study data primarily describes entrepreneurs, not small business owners. I have read academic studies from the likes of Harvard, Stanford and Berkley. I reviewed work done by private organizations such as Ernst & Young, *The Globe and Mail*, and *The Wall Street Journal*, etc.

From what I could discern, most of them did their best to describe the personality traits of the high-tech elite. People like Mike Lazaridis, Steve Jobs, Steve Wozniak, Bill Gates, and Michael Dell were often referenced, as they should be. The more we learn about what makes these guys tick, the better off we much smaller capitalists will be.

I struggle, however, with how much benefit there is in listing the personality traits of these icons for the SBO? Yes, many of the same attributes are shared by both; however, some will be different, or absent, and some will be shared in varying degrees. For example, few can compare to the level of passion and vision exhibited by Steve Jobs. Nonetheless, they may still become successful SBOs.

I then compared my humble list to see if it resonated with studies more closely aligned with the personality of the SBO rather than the high tech entrepreneur.

One of the more referenced studies targeted to the small business owner was created by The Guardian Life Small Business Research Institute. I favor this study over many others because the researchers actually asked success-oriented SBOs what they thought was necessary to be successful. Fancy that.

Below are some excerpts from the Guardian report.[1]

The Guardian Life Index: What Matters Most to America's Small Business Owners, has identified six dimensions that characterize small business owners who exhibit a strong success orientation based on their desire to enjoy longevity in their businesses, expand revenues and grow the size of their companies.

In uncovering these dimensions, The Index polled more than 1,100 small businesses with 2-99 employees in May 2009. The research methodology employed a 21-point scale (from +10 to -10) that measured the positive and negative intensity of responses to a vast battery of issues.

Through the research analysis, The Index uncovered 60 critical factors that correlated with success-oriented owners.

---

[1] The Guardian Life Small Business Research Institute, "Six Dimensions That Characterize Success-Orientated Small Business Owners," June, 2010, 1-2.

The six dimensions, based on the 60 factors, paint a nuanced portrait and provide a deeper understanding of the success-oriented small business owner:

1. *Collaborative*

   Success-oriented small business owners understand how to delegate effectively to others within their business as well as build strong personal relationships with their management team, employees, consultants, vendors and customers. They are more committed "to creating opportunities for others."

2. *Self-fulfilled*

   Success-oriented small business owners place a high value on the personal fulfillment and gratification that their companies provide them, relishing the self-determination and respect that comes from being their own boss and being in control of their personal income and long-term net worth. They are more desirous of "doing something for a living that I love to do," "being able to decide how much money I make" and "being able to have the satisfaction of creating something of value."

3. *Future-focused*

   Planning for both the short- and long-term future are key traits that characterize success-oriented small business owners. They are more focused on cash flow and more likely to have "a well thought out plan to run our business for years into the future" as well as "a well thought out plan to run our business day to day."

4. *Curious*

   Success-oriented small business owners are more open to learning how others run their businesses. They actively seek best practice insights regarding management, business innovation, prospecting and finding/ motivating/retaining employees.

5. *Tech-savvy*

   Technology is a key point of leverage for success-oriented small business owners. They more intensely value their company's website and are significantly more likely to "rely a great deal on technology to help make our business more effective and more efficient."

6. *Action Oriented*

Finally, success-oriented small business owners are more proactive in taking initiative to build their businesses. They are more committed to "taking the business to the next level," "differentiating ourselves from our competitors" and "having something to sell when I'm ready to retire." They also see adversity as "a kick in the rear to help move you forward." Not surprisingly, they are less concerned than other small business owners about the overall state of the economy.

Possessing many or most of these factors may prove to be the key in predicting success in establishing, maintaining and growing small enterprises.

If this were a test and we assumed the Guardian study to be 100% correct, then it appears my list is lacking. However, in my defense, I feel that some explanation/clarification is in order.

Firstly, the traits on my list are based on my experience, so "it is what it is". I believe them all to be important and relevant.

I should get a pass for not including specific reference to Guardian's fourth point, "Curious". Remember, this chapter was written long after I had already covered much of what this trait describes. As evidenced by my chapter on Key Performance Indicators, I happen to believe very strongly in emulating the leaders in your industry. Still, this was "my bad" for not including it on my list.

Personally, I would classify tech-savvy as more of a "want" than a "need". Don't get me wrong; a fundamental understanding of technology is critically important, but could one succeed without it? I believe so, because it is a service that can be bought; however you can't buy common sense or people skills. Similarly, I wouldn't have accounting knowledge on my list (and nor does the Guardian report). However, a fundamental understanding of financial management is just as important as being technologically adept.

If you are contemplating going into business for yourself, perhaps a soul searching review of both lists will help you decide if you've got what it takes to succeed in the challenging world of small business.

Chapter Takeaway

There is predictive value in studying the personality traits of successful business owners; however, there is nothing more important than an honest and introspective assessment of one's own strengths and weaknesses.

CHAPTER 18

Is Passion Really Necessary to Become a Successful SBO?

THIS IS LIKELY A personal question, and the answer is highly dependent upon who you ask and what they are experiencing in their business cycle. As difficult and perhaps unanswerable as this question may be, I feel that it is still an important question to discuss for those thinking of a career as a small business owner.

As I contemplate my past thirty-five years as an SBO, and ask myself if I had a passion for every business I have been involved in, I guess the honest answer would have to be, no. It would depend on when I was asked. The start-up and growth phase can be downright exciting, the maturation phase can be a drag (for a guy like me) and the exit is always, and I mean always, a traumatic and exhilarating experience at the same time, especially if there are employees involved.

I suppose one could line up 100 employees and ask if they are passionate about their jobs, and one could do the same for 100 SBOs. I don't know if this has ever been done before, but I would certainly hazard a guess that the former group would be much less likely to be passionate than the latter, and probably by a long shot.

I would say that although I absolutely love small business in a general sense, I was not passionate about all of our ventures and, interestingly enough, I failed big on the one I was most passionate about, new product development.

Yes, we made a decent living without having a real passion for each and every one of our ventures. In fact, there were a few businesses that I didn't enjoy at all. My passion, I suppose, was to simply be on my own.

I believe that having a passion for the business you choose can be very important in terms of the overall satisfaction and the enjoyment you might experience; however, I also think that there must be some sort of balance between that passion and the economic reality of the venture. You can't pay the bills with passion, but you may become fulfilled with the independence you experience, and pay those bills at the same time.

As I write this book, I am also doing some swing/momentum trading in the equity markets with which I have a love/hate relationship. In addition, JoAnn and I are starting a product development business designing and licensing new products. This really gets me excited! Right now, I would rather spend my time writing, so perhaps I have a new passion. But, will I make any money doing so?

Chapter Takeaway

Having passion for your venture will increase your chances of success; however, passion alone will not guarantee it.

CHAPTER 19

Pros and Cons of Owning a Small Business

OBVIOUSLY MY OPINION IS that the advantages of being self-employed definitely outweigh the disadvantages, or I wouldn't continue to choose the SBO career path. After I first set out on my own, it was rare for me to ever seriously consider working for someone else. Such feelings did occur occasionally, but usually when I was bored or couldn't find an opportunity that made sense at the time.

PROS:

- *Master of Your Own Destiny:* For some, this benefit alone may be enough to offset all of the cons; at least it was for me!

- *Self Fulfillment:* It is an amazing feeling to succeed through your own efforts. It's a high that is difficult to duplicate as an employee.

- *Opportunity:* There is opportunity for both financial and personal growth. The numbers at the back of this book will help you determine how a small business income might compare to your job. In theory, an SBO's income is limitless; however, these statistics will help keep things real. As for personal growth, all I can say is that the SBO is the leader, and business growth depends on good decision-making by the SBO. Now, that's empowerment and accountability which can lead to a great deal of personal satisfaction!

- *Pride:* It's pretty cool to be able to say, I "own" that business, rather than, I "work" for that business. I believe that when you are proud of what you do, you will be much more effective at what you do.

- *Flexibility:* Although I rarely capitalized on this, I loved being able to come and go as I please. Just the notion that if I wanted to go golfing mid-day, I could, and that helped me push on.

- *Tax Benefits:* There are more tax benefits for SBOs than there are for employees, especially if you include the big kahuna of tax benefits: the lifetime small business capital gains deduction/exemption. See Chapter 33.

CONS:

- *It Can be a Lot of Work:* Although this can be true especially at the start, it is not a killer amount, in my opinion. In fact, I put in as many (or more) hours as a Chief Executive Officer (CEO) than I did as an SBO; however, I had over 100 employees as a CEO versus an average of about six as an SBO. It can vary greatly, but count on about 50-60 hours per week.

- *Higher Risk:* I believe this negative has edged slightly closer to the risk that employees face these days. Gone are the days when one worked for the same company for an entire career. Employees are forced to change jobs, and sometimes occupations, much more frequently these days, and as a result there is increasing risk to their livelihood. Having said this, employees are usually protected by employment insurance. In contrast there is no such insurance for SBOs, and only about half of small businesses last longer than five years![2]

---

[2] Industry Canada, Small Business Branch, "Key Small Business Statistics," July 2012, p. 4.

- *Can be Stressful:* There is nothing like having your own money on the line. No more spending of other people's money (OPM). It is a weird and sobering feeling reaching into one's own pocket to pay an expense that was once paid for by others.

  Aside from financial concerns, managing people is by the far the biggest stress one will face. Yes, good staff can become your biggest asset, but along the way some may steal from you, some will quit when you need them most, and some will compete with you after you have trained them.

- *It Can be Lonely Out There:* I haven't experienced this emotion as my wife JoAnn has been my partner on four of our ventures, and I have usually had some staff to keep me company in most of the others. I can, however, see how some one-person operators may need more social interaction than others. Luckily, there are many networking clubs and business associations to keep you company after hours. I will cover more on networking later.

- *Must be Able to "Wear Many Ugly Hats":* Yes, there will be many jobs to do that you won't necessarily enjoy, and it may be a long time before you can afford to have someone else do them. It's just a fact of small business life.

- *Lack of Time Off:* If you are the type who needs a regularly scheduled holiday break or regular hours of work, then self employment may not be a good fit for you.

Chapter Takeaway

Independence may tip the scales for many considering the self-employed lifestyle.

CHAPTER 20

Comparisons to the Corporate World

I HAVE HAD THE PRIVILEGE of working in both the larger corporate world (13 years) and in the small business world (22 years). I have been asked how these two environments compare.

At one point in my life, all I dreamed about was getting my first management position, moving up that corporate ladder, and then perhaps, one day, the executive suite!

Interestingly, the more I looked at the executives in my world, the less I saw that they had anything I really wanted. I adopted (stole) this notion from my older brother, Bob, who at the time was a senior executive himself.

In fact, early in my career I started to want more of what successful SBOs possessed. It seemed to me that these owners may have had less prestige, fewer employees, and smaller offices than large company executives, but they seemed to have much more control over their time, destiny, and financial security. I believe the more control you have over your time and decision-making, the less stress you will endure. Also, the fewer employees you have, the less stress you may encounter.

Being an SBO affords one the opportunity to be in greater control of one's future, with fewer bureaucratic and/or political hurdles to overcome in order to effect change. You are the "owner"; if you don't like something, simply change it, and deal with the consequences. The executive, on the other hand, may not have such "pure" autonomy.

So, which path is more stressful? I can only speak for myself, but having worn both hats, I would have to say that the Corporate world was more stressful, but for different reasons. The SBO will likely stress more over money as there is no assured income like there is in an executive position. Yes, the executive risks getting fired, but he or she is not likely to lose their nest egg in the process.

The executive, or senior manager, will likely experience more stress due to having more employees, and not having absolute independence in making decisions. There is always someone higher, or ultimately a Board of Directors, to answer to.

Who works harder? I really can't say for certain as this question is subjective and there are so many variables involved. I would say, though, that on a start-up, the SBO will work many more hours (at a lower stress level) than say a middle manager in a large corporation. As the SBO's business grows, however, the hours per week may taper off, while the middle Manager's hours will likely increase as he or she climbs that corporate ladder. Unfortunately, I have no studies to support my thoughts; they are based solely on my experience.

I suppose, if your goal is to achieve a higher level of power (measured by the number of employees under your supervision) and prestige (measured by the size and location of your offices), you are more likely to aspire to becoming a corporate executive or senior manager. If your goal is to maximize your independence and opportunity for financial freedom, you are more likely to aspire to a career as a small to medium-sized business owner.

No doubt you have detected my bias toward SBOs versus larger company managers. I make no apologies because I don't believe that one is a true businessperson unless he or she has put their own money on the line, and I don't mean cheap stock options either.

There, I have said it. Corporate executives without major skin in the game may be highly skilled managers of assets, but not necessarily true-blue business people. Yes, they may be very intelligent, talented, and powerful people, but they are not quite complete business people until they have risked their personal capital in a significant way.

Lastly, another way to describe the differences between these two career paths is to discuss what they have created at the end of their working lives. The successful SBO will likely have built "equity" in a going concern that can one day be sold or, perhaps, carry on indefinitely; a legacy of sorts.

The executive on the other hand (unless he has ownership in the company) will certainly have contributed to the growth of the company; however, on less risky terms. Of course, there is nothing wrong with that, and I admire all executives for their accomplishments and contribution to the Canadian economy; I just admire SBOs a tiny bit more for the risks they take.

Chapter Takeaway

If you seek independence, then a small business career may appeal to you. If you seek power and prestige, Corporate Canada may be a better fit. The executive builds "credentials", while the SBO builds "equity".

CHAPTER 21

The Big Picture

I STRONGLY SUGGEST THAT BEFORE you spend too much time or money on any business opportunity, you test the concept against these "big picture" criteria. These questions should be answered long before you get to the business plan stage.

1. *Is your concept in a growth industry?* If not, stop here and look for another concept. There is no use fighting an uphill battle no matter how much you like an idea.

2. *How much money do you "need" to make, and how much would you like to make, to keep you motivated?* Specifically define your target income and write it down. Can the concept you have chosen realistically support your needs and offer higher income potential at the same time? If not, take a pass. The statements in the reference section of Part Six will help you with this.

3. *Do you have the skill set required to succeed, or the money to hire those that do?* It is time again for some soul searching. You may wish to ask a mentor-type person for his or her opinion concerning your abilities. For example, people often mistakenly think that selling is easy. In fact, selling can be quite a challenge for some, and almost all business activity is about selling something.

4. ***Does this concept stroke your ego?*** I have made this mistake. I didn't really think about it until I got into something that I wasn't too proud of, not for nefarious reasons, of course.

5. ***Will you be able to sell this concept after you build it into a profitable business?*** If your goal is to retire off the proceeds of a sale down the road then now is the time to start thinking about it. We will discuss this in much more detail later on.

6. ***Does your preliminary market research suggest viability?*** Thanks to the power of the internet, you can quickly search for competing products or services, and receive almost instant feedback, which can save a lot of time and money down the road.

7. ***How many products or services do you have to sell per day in order to break even? Does this sound feasible?*** We are just talking rough calculations here, but they can be a preliminary "acid" test which will prove beneficial if you proceed to the business plan stage.

8. ***Does your family support you 100%?*** Spending a bunch of time or money may be useless until you are sure that you have this support.

If you answered yes to all of the above for each opportunity presented to you, then it's time to proceed.

Chapter Takeaway

When you get an idea, step back and consider it from a big picture perspective before you dive in prematurely.

CHAPTER 22

How Much Money Can You Really Make and How Many Widgets Do You Have to Sell?

AS MENTIONED IN THE introduction, this book is a bit of a hybrid between a "how to" publication and a "reference manual". Many of these pages are filled with numbers . . . very important numbers. These numbers can tell you how much money you can **realistically** make as a small business owner in Canada. In fact, these are numbers you can literally "take to the bank!"

I find that people, including myself, don't really want to look at boring data for any length of time. It's more fun and exciting to think up new business names, or design a fancy new logo, or dream about where to locate that new office.

Often, there is no money for that new office and, if there is, it quickly becomes filled with stock or supplies of some kind. This is why many SBOs end up doing their administrative work at home, at night or on week-ends. Office space is costly!

I am not trying to dissuade or discourage, but the early life of a small business owner is often one of considerable sacrifice and long hours. Knowing your numbers will go a long way to preventing you from getting into something that has little chance of being financially rewarding.

At this point in our discussion, we are still at the research stage of starting a new business or, the due diligence stage, if buying an existing business. We want a preliminary look at how much money we can make before wasting too much time on a particular opportunity.

Before I do a formal business plan, I always rough out some numbers often referred to as "back of the napkin calculations". My intention here is to do some very early viability testing to see if the "numbers" make any sense.

Let's say you're thinking of opening a new car wash. Do you really know how much car wash owners actually make? I don't mean what you heard from your friends at the local bar or from your brother-in-law in Fort McMurray, but from real data? Luckily you bought this book . . . just turn to page 336 to see some reality. We'll talk more about how to use this new-found data a little later.

There are 100 different business types included in the reference section of this book. The data is based on 2011 tax returns from Revenue Canada, so it can't get much more factual than that! It includes both incorporated and unincorporated businesses with gross annual sales between $30,000 and $5,000,000 which is our definition of an SBO. This data is complied by Stats Canada, and published by Industry Canada.

If you are currently employed, it may be a good exercise to compare this data to your current annual income and what you expect it might be for the next five years. Then assume you are capable of becoming an average business owner, and compare the two sets of figures.

I realize that there are a lot more benefits to owning your own business then just financial rewards, i.e., freedom from current boss, flexibility, job satisfaction, etc. But does it make sense financially? If not, you may wish to keep your job until another opportunity comes along that might compare more favorably. Remember you still need to pay the bills and get some return on your invested time and capital.

When you look at the statements in Part Six, it is a useful exercise to think of it in terms of dollars per hour. Often, an SBO puts in many more hours than in a typical job.

In 2011, the average net income of unincorporated businesses in Canada with revenues between $30,000 and $5 mil was $43,000 per year (see page 311). This figure generally represents the average owner's taxable income. If you figure that this income level sounds pretty fine (especially because you are just not average), you need to understand that it may translate into much less per hour than a typical job.

Employment Canada reported that in 2012 the average number of hours worked by Canadian employees was 36.6 per week. Based on personal experience, I suggest SBOs average about 55 hours per week.

If we put this all together, the "job" might pay $22.60/hour, while the SBO might earn only $15.04/hour given the extra hours they typically put in. ($43,000/52 weeks = $827/week divided by 36.6 average hours/week = $22.60/hour, and $827 divided by 55 hours/week = $15.04/hour)

This non-scientific, yet logical, example is just another way to think about self-employment. There are also employment benefits to consider which can add 10% to 15% of value to the employee compensation package. These might include health, dental, life insurance and employer pension contributions.

Often I hear people say, "That's not a business . . . you're just buying yourself a job." While I believe this statement can be true, I also believe that it may be okay to do so, as long as you understand that is exactly what you are doing . . . buying a job, not necessarily an investable business.

Let me explain. In our definition of a "real" business, the owner/investor needs to get a decent return on investment (ROI). Let's assume that a new venture costs $250,000 to set up. The owner manages the business full-time. Let's further assume that he nets $50,000/year before taxes and depreciation (more on depreciation later). If the owner has paid himself a market value salary and still nets the $50,000, we could say he has a "real" business with a ROI of 20% ($50,000/$250,000).

If the business shows a net income of $50,000, but hasn't yet paid the owner, this venture has zero ROI (assuming the market value of his management time is $50,000); thus he may have bought himself a job with his $250,000. In other words, someone must be paid to manage the business, and this is an expense which much be deducted in order to determine the real income for calculating ROI.

Again, there is nothing wrong with the scenario I just described. The point is that one must understand the difference before capital is committed. Buying a single franchise can fall into the category of "buying a job" as its royalty structure and capacity limitations often make it difficult to make a real ROI (after the owner/operator is compensated at market rates). We have owned two different franchises, and I will elaborate on this point in a subsequent chapter.

Please keep in mind that the reports in the reference section are averages, and the age of the reporting businesses is not taken into account. It might take five years to reach these averages, so think about what the first year or two might be like. It is quite possible that the SBO won't be paid a nickel of salary for a year or so. I'm not trying to be negative, just realistic.

I love rules of thumb (ROT)! Merriam Webster defines a rule of thumb as:

> *a method of procedure based on experience and common sense; a general principal regarded as roughly correct but not intended to be scientifically accurate.*

Assuming they are based on factual data, like the statements included in this book, ROTs can really help save you time and energy when analyzing potential business opportunities and managing your small business.

The only problem with ROTs is that they are difficult to come by. Usually business ROTs are developed by professionals like accountants, bankers, lenders, business brokers, etc. over many years of observation.

Another good source of ROTs is industry associations which compile financial and operating data from their members. ROTs are not to be confused with Key Performance Indicators (KPIs) which will be discussed in a later chapter. ROTs are very high-level indicators of relative comparisons, whereas KPIs are much more specific to a particular business type.

For example, let's take a look at retail stores. An ROT in retail is that you need a gross margin of at least 50% to make a go of it. This means, if you buy your goods for a dollar, you must be able to sell them for at least $2 (including discounts) in order to produce positive cash flow (bring in more cash than you spend each month). Pretty simple stuff, I know, and most people already know this, but I mention it here only to illustrate the ROT principle.

Everyone knows full-service restaurants need a gross margin of at least 55% to be viable, right? How about new car dealerships? Most people think those guys make tons of money. You just have to look all those shiny new cars on their lot. In fact, new car dealerships have tight gross margins (about 20%) and they make most of their profit from repair and warranty service, but everybody knows that too, right?

One ROT that has been around for a long time is that you can usually sell your business for about one times the gross revenue. Boy, this is one dangerous assumption! In fact, this ROT may hold true for only a few business segments (i.e., accounting firms and small manufactures), but it is far from reality for almost all other sectors. I have included some sample ROTs for business valuations in Appendix 3 which will be discussed in more detail in Chapter 31.

Let's start our own ROT and see if it might help us make better decisions concerning starting a new business. Let's assume you are thinking of opening a coffee shop. Yep, just like everybody else.

Based upon my experience in helping people sell coffee shops, a typical outlet needs about $400,000 in gross sales in order to break even and start to pay you (the owner) a market salary. This is the sales level one needs to reach where total costs equal total sales revenue. I often use this type of ROT to answer the question, "How many widgets (or, in this case, cups of coffee) do I have to sell to break even?"

I like to calculate how much product needs to sell each and every day the shop will be open for business in order to break even.

In this case, $400,000 divided by 350 days = $1,142/day. At an average sale of about $6.00, you would need to serve about 190 customers per day.

Now, does this sound feasible? Will your location deliver this level of traffic? How much traffic does your competition get daily? Yes, you should go and count their traffic a few times. Who is going to serve this many people?

The point here is that this kind of simple analysis can be very beneficial as a quick feasibility study. It helps us focus specifically on what it would take to break even. It raises great questions which need to be addressed, and it saves a lot of time in the event our cursory analysis points to a lack of feasibility.

Chapter Takeaway

Make sure you have a "realistic" idea of how much money you can make before you commit too much time or resources to a business opportunity.

CHAPTER 23

Do You Really Need a Business Plan?

AH . . . THE OFTEN DREADED business plan. Why do so many SBOs and entrepreneurs wish they could just skip this stage of starting or buying a business? It's likely because it can be an uncomfortable process. Most people seeking a job don't write up a three year employment plan before they apply for the job, do they? Perhaps they should, but when it comes to starting a business there is a whole lot more risk involved. Is this risk reduced if one takes the time to write a business plan?

I have discovered three credible studies which try to answer this question.

1. ***Babson College Study (2007)***: Babson is regarded as having one of the top entrepreneurship programs in the US and I quote from their study as follows:

   > *This study examined whether writing a business plan before launching a new venture affects the subsequent performance of the venture. The data set comprised 116 new ventures started by Babson College alums who graduated between 1985 and 2003. The analysis revealed that there was no difference between the performance of new businesses launched with or without written business plans.*

> *The findings suggest that unless a would-be entrepreneur needs to raise substantial start-up capital from institutional investors or business angels, there is no compelling reason to write a detailed business plan before opening a new business.*[3]

Before you say, "That's great to hear; now I don't have to write that damned business plan," please read on.

2. *University of Oregon Study (2010):*[4] Palo Alto Software founder, Tim Berry, completed a survey which asked 2,877 users of its Business Plan Pro software questions about their businesses, goals and business planning. The responses showed that those who completed business plans were nearly twice as likely to successfully grow their businesses or obtain capital as those who didn't write a plan.

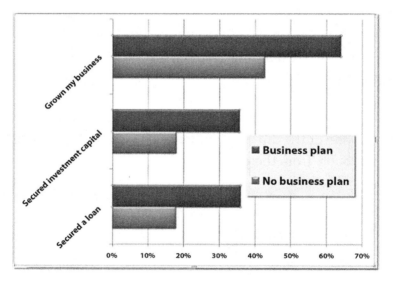

---

[3] Julian E. Lange, Aleksandar Mollov, Michael Pearlmutter, Sunil Singh and William D. Bygrave, "Pre-startup Formal Business Plans and Post-startup Performance: A Study of 116 New Ventures," *Venture Capital Journal* 9:4 (October 2007): 1-20.

[4] Eason Ding and Tim Hursey , "Evaluation of the Effectiveness of Business Planning Using Palo Alto's Business Plan Pro," (Authored report under the supervision of Professor Joe Stone and presented to the Department of Economics, University of Oregon, June 7, 2010).

Now, Mr. Berry is in the business of selling business plan programs and, therefore, he and his study may be a tad biased. In order to respond to such potential bias, Mr. Berry asked the University Of Oregon Department Of Economics to evaluate the validity of his data.

Eason Ding and Tim Hursey authored a report on the data under the supervision of Professor Joe Stone. "Results suggest that planning with software is highly correlated with subsequent successes for a variety of firms," they wrote.

Even more to the point, Ding and Hursey's analysis found that, "Writing a business plan correlated with increased success in every one of the business goals included in the study". These incorporated obtaining a loan, getting investment capital, making a major purchase, recruiting new team members, thinking more strategically, and growing the company.

The authors further concluded that:

> *Except in a small number of cases, business planning appeared to be positively correlated with business success as measured by our variables. While our analysis cannot say that completing a business plan will lead to success, it does indicate that the type of entrepreneur who completes a business plan is also more likely to run a successful business.*

3. *The "How Much Money Can I Make?" Study*: Truthfully, I have started or purchased ventures without doing a business plan, or I have completed only certain parts and not finished other parts, i.e., toys, home flips, MLM, new product. I was either too lazy, too cocky, or too excited, and as a result three of these four were losers, one a big loser. On the other hand, our eight winners did start with some sort of written plan.

My opinion of the first two studies relates more to the participants included in these studies rather than the actual results.

Study one focuses on university-educated "entrepreneurs" who, because of their business education, may not need to do a formal business plan as much as potential small business owners who likely have less formal business education. Also, study two includes a much broader range of participants and is much more relevant to the potential small business owner targeted in this book.

The Babson study also revealed that almost 78% of the top 100 American universities had at least one class dealing with business plan education. I wonder why?

I also wonder why larger and more mature corporations generally always have an annual business planning process. Is it because they like to waste time and energy on something that won't help improve their bottom line? Of course, that is not the reason. If a business plan is good for huge and often growing existing businesses, why on earth would it not help a new business?

For me, I base my answer to this question on what I have personally and practically experienced from our dozen ventures. My small "study" strongly confirms for me that doing a business plan greatly improves one's chances of success.

I know that writing a business plan can be uncomfortable because it forces the author to be realistic and answer questions that can be challenging to answer. You have to make assumptions that may make you feel vulnerable to criticism in the event those assumptions are later proven wrong. I also think that deep down we don't want to find reasons why we "shouldn't" do what we think is a good idea, preferring to move on to the more enjoyable parts of starting a new business.

Whatever the reason, the fact is that it absolutely needs to be done . . . so JUST DO IT! I guarantee you will never ever look back and say, "Boy, I wish I hadn't wasted time on that business plan." On the contrary, you'll be very glad you did, for a myriad of reasons.

It is not my objective to teach anyone how to write a business plan. Many good books are available on the subject, and there is a wealth of easily attainable information available on the internet, so there is no need to reproduce it here. Appendix 4, however, does list elements of what should be included in an effective business plan for a small business start-up or purchase.

If you have to borrow money to start your venture, which many people do, then you will most likely require a written business plan. And please, don't insult your friends or family by asking them for their hard earned money without showing them that you have at least gone to the trouble of writing even a brief business plan. I have seen this happen, and, frankly, it annoys me; so don't take advantage of people that love and trust you. Also, they may have an idea or two that might help you if they have had the benefit of reading about your business opportunity.

Banks and other lenders may not require a formal business plan, but they are very likely to require cash flow projections. Both my experience and the study results referenced earlier suggest that your odds of receiving funding will increase immensely, if you have a complete business plan in place.

Why is the thought of writing a business plan so intimidating for some? Do you need an MBA or an accounting degree to write an effective business plan? No! In fact, as suggested earlier, these types have a lower need to write a plan. They should already be familiar with what needs to be done to start a business, and they can incorporate their training on the fly, so to speak. My recommendations are directed to those with an idea and a dream who have much less, if any, formal business training.

It doesn't need to be, nor should it be, a long and tedious process. The last thing you want to do is analyze things to death. In fact, the shorter and simpler, the better. About four to five pages should do fine, and hand-written is acceptable if it is not being presented to outside parties. I suggest that the business plan address much of what I have outlined in Appendix 4. If you haven't covered each of these areas, you're just not ready to ask dear old dad for his hard earned dough!

At the absolute very least, I suggest you write down a brief answer to the following questions:

1. Is your concept in a growth industry? Some back-up data would be nice.

2. Who is your target market? I am specifically referring to gender, age bracket, income level, geographic location.

3. Have you talked to some of your target market? If so, what did they say?

4. How will you reach/communicate with your target market?

5. Who is your competition and how will you beat them?

6. How and who will sell your product/service?

7. What is your break-even, in dollars & units per day, week, or month?

8. What does your twelve month cash flow statement look like, and what were your assumptions? How long do you estimate it will take to become cash flow positive?

These are only eight questions, so please answer them before you put your money or someone else's money at risk. Much of the work involves common sense, not a business degree; if you need help with the last two points, then by all means, get it. At some point you will need a bookkeeper and/or an accountant, so now might be a good time to find one that you are comfortable with. Alternatively, there are plenty of resources online which will teach you what you need to know about cash flow statements.

I want to mention something else here that might be helpful. When I was in university, they taught us about the 4 P's of marketing (now it's the 5 P's of business). This might seem too simple in this day and age given our complex high-tech world, but for regular folks it is still a good practice to consider these as a business owner: Product, Price, Promotion, Place, and People.

Each of these will be discussed at greater length in Chapter 37.

Often, the greatest benefit of doing a business plan is the "process", not necessarily the final product. In fact, you may never even look back at your plan once you get your business going; although, I do recommend you revisit things monthly, or at least annually. Creating a business plan will teach you a lot about yourself, in addition to the viability of the venture you are planning, or operating.

Keep it brief and simple, and try to address the key elements of "what you will have to do well in order to succeed."

It is also important to understand that a business plan is not carved in stone. It should be viewed as a dynamic tool that should change and adapt to ever-changing market conditions.

Lastly, completing a business plan will make you feel better about yourself. You will have more confidence having done your homework; and this increased confidence will also increase your chances of success as you will be less likely to give up when you encounter challenges.

Chapter Takeaway

If you are seriously committed to success as an SBO, then you <u>absolutely must</u> complete a business plan.

CHAPTER 24

Mentors and Professional Advisors

I MENTIONED EARLIER THAT MOST people who own their own businesses or lead large corporations have large egos. I suggested that such a trait is a good thing. However, that ego can sometimes prevent us from developing a very important business relationship . . . that of the mentor and protégé. There are times when we need help, and we must keep our egos and pride in check long enough to seek out and accept that help. Mentors can offer such assistance in a highly rewarding and cost-effective manner. A mentor is a person who has specialized skills, experience, knowledge, and/or contacts that can be beneficial to the successful development of the protégé's business endeavours.

Mentors

Earlier, I mentioned Keith Critchley who was my mentor during my Yellow Pages days. We worked together on a daily basis for only three years; however, we continued to interact as invested members on the Board of Directors of a private company. To this day, I am still comfortable calling Keith for business advice.

Mentor/protégé relationships have grown a great deal in recent years. In fact, one is viewed as lacking an "edge" if he or she lacks a mentor; so, if you don't yet have one, I strongly suggest you find one, especially if you wish to be in the top 25% of your industry.

I have outlined a few of the possible benefits you may experience if you are fortunate enough to find a mentor.

1. *Grow Your Business Faster:* Two heads are always better than one, and a mentor's experience can help you avoid costly and time-consuming mistakes which will help your business grow more quickly.

2. *Expand Your Contacts:* It's often who you know that can make all the difference in business. Mentors provide introductions to important people and markets which otherwise might never come to fruition.

3. *Fantastic Return on Investment:* There is no other initiative as cost effective.

4. *Reduce Stress and Make Better Decisions:* Bouncing ideas off an advocate and discussing economic trends, etc. can be beneficial to one's health and bottom line.

Advances in technology will greatly improve the opportunities for SBOs to find a mentor match. Think about the rapid growth in online dating services. Eventually, online mentor matchmaking will become commonplace. It doesn't even matter if participants are located in another city or country. Services such as Skype or FaceTime can facilitate fast and efficient communications for SBOs to connect with mentors who can help their businesses grow, and provide an edge over their competition.

Professional Advisors

Let's talk professional advisors for a few moments, accountants in particular. When we moved to Kelowna, we knew no one and had no business contacts. I called my network back home to see if anyone could refer a good accountant out west. Somebody knew somebody, and a name surfaced.

This accountant's name was John, and he was a partner at a larger regional firm. I set up a meeting to introduce myself and see if he was somebody I could work with, even though I had no idea what that work would be. We seemed to click; John came across as a positive type which is not always a common characteristic of an accountant. John became our accountant on five different ventures over a thirteen year period.

Choosing professional advisors is such an important decision for SBOs that I think we should discuss it further. You will be entering into a business relationship that may last for many years; it can also be a difficult, uncomfortable, and costly relationship to break. Think about that for a moment. All of your business numbers and tax returns, likely both business and personal, will be passed to this person/firm, so choose wisely. The last thing you want is an uncomfortable feeling when you pick up that phone to ask for advice.

I suggest that you meet with as many accountants as it takes to feel comfortable, and remember they are in business to make money, just like you.

Once you have narrowed your list down to a couple of candidates, call them and explain to them that you are interviewing people to work with as you start up a new venture. Explain that you are not seeking accounting advice; however, you have some questions about what their particular firm has to offer. There should be no confusion about the purpose of the meeting. You do not want to later receive an invoice in the mail.

Here are a few questions to ask during that meeting, and don't be shy:

1. What experience do you (not just the firm) have in my industry?

2. Do you have other clients in my industry? i.e., competitors?

3. What do you charge per hour for accounting/tax advice? Depending on their professional designation and the type of work they do for you, this can range from $150 - $400.

4. What do you charge per hour for general bookkeeping duties? Sometimes it is wise to hire an outside bookkeeper for about $25.00 per hour rather than pay the $50.00 - $75.00 per hour charged by accounting firms for this service. With this scenario, you simply pass on the year-end statements from your bookkeeper to the accountant for year-end adjustments and tax returns.

5. What is the rate per hour for telephone calls made directly to you? How are these calls billed? i.e. per quarter hour? This is important, so you may opt to use email rather than play a game of telephone tag.

6. What will a non-corporate tax return cost?

7. What will a corporate tax return cost?

8. If applicable, will you refer business to me?

9. Why should I become a client of this firm?

10. Will I receive a discount on rates for my first year since I am just starting out? . . . well it's worth a try!

11. Do you have some client referrals that I can contact?

12. Do you have a legal firm that you can recommend? They may not want to use the word recommend, but you can bet they have their favorites, which may save you time and money if it is someone you can work with.

13. Who do you recommend to use as a commercial insurance broker?

If you handle these inquiries in a friendly and business-like manner, I believe you will gain the respect of the individual you are interviewing.

Lawyers are obviously less of a necessity if you choose not to incorporate right away; however, if you do incorporate or form a partnership, I suggest you take almost the same care in choosing a lawyer as you take in choosing an accountant. Again, the relationship you start today can last many years, so invest a little time meeting with a few potential legal advisors.

I recommend that you ask other SBOs or people in your network for referrals. Once you get a few names, you should narrow it down to include only those that specialize in commercial law. Most lawyers, particularly in smaller centres, operate as "generalists"; they do a bit of real estate, a little family law, some personal injury, and so on. Why spend time with a lawyer who spends most of his or her time on divorce cases when all you require is business advice?

At a minimum, you want somebody who has experience reviewing leases and writing partnership agreements. You also want someone who has done at least a few business deals, including both asset sales and share sales. If you happen to be buying a franchise, pick someone with experience in franchise agreements, even though these agreements are extremely difficult to change. He or she will at least be able to properly explain what you are getting into.

If your business model requires intellectual property protection and/or a successful patent application, you need to seek a specialist in that field.

After you have identified your candidates, call them and explain that you are interviewing a few people to work with as you start up a new venture. Explain that you are not seeking legal advice; however, you have some questions about what their particular firm has to offer. Again, there should be no confusion about the purpose of the meeting as you don't want to receive an invoice at a later date.

Here are a few questions to ask during your lawyer interview, and again, don't be shy:

1. What area(s) of law do you personally specialize in?

2. I plan to purchase XYZ company. Do you have any first-hand experience in this industry? Do you have other clients in this industry? This is important to flush out so that any conflicts of interest can be identified early on. They may not be able to work with you if they already represent a competitor.

3. Which of these do you work with most: sole proprietorships, partnerships, or corporations?

4. How many business sales have you completed? In which industries? Were these asset sales or share sales?

5. Kindly explain your fee structure for incorporation and/or partnership agreements?

6. How much should I budget for legal fees for my start-up in the first year?

7. How much do you charge per hour?

8. Why should I become a client of this firm?

9. I am in need of an accountant, whom do you recommend, and why?

Now you may be thinking, "Tim, I'm just a little start-up. I can't go into these professional offices and ask them all those questions; I'm just peanuts to them. They're only interested in bigger fish that can afford to pay for many billable hours. They'll just think I'm a waste of their time and they won't even get paid to do it!"

Well I can tell you, I had those same thoughts, and how wrong I was. The fact is, these professionals will be glad to hear from you and happy to spend a half an hour telling you why you should choose them.

They understand that this is a great opportunity to gain a client they can bill for many years, and they're in the business of "billable hours", plain and simple. So, go to these meetings with a long-term view. Who knows, you may become a big fish and they'll be taking you to lunch someday soon!

Chapter Takeaway

Having a mentor is a great business "edge"
and a privilege!

CHAPTER 25

Sole Proprietorship, Partnership or Incorporation?

I HAVE DECIDED TO take the easy way out on this topic and reproduce data from TaxTips.ca. This information seems complete for our purposes; however, you should seek professional advice before making a decision on which structure best meets the needs of your new venture. Familiarizing yourself with this information beforehand will certainly help you be much better prepared when you meet with your advisors. To help with your decision, I have added a few comments/opinions after this plagiarism.

Sole Proprietorship

A sole proprietorship is one person operating a business, without forming a corporation. The income of the business is then taxed in the hands of the owner (the proprietor), at personal income tax rates. The income is considered income from self-employment, and is included on the personal income tax return of the owner.

Advantages of proprietorship:

- *Setting up a business in the form of a proprietorship is relatively simple and the costs are low.*

- *If the business loses money, the losses can be written off against other income of the proprietor.*

- *Proprietorships are less regulated than corporations. The administration of a proprietorship is less costly than that of a corporation. However, proprietorships are regulated by the provincial/territorial governments, and the proprietorship may have to be registered.*

- *The proprietor is in control of all decision making, and receives all profits of the business.*

Disadvantages of a proprietorship:

- *The biggest disadvantage of a proprietorship is unlimited liability. The proprietor is liable for all debts and other liabilities of the business. If the business is sued, all the business and personal assets of the owner are at risk.*

- *If the business is profitable, it will usually be paying higher taxes than if it was incorporated as a <u>Canadian Controlled Private Corporation (CCPC)</u>. The lowest personal income tax rate paid by a proprietorship would range from approximately 20% to 29%, depending on the province/territory. This rate increases with income. Taxable income over $120,887 (in 2007) is taxed at the highest marginal rates, which range from approximately 39% to 48%, depending on the province/territory.*

- *A proprietorship has a lack of permanence - if the owner dies, the net business assets pass to the heirs, but valuable leases and contracts may not.[5]*

Partnership

A partnership is also an unincorporated business. It is similar to a proprietorship, except two or more entities are partners in the business. For partners who are individuals, the income from the partnership is taxed at personal income tax rates, and a percentage of the income is included on the personal income tax return of each owner.

---

[5] "Canadian Tax and Financial Information - Should You Incorporate Your Small Business?" Boat Harbour Investments Ltd., accessed April 23, 2014. http://www.taxtips.ca/smallbusiness/incorporate.htm.

Advantages of a partnership:

- *The setup costs of a partnership are relatively low.*

- *A partnership is less regulated than a corporation. A partnership agreement should be drawn up to outline the terms of the partnership, what happens in the event of a dissolution, and what happens in the event of disagreements among partners. In the absence of an agreement, or if certain provisions are not addressed in the agreement, provincial or territorial laws will determine some or all of the terms of the partnership.*

- *Business losses can be written off against other income of the partners.*

- *Broader base of experience, knowledge and skills to draw from.*

Disadvantages of a partnership:

- *The biggest disadvantage of a partnership is unlimited liability. The partners are jointly liable for all debts and other liabilities of the business. If the business is sued, all the business and personal assets of the partners are at risk. An exception to this is a Limited Partnership. Limited Partners, who contribute capital but do not participate in the management of the business, will have their liability limited to the amount of capital that they have contributed. The partners who participate in the management of the business are called General Partners, and will still have unlimited liability.*

- *Decisions must be made jointly.*

- *If the business is profitable, it will usually be paying higher taxes than if it was incorporated as a <u>Canadian Controlled Private Corporation (CCPC)</u>. See this same topic above under proprietorships.*

- *The death or retirement of a partner will not end the partner's liability for debts and obligations of the partnership that were incurred prior to the death or retirement. Also, if a partner retires and does not make the retirement publicly known, he/*

she could still be held liable for obligations incurred by the
partnership after the retirement.[6]

Corporation

A <u>corporation</u> *is a separate legal entity, which is formed by*
application to either the federal government, or one of the
provincial/territorial governments. The corporation issues shares
to the owners, or shareholders. The funding of the corporation can
be done through the issue of shares, or by borrowing. Instead of
investing a large amount in shares, shareholders can lend money to
the corporation, and invest only a minimal amount in the shares.
This way, when the corporation has available cash, the shareholder
loans can be repaid without attracting personal income tax.

Being a separate legal entity, a corporation pays corporate
income tax, which is calculated completely separately from the
owners' personal income tax. If the corporation pays wages to the
shareholders, income tax and Canada Pension Plan contributions,
and sometimes <u>Employment Insurance</u> *premiums, must be*
deducted and remitted to Canada Revenue Agency.

Advantages of incorporation:

- *One of the biggest advantages of incorporating a business*
  is limited liability. This means that the liability of the
  shareholders is usually limited to the amount that they have
  invested in their shares in the corporation. However, many
  incorporated small businesses are not able to get bank loans
  without the personal guarantee of the shareholders, so this
  eliminates part of the advantage of limited liability. The
  personal assets of the shareholders are protected from lawsuits
  against the corporation. However, shareholders who are
  directors of the corporation can be held legally liable for some
  debts of the corporation (such as GST/HST and payroll taxes)
  in certain circumstances.

---

6 "Canadian Tax and Financial Information - Should You Incorporate Your
Small Business?" Boat Harbour Investments Ltd., accessed April 23, 2014.
http://www.taxtips.ca/smallbusiness/incorporate.htm.

- *Another major advantage for a profitable small business is the income tax advantage. A _Canadian controlled private corporation_, or CCPC, pays a much lower rate of federal tax (small business rate) on the first $400,000 (in 2007) of _active business income_ than would be paid by an unincorporated business, due to the _small business deduction_. Active business income generally does not include investment income or rental income, which is taxed at regular _corporate tax rates_. The combined federal + provincial small business tax rate varies from approximately 16% to 22%, depending on the Province. The threshold amount subject to the lower small business rate also varies between Provinces. Keep in mind that this tax advantage is mainly a deferral of taxes until the profits are paid out to the shareholder. If all the profits are paid out to the shareholder as they are earned, leaving the corporation with little or no taxable income, then they will be taxed entirely as income of the shareholder, at personal income tax rates.*

- *Another tax advantage of incorporation is the _$800,000 capital gains deduction_ on the sale of shares of a qualifying _small business corporation_. One of the qualifications is that the corporation must be a CCPC with active business income.*

- *_Private Health Service Plans_ can be used to provide tax-free benefits to employees. This deduction is also available to sole proprietors and partners, but the treatment for corporations is more favorable than that for unincorporated businesses.*

Disadvantages of incorporation:

- *Incorporation is the business structure with the highest setup and administrative costs.*

- *Incorporation is the most complicated business structure. It is very important to take extreme care in setting up classes of shares, deciding who will be shareholders (spouses, children) and how much control they will have (control is determined by % of voting shares owned). Professional advice can avoid serious problems.*

- *Business losses cannot be written off against other income of the owners (shareholders).*

- *More administrative work is required for a corporation. This includes annual reports filed with the corporate registry, and corporate tax returns which are filed separately from the owners' personal tax returns.*

Generally, the higher the net income of your small business, the more advantageous it is to incorporate instead of remaining as a proprietorship.

*No matter what the type of business structure, spouses and children can be employed by the business, thus effectively splitting income. However, amounts expensed must be reasonable amounts based on services provided, and must actually be **paid** to the spouse and/or children.[7]*

I have operated within all of the business structures described above, except the "Limited Partnership". In Canada, there is also the "Limited Liability Partnership" which is usually only available to groups of professionals such as lawyers, accountants, and doctors. I will limit my comments to what I have experienced, namely sole proprietorships, general partnerships, and corporations.

As you can see from the pros and cons discussion above, your choice primarily boils down to liability and taxation concerns; therefore, you must seek the guidance of both a lawyer and an accountant. The point I want to make, and where I disagree with many lawyers and accountants, is that it is not a matter of whether or not to incorporate but, perhaps more a matter of, when. In addition, I will offer my two cents regarding partnerships.

---

[7] "Canadian Tax and Financial Information - Should You Incorporate Your Small Business?" Boat Harbour Investments Ltd., accessed April 23, 2014. http://www.taxtips.ca/smallbusiness/incorporate.htm.

I believe there are times when it makes more sense to start out as a sole proprietorship with a view that at some point you may convert to a corporation. There is no need to rush into incorporating if the risk of being sued is low. Do you really need limited liability in order to operate a beauty salon, design websites or start a nursery?

The legal costs and filing fees associated with incorporation will likely run from about $1,000 to $2,500, plus annual fees of about $500. In addition, the accounting fees to set up a corporation will run about $1,000 to $2,000, and the annual corporate tax returns will run about $1,000, or more. These can be onerous, ongoing expenses to the new SBO.

A sole proprietorship, on the other hand, may only need $150 or less to get rolling, and much, much less for an annual tax return . . . about $300 to $400 per year. As you can see, there is a significant cost difference.

On the tax side of the consideration, I would suggest that another rule of thumb is in order: if your sole proprietorship has a taxable income of less than $65,000 per year, then it may make sense to remain a sole proprietorship until it exceeds this level. The reason for this suggestion is to minimize taxes payable. Please discuss this with your accountant, taking into consideration that very few SBOs make this kind of profit in their first few years. Why pay all those professional fees when there is no need to do so? The time will come when it will make perfect sense to incorporate. I'm just not sure the start-up phase is the best time, especially for businesses with a low risk of being sued.

Another point to keep in mind is that if you run your corporation at a loss and then you close it, you can't claim the business losses personally. In this case, all you are able to claim personally is money you lent or invested in the business; whereas, in a sole proprietorship, you may be able to claim the full amount of your losses against other income. Again this is something you should discuss with your accountant.

One of the most important advantages of incorporation is to be sure that you qualify for the $800,000 capital gains deduction when you sell your business. Being incorporated is one of the qualifications; thus, you will eventually want your business incorporated. Interestingly, few small business owners are aware of this exemption and how important it is. This is the "Holy Grail" of the SBO movement. I know there is no such movement, but there should be!

My goal has always been to maximize this deduction because, if you don't use it, you'll lose it forever. This is a powerful incentive for SBOs to grow their business and manage it in such a way that makes it saleable some time down the road. Essentially it means that half the gain you make on the sale of your qualifying business shares is TAX FREE!!! I will discuss this in greater detail in Chapter 33. Please make sure you read it.

I would also like to reiterate something that was mentioned in my earlier quotation. If you need to borrow money, as do most SBOs, don't be surprised when the lender requires that you "personally guarantee" the loan. This means that if you run into trouble and can't repay, the lender can go after all of your personal assets (home, car, etc.). This is true regardless of the business structure you are operating under, even a limited liability company.

And now it's time for "Partnerships". I have had two formally structured partnerships where legal partnership agreements were signed. One went famously well and the other, well, let's just say it was challenging and I lost a lot of money! See Chapter 9.

I would have to say that there are few circumstances where I would get into another partnership if I didn't have at least 51% ownership. Besides protecting my interests by maintaining control, businesses generally run better when there is one final decision-maker. I recommend a 50/50 split as a minimum, with dual signatories on all cash outlays over a reasonable dollar amount.

Why do people consider getting into a partnership in the first place? I suppose they feel a little "safer" with a partnership versus going it alone. They can share the enormous work load often associated with a start-up, and also share the financial risk. Some people are such social beings that they may "need" to work closely with others in order to be fully satisfied in their career.

On a more practical note, it may make sense to partner up when each partner offers a skill set that the other partners don't possess. Personally, I might consider a partner with technology skills, an area where I am weak, but not a partner with marketing skills, since that's one of my strengths. Also, keep in mind, a gifted sales professional is always worth their weight in gold and worthy of consideration as a partner.

I have tried to find statistical research on how partnerships stack up against sole proprietorships and corporations in terms of success rates and longevity. Unfortunately, I have been unsuccessful. So, let's do a little test ourselves.

Think of as many SBOs as you can . . . your auto dealer, your home builder, or your insurance broker, for example. Now, what percentage of these are partnerships? You are apt to find the percentage is low, and there are likely good reasons for this. My sense is that this structure has more potential issues than one might guess.

You may sense that I have a slightly negative bias toward partnerships, at least toward those where I have less than controlling interest. This is because I have had a negative experience using this structure. It is also because I really haven't seen many equal partnerships succeed for the long term.

Yes, we are all familiar with some very famous partnerships like Bill Gates/Paul Allen (Microsoft); Bill Hewlett/Dave Packard (Hewlett Packard); Steve Jobs/Steve Wozniak (Apple); however, not even these partnerships lasted as long as the ventures themselves. I speculate that these are exceptional situations, and not the norm. When you look at the millions of successful proprietorships and corporations, I believe the odds favor going it alone.

If you are considering a partnership because you like to work with others and bounce ideas around, may I offer two possible solutions for you to consider. Firstly, try to find a mentor that you can sit down with on a regular basis. There are likely many retired business people who have succeeded in your industry.

Secondly, look to your accountant as your "non-partner" partner. If you have chosen him or her wisely, enjoy their company, and feel they can add value, why not sit down with them every week or so? I know it can be costly, but it could be a lot less costly than giving up half your business or suffering a soured partnership.

For example, if you sat with your accountant for one hour per week (less time will be needed later on) at $150 per hour, it would cost you about $600 per month or $7,200 per year. Also, don't be shy about asking for a lower rate than normal, due to the regularity of meetings. I doubt you would need this much time but, even if you did, it may be worth it for the first year. Again, I assume you have chosen an accountant that can add value to your business so that you get a positive return on your investment.

If the start-up you are considering requires a huge workload and you are looking for a partner to help share in that workload, you should always calculate what it would cost you to buy that service. If that cost is too high, a partner may be needed, but if the cost is manageable, reconsider the partnership.

Once again, I am talking about partnerships involving giving up control of your business in order to strike a deal. Junior partners or employee partners are indeed a whole different ballgame, and they are worth considering at every opportunity.

Chapter Takeaway

Unless you have significant liability concerns, don't be too quick to pay the added costs of starting and maintaining a corporation.

CHAPTER 26

Start-up, Purchase or Franchise?

WHEN YOU DECIDE TO seek your version of "Independence Day", you will ask yourself how best to proceed: start something from scratch, buy an existing business, or purchase a franchise.

There are so many variables involved that it would take an entire book to address them all adequately. As we have taken each of these paths at one time or another, I will offer some factors you should consider while you plan your entry into the small business world.

First, I have listed some questions you should ask yourself as you consider these options. There is no right or wrong answer; it's all about being brutally honest with yourself.

1. How much money (capital) do you have to invest?
2. How long can you last before you need to draw a salary, and how much do you need to draw each month after that?
3. What are your business strengths and weaknesses?
4. How confident are you in your ability to manage your own independent business?
5. Are you a business builder/flipper (like me), a long-term investor, or are you looking to buy a job?
6. How long do you plan to own this business?
7. Do you prefer to manage people, or do things yourself?
8. Do you like to frequently change what you do for a living?

9. How independent do you want to be?

10. Could you accept suggestions and/or direction from a franchisor?

Start-Ups (Independent)

Pros

- Greatest potential return on investment. You are not paying a premium for goodwill; you create it yourself.

- This may be the lowest cost option given that all of the work involved is completed by the new owner.

> *The average micro-business (1-4 employees) in Canada, has invested about $118,136 into its operations. It includes the total initial investment upon start-up as well as any additional capital contributed to the business through operations, less any capital withdrawn through dividends.*[8]

- Possibility of starting out slowly or working part-time.

- Greatest freedom and flexibility in setting your own operating guidelines.

- You will own everything you develop for your start-up, including the name, the brand, the IP (intellectual property), as well as all other assets (no exclusions). This is not true with a franchise.

Cons

- May be the highest risk option, especially if starting full-time.

- Definitely the most work involved.

---

[8] "Survey on Growth and Financing of Small and Medium Enterprises," Statitistics Canada, 2011.

- Low levels of support. With this option, you are basically on your own; however, you may find a mentor to help and guide you. Trade associations and/or supplier support can also be very helpful.

Buy An Existing Business

Pros

- Concept is proven.

- May have good, trained people in place.

- Business is likely cash flow positive (or you wouldn't consider purchasing it).

- Less risk than a start-up.

- At least some goodwill is established, i.e., customer base, business name and/or brand recognition, supplier relationships, location, intellectual property, functional operating procedures, and/or systems.

Cons

- Second highest cost of entry option. This is debatable as it depends on how well you do on the purchase price versus how well you control costs on a start-up.

- May unknowingly take on hidden liabilities. This can occur even if you buy only assets and not shares, which we will discuss in Chapter 29.

- Very difficult to find. It could easily take years to find a good business at a fair price, and one that realizes a decent ROI (return on investment).

Franchise

Pros

- May be the lowest risk option? Refer to "The Franchise Myth?" on page 141.

- Highest level of support. The franchisor should supply all kinds of ongoing support, including advertising, marketing materials, promotion ideas, market research, product development, training, annual conferences, key performance indicators, operating guidelines, systems support, etc.

- Brand awareness "may" already be established in your market.

- Least work to set up as franchisor usually finds a location, manages leasehold improvement process, and sets up most operating systems as part of the initial franchise fee. It should be a proven and turnkey opportunity.

- May be most appropriate for those with limited business experience as training and on-going support is provided.

- May receive supplier discounts as a result of volume buying of the franchise network.

- Likely to provide ongoing research and development which independents may not be able to afford.

- It may be easier to get financing for an "established" franchise, but it will still be tough if you have no previous business experience.

Cons

- Likely to have the highest cost of entry. The initial franchise fee will vary from $5,000 to $75,000 or more.[9] The average initial franchise fee in Canada is $23,000 and the average

---

9   "Franchise Tutorial 2: Intro to Franchise Fee Fundamentals," Canadian Franchise Association™, accessed April 24, 2014, http://lookforafranchise.ca/franchise-resources/franchisee-tutorials/franchise-tutorial-2-intro-to-franchise-fee-fundamentals.

franchisee investment is $160,000.[10] Personally I find these numbers to be quite low, so you must be sure to do your homework. Training costs are usually included in the initial fee; however, travel costs and accommodations are rarely included.

- Ongoing royalty payments can be onerous, especially for newer franchise organizations with limited brand recognition. Rates range from 0% to 20% of gross revenue, with 6% to 10% being typical. This includes the portion for an advertising and promotion fund.

- Limited operating flexibility. There will be plenty of rules and restrictions limiting how you operate your franchise and what you are allowed to sell.

- The franchisor's problems can easily become your problems. If the franchisor is not properly managed, you'll most likely be affected. You are inevitably tied to the franchisor, not only by contract, but by concept, name, product and services sold.

- You really only own the "right to use" the brand name while in good standing of the franchise agreement for a fixed period (usually 5, 10, 15, or 20 years). This time period depends on the amount paid to set up the franchise. The more you pay, the longer they should give you to get a return on your investment.

---

[10] "Canadian Franchise Statistics & Info," Franchiselink, accessed April 24, 2014, http://www.franchiselink.ca/canadian-franchise-faqs/canadian-franchise-statistics-info.

- There are usually franchise renewal fees involved. The renewal fee for one of our franchises was $3,000 after five years, and the other was $5,000. These fees are almost certain to be higher today.

  It is important to note that there is often a requirement for the franchisee to undertake substantial upgrades, or a complete redesign to the premises, in order to be granted a renewal. For example, the franchisor may require that you re-paint the entire premise, replace equipment, counters, flooring, signage, etc., all at your own expense. If you don't comply, you risk losing your business!

The Franchise Myth?

For many years I believed that buying a franchise was a much safer way to enter the world of small business. It turns out that I may have been wrong. While we were reasonably successful in both of the franchises we operated, most of that success was due to our efforts as opposed to franchisor support. I know this may sound like sour grapes, but I base this opinion on the results we attained versus the average results attained by our peers, and the results attained by the growth of the franchise network across Canada.

Why have I changed my opinion on the risk level of owning a franchise? In addition to our practical experience, it turns out that many of the claims made by the franchise industry may not have been accurate. The International Franchise Association, for example, has greatly softened its claim that franchises have a much higher success rate than independent businesses.

Many believe that the franchise industry has backed away from such claims as a result of a study done by Dr. Timothy Bates of Wayne State University in Detroit, Michigan. The study is based on a survey of 125,000 firms.

I urge readers to take a look at the complete results of this study by visiting *www.sba.gov/advocacy/7540/40341#*. I have included the study summary below:

> *The study challenged the presumption that the franchise form of business ownership offers a better chance at success than does an independent startup.*
>
> *While the dataset used for this analysis was not without limitations, the results, tested in a variety of different contexts, remained consistent: opening a new, non-corporate independent small business provided a better chance of success than starting or buying a non-corporate franchise. Corporate franchised establishments performed much better; they were generally more heavily capitalized; their survival rates were higher than those of corporate independents.*
>
> *Despite some strengths of young non-corporate franchise firms, they were dramatically less profitable than young independent small firms of the same age, and they exhibited a lower survival rate -- 61.9 percent compared with 68.1 percent for non-franchised firms -- over the time period studied.[11]*

At the very least, this study raises important questions that should be considered by anyone contemplating the start-up or purchase of a franchise, particularly from smaller, less established franchise networks.

Below are some of the lessons we learned from being franchise owners.

1. ***Determine Return on Investment (ROI) Not Only Cash Flow:*** Franchises are often sold on the basis of cash flow from which you must draw a salary. After your salary is deducted, will you still make a good ROI? If you aren't getting a 10% to 20% ROI, you may be buying a job.

---

[11] Dr. Timothy Bates, "Survival Patterns Among Franchise and Nonfranchise Firms Started in 1986 and 1987," (Wayne State University, Detroit, Michigan under contract no. SBA-8121-OA-94), 1996.

2. ***Don't Think You Can Change a Franchise Agreement:*** This just won't happen unless there are very unique and one-time circumstances. Even if you get sick and aren't able to work, don't expect the franchisor to stop collecting their royalty. The only clause I was able to change in a Franchise Agreement was to increase the size of our exclusive territory.

3. ***Contact Veteran Franchisees Before You Buy In:*** This is so important, and it once saved us from making a huge mistake. Ask them what they like and dislike about the network, and don't forget to ask them the important question. . . which is the title of this book! Some will be reluctant to share, but many will, so you must be persistent. See Appendix 5 for a sample list of franchisee interview questions.

   You may want to check out some independent internet sites which support franchisee interests. Blue Mau Mau at *www.bluemaumau.org* is a good one, and if you want to learn which franchises are most complained about, visit The Unhappy Franchisee at *www.unhappyfranchisee.com*.

4. ***If the Franchise Brand Isn't Very Familiar to You, it Certainly Won't be Familiar to Potential Customers:*** It will take longer and cost a lot more to educate your market on a new franchise concept. We know this because we were in this position twice. It may be worthwhile to pay more for a nationally recognized brand than a new concept. The royalties charged are likely very similar; consequently, you will likely reach profitability much sooner.

5. ***Check Franchisor Credentials:*** Do the people running things in head office have experience managing a franchise organization in your specific industry? At Mail Boxes Etc., our CEO came from Little Caesars Pizza. Yes, he had franchise experience, but he still had to learn the business services industry. In fact, because it was a new concept in

Canada, I don't recall any of the head office staff having franchise experience of any kind. This was disappointing and frustrating at times.

6. ***Check Franchisee Credentials:*** If you determine that the franchisor will accept anyone with cash and a "pulse", then I recommend you take a pass. The network is only as strong as the abilities of its franchisees to grow their businesses. For example, if the franchisor accepts people without past business experience, the network is likely to grow slowly, if at all.

7. ***Open With a Bang!*** I know that it can cost a lot to promote a "Grand Opening" but, if we could do it over again, we would definitely try to find the money. One way to reduce costs is to lean heavily on suppliers to pay for part of the advertising or offer special discounts on opening day.

8. ***Try all Franchisor Promotions:*** We missed one promotion because I didn't believe that it would be profitable. I was wrong, and we had to wait until the following year to participate. In general, we have found that following franchisor suggestions is a good idea. Many franchises don't offer a choice and you must participate in all promotions.

9. ***Participate in all Peer Networking Opportunities:*** I realize it can cost a lot of money to travel to franchise events but, in the majority of cases, it will pay off. The key is to seek out the best operators and ask them how they have become successful, and then go home and do the same!

Chapter Takeaway

All three options are viable, depending upon one's skill set, goals, and personality; so the better one knows oneself, the better the decision will be.

PART THREE

BUYING A GOING CONCERN

CHAPTER 27

Personal Search Criteria

S OME YEARS AGO I developed a "personal" checklist comparing various business acquisition criteria that I felt were important to me at the time. I consider the checklist personal because everyone's criteria will be different, depending on their life goals, available capital, market conditions, etc. I found this checklist particularly useful when comparing a number of different opportunities.

I've been asked many times by business brokers and even friends, "What kind of business are you looking for this time, Tim?" It seems like an easy question to answer, but it wasn't easy for me until I completed my checklist. I am the type of guy who believes that a good manager can manage almost any kind of business. As a result, this belief made it difficult to pinpoint what I was looking for. There are exceptions and people have limitations, but this is generally how I looked at things for most of my business career.

I was searching for a business that made sense according to my criteria at the time: my interests, my age, and the amount of capital I had available. It was also more about knowing what I didn't want as opposed to what I did want. For example, I rarely had an interest in restaurants as it ticked so few of my boxes. In addition, I never again looked at retail after we sold Mail Boxes Etc., as the barriers to entry are too low. Such barriers or obstacles are situations that make it difficult for a new business to enter a particular market. Some examples include a requirement for a high cash investment, patent protection, highly skilled labour, government approvals, etc.

Below are the criteria I have used in the past. You will relate to some and not to others, which is fine; the point here is to develop your own set of criteria to help you choose the kind of business that suits you best.

When I was comparing a few different businesses or concepts, I would rate each on a scale of 1 to 5 so that I could get a more analytical view of which option was best for me at the time.

1. ***Return on Investment (ROI):*** Please remember that you are only profitable if there is money left over after the business pays you a market rate salary for managing the business. To determine your ROI, take this remaining profit and divide it by the amount you might pay for the business under consideration. Hopefully, the result of this calculation is larger than what you could get if you invested your capital elsewhere. If it is, you are the owner of a profitable, as well as an "investable", business.

2. ***Does this Opportunity Fulfill a Market "Need" or "Want"?*** I would generally rank "needs" as higher than "wants", especially if the economy is struggling.

3. ***Long-term Growth Potential:*** Is this opportunity in a growth industry? Will this industry be around in ten or twenty years?

4. ***Ego Factor:*** Does this concept make me feel good, and will I be proud to own it? Depending on your personality, you may be surprised by how important this factor can be.

5. ***Managing vs. Doing?*** Personally, I ranked this criterion high if there was a greater opportunity to manage assets (particularly people assets), and less chance of having to perform day-to-day tasks myself.

6. ***Barriers to Entry:*** After selling Mail Boxes Etc., this became one of the key criteria for me. Retail generally has low barriers to entry. People often came to our MBE store just to take photos of this new and fresh business model. Within six months, we had three competitors in close proximity; two of these were new franchises and one was an independent. I note that none of these businesses survived; however, Mark and Deb (who bought our store) are still successfully operating today, twenty years later!

7. ***Do I Have the Skill Set Needed?*** This is where one must be brutally honest. If necessary, bounce the idea off people who are familiar with your business skills. A mentor is an ideal choice.

8. ***Is the Market Local, National, or International in Scope?*** At one point I wanted a business that catered to customers outside of our local market. If you work in a market that is popular as a lifestyle destination, it can become saturated quickly, leaving less opportunity for growth.

9. ***Low Start-up Capital Required?*** This seems too obvious to mention, but remember that we may be using these criteria to compare one opportunity to another, so it must be ranked.

10. ***Re-sale Opportunity?*** Personally, this is one of the most important factors that I consider; however, it may rate very poorly for you if your goal is to start something that you can leave for your grandkids. I, on the other hand, need to see an exit opportunity in the shorter term, due to my "three year itch syndrome".

11. ***Enjoyment Factor?*** This criteria was added to my list after my stint as a realtor. I have nothing against being a realtor; it just wasn't for me. Enjoying what you do for a living can be a big factor in your business success.

12. **Low Risk of Capital?** As I am a low to moderate risk taker, this one weighs heavily in my decision-making.

13. **Is it "Scalable"?** Is the opportunity one that can be readily increased in size (sales volume) while maintaining or improving profit margins? For example, does the venture allow for duplication of a successful system in multiple locations and markets?

I would add one more criteria to this list: can the product or service offering be leveraged (rapidly increased in size) by the use of internet marketing? Obviously, the easier it is to sell your concept online, the higher the score.

Chapter Takeaway

When comparing business opportunities, adding some structure to your decision-making process will greatly improve your chances of choosing the best fit for you.

CHAPTER 28

Where to Look?

GIVEN THIS SECTION DEALS with "buying" a business, I felt it necessary to briefly discuss the question of "where to look for opportunities?" As there are obvious overlaps, I have gone into more detail on this subject in Chapter 35 which covers methods I have used to "sell" a business.

There are literally thousands of websites offering small business opportunities, so take your pick. If I were looking to buy a business today, I would narrow my search vehicles down to the list below. These are offered in no particular order, as much depends on the size and location of the business sought.

- businessesforsale.com
- Business Brokers
- Print and online versions of *The Globe and Mail* and *National Post* newspapers
- *The Western Investor* newspaper
- Multiple Listing Service - icx.ca
- kijiji.ca and craigslist.ca
- Professional and personal contacts (your network)
- Those that are "not" for sale

Finding a decent business to purchase sounds like an easy task; however, it can be quite a major undertaking. In fact, it can be a fulltime job, as it has been for me on occasion. You may have to look at about one hundred business opportunities to find one that is worth pursuing with an offer. The reason for this is mostly due to valuation challenges (code for overpriced listings), but it is also due to the great number of variables involved in this process.

The time frame involved in finding a good business that fits your purchase criteria should be measured in years, not months.

Because buying a business can involve the acquisition of real estate, the two processes are often compared. However, if you think buying a home is an emotional and complicated task, then get ready for a challenge. I don't mean to frighten you, but we must always keep it real. Finding something that will provide a good return on your investment, with reasonable risk levels, and something that you will enjoy, is a little harder than three bedrooms or four? Personally, I enjoy the challenge of both buying and selling a business, and perhaps you will too.

The question of whether a buyer should use a business broker is pretty simple . . . why not? I would suggest searching for one that has personally owned and operated at least one business, and preferably more. If you are looking to buy something local, then look for a broker that has been in your market for a long time. This individual will have a longer list of contacts in the business community.

I believe that all businesses are for sale for the right price. Now don't get me wrong; I'm not suggesting that you overpay for an opportunity, because your goal should always be to buy a "good business at a fair price". I also believe that if you widen your search to include those businesses that are not listed for sale right now, you will increase your chances of finding a business that best suits you.

As an example, observe businesses that you patronize. Do you see big potential despite how the business is managed? If so, add it to your search list and discreetly approach the owner. You never know what might happen and, at the very least, you could learn something, and make a new business contact at the same time.

Chapter Takeaway

Finding a good business at a fair price can be challenging and take much more time than you think.

CHAPTER 29

What Are You Buying . . . Assets or Shares?

T O ANSWER THIS QUESTION, I strongly advise you to seek the assistance of your accountant for tax advice, and your lawyer for liability advice. My goal is to give you some general information regarding this topic so that you might better understand the implications of each type of transaction. This needs to be done before you begin your due diligence (research) on a specific business you may wish to purchase.

Most small business transactions in Canada are for assets as opposed to shares. The primary reason for this is one of liability which will be discussed later. In general, the buyer of a business wants to purchase assets, and the seller wants to sell shares. This paradox can only be solved through negotiation.

In an asset purchase, you are buying "some or all" of the specific hard (tangible) assets such as inventory, signage, office supplies, vehicles, tools, equipment, etc. You are also likely to be buying access to softer (intangible) assets like business names and logos, customer lists, goodwill, intellectual property (IP such as trademarks & patents), operating manuals, websites, telephone numbers, etc.

In a share purchase you are buying all of the assets of the corporation (you can't pick and choose), and all of the liabilities. This is critical to understand. Assuming the liabilities of a company is where some serious potential problems can arise.

For example, when I bought our swimming pool business, which was a corporation, I purchased only assets from the seller. Had I purchased shares, I would have been liable for the hundreds of pools constructed by the corporation prior to my taking ownership.

In addition, I could have been liable for other customer claims, third party claims from sub-contractors, Revenue Canada tax re-assessments, and who knows what else? In fact, during my first few months of ownership, a few pool customers came knocking at my door for significant repairs. They weren't interested in whether I bought assets or shares; they just wanted their pools fixed! In order to maintain a good reputation and to keep valued customers, I "worked with" as many reasonable requests for assistance as I could; however, I did so on my terms.

If I had assumed all of the liabilities of the previous owner, it could have been very detrimental to the future of this venture. Hopefully, you now better understand why most small business sales are for assets as opposed to shares.

There may be instances where buying shares makes sense; that is where your professional advisors can help structure a deal that can reduce your risk. Unfortunately, the cost to do the proper due diligence on a corporation is much higher than that needed for an asset sale. On the other hand, you are more likely to get a better price for shares than for assets.

A business sale transaction is all about negotiation between two willing parties. For example, I have found that a sizeable (15% to 25%) holdback for at least a year can reduce risk for a buyer of shares, and be agreeable to a seller who has nothing to hide. There are, of course, a number of ways to structure a win-win deal.

If you are looking at a larger small business (say, $2 to $5 million in gross sales), and the owner insists on selling shares, it is very likely his or her corporation is a "qualifying small business" (which we will discuss in Chapter 33). This means the seller is able to take advantage of the $800,000 capital gains deduction and wishes to sell shares, not assets. This type of motivation may lead to a better price for the buyer versus buying assets. Again it's a matter of negotiation, and you will need the help of a good accountant to navigate such tax implications.

Chapter Takeaway

*As a rule of thumb, look to buy assets, not shares,
unless there is a compelling reason to do otherwise.*

CHAPTER 30

The Due Diligence Process

F OR OUR PURPOSES, DUE diligence refers to the research and investigation that is completed on a particular business of interest, for the purpose of establishing the value that business may have to you as a potential buyer.

The vast majority of due diligence on a small business asset purchase (sole proprietorship or partnership) is done by the purchaser. In the case of the purchase of shares (buying a corporation), some of the due diligence work is best left to your lawyer. For example, your lawyer will check to see that the shares are free of claims and encumbrances, and also check for governmental claims from the likes of the GST office, the PST office, Revenue Canada, and municipal taxation departments. You will also need the help of your accountant to review any complicated financial statements. In the end, the lion's share of this process is, and should be, the responsibility of the buyer . . . so get ready to dig, dig, dig!

I have been through this process many times and, while some of the investigation is common from one business to another, much of it is unique as no two businesses are exactly alike.

These days, every due diligence process begins with a simple Google search. One can learn a great deal about a business and the industry it's in by studying the seller's online presence. For example, an up to date professional website tells you something about how a business is run. I also find it helpful to read employee profiles to get a sense of how the business is structured.

The buyer/seller dynamic can run the spectrum, from being positive and respectful to downright adversarial. Personally, I think a buyer owes the seller a duty of respect. After all, it is the seller who has to totally open up to a complete "stranger" about all aspects of their business. This can be quite uncomfortable, especially if the business is suffering.

My advice to buyers is to be well prepared, and prove to sellers that you are qualified and serious. Sign a confidentiality agreement without argument; show that you have the funds to buy; and be discreet in all dealings with the seller, their employees, and their competitors.

When I was on the sell side, I went to great lengths to qualify potential buyers, and I had zero time for "lookie-loos". If you want a win-win transaction, treat people the same way you would like to be treated.

Again, I could write an entire book on this topic; however, my purpose is to highlight key points that will help you understand what normally transpires in a business sale transaction, from the buyer's perspective. There is an old horse trading quotation, "The buyer needs a hundred eyes but the seller not one," that may help you better understand as you read on.

Once I discover a business of interest, I go through a due diligence process which includes the following five steps.

1. **Data Gathering:** Before you meet with the seller, there are a few pieces of information you absolutely must have:

    a) *Financial reports for the last three years:* Both the profit & loss and balance sheet statements. These must have been prepared by the seller's accountant which in turn were used to complete the business annual tax returns. In-house bookkeeper reports are **not** sufficient.

b) *List of all assets included in the sale:* This list should include the year of purchase for each item over $500; the purchase price (cost); and the depreciated value of each item, if available.

c) *Lease terms:* A brief summary of the lease, if any, including total cost per square foot; the expiration date; and renewal terms. A complete copy of the lease will be required later.

d) *List of items that are "excluded" from the sale:* These are personal things, such as artwork, which may be on the business premises but are not part of the deal.

You will have to look at many business opportunities to find a good business at a fair price; therefore, it isn't practical to run to your accountant each time you receive financial statements from different sellers. If you are weak in financial analysis, don't fret; we will be covering some material here, and in the next chapter, which will help you whittle things down so that you don't have to spend all of your purchase funds on accounting fees.

2. **Determine if Reasonable Value Exists:** The last thing you want to do is waste a bunch of time on an overpriced venture . . . and you are going to see a lot of them. . . . perhaps even 80% will be overvalued! If the financial reports don't support at least three quarters of the asking price, take a pass. Because this topic is so important, I will deal with it in more detail in the next chapter.

3. **Meet with the Owner:** This is a very important meeting, and I suggest you tread lightly here. Your goal is to ask carefully prepared questions in a professional and respectful manner that don't put the seller on the defensive.

You still need to be persistent and dig deep for information in order to make the best decision; after all, we are talking about your livelihood. Here are questions that must be asked:

- Please tell me about your business? After asking this question, I suggest that you keep your mouth closed and listen until the owner stops talking.

- How long have you owned this business?

- Why are you selling your business?

- If I may ask, what is your business and educational background?

- What percentage of time do you personally spend on marketing, sales, operations, and financials?

- Please discuss your internet exposure and any social media campaigns you fund. What percent of gross sales does this expense represent?

- How many hours per week do you work at this business?

- What would happen to this business if you were gone tomorrow?

- How much vacation time do you take per year and when?

- How much salary do you take?

- Do you have a business plan, and may I have a copy?

- Do you belong to any industry associations and, if so, which ones?

- Tell me about your main competitors?

- Do you have an edge over your competition and, if so, what is it?

- Tell me about your target market?

- Who are your main suppliers?

- May I contact your main customers, competitors, and suppliers?

- Do you have any single customers that represent more than 20% of total revenues?

- Are there any partners or family members involved in this business?

- What can you tell me about your "key" employees; and how much are they paid?

- What do you like most and what do you like least about operating this business?

- Can we now review the financial statements?

- Is your gross profit above or below the industry average?

- What are your main profit centers, and what percentage of gross revenue does each represent?

- What is the current value of your inventory at cost?

- Are you willing to carry a portion of the sale price, and on what terms?

- When can we tour the premises and view the assets?

- Is there anything else I need to know about this business that we haven't yet discussed?

- Will you sign a non-compete agreement? (Typically, these are for three to five years and cover a radius of five to ten kilometers for an urban retail business. Other types of businesses can be regional, provincial, or national in scope. Some agreements might preclude the seller from competing in the same industry altogether.)

- How was the asking price determined, and how willing are you to negotiate?

4. ***The Investigation Begins:*** You should now have ample information to review and corroborate. Below are some additional initiatives you may want to consider:

a) *Customer impersonation:* Where possible, I will become a customer of the business to determine customer service levels. If applicable, I will also monitor customer traffic and do customer counts at various hours of the day. If agreed by the owner, I will call customers and ask why they patronize this business.

b) *Check out the competition:* I will discretely check out the competition by patronizing their operation. I will study their websites and social media campaigns.

c) *Contact owners of similar businesses:* Whenever possible, I like to talk to a similar business owner in another market to see how things are going. This helps me determine if this industry is growing or shrinking, and what the major challenges might be.

Years ago, when I considered opening a "Play It Again Sports" franchise, I called a franchisee in Winnipeg. I found out the challenge of this business wasn't getting sales, it was getting product to sell! In this business, you can't just pick up the phone and place an order for inventory, you have to go out and find it. This can take a significant amount of time that most SBOs don't have in abundance. As a result, this fellow was working seven days per week in order to keep his store fully stocked.

Making this one call taught me the key challenge facing this business model. This franchisee was happy to offer advice because I wasn't going to compete in his market, and he didn't want me to make the same mistake he had made.

d) *Contact trade associations:* The goal here is to determine how well this industry is organized. I am also looking for financial key business indicators that I will use to compare to the venture under consideration.

e) *Accountant meeting:* If you are comfortable with the results of your investigation thus far, now may be a good time to meet with your accountant. The objective of this meeting is to review the financial reports and determine a valuation range. In order to save time and money, you may wish to prepare your own price range and have your accountant review it. We will discuss how to do this in the next chapter.

f) *Landlord meeting:* If a leased premise is involved, you will need to meet with the landlord to ensure that there won't be any issues in taking over the existing lease. In most cases, this is not a problem; however, the landlord may have someone else in mind who is willing to pay a higher rate. He may use this change in ownership as an opportunity to make changes.

When you are assuming an existing lease, there are few things that you will be able to alter. However, if the landlord wants to make a change, like extending the term, which is common, then every clause is fair game. For example, you may wish to change such things as signage flexibility or additional parking spaces.

g) *Key employee interviews:* Near the end of your due diligence, or as part of the conditions of your offer, you must interview the key employees. This is always a sensitive area for sellers, but it must be done, nonetheless. I suggest that you prepare a list of questions to be asked of each employee. The obvious question you want to ask is whether or not the employee plans to stay on after the sale. I also like to ask the question, "On a scale of 1 to 10, what is your current level of job satisfaction?" Answers to such questions can tell you a lot, and they will often lead to candid discussions which should prove valuable in your assessment of the "team".

5. *Prepare Verbal or Written Offer:* My first offer is usually a verbal one, even if I am working through a broker. My reasoning is that I don't want to waste my time, or that of the seller, with a bunch of unnecessary paperwork if we are so far apart that a deal is unlikely.

If we do reach a verbal agreement, and no broker is involved, I will often put together a one page non-binding "letter of understanding" (LOU) which will outline the main points of our deal. See Appendix 6 for a very basic, but functional, sample. I do this because it saves time and legal fees. Also, the lawyers need something to work with in order to produce a formal asset purchase and sale agreement, or a share purchase agreement.

I should mention that regardless of whether you use a broker or a realtor there is always a formal agreement prepared by the buyer's or seller's lawyer. These can be costly documents to produce, so I usually let the other party's lawyer produce it, and have my lawyer review it to ensure that all points in the LOU are properly covered, and my interests are protected. The issue of whose lawyer does what, and who pays, is always a matter of negotiation. Most people want their lawyer in charge of the whole process. This is is usually fine with me, as long as my lawyer gets to review it.

It is very important to determine if the owner of this business "is" the business. You must determine what impact the present owner leaving will have on future growth. Sometimes it can be obvious that the owner, like an accountant or jeweler, has specialized knowledge which can impact future growth when they exit.

Sometimes it may be less obvious; such as when the current owner has built special and close relationships with key customers. If 25% of revenue comes from one customer, and that customer went to school with the current owner, then you need to ask yourself, what happens if I lose that business?

Something else to keep in mind, which caught me off guard one time, is that of supplier credit. I trust you will have available cash, or a line of credit, to pay for expenses that occur right after you take possession of the assets. I, however, am the type who hates to pay for things like inventory before I receive them. I prefer to have time to pay (called credit terms) of thirty days, or more, if possible. The current owner will likely have built up such favorable credit terms; however, these **do not** extend to you as the new owner. You may have the same business name as the previous owner, but you may not receive the same credit opportunities until you prove yourself.

If you have not made prior arrangements, most suppliers will treat you like a new customer and request that you "apply" for credit. You will need to fill out as many credit applications as you have suppliers, so ensure that your credit record and score are in good standing. In the meantime, you will have to pay in advance for almost everything you buy, even utilities.

This point is particularly important for businesses that turn their inventory over very quickly. The last thing you want when you take over an enterprise is any disruption to operations which might negatively affect customers. Dollar Store type operations are a good example; if shelves look sparse, even for a short time, you may lose customers until your credit issues are resolved, and new product arrives.

Chapter Takeaway

Inadequate due diligence will result in multiple negative surprises, all of which will cost you money and/or unnecessary stress.

CHAPTER 31

How Much Should You Pay?
Valuing a Small Business in Canada

A FELLOW SBO ONCE ASKED me, "Hey Tim, how much did you get when you sold your pool business?" To which I replied, "Oh, I got about 3.5 times . . . and I think it was a fair deal at that."

Although my response was honest and accurate, it was met with a "what the heck is that supposed to mean?" type of stare. You see, I gave my friend, who happened to be in the same industry, some very useful information. I shared with him the only information he needed to know about my transaction that might one day help him if he decided to sell his business. I gave him my multiple, and I don't share that number with very many people!

Many books have been written on how to value a business as a going concern. My goal in writing this chapter is to help readers gain a general understanding of the process so they are better able to work intelligently with their advisors on valuing different business opportunities.

I find most SBOs don't know much about this topic because they don't think about it until they go to sell their ventures. I suppose this makes sense, but I believe that every business owner should have a good idea of what their "multiple" is throughout the life cycle of their business. It's something like the average employed person keeping an eye on their RRSP account or investment portfolio so they can plan for their retirement. It's the same for the SBO because much of his or her portfolio is likely made up of the current value of their business, and what is that worth? In my opinion, and that of many experts, it is worth a "multiple" of the businesses "earnings", and little more.

Valuing a business is definitely not a science. The process is usually more a mix of quantitative and qualitative factors. The reason for this is because no two businesses are exactly alike, and human emotion plays a huge role in determining the final selling price of most businesses. The fact is, buyers drive market prices, and I believe buyers should only pay what the business is worth to "them" personally.

Some business brokers, usually those representing sellers, say that a business should be valued on future earnings "potential", and not on the past results. Personally, I couldn't disagree more. This kind of thinking only makes sense for very large and stable corporations, or publically traded companies, where the risk profile is much lower than that of a small business.

I believe that a buyer of a small enterprise should only pay for the past. Yes, we may "buy" a business based on what we think we can do with it going forward, but we should only "pay" a price based on what we actually know for sure. Why would a buyer want to pay a price based on the projections of the seller, when it is the buyer who will have to do the work and take the risk of realizing those projections? Even when I have been on the sell side of this equation, I saw little merit in this kind of thinking.

If you want a gigantic headache, go online and search "business valuations". You will find a dozen or so different methods, a hundred or so different opinions, and thousands of permutations of each of these. Bottom line: it can be as much a subjective process as it is objective.

Let's cut through the clutter and focus on what is happening today for most small businesses sold in Canada. Canadian statistics in this area are extremely limited; therefore I base much of my opinion on personal experience in closing eleven small business transactions. My experience and research suggests that most profitable businesses in Canada are bought and sold based on the average of the net earnings (not sales) over the past three or four years, times a market multiple.

We now need to define "earnings" and "multiple" in simple terms. Remember, you are going to be talking to your accountant about all of this when the time is right, but let me try to prepare you for that day.

Earnings (or profits) are usually defined in one of two ways:

1. **SDE - Sellers Discretionary Earnings (also called discretionary cash flow):** This is most often used when valuing a smaller owner-operated business, with say, less than $350,000 per year in gross sales. Most Canadian business brokers use this term, and it is defined by The International Business Brokers Association (IBBA) as:

   > *The earnings of a business enterprise prior to the following items: Income taxes; nonrecurring income and expenses; non-operating income and expenses; depreciation and amortization; interest expense or income; owner's total compensation for one owner/operator, after adjusting the total compensation of all owners to market value.*

   Stated another way, SDE are determined by adding back items to the reported income which may not to be required by a new owner, and are thus called "discretionary". Additional examples of items added back to income include personal vehicle expenses, personal insurance, wages to family members for income-splitting purposes, perks, incentives/bonuses, personal travel, and the list goes on.

It is important to ensure that items are not added back which are actually required expenses in operating the business going forward. For example, depreciation is always added back because it is a non-cash expense, but you need to understand that those assets are wearing out (which is why they are depreciated), and they will one day need to be replaced at the buyer's expense; thus, as a buyer, you may not wish to give the seller full credit for this addition.

This process is often referred to as "recasting" or "restating" the income statement. It is an attempt to present an amount of cash that "might" be available to a new owner.

In order to illustrate this definition, a financial statement which looks like this:

Total Revenue	$1000
Less Cost of Goods Sold	600
Gross Profit	$ 400
Less Expenses	350
Income	50
Less Income Tax	10
Net Income	**$ 40**

May end up being recast to look like this:

Net Income	$ 40
+ Income Tax	10
+ Owner Salary At Market Value	35
+ Personal Use Of Vehicle	5
+ Personal Travel	3
+ Depreciation & Amortization	3
Sellers Discretionary Earnings – SDE	**$ 96**

As you can see, the SDE paints a much brighter picture than the actual financial report. Is this a legitimate way to present a potential opportunity? I suppose it has some merit in certain circumstances, particularly for smaller businesses with no net income after the owner's salary is deducted. This method attempts to present value by suggesting, "Here is the available cash flow; it's up to you to decide how much to pay yourself". Further, it does provide a quantitative mechanism where one business can be compared to another. In other words, it provides a way to compare unprofitable businesses and determine what they might sell for in the marketplace.

2. *EBITDA (Earnings Before Interest, Taxes, Depreciation, and Amortization):* This is a non-accounting term which is defined by Investopedia as:

> *Net income with interest, taxes, depreciation, and amortization added back to it, and can be used to analyze and compare profitability between companies and industries because it eliminates the effects of financing and accounting decisions.*

This measure of earnings is used most often when comparing larger businesses with revenues greater than roughly $500,000 per year. Obviously, the EBITDA metric can only be used to compare truly profitable enterprises. Such enterprises are those with a net income after all salaries are paid, including those of the owner.

Next we need to discuss this thing called a "multiple".

Simply put, the multiple is a factor of earnings, generally between 1-10, which is multiplied by the SDE or EBITDA to come up with a measurement of the value of the business. The multiple is what the marketplace is telling you an enterprise may be worth today, in a specific industry, in a specific geographic area.

For example, if your EBITDA is $100,000, and you are in the car wash business in Calgary where most car washes sell for three times, then you might expect to receive $300,000 for your car wash business. Real estate and inventory are almost always excluded from this calculation as they are deemed to have a much lower risk profile than the business itself. Therefore, if you are buying assets, you will likely be paying extra for the real estate and/or inventory on top of the purchase price.

Valuation multiples will change according to the economic conditions in each market. If the risk of owning a business goes up (due to an economic downturn or increased competition, for example), the multiplier will, of course, go down. For instance, a common rule of thumb used before the financial crisis hit in 2008 suggested that a well-run clothing retailer in Western Canada could expect five times EBITDA. After the crisis, however, that multiple fell to about two and a half times.

It may seem obvious, but note that the multiple for a business using SDE will be quite different (lower) than one used for a business valued according to EBITDA. It's all about the higher risk involved in smaller enterprises.

So where do these "multiple" values come from in the first place? They are derived from what businesses have sold for in the recent past, in a given market. Unfortunately, Canadian data is extremely scarce, so business brokerages and data mining companies rely primarily on American business sale data which then become the current multiples used in the marketplace. (Refer to sample multiples in Appendix 3)

The multiple a buyer may be willing to pay can be greatly influenced by factors such as:

- length of time the business has been established
- strength of key staff
- unique qualities of products or services
- reputation
- "scalability" of the business (refer to page 149)
- opportunity for the business to run without the owner present

- barriers to entry from competitors
- patents, trademarks, or other intellectual and material property protection
- location of business premises
- general condition of tangible assets
- exclusive supplier relationships

The above variables further support the premise that business valuation is more an art than a science. They also confirm that using an earnings multiple (or any other kind of multiple) is only a starting point from which to launch an effective due diligence process. As I mentioned in the previous chapter, as a buyer, I will use an earnings multiple examination as a filter to weed out grossly overpriced business listings. I will use the same process to give me a goal to drive my bottom line when I am thinking of selling.

Personally, I consider three financial goals when I am carrying out due diligence on a new business opportunity.

1. **EBITDA Multiple of Less Than Five:** I use five as a top-end guideline in order to filter out potentially overpriced listings. In fact, it would take a very special situation for me to pay more than three or four times EBITDA, given the uncertain market conditions we face today. It also greatly depends on whether or not the opportunity is in a growth industry.

    I look in the area of two times SDE for the same reason. You may think otherwise, and that's fine. Again, a business is worth what you as a buyer are willing to pay; it is a very personal thing.

2. **Return on Investment of 15% to 20%:** This has been a historical target of mine, but given the extremely low interest rates we are experiencing, I may go a bit lower these days. As you may recall, profitability is determined after the owner

is paid a market rate salary; therefore, our ROI calculation is the profit left over after all salaries are paid, divided by the total cost of starting or buying the business. I compare this ROI to other types of investments, i.e., stocks, bonds, savings accounts or real estate, and then I ask myself how this business opportunity compares. Is the expected return worth the added risk and the amount of work involved to run a small business? I know some people who expect an ROI of at least 25% before they will risk their capital; however, they usually have to wait an awfully long time to find such a gem, if they ever do.

3. *Estimated Cost to do it Myself:* When I consider buying a business, I like to come up with an estimate of what it would take for me to reproduce the business myself. This is a good exercise for me if I like the concept, but feel it is overpriced. Most times it is a reality check of how costly it can be to do a start-up. It is sometimes better to pay a fair price for a good existing business, particularly those businesses with significant tangible assets that are still in good and productive working order.

So, these are my financial criteria which I add to the murky mix of variables that one might consider when evaluating and comparing various opportunities. Your criteria may be materially different and that's fine, as long as you have some relative guidelines to help you compare one business to the next. Without guidelines, the process could drive you crazy. You may then do nothing, or, worse yet, buy something and pay much more than it may actually be worth.

I know exactly what you're thinking right now. Where the heck are all the Canadian multipliers and rules of thumb that you were expecting? As I mentioned earlier, there is only a smattering of data on Canadian deal flow. This data is usually held by various broker agencies, and larger accounting firms. Most Canadian business brokers use US data as a starting point and work from there.

I contacted Greg Kells who is the President of Sunbelt Business Brokers Inc. in Ottawa. This is an international organization declaring that, "They sell more businesses than anybody else in the world."

According to Greg, their Canadian offices use a mix of US data from Bizcomps, Pratt's Stats, and the IBA (Institute of Business Appraisers).

They adjust values based upon their experience in order to reflect the differences in access to capital, taxation, and the entrepreneurial spirit of the USA. The structure of the transaction also affects values, and in Canada we do a much greater percentage of share sales in order to take advantage of the Capital Gains Tax Exemption.

My search for Canadian deal flow data also included communications with Allister Byrne who is the President and CEO of The Canadian Institute of Chartered Business Valuators located in Toronto. It seems that Mr. Byrne concurs with Mr. Kells when he stated, "Information for smaller businesses is usually not publicly available."

I have found Pratt's Stats to be a good source of data, although it can be a bit pricey for small operators. I suggest that you ask your professional advisors if they have access to this data bank or, if you are using the services of a business broker, they should certainly have access.

Pratt's Stats can be found at BVResources.com. This is the only source I could find that had any Canadian deal flow data. From 1996-2013, only 184 Canadian transactions were captured, versus 12,824 for US businesses during 1990-2013. Now you can understand why American data is so widely utilized. My search included only those businesses with less than $5 million in annual sales.

This illustrates just how far behind Canada is in tracking it's deals. I believe the main reason for this is that the growth in transactions by certified business brokers in Canada has been rising only in recent years, whereas in the US it has been growing for much longer. The primary data source for business sales is from these brokers. The more deals done by brokers, the better the data flow. This is because brokers are encouraged (and sometimes compensated via free access to data sites) to provide details on each transaction completed.

I was granted access to Pratt's Stats database for a brief period thanks to Sarah Anderson, the Publisher of Business Valuation Resources, LLC. Appendix 7 is a summary of my research of their database. Due to the lack of Canadian data (a mere 184 deals), it is difficult to say whether we track closely with American results; however, it definitely points one to that conclusion.

For example, the median EBITDA earnings multiple for 184 Canadian deals done over 17 years to May of 2013 was 3.75 times. In the US, this multiplier was 3.46 times EBITDA based on 8,560 deals done over 13 years to June of 2013; thus, the results look quite similar.

Interestingly, the Market Value of Invested Capital, or selling price, for 12,824 US businesses sold was a median average of $180,454. Of the 184 Canadian deals, the median average selling price was $242,875.

Please don't try to use the data in Appendix 7 to judge an individual business. You must keep in mind that these are averages and, as mentioned earlier, individual values can vary greatly by industry, geographic location, and many other factors. Having said that, you now know where to locate specific data (albeit, mostly American) that can be directly compared to the business you are evaluating. Sources such as Pratt's Stat's are what the professionals use, and you too are now able to estimate the value of your current or future enterprise.

I might also note that of the 184 Canadian deals referred to in Appendix 7, approximately 64% were asset sales and 36% were share sales. These results seem to contradict comments quoted earlier from Greg Kells who said, "In Canada we do a much greater percentage of share sales in order to take advantage of the Capital Gains Tax Exemption;" however, much depends on the business size being discussed. Generally, the larger the business, the more likely it is that shares and not assets will be sold due to the tax benefits referred to by Greg. As there are many more small businesses in Canada than larger ones, it stands to reason that 64% of these were sold for assets.

Another US data source you can use to get that valuation metric or rule of thumb that you are looking for is The Business Reference Guide published by Business Brokerage Press (BBP). BBP Founder, Tom West, is a founder, past president, and former executive director of the International Business Brokers Association (IBBA). I spoke with Tom, and received permission to publish the rule of thumb data in Appendix 3. This should give you a better sense of the kind of data that is tracked in the US.

Valuation metrics for internet based businesses such as websites, domain names, and mobile applications are of increasing interest to technology-minded entrepreneurs. I suspect that most readers would be surprised by how much such enterprises sell for, and how long they take to become profitable once the developer's salary is deducted.

I found an interesting post on this subject from Matt Paulson, one of my LinkedIn contacts. Matt is the author of *40 Rules For Internet Business Success*. He recently sold one of his websites for $6,181.20, and this is what he had to say about the valuation and marketing process:

When you have a website that you want to sell, it will typically be valued based on a multiple of its monthly revenue after expenses. A site less than a year old may only sell for six to twelve times monthly revenue. An established website that has had two or three years of relatively steady traffic and income can sell for as much as twenty or twenty five times monthly revenue. The general rule of thumb is that the longer a website has been around and has been receiving steady traffic and income, the greater revenue multiple it will receive. For example, if you had a website that was three years old and earned $100.00 per month, you might get a 20x revenue multiple, or $2,000.00.

Most websites are sold on public marketplaces that list websites for sale. The largest of these is Flippa.com. Typically, someone with a website for sale will create a listing on a marketplace like Flippa detailing the history, traffic and revenue numbers for a site. After the listing is created, an eBay style auction will commence where potential buyers can make bids on the site. After a set period, usually 7 or 10 days, the highest bidder will win the auction and buy the website. Since there's often very little trust between the buyer and seller on Flippa, usually the sale is facilitated by an escrow service, like Escrow.com.

Remember, "thumbs come in all shapes and sizes" and such rule of thumb data is only one piece of the valuation puzzle that you should address before you decide how much you are prepared to pay for a business and, conversely, how much you might ask when you go to sell.

Chapter Takeaway

*Valuing a profitable small business comes down to return on your investment **after** you have paid yourself a market equivalent salary. Everything else is basically dreams and emotion.*

CHAPTER 32

What to Look for in Financial Statements

I RELY ONLY ON FINANCIAL statements produced on an accountant's letterhead. Having said that, I have encountered instances in smaller enterprises where a bookkeeper, or a significant other of the owner, has produced orderly and complete reports. I then compare these to the corresponding business (or personal) tax returns for verification.

These days, most SBOs use a bookkeeper to produce monthly reports because it is much less costly than having their accountant do it. Also, much of this function has been automated through effective accounting software packages which makes it more difficult to screw up too badly, for too long. The SBO's accountant then takes this information and makes any necessary year-end adjustments to the annual financial report to be used to file the corresponding tax return.

Again, please remember that you will seek assistance from your accountant on this subject; however, it is not practical to have your accountant look at every set of statements that you come across during your search for a new business. My goal is to highlight some areas you should pay attention to on your own which may help you narrow down your search.

Income Statement Items

1. *Growth in Gross Sales:* This is my most important line item in determining if I want to pursue a particular opportunity. If I don't see growth in this top line over at least the last few years, I will likely take a pass. The exception to this may be if there is a logical and verifiable reason why revenues are not growing, i.e., temporary product supply issues; poor broad economic conditions where all businesses in this industry are down; or loss of key sales people. This is more important to me than the bottom line (profit). I believe I would have a better chance of improving marketing and cost controls, which will drive profit, than I would have in increasing sales in a declining market.

   You must be on the lookout for large, one-time sales that are not very likely to be repeated. Also, check for large percentages of sales from one or two customers. I generally assume that I will lose one third of this business and I will recast the revenues on that basis, obviously reducing the amount I am willing to pay.

2. *Management Salary Expense:* To me, a business is not truly profitable until all those who work on the business have been paid at current market rates. It is, therefore, critical to quickly determine if the expenses include a market rate salary for the management of the business. Businesses are often touted as being "profitable" or "cash flow positive"; however, if you take into account that the owner/manager must be paid, there may be little or no real profit in the business. This is perhaps why the business broker industry came up with the acronym SDE (Seller Discretionary Earnings). Yes, it is a way to describe the possible benefit to a potential buyer, but by no means is the business profitable

and providing a real return on investment to the owner over and above a salary. Such a scenario confirms that the buyer is acquiring a "job" with perhaps the potential to become a profitable business.

There is another important point that I should mention here and will be covered in more detail in Part Six. Income for incorporated businesses and unincorporated businesses are reported differently for tax purposes. For example, a sole proprietor shows his or her compensation as net income, while a corporation typically reports net income after all wages and salaries are expensed. One can, therefore, generally assume that a sole proprietorship (or partnership) net income is the personal income of the owner, and not necessarily the profit of the business since all salaries have yet to be expensed.

3. *KPI Comparisons:* We are going to discuss KPIs (key performance indicators) in an upcoming chapter, but in a slightly different context. Our purpose here is to do a line-by-line financial comparison between the business you are considering purchasing and the actual results of directly comparable businesses. The data supplied in Part Six will help with this process. Let's look at car washes on page 336, as an example. It shows the average Canadian car wash has a gross profit of 74.8%. How does the car wash business you are looking at compare? If there is a material variance, you absolutely need to know why!

4. *Large Reductions in Variable Costs:* You will frequently see this in the advertising and promotion expense. Once they decide to sell, a seller will often cut this, and other variable expenses, in order to improve the look of their bottom line. This is another good reason to have at least a three year history so you can pick up on such abnormalities.

Also, if the business you are considering has a lot of vehicle and/or equipment type assets, keep an eye on the repairs and maintenance line. You want to be sure that these assets have been properly serviced on a continual basis.

5. *Cash Sales:* Now this is a delicate topic, indeed. I have encountered everything from a mild reference, to an overt declaration that I could save a ton on income taxes if I were to buy a particular business that has a lot of cash sales. Such inferences are obviously made to suggest that a business that transacts much of its revenues on a cash basis is somehow more valuable than one that does not. Yes, it is true that we all would like to be paid in cash to avoid collection fees like those from credit or debit card companies. From this standpoint, a cash business may be worth slightly more than one using credit, but let's get real for a moment. When someone tells you that they have a lot of cash sales, they usually aren't talking about revenues recorded on their books. They are suggesting that their business is worth so much more than another business because they don't claim this revenue and are lining their pockets with tax free cash payments every month.

So what do you do if this happens to you? My advice is to never pay for anything that can't be proven. Aside from the moral and legal issues, why take the chance that those implied revenues are real? They might be real, but should only be viewed as nice to know, or as a potential bonus to the buyer. If the seller presses you, and says you are undervaluing his business or, worse yet, that you are trying to rip him off, then politely explain to him that he has reaped the benefits of such cash payments in the past. In other words, he is trying to double dip the market. This sounds a bit greedy to me, not to mention illegal and offensive. Buying a small business is risky enough, so why take a chance based on the seller's word alone; someone you don't even know!

Balance Sheet Items

Balance Sheet items are usually of less interest to buyers of a small business because, in most cases, the buyer is buying only assets; therefore, liabilities are of little concern. Personally, when investigating a business, I will look at anything and everything for clues about how it has been run in the past.

Discovering such clues may lead to identifying missed or hidden opportunities, or they may save you from making a huge mistake. For both income statement and balance sheet items, look for large variances from one reporting period to another, and then ask, why the difference? You will be amazed at what you will learn.

Below are some areas you may wish to focus on:

1. *Assets That are no Longer Assets:* Sometimes you will find items that continue to be listed on a balance sheet when, in fact, they no longer have any value left. For example, accounts receivable over 60-90 days should raise concern. If the current owner is having trouble collecting on outstanding accounts, think how hard it will be for a new owner! Debtors seem to vanish in a hurry once they hear a business has been sold.

   Your best bet is to give near zero value to the seller, or let the seller try to collect on these debts because they will have the greatest chance of success. As the new owner you should agree to accept any payments that come in after you take over, and pass those payments back to the seller, less a reasonable collection fee, of course.

2. *Assets That are Overvalued:* In most cases, the seller will supply you with a list of included assets along with their cost

and date of purchase. Some sellers think a buyer will simply accept that the assets are still worth what was paid for them. That's ridiculous, of course. Balance sheets should show the depreciated values, but often you receive only the asset list, which requires some digging to find the current market value.

Ask yourself what price you might get for each asset if you were to try to sell it on the street tomorrow. You should be paying the seller as close to that figure as you possibly can. If things don't work out, you may have to liquidate; if you keep this mind set, you are more likely to determine the true market value of the assets.

3. *Assets That are Undervalued:* Yes, this can and does happen, at least in a manner of speaking. I once tried to buy a fishing lure manufacturing business. It was a great little twenty-five year old business with a good reputation and decent on-line potential. Unfortunately, someone else was willing to pay a lot more than I was, and I lost the opportunity.

The seller had one piece of key manufacturing equipment that was fully depreciated; therefore, it didn't show much value on his balance sheet. When I toured the premises, I took my son, Matt, along in order to have more eyes and ears to inspect things. We paid particular attention to this piece of machinery and asked if we could see it in action. It looked really old, and we wondered if it would even start? Well, it surely started and just hummed along like the well-oiled machine that it was.

The fact that the owner had purchased this machine new, and had it on a regular maintenance contract, was music to our ears. I was convinced that we wouldn't have to replace this machine for many years, thus delaying a $60,000 capital outlay until cash flows could be improved, and we could better afford such a purchase.

If you discover older pieces of key productive equipment, they may be worth more than their depreciated value due to meticulous maintenance carried out by the current owner. This is something positive to watch for.

4. ***Inventory That is Overvalued:*** I don't care what business we are talking about; there will always be inventory that is no longer saleable at full profit margin, and this will put the buyer at great risk. It can be very difficult for a new owner to determine what is saleable and what is not, particularly if that person is new to the industry.

   When I was negotiating the purchase of our pool company, I had little idea which of the current product inventory would sell and which wouldn't. I was fortunate to have trustworthy sellers, and we were able to cut a deal whereby I paid 85% of the cost of the inventory which we counted together at the close. I suggest that a 15% discount to the net landed cost of any inventory is the minimum. In the case of fashionable, trendy, seasonal, or perishable inventory, this discount could be much higher.

5. ***Missing Liabilities, Unwritten Deals, and Warranties:*** I recommend that you always ask the seller if there is anything of material importance that you as the buyer should know about this business before you buy it. Obviously, you are trying to shake the trees for potential rotten fruit that could impair your opportunity for profits going forward.

   Sometimes this question will jog the seller's memory about a verbal agreement he made with a customer, or a contra (trade) deal he made with a supplier. As most buyers purchase only assets and not liabilities, you may not be legally committed to honor such agreements; however, you may find yourself morally obliged, nonetheless. There will also be times when such deals contribute to the success of the business.

Such obligations surfaced in a small way in our alarm business, and in much more substantial ways in our swimming pool business. I had to do work at a loss or break even in order to keep some pool customers, but I'm glad I did. Negative news can travel fast, especially in a smaller market like ours. When you buy a business, bad things are going to happen . . . it's all about how you manage it. Keep in mind that a lot of good things can happen too!

Something that never occurred to me when we bought the pool business, but should have, was warranties on products sold by the previous owner. For example, customers would try to return used pool equipment like a pump or filter, claiming it was faulty or unsatisfactory. As a buyer of assets, I wasn't legally responsible, but I felt I had to help the customer, in some way.

I approached the manufacturers on behalf of these customers and, in almost all instances, I was able to make things right without incurring too much of a loss. Thankfully, most of my suppliers were willing to work with me. We bought a lot of pool equipment; therefore most suppliers wanted to keep us happy and maintain a positive reputation in the market.

If you are buying a business dealing in very large ticket items or service contracts, you may wish to ask your lawyer if a holdback from the purchase proceeds is necessary in order to protect you from unanticipated customer claims.

6. *Goodwill:* This is an intangible asset class, as opposed to physical assets like inventory or equipment. Some examples include a positive brand name and/or reputation,

experienced employees, and intellectual property such as patents or web domain names.

If you see this asset on the balance sheet of a business you are investigating, it may suggest that this business was previously purchased as a going concern. The current owner is now depreciating this goodwill asset, and reducing potential taxable income by recording the depreciation as a non-cash business expense.

Basically, goodwill is the amount that you might pay for a business over and above the current market value of the business's physical assets. Most bankers cringe at the idea of paying very much for goodwill, and they usually won't finance it. If they lend you money and the business fails, they can't sell the "goodwill" on the street like they could a tangible asset such as a truck or a trailer. If it is a profitable business, however, you are very unlikely to do a deal by attempting to pay only the net asset value. Remember, you want to pay for a multiple of "earnings", not goodwill; therefore let similar business sales transactions be your primary guide in determining fair value. Refer to Chapter 31 and Appendix 3.

Chapter Takeaway

Potential business buyers should become reasonably proficient at interpreting financial statements. Comparing data from similar businesses is the most effective way to uncover issues and opportunities.

PART FOUR

SELLING YOUR BABY!

CHAPTER 33

$800,000 Tax Exemption - The Holy Grail of Qualifying Small Businesses in Canada!

I F THERE IS A holy grail for Canadian small business owners, this is definitely it! After all the years of hard work, long hours, and often very high stress, we finally get a break from our friends at the Canada Revenue Agency (CRA). This exemption is to the SBO, what the RRSP is to employee tax payers. Yes, it's that important, and I'm often surprised that many SBOs I talk to still aren't aware it exists, even though it was first introduced in 1985.

This is a very short chapter, for two reasons. First, tax issues are boring. Second, tax issues frighten most of us.

The point in writing this chapter is to ensure that readers are made aware that this opportunity exists, and to offer a little insight into how it works, as it can get quite complicated. I have always left my tax matters to my accountant, and I strongly recommend that you do the same. Just ask him or her to be sure that your business is structured so that it qualifies for this opportunity when you become ready to sell.

This Holy Grail lifetime exemption excludes up to $800,000 in capital gains from tax on the sale of Qualified Small Business Corporation (QSBC) shares, qualified farm property, and qualified fishing property. If the full $800,000 capital gain qualifies for this capital gains exemption, you would be eligible to claim a $400,000 capital gains deduction. Why only $400,000? It's because you only pay tax on half of your capital gains, thus you can only deduct half when your business is sold.

The key words here are "Qualified" and "Corporation".

In order for your shares to qualify, they must:

a) be shares in a Canadian controlled company where at least 90% of its assets are used primarily in an active business, and where at least 50% of those assets are located in Canada, and

b) have been held by qualified shareholders for at least two years prior to a sale.

It may seem obvious to most from the above reference to "shares", however, I should reiterate that in order for your business to qualify, it must be incorporated. If you operate your business as a sole proprietorship or partnership, you won't be eligible for the capital gains exemption when you sell. You may, however, be able to transfer your unincorporated business into an incorporated entity prior to a sale in order to qualify so be sure that you seek professional advice.

There is a lot more to this exemption, and the complexities can be daunting; however, if you keep the above points in mind and work with an accountant who is well versed in taxation issues (not a bookkeeper), you should be fine.

This exemption also applies to capital gains that are flowed to individuals through partnerships, trusts, and certain other types of investment vehicles. You may want to ask your tax advisor whether you can increase your exemption by the number of shareholders in the QSBC. If your spouse or children are shareholders, then each may be able to claim the exemption. For a family of four, that can be a $3,200,000 tax exemption! Sweet!

In an earlier chapter, we discussed how a share sale generally benefits the seller and an asset sale generally benefits the buyer. We have talked about how most small business sales in Canada are asset sales, not share sales. So you may ask, "Why would a seller want to sell assets and forgo this tax exemption?" The answer is because he may get a higher price which may offset a large part of the tax exemption benefit. The buyer is not taking on the seller's liabilities which is why he may pay more for assets than he would for shares.

As mentioned earlier, whether you sell assets or shares, it is always a matter of negotiation, and the tax implications are a major part of that negotiation process for almost any business sale. Again, you must consult with your accountant long before you put your business on the market so that you understand the implications of each type of offering.

Chapter Takeaway

This exemption is the best tax break in Canada for small business owners!

CHAPTER 34

How to Prepare Your Business for the Ultimate Payout

T HIS CHAPTER FOCUSES ON SBOs who have had their businesses for a good number of years and are looking to retire, as opposed to business "flippers" like me. While many of the principles will apply to both groups, from a practical perspective, the latter group will obviously have less time to prepare. In addition, we will be focusing on operations that have more than one or two employees which is likely to be the case after many years in business.

Ideally, the process of preparing one's business for sale should start two to three years prior to going to the market. Personally, I usually think about my exit when I buy or start a business. Yes, there have been some ventures that I honestly felt would be the one I would retire from, but it just never seemed to work out that way. I realize thinking about an exit at the start of a venture is unconventional; however, I don't think it hurts (and can be quite beneficial), even if you believe you are in it for the long term.

As a seller, you should prepare your business in a way that will minimize negative surprises for the new owners. Such initiatives will keep your reputation in good stead.

While you can do little about the management capabilities of the new owner, the last thing you want is for him or her to fail, or talk poorly about the deal to other SBOs. Think about your employees and loyal customers. What will they be saying about you a year after the sale? In each of the retail businesses we have sold, we still remain customers of the new owners. You don't want any awkward feelings when you go back to patronize what is now their operation.

There are things to do and plans to put in place long before you go to sell, and there are other things that need to be accomplished just prior to listing it for sale.

In the longer term:

1. ***Structure Your Business so it can Operate Profitably Without You:*** Begin this process by asking yourself what would happen to your business if you had to go away for six months? If the answer is disaster, you have some pre-sale preparations to do. If you want to maximize your return, it is critical that you are able to prove to prospective buyers that, when you walk out that door, the place won't take a nosedive. So how do you do this?

   - Cultivate a 2IC (second-in-command). Challenge your best person to do as many of the same tasks that you do so they are ready and capable to run things profitably. You may wish to consider an ownership buy-in strategy for such a protégé.

   - Hire a General Manager, if the business can afford it.

   - Cross-train your staff in different areas so they can cover for one another; this will also improve morale.

   - Create job descriptions and prepare procedure manuals for every job, including your own.

   - Design and implement as many effective "systems" as possible in order to maximize staff productivity. Buyers will pay a premium for efficient operations.

   - Test your structure, frequently. Go away on business or holidays, leave someone in charge, and see what happens.

I should have done this more often; however, when I did, I was pleasantly surprised.

2. *Identify Your Target Buyer:* Try to identify, as specifically as you can, who would most likely buy your business and where that person is located geographically. This will make it much easier to market or advertise your business when the time comes. Is it an individual or a larger enterprise? Is it one of your competitors, a supplier, or possibly a customer?

3. *Identify Key Employees:* You need to think through who is key to the success of your business. If changes need to be made in this area, you will require a long lead time, so now is the time to start. As part of their annual performance review, I always ask the question, "On a scale of one to ten, how satisfied are you with your current position?" This is important information for any SBO, regardless of a pending sale, and it will offer comfort to a buyer to see in writing what key employees think of their situation.

In the nearer term, six months to one year before you go to market:

1. *Be Certain Your Financial Reporting is up to Scrutiny:* You will need at least the last three years of financial statements. Well managed operators will also have a list of key performance indicators (KPIs) defined, and a report to show how you have performed compared to the industry. We will discuss KPIs later, but think sales per square foot, gross margins, revenue per employee, etc.

2. *Prepare a Brief Business Plan for the Following Year:* A one or two page plan is all you really need to show a prospective buyer. You should have such a document as part of your normal course of business anyway, but you can tailor this

one more toward how this business can run without you personally being there.

3. ***Clear up Outstanding Issues***: There may be things that need to be rectified between you and your customers, employees, and often your suppliers. It is also a good idea to transform any verbal agreements you have into written agreements. A verbal agreement is just talk, and a written agreement is an "asset"!

4. ***Be Aware of Changes to Competitive Threats***: If there are new competitors entering your market, you need to know about it, and have a plan as to how your business will deal with them. Conversely, if your competitors are hurting or closing, you certainly want to highlight that for prospective buyers.

5. ***Ensure all is Good With Your Lease***: I almost got tripped up here in my early days. Selling a business can be a long and difficult process, and the last thing you need is trouble when the buyer goes to get the lease transferred, and finds out that the landlord has other plans.

   If your landlord is local, I suggest that you sit down with him or her, and ask about their plans going forward. All you can do is try to get a feel for anything that may disrupt your sale. For example, if your lease is coming due, and a strong national tenant is next door, you run the risk of getting booted if that tenant wants more space. This is more likely to happen in the retail arena, but I have definitely seen it happen.

6. ***Google Your Business***: You know that potential buyers are going to do this, and you should do the same. It's an important exercise to take a look at what others see when they do an internet search on your business. Are you easy to find? How do you rank? Do things look up to date? Are there any customer complaints online? This is your window

to the world, so spending a little extra time and expense should pay big dividends when you go to sell. In fact, you should view this as one of your primary marketing tools for attracting potential buyers.

7. ***Collect or Write Off Accounts Receivable:*** It's a good idea to get ahead of the game here, and call a spade, a spade. If you have accounts over ninety days, write them off. In fact, the more effort you put into collecting past due accounts while you own the business, the better off you will be. As I mentioned before, it is much more difficult to collect after a business has sold because debtors become much tougher to deal with. Also, the buyer is likely going to discount these debts heavily, or leave the collections entirely to you, anyway.

8. ***Keep Accounts Payable Current:*** Overdue payables can alarm potential buyers. They may interpret this as risky because they might lose a key supplier. Overdue payables will make it much harder for a new owner to get good supplier credit terms, or any terms at all.

9. ***Make Necessary Improvements to Assets:*** A little spit and polish can go a long way to increase the amount you will get for your baby. I suggest you spend money where you feel you can get a return of double your cost. In many cases, you will qualify for a tax exemption on the gains you make from a sale (see Chapter 33) which makes it worth spending a dollar for additional tax free dollars. Wherever possible, do the work yourself, and use staff downtime to complete the rest.

10. ***Keep Driving the Top and Bottom Lines:*** Now is not the time for the owner to slack off. In fact, I believe the most difficult years for an SBO are their first and last year in business. Obviously, the first year has a huge learning curve, and the last is tough due to the added emotional burden of finding a buyer, worrying about employees, and staying motivated.

Some sellers will greatly reduce their operating expenses in an attempt to show a better bottom line, but a savvy buyer will figure that out pretty quickly. Advertising is a popular place to cut expenses. You're selling the business, after all. Why advertise, right? Wrong, in my opinion. You never know when your business is going to sell. It could easily take a year or more. If you start cutting expenses that are needed to support sales, then you risk negatively affecting the profit line. It is this number that is most widely used to value your business, so protect it, and do your very best to grow it . . . it's your last chance to do so!

I recommend business as usual, for the most part. You might delay non-critical large asset purchases. You might nix a new and unproven advertising campaign. You might pass on introducing a new product line. You are also likely to hold off on new hires, but overall, I think you are best served by continuing operations within the averages of the past few years. This is a prudent and responsible approach for all involved.

Chapter Takeaway

*Keep your exit strategy in mind from day one
to ensure you maximize your returns when
you decide to sell.*

CHAPTER 35

How to Market Your Business Opportunity and the Discretion Paradox

THERE ARE THREE PROCESSES a seller can use in order to reach a buyer and transact a business sale. To me, two of them are viable, and the other one, in most cases, should be avoided. Before we cover these three options, I want to take a few moments to discuss what I refer to as the Discretion Paradox.

When I was a residential realtor, I was taught that the more people who "looked" at a property, the higher the price received for that property. Although I can't prove this theory outside of my practical experience, it seems like a reasonable assertion. If this theory is true in the real estate market, it seems logical for it to be true in the case of selling a business, right?

Why then are so many business owners, including myself, afraid to make it public that their business is for sale? Herein lies my paradox reference. If you actively try to suppress the number of people who know your business is for sale, how can you expect to get a good price for it, or sell it at all, for goodness sake?

This is a risk most business owners seem willing to take. Many argue that if it becomes known that their business is for sale, it can be destructive to the relationships the business has in place, and, thereby, reduce the value of the business. Such affected groups include:

1. *Employees:* News of a sale can be very disruptive and stressful to staff, and it heightens the risk of losing key employees if not managed properly. It can also reduce productivity at a time when you need it most.

   Some may say that trusted key employees are entitled to be told out of some sense of respect and loyalty; however, I don't buy it. Employees are not paid to stress about what "may" happen. Circumstances often change, and a sale may never occur. Perhaps no sale takes place because the current owner's spouse loses a job, and they need the income from the business.

   I believe business sale plans are best left to those individuals who "need" to know, such as operating partners, or others with skin in the game.

2. *Competitors:* Some competitors can be ruthless in this regard, and spread negative rumors that can be disruptive to business activities. I have had my competitors try to get my financial information by posing as a potential buyer. It is not an uncommon practice, I can assure you.

3. *Customers:* What do you as a consumer think when you hear that a business you patronize is for sale? Certainly it depends on the type of business, but don't you get a little concerned that you may not be able to use that gift card, or that your product warranty may be in jeopardy? I can tell you this was a big concern for me when I was selling my pool business. Some people may hesitate signing a $50,000 pool construction contract if they discover that the business is for sale.

4. *Creditors:* Okay, so my business owes you a pile of dough, and you hear that I am selling. How does that make you feel? A little uneasy, I suspect. Landlords are creditors too, and they generally view such news as potential trouble.

You may be thinking, what's the upside to telling any of these people that your business is for sale? One important upside is that some of these people may be qualified potential buyers, another aspect of the paradox a business seller faces. I believe it's all about how the marketing process is managed.

Now let's discuss the options a seller has when making this critically important decision.

Hire a Realtor

There are two types of realtors, and we should distinguish their specialties. There is the residential realtor whose primary focus and source of income is that of selling homes, and perhaps the odd business. Then there is the commercial realtor whose primary focus is selling and leasing commercial properties. Commercial realtors are more likely to have some specialized training in the area of selling businesses, but this is more of an offshoot of selling or leasing real property such as land and buildings.

During my year and a half as a residential realtor, I listed a few businesses, sold only one, and bought one personally. I did this because I had experience selling and operating my own businesses and felt that I could add value to the process. My primary focus was always on the residential side, as this is where the money was, although I enjoyed the business selling side much more.

My experience as a realtor confirmed my earlier suspicions that business owners are much better served by the next two options than they would be by a realtor of either description. One might make an exception for a commercial realtor that has owned a business before, or has done a dozen or so business deals in the past. I think that most realtors would agree when I suggest that they are not properly trained to do business transactions, even though they may be licensed to do so.

Realtors may also lack motivation in this area because business deals can be complex, take a lot of time, and they are difficult to compare. Again, most realtors believe that the more people that see an asset for sale, the higher the price received by the seller, and the less time it takes to sell. This is a key motivator for realtors and, as a result, they are less likely to be discreet when marketing a business. Further, I have searched many business listings on the Multiple Listing Service (MLS) across Canada, and I have found relatively few that were properly priced, and even fewer where the listing agent used much discretion in their dealings with the seller's confidential financial information.

In general, realtors primarily market businesses with a value of around $100,000. They typically charge a flat fee of $10,000 or a commission of 10% of the selling price, not including the value of inventory, or real estate. There are those who suggest that 90% of small businesses, particularly those at this value, never sell. While I can't prove this to be the case, my experience suggests something approaching this level sounds about right. If this is true, it is understandable that realtors are not very motivated to sell businesses, because they can't make a decent living chasing deals which are highly unlikely to close.

Hire a Qualified Broker

The occupation of Business Broker, often called an Intermediary, is a relatively new one in Canada. The number of brokers, however, has grown steadily over the last five years, particularly in the larger centers like Toronto and Vancouver. Hiring such a trained and, hopefully, experienced person is definitely an option for many SBOs. Although I have had some interaction with numerous brokers, I have yet to use one to complete a deal.

In my opinion, the most important value-added component that a broker brings to the table is his or her ability to properly value your business according to your specific industry, and the market in which you operate. A broker should have access to the most relevant and timely data to prove to potential buyers that your business is worth what you are asking. Proper pricing is the key factor that ensures your "baby" gets sold. Sadly, it is an area that so many SBOs fail to get right.

Human emotions like pride and fear can cloud reality and good judgment. After all the sweat and tears, it has to be worth millions, right? Well, perhaps, and perhaps not. If your "baby" isn't priced right the first time, it can cause a mountain of anguish for you, the owner. This process can be stressful enough as you try to keep operations running profitably, while at the same time keeping a lid on things so that staff and customers don't become alarmed. Pricing it right the first time is of paramount importance.

Utilizing the services of a qualified broker has other advantages. The seller's focus should be on driving the top and bottom lines in order to show potential buyers that the business is growing, not shrinking. This extra push takes a lot of time, and a good broker should be saving you time to do that. He or she should act as an effective intermediary between you and potential buyers. Only the most promising and credit-worthy parties should be brought to the busy seller's attention.

A good, experienced broker should have a large network of contacts, and a book of buyers ready for an opportunity that actually makes sense from a financial perspective. He or she should also have some good insight into how to prepare your business for sale, so listen and heed such advice.

Now, before you accuse me of working for the Business Broker industry, please understand that I also see significant disadvantages in using a broker. The most notable downside is that they don't know your business as well as you do. And how do you think all that knowledge is going to get to potential buyers so they can properly assess the opportunity? Yep, they'll need to talk to you, and you'll want to talk to them to ensure the information is properly understood. So there is the potential that adding a third party to the mix may increase the odds that important information about your business is improperly disseminated, thus increasing the chance that it is misunderstood.

A broker may save some time by keeping tire kickers at bay, but I question how much time they can really save you, overall? Another thing that frightens me is the lack of control I would personally have over how, and to whom, my confidential information flows. Brokers say that they will provide confidentiality and discretion, but it is certainly on a best efforts basis which, I suppose, is only fair. I just don't know. I'm not comfortable with having someone from outside my business trying to explain my business. It doesn't work for me, personally. Some SBOs may be fine with delegating their information flow. It depends on one's personality. I am a control freak when it comes to explaining my business, which is part of the reason I have never used a broker.

Another potential disadvantage of using a broker is the cost. Although I see this as less concerning compared to the issues I raised above, it is certainly worth mentioning. For businesses with a value between $100,000 and $1,000,000, a broker will usually charge a commission of between 8% and 12% of the sale proceeds. This may sound like a lot, and it is, but if that broker brings a buyer and closes the deal, it won't sound like such a bad arrangement after all. Selling a business is nothing like selling a house, and I can say this based on my experience doing both. Effective marketing of a business involves a great deal more time and effort per transaction than that required to sell real estate. It makes sense that the broker is paid more given the extra work involved.

Should you decide to hire a broker, here are some tips to help you choose the right one for you:

1. ***Check Experience:*** You may be able to get away with hiring an inexperienced realtor and still sell your house, but hiring an inexperienced business broker can be detrimental to your retirement plans. If the person hasn't owned and operated at least one of his own businesses, <u>and</u> brokered at least a half a dozen deals, I would take a pass.

2. ***Check References:*** Most SBOs won't ask for references, let alone call them, but you shouldn't hesitate.

3. ***Try to Find a Specialist:*** If possible, see if you can find someone who has experience in your industry. A person who is familiar with how your business operates will add more value to the project.

4. ***Google Search:*** This is a simple and quick method of determining if there are any red flags that you should investigate.

5. ***Have Them Explain Dual Agency:*** Be certain you understand who is representing whom. Under dual agency, your broker may be representing the interests of both the buyer and the seller.

6. ***Have Them Explain Contract Terms:*** Make sure that you are crystal clear on all terms of the broker contract. The duration is typically twelve months with a six month minimum. Can you cancel before the term is up? At the end of the contract, are you still liable to pay a commission if you sell the business on your own? In some cases, you are.

7. ***Ask for Local Stats:*** A good broker will know your local market and be able to quote some stats on the average length of time it takes to sell a business, and what the average sales multiple is in your region or province.

For example, various US data sources suggest that, on average, it takes six months to sell a business. The website

Businessesforsale.com (international results) suggests that "80% of businesses sell within twelve months." The only Canadian data I could find were the results from Pratt's Stats which showed that of 184 businesses sold up to May 2013, it took an average of 6.6 months to sell. It seems that we Canadians track slightly longer than the US on this metric.

For Sale By Business Owner (FSBBO)

This option is not for every SBO; however, it may be a viable and rewarding option for some. I have written this section for those who have a modest amount of time and would like to maintain control over how information about their business is distributed.

During the period I was most in need of a specialized business broker (1985-2005), there were none to be found in my market. I assume most deals were being done by commercial realtors or FSBBO sellers, like me. I really didn't know who was doing what at the time. I do recollect asking my accountant, who was well connected in the local business community, for leads on businesses for sale, and his response was that he was usually the last to know when or how a business was sold.

To be honest, it really didn't occur to me to use an intermediary to sell the four businesses that I sold on my own. It just wasn't in my DNA to delegate such an important part of my livelihood to a stranger; therefore, I devised my own marketing plan and controlled the entire process myself.

Yes, it took extra time, but isn't that what evenings and weekends are for? At least that's the way I looked at it. If you set things up properly and use effective screening tools, you will be surprised how little time it actually takes. I'd say maybe an hour per week, on average, is all that is required.

Your goal should be to talk to only the most qualified of potential buyers, and there will be only a handful of them at most.

As mentioned earlier, this process is very unlike selling a home, especially in terms of how few people will be looking at your business.

Although your home may have sold in two months, and you had thirty people come and see it, with a business, it may take six to twelve months to sell, with only two or three people having taken a close look. Clearly this is an unscientific analogy, but I want you to understand that, in most cases, your phone isn't going to be ringing off the hook and distracting you from properly running your business. If this does happen, you may have underpriced your enterprise.

The reason I am so confident on the FSBBO option is because I have developed a simple, successful system to market my businesses and the businesses of others. This system can save a lot of your valuable time, and maximize your opportunity for a successful sale. Don't worry, I'm not going to direct you to my website to purchase my system. Everything you need is right here!

First, you need to develop some tools that will ensure your marketing efforts are both professional and effective. Later, we will discuss how and when to use them.

1. ***Request a One Page Valuation From Your Accountant:*** This is the key to a successful FSBBO sale. You need to go to your accountant and ask for a "one page valuation estimate" of your business, based on your last three to four years of business activity. You are not asking for an "opinion" or a professional valuation that can cost many thousands of dollars. This summary should cost about $500. You are simply asking your accountant to organize your own data in a format similar to what I have shown in Appendix 8, Sample FSBBO Valuation Range.

   This is exactly the same format I have used, and it must absolutely be printed on your Accountant's letterhead. Please note that you may save some money if, at the same time, you also ask for a one page "cash to seller" worksheet. Your accountant may call it something different, but this analysis estimates what you might receive from the sale of your business after all taxes for various assumed selling prices.

Now, let's get back to our one page valuation in Appendix 8. This example shows three valuation methods; EBITDA, SDE, and ROI, all of which were described in Chapter 31. The primary purpose of completing this brief valuation estimate is to give credibility to your asking price so that you can create and maintain buyer interest. It is a platform for discussion and negotiation. When I received my one pager from my accountant, I didn't ask him to make any changes whatsoever; it was what it was, a credible starting point.

You should encourage your most qualified potential buyers to show your valuation page to their accountant, and have them call your accountant directly with any questions. By the way, I fielded very few questions about my numbers, and my accountant was never called until an offer was on the table. As you will discover, very few people will actually see this information.

2. *Create a Confidentiality Agreement (CA):* This document may also be referred to as a Non-Disclosure Agreement or NDA. This is a tool that will help you in maintaining an acceptable level of confidentiality in your dealings with potential buyers. However, the main reason you should use one is to conserve your precious time and energy by discouraging non-serious buyers and competitors from making inquiries in the first place.

Believe me, a serious and financially qualified buyer will jump through this hoop without hesitation, so there is no need to be concerned that someone who is legitimately interested will be put off. The fact is, most savvy buyers know that this agreement, though legal and binding, is very difficult to enforce, and few put much credence on its value from a purely legal perspective.

A confidentiality agreement will discourage the types of individuals you don't want reading your financial information. The vast majority of realtors will not bother with this step; on the other hand, the vast majority of licensed Brokers will. A sample agreement is included in Appendix 9.

I will confess that, if I don't have a numbered company to use as a business name, I may make one up in order to keep my business name confidential. I realize that the buyer can search this; however, it is worth the risk to me. You may feel differently and, of course, that's fine.

Another benefit of a CA is that you get to see who the inquiring party is before you give up any information. I believe it also tells you something about the individual if the information supplied is incomplete or unclear. In these instances, I automatically turf them from my short list. I can't be bothered with people who don't respect seller due diligence.

3. *Create a One Paragraph Advertising Plan and Budget*: Yes, one paragraph should do it. Decide where you are going to advertise your business, and check their rates. I have never spent more than 1% of my selling price, or about 10% of a broker commission, on the sale of any of my businesses. In fact, in most cases I spent much less. In addition to the suggestions outlined in Chapter 28 on where to look for a business, below are some marketing opportunities I have successfully used to sell my babies in the past:

a) *Businessesforsale.com:* This is the only on-line site I have used, and I was generally pleased with the results; however, I have not actually sold a business using this vehicle. I have used it to help friends market their opportunities, and I have come close to buying a business listed on this site. Interestingly, many brokers list their businesses here, as you will see when you request more information from a listing. This service is free to buyers and the listing cost to sellers is reasonable at about $50.00 per month.

b) *The Globe and Mail Newspaper-Business Opportunities Classified:* You may be thinking that I am out of touch here but, believe it or not, this vehicle has been the best source of quality leads of any I have tried. I also bought a franchise as a result of an advertisement in this publication. I realize that print media is under tremendous pressure from on-line news sources, but you may want to consider this option, nonetheless. All you need is a brief, well-worded advertisement of about four or five lines, which we will cover in a moment.

I admit that I have not used this vehicle for a few years, and it may be out of favor, but please don't underestimate the quality of *The Globe and Mail* readers as valuable leads. They are usually well-educated, cashed up, and often mobile. Both *The Globe and Mail* and *The National Post* have an online version with a classified section covering business opportunities.

c) *The Western Investor:* This is a monthly print and digital publication covering Western Canadian commercial real estate and business opportunities. It is definitely "the" place to advertise if you have a business that includes real estate. I have had good success with this publication, having sold one of my biggest ventures using a small, quarter column advertisement. The rates are not cheap, but the quality of leads is quite exceptional.

d) *Business Immigration Programs:* As a potential business seller, I think you should at least be aware that programs for immigrant investors, entrepreneurs, and self-employed people do exist in Canada from time to time. The types of eligible investments are frequently changed as the Canadian Government adapts to the needs of our country.

In other words, the business you are selling may not qualify to be sold to an immigrant, especially if no jobs will be created; however, if you own a small farm or agricultural business, this may be a good source of leads for you.

4. ***Create a One Page Sell Sheet:*** This is a list of preliminary information given to the prospective buyer after you have approved their CA, and prior to releasing any detailed financial data. It must give potential buyers enough key information about your business so they can decide if they are willing to pay something near the asking price . . . or not. You may or may not have disclosed the actual name of the business, perhaps only the industry and the city, or region. I have created a sample sell sheet in Appendix 10 which you may want to use as a guideline. It is very similar to one I have successfully used in the past.

5. ***Create a Blind Email Address:*** Since you are not using an intermediary, you will need a way to communicate with potential buyers in a confidential manner, at least until they have completed your CA. For example, I have used businfo@ shaw.ca.

6. *Create Advertisements:* By now you will have everything you need to create an exceptional advertisement. I say exceptional because you are going to include information most others, for some reason, neglect to mention. Think about it. If you are a buyer, what is the most important thing you want to know? Certainly, it's **how much money you can make**, right? That's what I want to know, and if I can learn that, in addition to the industry it's in and the approximate location, then I am an informed potential buyer. Wouldn't you be, if you got all this information without picking up the phone? The buyer has no broker to call, no confidentiality agreement to fill out, and no time is wasted. The key elements of an exceptional ad are:

   a) Return on Investment (ROI)

   b) Approximate Location

   c) Industry

   d) Asking Price

   e) Direct Contact Information

Take a look at Appendix 11 to see these elements in action. I have used a close facsimile of this example in print media with very good results. It can be easily adapted to on-line advertising, as long as all of the elements are included. I haven't referenced whether it is an asset sale or share sale in my advertising, but you may wish to do so if you are certain which way it will go. Also, if your business is structured such that it is easily "scalable", you may choose to mention this in your advertisement.

Now that you have created the tools necessary to successfully market your business, you need to create a process of disseminating this information to only highly qualified potential buyers. You need to do this very quietly, so as not to disrupt your current business activities. It is important to distribute information in a disciplined manner. I suggest that you do things in the order presented, and don't waste time on people who don't want to follow your process.

1. Place advertisements.

2. Respond to blind emails by emailing or faxing your CA.

3. Send your one page sell sheet (Appendix 10) to those who properly completed the CA. Some of you may think that this step is a waste of time since the CA has been signed, and that's okay. I use this step to weed out less serious players, and, thereby, reduce the risk of leaking my financial data. All I can say is that it has repeatedly worked for me.

4. Financial Qualification (Optional Step). For higher priced businesses, I have used this step to ensure that the interested party has the financial capability to transact a deal. I have asked that they send a simple note from their banker or accountant stating that they have the financial wherewithal to complete a deal of this size. I, myself, have complied with such a request, and I made a successful sale using the same qualification. Why would a potential buyer say no to this request if they were serious about buying? Again, savvy buyers will jump through many "reasonable" hoops to pursue a properly priced business with a good ROI. They understand that such opportunities are rare. I am speaking from experience, as it took me quite a long time to find our pool business.

5. Send the one page valuation document from your accountant, along with your personal contact information. If you have been diligent, this is the first time the buyer has learned the name of your business. You now know that you are dealing with a qualified potential buyer so you

should respond to all subsequent inquiries from this party, expediently.

6. Buyer due diligence begins. See Chapter 30 for a summary of the kinds of information this person may request. Now it's your turn to jump through a few hoops. There is no need to worry because you have prepared your business well and you should now be ready to answer all operational type questions. Complex financial and/or tax questions go to your accountant.

7. Decide on the offer process. If a potential buyer wants to make an offer, there are a few ways to go about it. I suggest that one of you, or both of you, draft a Letter of Understanding (LOU) as per Appendix 6. This document will reduce the amount spent on legal bills by giving the lawyers clear direction on the most important terms. As always, it's a matter of negotiation as to whose lawyer creates the formal asset or share sale agreements. If the seller's lawyer has dealt with the business for some time, it may be most expedient for him or her to do the work, and allow the buyer's lawyer to review the same, each paying their own legal fees.

If you think about it, what we have done by combining the six tools and the seven step process of dissemination, is to create a do-it-yourself business marketing "system". It is a simple system to follow and, once set up on your computer it is fast and efficient. It can be used over and over again, should the need arise.

I have successfully utilized this self-designed "system" for myself and close business associates. To date, no one has discovered I was selling a business until I was comfortable telling them, and all businesses I tried to sell, using my "system", were sold.

Finally, I must reiterate that if you don't prepare your business properly, and value it according to current market conditions, all the fancy marketing systems on the planet won't help you sell it . . . not even mine.

Chapter Takeaway

A simple and professional For Sale By Business Owner (FSBBO) marketing "system" can save a seller a lot of money and maximize ROI. It may be worth the minimal extra effort for those so inclined. The process is a natural extension of what SBOs already know. After all, who knows your business better than you?

PART FIVE

HOW TO GET IN THE TOP 25% OF YOUR INDUSTRY AND STAY THERE!

EFORE WE BEGIN THIS section, I would like to clarify my intentions in writing the next few chapters. First, I don't want to imply that the following initiatives are the "backbone" of a successful business. Undoubtedly, the backbone is comprised of offering quality and desired products or services at an attractive price, utilizing superior customer service practices.

These days, however, such components, while challenging to deliver, are expected as a baseline, and taken for granted by your customers. What we are going to discuss next is how to strengthen that backbone so we can grow an entire ribcage, protecting our assets from competition, thus allowing the heart of the business to flourish. After all, a business is a living, breathing, going concern. So please keep in mind, the initiatives we are about to discuss are activities required to build an exceptional business, assuming the backbone is already in place.

This entire section is about how to become a top performer in your market and maintain a competitive advantage. We will investigate some tactics and strategies that will help propel your business to its next level of competency.

CHAPTER 36

What Business Are You In?

I N ORDER TO GET into the top 25% of your industry, it is critical that you understand precisely the business you are in. You must be able to clearly communicate this to all stakeholders in your organization. This is very important for all SBOs to nail down, and I mean really nail down. It sounds so simple, but it can take months or years to understand the real business you are in and to become able to clearly articulate it in only a few words.

If you ask an SBO what business they are in, you will often hear such things as, "I sell air conditioners", or "I create software applications", or "I install swimming pools". Yes, these descriptions are simple and concise, which is what you want; however, they describe a business by the product or service that is sold, not by what the business does to meet customer needs. To broaden opportunities, perhaps it would be better if these businesses were defined as offering "home climate control systems", or "designing smooth web customer interfaces", or "creating backyard leisure spaces".

Harvard Professor, Ted Levitt said it best when he told his students that, "People don't want a quarter inch drill . . . they want a quarter inch hole!" What he meant was that business people shouldn't focus on the product, but instead focus on the benefit it delivers to customers. If SBOs want to grow, they need to broaden their thinking so they don't miss opportunities often presented to them by their very own customers.

If you are struggling with how to define what business you are in, try asking yourself the following:

- The majority of my customers are _____. Include specific information such as gender, age, location, income level, habits, etc.
- Which of my products or services are growing the fastest?
- Why do my customers return to me?
- What makes my customers most happy?
- If I lose customers, where are they likely to go? What is the other business doing to better serve their needs?

I can think of four examples in my business career which may help you understand the concept of correctly knowing what business you are in.

1. *The Evolution of the Telephone Book*: As you may recall, I spent time in the "Directory" Division of a telephone company. It wasn't until we fully understood "what business we were in" that this business really took off. We went from referring to ourselves as Directory Publishers, to Telephone Book Publishers, to Yellow Pages Publishers, to being in the Advertising Business. In only a few years, our target market went from consumers looking up a telephone number in the White Pages, to the business customers buying a Yellow Pages advertisement, to consumers looking for a business in the Yellow Pages. Phew, that's a lot of change in a short time, but we did it by listening to our customers, and attempting to meet their needs.

2. *Mail Boxes Etc. / UPS Store:* Now, I am certainly not going to claim much credit for this one. We simply purchased a franchise in a growth industry; however, it had an identity crisis early on. We struggled to wean ourselves off the idea that we were a post office alternative with a consumer focus, and began to view ourselves as a business service center where small business owners were our primary target. Once we and our customers were clear what business we were in, things turned positive.

3. *AlarmForce:* Again, I won't try to take credit for this business model. Joel Matlin, the Founder and CEO of AlarmForce Industries Inc. broadened an existing business model of selling security system equipment to one of being in the monitoring business (equipment was free, so to speak). I never questioned whether Joel knew exactly what business he was in. His clarity of concept was one of the reasons why he was so successful.

4. *From Swimming Pools to Back Yard Living:* I must admit that when we purchased Sunshine Pools & Spas all I thought about were swimming pools, hot tubs, and not much more. During my second year, it became apparent that this industry was transforming from installing swimming pools and selling spas to creating entire back yard leisure spaces. This included pools, spas, barbeques, toys, water features, outdoor furniture, gas fireplaces, etc. The Canadian industry even embraced a common trade name called "Leisurescapes". While I endorsed the concept as being quite exciting, it was a long-term transition which would be up to the new owner to fully implement. Nonetheless, this is a classic example of redefining what business you are in.

If you own a very small enterprise, or you are doing a start-up, it may seem like this chapter doesn't really apply to you. I can ensure you, however, that if you want to be a leader in your industry you must clearly understand your business model. You must be able to articulate it quickly, and confidently when asked by employees, customers, suppliers, creditors, and other stakeholders.

Chapter Takeaway

Define your business in terms of the benefit it brings to your customers. Think "holes", not "drills".

CHAPTER 37

Sex and Marketing!

I F THERE IS ONE lesson you learn from this chapter, I sincerely hope that it is this . . . In Business, It's All About Marketing! My goal in writing this chapter is to help the SBO understand the marketing concept and how to use this understanding to grow their business into the top quartile of their industry.

Let us begin with some definitions of marketing.

Investopedia.com: *The activities of a company associated with buying and selling a product or service. It includes advertising, selling and delivering products to people. The four 'Ps' of marketing are product, place, price and promotion.*

American Marketing Association: *Marketing is the activity, set of institutions, and processes for creating, communicating, delivering, and exchanging offerings that have value for customers, clients, partners, and society at large.*

Author's Definition: *Marketing is any activity that results in sales to new or existing customers.*

SBOs generally define marketing as advertising or sales, or a combination of both. Yes, marketing includes both, but it is, in fact, so much more. Obviously, I am biased toward my definition because it is so broad. I like to say, "If it results in a paying customer it's marketing!"

How you answer the phone, how you greet customers, how fast you respond to customer concerns, how much your staff smiles, how presentable you and your staff are, how clean your premises are, and how up to date your website is are all important aspects of marketing. These things affect how your customers perceive your business, and whether they will return or recommend you. By the way, employees may answer the business phone, but it is up to the owner to make it ring; therefore, SBOs must take their marketing responsibility very seriously.

Let's drill down a bit and use the 5 P's (Product, Place, Price, Promotion, People) of marketing to further clarify what marketing might entail for the SBO. Traditionally, this marketing mix is referred to as having only four P's; however, I favor including "People" who are of paramount importance to SBOs.

Each of these categories must be addressed when putting together an effective marketing plan. It is the interrelationship and management of these five areas that creates a marketing mix unique to your enterprise, and it must focus directly on your target market.

Study results published by the Harvard Business Review in 2013 provide a fresh and valuable view of how marketing efforts should be focused in the future. It is called *Rethinking The 4 P's*[12] and it involves a five year study of more than 500 marketing managers and customers in multiple countries. The study focuses on the business-to-business relationship; however, it also has important implications for how businesses target consumers. This study doesn't suggest the original four P's are irrelevant; however, they do suggest shifting emphasis from *products to solutions, place to access, price to value, and promotion to education* . . . SAVE, for short.

I have discussed the following five categories in a way that will help the SBO understand some historical context, in addition to more current thinking from the SAVE study. Please understand

---

[12] Richard Ettenson, Eduardo Conrado and Jonathan Knowles. "Rethinking the 4 P's," Harvard Business Review, January 2013.

that these two types of thinking are not mutually exclusive. In fact, utilizing both in your marketing initiatives may provide you with a strong edge over your competition.

Product

Traditional Thinking: Product includes both tangible items that one can touch and feel, and intangible service offerings like web page design or window cleaning. We are talking about how you present your products or services in terms of quality, design, variety, features, benefits, sizes, brand name, warranties, return policies, etc. Also included here is how your product is packaged, although sometimes packaging is a category on its own.

Contemporary Thinking: Today's market leaders tend to think about their product in terms of the problem it solves or the **solution** it provides. As mentioned earlier, if you market drills, think about the type of holes they produce.

Place

Traditional Thinking: The most obvious example of place is the physical location of the business where customers are served. Traffic counts, street exposure, signage, lighting, customer security, access to parking, loading zones, and business hours are all "place" considerations. Place also refers to the type of distribution channel or sales method being used. Are you in need of a sales force? Are you in need of telemarketing people, or boots on the street? Perhaps your sales channel is online, or through a catalogue, or via tradeshows.

Contemporary Thinking: The internet has driven this marketing segment to a whole new level. The SBO needs to think in terms of customer **accessibility** to products and services in a much broader context. Both physical and virtual accessibility require thoughtful consideration going forward. How many ways can customers gain access to your business? Is that experience smooth and consistent?

Price

Traditional Thinking: How you price your products or services can sometimes help differentiate your business from the competition. You might offer large discounts in order to drive volume, or you might never discount in order to suggest your everyday prices offer the best value. Offering volume discounts, credit terms, trade-ins, and cash discounts are all a part of "price".

Contemporary Thinking: More and more emphasis is being placed on **value** instead of price alone. Yes, customers may look at price first, but then they ask themselves, "Is it worth it?" If you can increase the perception of that worth, you may not need to lower your price.

Promotion

Traditional Thinking: This part of the marketing mix includes all types of traditional media advertising such as TV, radio and newspaper. More importantly for SBOs, it includes those that are sometimes more affordable and often more effective means of advertising. These might include networking, social media advertising such as Facebook, Twitter and Google Ads; event sponsoring; direct marketing by flyer distribution or mail-outs; co-op advertising with vendors, etc.

Contemporary Thinking: A move towards **educating**, as opposed to directing customers, can lead to higher levels of customer satisfaction. If you offer information relevant to customer needs, you may build trust and loyalty long before they make a purchase.

People

Traditional Thinking: This 5th P refers to how your level of service, and the expertise and skills of the people who work for you, can be used to set you apart from your competitors.

This Author's Thinking: Every direct or indirect interaction a potential customer has with your business and your employees is a marketing opportunity. Skillfully determining a customer's needs (by listening) and then satisfying those needs (by following through) leads to business growth. Training and supporting your staff to be more **relationship** focused can become a powerful and long lasting edge over your competition. The challenge going forward is how to build long-term relationships with your customers over the internet. You may never actually talk to your customers, but you can still build a positive and lasting relationship. Could it be as simple as consistently doing and delivering exactly what you promise?

Hopefully you now have a better understanding of how broad the scope of marketing actually is. I'll wager, however, that you didn't consider marketing to be a concept broad enough to include human reproductive activity as referenced in the title to this chapter. In fact, it is so vital for SBOs to understand marketing that I will risk the wrath of my brother Bill, an ordained Catholic Deacon, and use sex to further explain marketing.

Actually, marketing is more appropriately related to what occurs just prior to the act of sex, for most species, I suspect. If you think about it, the terms marketing and foreplay are quite interchangeable.

Healthy and loving sexual activity rarely happens suddenly, from out of nowhere. Similarly, the sale of a product or service doesn't usually happen for no apparent reason. No, there is some sort of marketing going on prior to the consummation of any deal.

When your spouse or partner offers a suggestive look or a wink, that's marketing. When he or she dresses or smells a certain way, yep, that's marketing, too! In some cases, a whole lot of this type of marketing has to happen before couples . . . um . . . copulate.

It's the same in business. You must often attract attention, overcome objections, and explain the benefits to customers before they will buy what you are offering.

We have already discussed annual business plans and how the marketing plan is a critically important subset of that process. So here might be a good place to discuss the marketing budget. How much should an SBO spend on marketing each year? This will be determined by the size of the business, the type of industry the business is in, the length of time in business, among other factors.

A general rule of thumb for SBOs to consider is 5% to 8% of projected annual revenue. It could be as high as 10% or 20% for a retail start-up, and as low as 1% to 2% for a well established manufacturer.

Given the above suggestion, you may find it interesting to learn that of over 1.8 million Canadian businesses with revenues between $30,000 and $5,000,000 in 2011, the average amount spent on advertising and promotion was only $5,100 or 1.4% of revenues.[13]

This may be an interesting statistic, but it is not very helpful to your specific business type. You must dig deeper to find a more meaningful comparison. The data supplied in Part Six will help you narrow things down to your specific industry.

People thinking of starting or buying a business will frequently make the mistake of underestimating the importance of marketing and overestimating the importance of operational activities. They have a talent, an interest, or a skill, and they crave independence, but this is not enough to become a successful business owner.

For example, you may be a very good electrician, but managing and marketing an electrical contracting business is another thing entirely. Or you may know a great deal about cars, but running an auto dealership involves much more than knowing what a flywheel

---

[13] Industry Canada, Financial Performance Data.

does. **Somebody has to continuously <u>sell</u> something in order to stay in business!** Further, if you can't sell or you are uncomfortable doing marketing, then I really must caution you about going into business for yourself. It's just that simple.

Marketing has become more and more complex, particularly over the last five years as technological advancements have offered so many new and exciting ways for SBOs to compete for market share. Today a small business without an effective on-line presence may be a lost business. Even small retail storefronts need a webpage that clearly defines what products or services they offer, and a map showing exactly how to find them. Personally, we don't patronize a restaurant unless it has an online menu. If a business doesn't provide such a basic convenience for their customers, why should a customer bother to visit their establishment?

A decent web page is now expected as par for the course, and there is increasingly more pressure on the SBO to begin social media marketing campaigns. Yes, it used to be a matter of sitting with your Yellow Pages Representative once a year and you were done; it's not like that anymore.

Understanding how to market using platforms such as LinkedIn, Twitter, and Facebook is crucial in today's market. As my Dad would have said, "Now, that's the ticket!" I believe it won't be long before half of the marketing budgets of Canadian SBOs will involve digital media.

Gartner Inc., a US information technology research and advisory company in Stamford CT, completed a study on digital marketing in 2012.[14] They studied over 200 companies covering six industries and found that digital marketing makes up about 25%

---

[14] "Key Findings From U.S. Digital Marketing Spending Survey," Gartner Inc., accessed April 25, 2014, http://www.gartner.com/technology/research/digital-marketing/digital-marketing-spend-report.jsp.

of their total marketing budgets. Gartner projects that this will grow by 9% in 2013. This survey was conducted with much larger organizations than we are talking about here, but the point is that SBOs need to be conscious of where things are headed, and try to adapt and prepare for the inevitable. If they do, their chances of being in the top 25% of their industry are going to be greatly enhanced.

I have personally tried a number of different marketing initiatives over the years, from cold calling customers with our toy business, to television advertising with our Yellow Pages and swimming pool businesses. In general, I have found that mass market media expenditures (TV & Radio) are not a great investment for SBOs, unless you have very deep pockets and can maintain campaigns over the long-term.

Below are some examples of marketing initiatives that have worked well for us, and where the return on the dollars spent was quite positive.

- **Trade Show Promotions:** This was probably the single biggest contributor to our success in the monitored security business. Our sales spiked up after every tradeshow we attended. Keep in mind that just showing up is never enough. In addition to product demos, we held a prize draw in return for contact information. We then had to follow up the hundreds of leads with warm calls, email, or a direct mail piece.

- **Award Competitions:** I had a Sales Manager in our swimming pool business come to me within a few weeks of my taking ownership, and request funds for a project I hadn't budgeted for. After spending what I considered a large amount of money to buy this business, I wasn't in any mood to spend more dough on a marketing initiative, especially one I had no experience with.

He wanted me to hire a professional photographer and travel around to take photos (in just the right light, of course) of some of the pools he had sold the previous year. He then suggested I enter the photos in our association's national pool construction competition. There was no prize money, just bragging rights among peers, and a picture in the association's annual magazine.

To cover the cost of judging etc., there was a hefty fee attached to each submission. My first thought was that this employee was on an ego trip of some type; then I realized, boy, what a clever idea . . . I could build a business around this marketing "edge", if it worked.

Our average selling price for an in-ground pool was about $50,000, and this idea could help propel sales of these high margin babies. My Sales Manager knew that if we won awards, it would help him sell more pools, and that meant more commissions for him. I was certainly okay with that. Our goals were nicely aligned, and I knew pool construction customers stay with you a long time because they require chemicals, parts, and service to maintain those pools.

We did win a few awards the first year, and many more in subsequent years. Can you imagine the credibility and leverage that comes with building the most beautiful pool in all of Canada, as judged by a panel of industry experts, no less?

I used these awards in every marketing opportunity available. We hung the award plaques on the walls of our store for all our customers to see. Some are still hanging there today, many years later. I had the magazine award pictures reproduced on flyers, glossy handouts, newspaper ads, magazine ads, and I even had them featured during our television spots. I then spent a sizable sum on a whole new website design and incorporated all of these awards to entice people to come in for a pool quote. We became "Sunshine Pools & Spas - An Award Winning Dealer".

We were able to increase gross revenues by 28% within our first two years, and this marketing edge had a great deal to do with that growth.

- *Limited Time Deep Discounting:* In our first franchise, Mail Boxes Etc., I was skeptical of a national promotion suggested by our head office. In fact, I waited until the second year to participate. At first I couldn't wrap my mind around selling photocopies for just one cent! Our average retail selling price at the time was fifteen times that, and to do this for a whole month . . . no way, I thought. I envisioned having to hire extra staff, increase our advertising budget to promote the sale, work our buns off, lose money, and attract the kind of customers we didn't want . . . the cheap kind that only want to pay a penny for a 15 cent copy! Nope, not for me; I'm too smart for that.

Well, you know what happened. It was a great success. You see, we worked with our copier vendor to cut our cost for a limited time to about 3/4 of a cent, including paper. Although it was not the goal, we actually made money that month due to the extremely high volumes. The purpose of this campaign was to create a buzz and drive traffic into the store so we could show people that we were much more than just a post office.

This promotion definitely put us on the map in our market, and we clobbered our competition, as one competing franchise closed its doors shortly after our second annual promotion. What was most interesting was that many of those cheap customers I spoke of turned out to be very appreciative, and they became regular, long-term customers. Who'd a thought?

I learned an important lesson here: smart marketing can be a long term investment, not just an expense.

- *Vendor Co-ops:* Participating in vendor-supported marketing promotions is something that all SBOs should consider. This is when a supplier pays for part, or all, of a promotional or advertising campaign. They may do it to promote their products or services, or they may just want to get their name out to a particular market.

For example, they will sometimes pay for up to half the cost of a newspaper ad, as long as their logo is included. Perhaps they will give deep discounts on products that you can promote for a special event. We had success with large companies like Canon, Xerox, Hayward, and ReMax, as well as smaller suppliers looking to grow. This worked very well in the pool business, especially with suppliers of chemicals and hot tubs. I recall that Joel Matlin, the CEO of AlarmForce, agreed to pay for a large portion of my Yellow Pages budget one year. Why not? I was promoting his brand!

My suggestion to all SBOs is that every time you think about doing any advertising or promotion, always consider who there is that might help you pay for it. Even if you get a 25% rebate, that's something, and it adds credibility to have your business name alongside big, well-known companies.

The key is to consistently "ask" your vendors what they can offer. If they don't have a formal program, then be creative and suggest one. You should reach out, and beg, if you must. They don't always come to you and, in this instance, the squeaky wheel definitely gets the grease.

Our Mail Boxes Etc. retail space was leased from a huge landlord headquartered in Toronto. This landlord tried to brush me off when I suggested a promotion including all the business owners in our strip mall. Eventually they came around and subsidized a newspaper and radio campaign for a big two-day sale which turned out to be great exposure for our new franchise concept.

- *Symbiotic Business Relationships:* Whenever possible, I like to control my marketing costs by sharing them with other like-minded SBOs. If you and another non-competing SBO have the same target market, consider working together to reach that market. Yes, it takes time to organize, but you may find an edge worth nurturing. Below are some examples of successful symbiotic business relationships:

  - Lawyers/Realtors: These two groups often co-host seminars for new home buyers.

  - Restaurants/Pubs/Liquor Suppliers: Most pub promotions are funded by the beer or liquor vendors.

  - Financial Advisors/Accountants: This is how I met my second financial advisor.

  - Realtors/Mortgage Brokers: This is a classic example of cross-referring and cost-sharing.

  - Commercial Printers/Advertising Agencies: This involves significant networking and it can be powerful.

  - Home Builders/Pool Builders/Landscapers: I've been there, done that, and yes, it works very well.

  - Insurance Brokers/Security Systems: This was clearly the best edge we had with our second franchise.

- *Yellow Pages:* Now before you call me an out of touch dinosaur, let me explain. I have used this medium with great success in numerous ventures, and although it is definitely a dying sector there may be the odd instance where this could become an edge for some SBOs. For example, if your target market is over the age of 60, there may still be value in a Yellow Pages advertisement. While many of the older baby boomers are embracing technology, many may still be "letting their fingers do the walking." All I am saying is that you shouldn't dismiss this vehicle without doing some research on how your customers are finding you.

Small business owners, including me, often find themselves in a situation where they "trip over dollars to find pennies." I don't know who coined this phrase, but it is a good lesson to remember. It can be a very uneasy feeling for an SBO to reach into his or her own pocket and spend money on what may appear to be a risky marketing initiative. It seems more natural to look for ways to cut costs. While determined expense control is prudent financial management, a balanced approach including a healthy marketing budget is the best way to grow a business.

In conclusion, I don't believe one can ever over-emphasize the importance of marketing to SBOs. It's the nourishment required for that living, breathing thing we call a small business. Without continuous feeding, all your efforts may be for not as your competition strives to beat you at your own game.

So remember, the next time you're in the mood to grow your business, don't forget the foreplay . . . 'er . . . I mean marketing.

Chapter Takeaway

Marketing is a much broader concept than most SBOs think; and effective marketing is the most important function of a successful small business owner. If you don't like selling and/or are not skilled in marketing, you may want to consider a different career!

CHAPTER 38

Develop and Track Key Performance Indicators (KPIs)

I F THERE IS ONE concept that you put into action as a result of reading this book, I hope it's the use of KPIs.

Management consultant, educator, and author Peter Drucker once said, "What gets measured gets managed;" or put another way, "If you can't measure it, you can't manage it."

Big business, particularly in North America, has been putting this maxim to the test since the 1950's. I believe that the growth in Corporate Canada is due in large part to increased productivity resulting from management practices which incorporate Drucker's measurement truism. If it works for big business, there is no reason why it shouldn't work for small business. Yet even today, few SBOs grasp the importance of developing their own set of key performance indicators.

The very best small business owners in Canada do some variation of what Peter Drucker taught over sixty years ago. These successful operators develop a set of key performance indicators (KPIs) that are relevant to their specific industry. They track and analyze these metrics to help drive their daily business efforts toward their annual goals. KPIs are a scorecard of key activities of a business. KPI tracking focuses on areas which are "important to do well in" in order to meet high level financial objectives such as annual sales and profit targets.

There are two main quantifiable KPI categories. This chapter will focus primarily on what I refer to as "operating" KPIs. These are the non-financial activities you need to track and measure on a regular basis (minute/hour/day/week) in order to effectively manage the day-to-day operations of your business. It is the results of these activities which ultimately determine the outcome of the second category: the financial KPIs. Financial KPIs include revenues, expenses, and profitability, and are most often reported monthly. If you are not attaining your financial targets, you are likely managing the wrong operating KPIs.

There are hundreds of different operating KPIs because they are often unique to specific industries. What may be important to track for day care centers is not likely important to car dealers. Below are a few traditional KPIs, many of which I have used. Hopefully, these examples will help you to better understand the concept. In all cases I have tried to gather as many specific details as possible from Canadian sources. Unfortunately, Canadian data was not always available.

Sample Operating KPIs

1. *Retail Sales per Square Foot:* This is a classic example that every retailer should know, and compare, constantly. Although shopping malls in Canada generally have larger national chain retailers as tenants, there are still many SBOs operating in malls. Below I have included data reported by Industry Canada which you may find both interesting and helpful.

> *As of 2011, Canadian malls have generated nearly US$600 in retail sales per square foot per year, compared with the American average of slightly above US$400 in retail sales per square foot. The Yorkdale Mall in Toronto draws the largest retail sales per square foot in Canada— approximately $1,200 per square foot—and ranks second in retail sales per square foot in North America, after the Forum Shops at Caesars Palace in Las Vegas ($1,400 in retail sales per square foot).*[15]

This metric is also monitored closely in the supermarket industry. In the US in 2012, the Food Marketing Institute reported that the average annual sales per square foot was $531.44.

2. ***Average Revenue per Employee per Year:*** Do you have too many staff? Not enough? This ratio also gives an indication of a company's productivity and financial health.

When I was managing DirectWest Publishers Ltd., our Yellow Pages company, this metric grew from approximately $80,000 per employee to approximately $172,000, in three years. This is quite impressive, even if I do say so myself.

The average revenue per employee per year in our swimming pool business was approximately $159,000 over the three years I owned it.

Based upon my experience, I would suggest that, on average, Canadian "retailers" produce about $125,000 per employee per year.

It is very important to compare apples to apples when using this or any other metric. To help demonstrate this point, I offer some research done for Investopedia.com:

---

[15] "Canada's Changing Retail Market Consumer Trends Update," Industry Canada Office of Consumer Affairs, Summer 2013, Cat. No. Iu22-1/1-2013E-PDF, 4-5.

> The sales-per-employee ratio is best used to compare companies that are similar. Retailers and other service-oriented companies that employ a lot of people, for instance, will have dramatically different ratios than software firms. For example, Starbucks Coffee is a highly efficient retailer, but because it employs nearly 74,000 full and part-time staff, its sales-per-employee figure of $55,000 seems to pale in comparison to Qualcomm's $690,000 per employee.

Further,

> The comparison of Microsoft and Walmart, two businesses in very different industries, illustrates how the sales per employee ratio can differ because of this circumstance. Microsoft relies on technology and brain power to drive its revenues, and needs a relatively small personnel complement to accomplish this. On the other hand, a mega-retailer like Wal-Mart is a very labor-intensive operation requiring a large number of employees. These companies' respective sales per employee ratios in 2005 were $670,939 and $172,470, which clearly reflect their industry differences when it comes to personnel requirements.[16]

Another illustrative example is that each full-time equivalent employee in US eating and drinking establishments averaged $72,880 in sales in 2012.[17]

3. *Daily/Weekly/Monthly Break-Even Dollars:* When I was in retail, I needed to know how much revenue we had to bring

---

[16] Ben McClure, "Doing More With Less: The Sales-Per-Employee Ratio," accessed May 6, 2014, http://www.investopedia.com/articles/stocks/04/110304.asp.

[17] "Restaurant Industry Pocket Factbook," National Restaurant Association, accessed May 6, 2014, http://www.restaurant.org/Downloads/PDFs/News-Research/research/Factbook2014_LetterSize.pdf.

in every day in order to break even. Knowing this number provides great focus for managing day-to-day operations.

4. *Inventory Turnover Ratio:* This is a figure that most retailers will have top of mind, and they should frequently compare it to the standards of their industry. This is basically the number of times per year that a business sells and replaces 100% of its inventory. It is calculated by dividing the cost of goods sold by the average inventory level.

   Low inventory turnover may be a sign of inefficiency. Inventory rarely increases in value; therefore, it usually has a zero rate of return. It also implies either poor sales or excess inventory. A low turnover rate can indicate possible overstocking and obsolescence.

   A high inventory turnover ratio implies strong sales. A high ratio can indicate better cash flow, but it can also indicate a shortage of inventory which may lead to missed sales. High inventory levels are usually bad news because they represent an investment with no return. There is also added risk to the business if prices fall.

   This metric is all about balance and requires constant monitoring. Trying to maintain inventory levels that are not too high or too low is a constant challenge for all retailers.

   What should your inventory turnover ratio be? There are no rules of thumb for interpreting inventory turnover ratios; it depends on the type of business you are in. For a fee, BizStats.com publishes some US national averages which are broken down by industry. For example, in 2010, the national average for hardware stores was 3.5 times per year. For grocery stores it was 12.7. For wholesalers of electrical goods it was 6.8. Clothing and accessory outlets had an average turnover rate of 6.4 times per year.

5. ***Write-Off Percent of Total Revenue:*** This is a measure of money lost due to errors in the delivery of products or services. Fix it quickly! If you are publishing telephone books or a similar type of directory, the industry looks to keep this metric at less than half of one percent.

6. ***Staff Absenteeism Rate:*** I have never encountered an issue with this metric, and don't see it as much of a concern for small enterprises. I mention it here purely out of interest. When you have only a half dozen staff or so, it has been my experience that pride and peer pressure played a big role at keeping this at a manageable level, and nowhere near national averages.

   In 2012-2013, the Conference Board of Canada reported that the overall absenteeism rate was 6.9 days per year.[18]

7. ***Staff Turnover Rate:*** Why are they leaving, and where are they going? It is essential to undertake exit interviews for all employees, especially the good performers. High turnover can be "the" most frustrating, stressful, and expensive challenge facing small operators, especially those who require staff with some level of skill.

   Your annual turnover rate is calculated by taking the number of employees that left during the year, and dividing it by the average number of staff you employed throughout the year. You then multiply the result by 100 to get your rate in percentage terms. For example, if two people left your business over the last year and your average number of employees was twenty, then your annual turnover rate was 2 / 20 x 100 or 10%.

   Generally, an annual turnover rate of 10% to 15% is considered healthy, and many human resource managers will target 10% in larger organizations.

---

[18] Nicole Stewart and Elyse Lamontagne, "Compensation Planning Outlook 2014," (report prepared for the Conference Board of Canada, October 2013), http://www.conferenceboard.ca/e-library/abstract.aspx?did=5737.

In 2013, the Conference Board of Canada reported:

The 2012–13 voluntary turnover rate was 7.3 percent. The retail sector is experiencing the greatest challenge with an average of 20.6 percent. Defined as exits from the organization that are initiated by the employers (severances, dismissals, etc.), the involuntary turnover rate for 2012–13 is 3.7 percent. Thus the Canadian total was 11% for this time period.[19]

This is definitely an important metric for those in the restaurant industry. According to The National Restaurant Association:

The turnover rate for employees in the restaurants-and-accommodations sector was 62.6 percent in 2013, compared to a 42.2 percent turnover rate in the overall private sector. Restaurant employee turnover is higher than the private sector due to several factors, including higher proportions of students and part-year employees in the industry workforce.[20]

8. ***Merchandise Return Percent:*** Is the quality of your product high enough? Are you selling the right product to the right customer?

   According to the US National Retail Federation, shoppers of all descriptions return between 7% and 10% of their

---

[19] Nicole Stewart and Elyse Lamontagne, "Compensation Planning Outlook 2014," (report prepared for the Conference Board of Canada, October 2013), http://www.conferenceboard.ca/e-library/abstract.aspx?did=5737.

[20] Bruce Grindy "Economist's Notebook: Hospitality Employee Turnover Rose Slightly in 2013," National Restaurant Association, accessed May 6, 2014, http://www.restaurant.org/News-Research/News/Economist-s-Notebook-Hospitality-employee-turnover.

purchases, depending on general economic conditions. In 2009, 8.4% of total retail sales were returned to merchants.[21]

Data compiled from about 50 clients of retail consulting firm Kurt Salmon shows that, on average, online consumers return 20% to 30% of orders of apparel and other soft goods. This compares to a return rate of less than 10% for hard goods like gifts, home products, and toys.[22]

If you are a retailer of almost any description, you would do yourself a great service by reading the research studies regularly produced by the Kurt Salmon organization.

9. ***Average Cost per Service Call - Average Number of Service Calls per Day:*** This is vital data for those in service businesses like plumbing, heating, electrical, and swimming pool technicians, too. Is repair work profitable? Is it efficient? How do your service people compare to the industry average?

10. ***Customer Acquisition Costs (CAC):*** This metric has gained most of its recent popularity from online retailers; however, it can also be important for bricks and mortar operations. CAC measures the total cost associated with acquiring a new customer, including all aspects of marketing and sales. It is calculated by dividing total acquisition expenses by total new customers over a given period. This tells you whether your marketing and advertising investments are paying for themselves.

In our monitored alarm business which had recurring revenue, we tracked our CAC in two key areas. We divided the entire cost of a trade show by the number of new

---

[21] "Customer Returns in the Retail Industry," National Retail Federation, accessed May 6, 2014, https://nrf.com/media/press-releases/customer-returns-the-retail-industry-2009.

[22] Mark Brohan, "Reducing the Rate of Returns," Internet Retailer, accessed May 5, 2014, https://www.internetretailer.com/2013/05/29/reducing-rate-returns.

contracts we signed; these contracts were a direct result of each show we attended. On average, it cost us about $40 for each new customer that signed a three year contract. This represented a value of about eight times the CAC.

The other CAC we tracked in this business was the insurance brokerage edge we had developed. As discussed earlier, this edge was a beautiful thing because it resulted in the lowest CAC we had ever experienced, approximately $33. This represented a value of just over nine times our CAC.

David Skok is a five time entrepreneur turned venture capitalist, and he is now a partner at Matrix Management Corporation. David suggests that for SaaS (software as a service) providers, CAC for subscription businesses should be recovered within one year. Further, he suggests that the

> *Life time value of a new customer should be about 3 times CAC and that most public companies like Salesforce.com and ConstantContact, have multiples that are more like 5 times CAC.*[23]

In his book, *The Fusion Marketing Bible,* author Lon Safko highlights some typical industry standard CAC values which include:[24]

- Travel: Priceline.com $ 7
- Telecom: Sprint PCS $ 315

---

[23] David Stock, "Startup Killer: The Cost of Customer Acquisition," accessed May 6, 2014, http://www.matrixpartners.com/blog/startup_killer_the_cost_of_customer_acquisition.

[24] Lon Safko, "The Fusion Marketing Bible," accessed May 6, 2014, http://www.entrepreneur.com/article/225415.

- Retail: Barnesandnoble.com $ 10
- Financial: TD Waterhouse $ 175

11. *Cost of Customer Acquisition Versus Customer Retention:* Strictly speaking, this point may not be a KPI per se, but it is critically important for all SBOs to understand. You may be surprised to learn that, depending on the industry, the cost to acquire a new customer can be as high as thirty times the cost of keeping an existing one!

Although I could find no definitive research, The Chartered Institute of Marketing states that, "In most cases, it costs between four and six times more to get a new customer, than it does to keep an existing one."[25] It seems clear that retaining as many repeat customers as possible will minimize marketing costs and improve profitability.

Sample KPIs By Industry

1. *Restaurants:* This is an industry where national chains and franchises dominate. Part of the reason for this is due to their relentless and systematic tracking of those things that need to be done well in order to succeed.

   Let's look at an example from Darden Restaurants, a huge publicly traded US company which operates a number of successful restaurant chains. In November of 2013, Market

---

[25] The Chartered Institute of Marketing, accessed February 11, 2014, http://www.camfoundation.com/PDF/Cost-of-customer-acquisition-vs-customer-retention.pdf.

Realist.com accumulated some public data from Darden Restaurants, as shown in the chart below.[26]

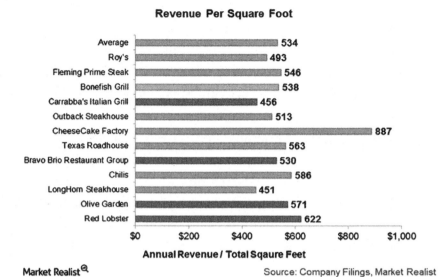

Revenue Per Square Foot

I realize that these examples comprise well-known, popular chains with great brand recognition. It would be difficult for independent restaurant owners to achieve these results. My point in showing you this data is purely illustrative, and offered in order to highlight the importance of KPI development and tracking. These are profitable operations, and setting goals based on KPI tracking is one important reason why.

2. ***Dentists:*** I include the dental industry in order to emphasize the positive relationship between tracking KPIs and enterprise profitability. This industry clearly demonstrates that if you do the first properly, the latter will usually follow.

---

[26] Xun Yao Chen, "Darden Analysis: Assessing the Success of a Darden Brand Spinoff," Market Realist, Part 13, accessed May 6, 2014, http://marketrealist. com/2013/11/darden-analysis-revenue-per-square-foot-essential.

It is no coincidence that dentists are one of the most profitable business enterprises in our country (see page 346 for details). One of the biggest reasons for their financial success is that this industry is generally very well organized and managed according to well-defined success criteria.

In addition to support from the Canadian Dental Association, there are a myriad of sources dental practitioners can turn to for help in managing and marketing their practices. One such source is expert Gary Takacs from Scottsdale, Arizona who is a recognized dental practice management consultant. Mr. Takacs strongly suggests that seven of the most important KPIs in a dental practice include:

- *Annual Production Per Active Patient: The suggested target is $800/year.*

- *Whitening Procedures Per Month: More whitening equals more engaged patients. Goal is one procedure per day.*

- *Accounts Receivable Aging Detail: The longer an account ages the less likely you are to be paid. The suggested goal by Takacs is to have no more than 20% of total accounts aged over 60 days. Other experts recommend that 95% of accounts are to be paid within the same time period.*

- *Annual Production Per Full Time Team Member: Staff wages are your single largest line item expense. Control this expense and you will have your overhead under control. Ideal goal is $200,000 in annual production per full time team member.*

- *Account Receivable Ratio: To compute your accounts receivable ratio, divide your total accounts receivable by your average monthly production. Goal is an A/R Ratio of 1.0 or less. That means that your total accounts receivable are equal to or less than one month's average production.*

- *Hygiene Production as a % of Total Office Production: Keeping your hygiene schedule filled and productive provides a host of benefits to the practice. Ideally, hygiene production should be 33% of total office production.*

- *Office Overhead: This may be the most important KPI of all. The goal is office overhead to be at 60% or less (all expenses before Dentist compensation).[27]*

I trust that the above example clearly illustrates how developing and tracking KPIs can lead to highly profitable enterprises. The only reason these professionals take the time necessary to set-up and monitor such programs is because it works! Think about it for a moment. Think back about twenty years. Do you remember how often (if ever) your dentist's office called you at home to remind you to get in for a check-up? Do you recall receiving cute little postcards in the mail telling you how good you could look if you would only come by for a cleaning? Next to real estate agents, I receive more marketing probes from my dentist than any other industry. No doubt about it, they are on their game, and you can be too.

3. **Wheat Farming:** Even though I grew up on the Prairies, I know absolutely nothing about the business of farming. Given my ignorance, I reached out to a friend in Saskatchewan who has been farming full-time for over thirty-one years. James Goby, from the Avonlea area, farms about 4,000 acres of wheat, canola, and flax. For perspective, the average farm size

---

[27] Gary Takacs, "7 Most Important Things to Measure in Your Dental Practice," accessed January 13, 2014, http://www.takacslearningcenter.com/ 7-most-important-things-to-measure-in-your-dental-practice.

in Canada is 778 acres, and the average in Saskatchewan is 1,668 acres.[28]

James told me, "I learned a lot in the first twenty years (school of hard knocks), but made no money. The last twelve, and, in particular, the last seven years have been what it's all about." He further explained to me that, "Farming can be very profitable or really suck, and the farmer can do all the right things and still lose. No matter how good you are at marketing, we 'commodity' farmers are price takers."

James shared his 2012 financial results with me, and I do believe I will ask James to buy the beer the next time he visits Kelowna. I can confirm that he is in the top 5% of this industry in all of Canada. James concedes that much of his recent success has been due to good markets (prices) and good weather. "This was the best year in thirty-three. Not typical. This was the boom to offset the many busts".

Knowing James to be a humble sort, I pressed him for more insight into how he and other top producers are able to lead the industry. His response was, "Knowing your COP or cost of production is THE most important thing, in my mind. I can know my cost for the upcoming year very accurately, but I can only estimate the yield (weather) and price (market)."

KPI development and tracking are what James analyzes during the long, cold winters so that he is ready for spring, year in and year out.

Yes, even farmers, at least the best ones, use key performance indicators to help set goals and maximize profitability!

4. **HVAC Contractors:** More and more of the smaller Canadian plumbing, heating, and air conditioning contractors are

---

[28] "Statistics Canada 2011 Census of Agriculture," (Component of Statistics Canada catalogue No. 11-001-X, May 10, 2012).

taking advantage of industry-supplied KPI data. Product manufacturers and distributors often provide guidance on which metrics are important to track in order to better manage and grow their operations.

The industry is also assisted by management consultants such as James R. Leichter, a life-long contractor, who offers assistance through his website MrHVAC.com. The following KPIs are a few examples included in James' research:

- *Conversion Rate to Service Agreement - Indicates how many service calls were made versus how many of those resulted in the sale of a service agreement. If you're in the service business, you should have approximately 300 SAs per billable employee.*

- *Gross Profit - Net sales minus the cost of goods and services sold (direct expenses). Service work should yield a GP of 70% or higher while heavy construction can be 20%. One of your manager's most important responsibilities is to protect profit margins on labor and materials.*

- *Call Back Percentage - A "callback" can be defined as return visit to correct an improper repair that cannot be billed. A good service department should have less than 2% of its service calls result in a callback.*

- *Sales to Technician (Field) Labor - indicates how much of your total sales revenue (income) is consumed by payroll and labor expenses related to the field (usually sales, technicians and installers). The lower the number the better, because it suggests that you are efficiently using your employees to create sales. Our recommendation is .2 or less.*[29]

---

[29] James R. Leichter, "Financial Rations and KPIs Used by MrHVAC," accessed January 16, 2014, http://www.mrhvac.com/2010/03/26/common-financial -ratios-used-by-mrhvac-com.

It has been suggested to me on several occasions that HVAC businesses have a very high failure rate, especially the smaller operators. Some industry experts suggest that up to 37% of these contractors fail within the first year! This seemed high, so I investigated.

In 2005, a study was done by Matt Michel, the CEO of the Service Roundtable (*www.serviceroundtable.com*), regarding the failure rate of HVAC contractors in the US. This organization is touted as the world's largest private contracting group serving plumbing and air conditioning contractors. Matt's research concluded that:

> *The close rate among non-payroll contractors (no employees) is projected to be 26.3%. When averaged with payroll contractors, the overall industry's annual close rate is 19.9%. In other words, one contractor in five closes every year. A 20% close rate is less than the conventional wisdom, however absent other research, this is the only empirically based statistic on contractor close rates.*[30]

A 2014 research study seems to confirm that the HVAC industry is plagued by high failure rates. This study found "plumbing, heating, air conditioning businesses to be number one in terms of businesses with the worst rate of success after the fifth year."[31]

Out of interest, this study showed that other businesses subject to high failure include single family home

---

[30] Matt Michel, M. "Business Closure Rates for Plumbing & HVAC Contractors," accessed May 6, 2014, https://www.serviceroundtable.com/freebies/viewfreebie.asp?PCID=850.

[31] "Startup Business Failure Rate By Industry," Entrepreneur Weekly, (Small Business Development Center, Bradley University, University of Tennessee Research, January 1, 2014).

construction, grocery stores, eating places, security brokers and dealers, and local trucking, in that order.

5. *Beauty Salons:* There are over 18,500 beauty salons in Canada who fall into our small business definition having revenues between $30,000 and $5 million. See the financial report on page 330. This is a significant portion of our service sector and deserves some attention.

Again, Canadian KPI data is scarce unless you become an association member and purchase one of their reports. If you are considering this business, I strongly suggest that you become a member.

Michael Lejeune is a business coach out of St. Louis who agrees with me on the importance of utilizing KPIs to manage your business. I have quoted some of Michaels' work below.

Michael says:

> *One of the most important factors in running a business is actually one of the most overlooked areas of business. I know this because I talk to hundreds of business owners every year and I only find about 5% of them that have a clue about KPI's.*[32]

Michael offers simple, practical examples of how tracking KPI's can work. Below are three examples based on work he completed for a salon client.

---

[32] Michael Lejeune, "Performance Tracking." Accessed May 8, 2013, http://michaellejeune.wordpress.com/2011/05/12/what-are-kpis-and-why-are-they-important.

Let's assume that the average clients serviced per day is 4 with an average sale of $45. If this person works 5 days a week we can come up with estimated revenues of $900 per week (4 clients per day times 5 days in a week times $45 average sale per client). Let's also assume that these numbers are the same for 10 stylists that you have in your business. So now the revenues are $9,000 per week ($900 times 10 stylists).

Now to put these KPI's to work for you, let's assume you can come up with 1 strategy (or edge, as I call it) for each KPI that will increase it by just 10%. That brings your average clients serviced per day to 4.4 and your average sale to $49.50. Doesn't look like much until we multiply it out. Now our weekly revenues per stylist are 4.4 customers times $49.50 in average sales for a new total of $1,089 per stylist or $10,890 for your whole team of 10. When you look at it over time it's even more attractive. That extra $1,089 per week turns into $56,628 over the course of just 1 year and over $283K over 5 years. That's a lot of money if you ask me.

But here's the fun part. If you know your average client visits per day and your average sale, it doesn't have to stop here. You could continue to work these numbers and improve them dramatically just by adding a single strategy here and there that will increase both areas.

Another KPI for this type of business is called, "Frequency of Purchase". To some people it can be referred to as average number of transactions per year, but I like frequency of purchase. Think about this for a minute. If your client visits you once every 8 weeks that winds up being about 6.5 visits per year. Not bad, but if I know this number I can now work to improve it by implementing simple strategies. So let's say I can reduce this to visiting me every 7 weeks. I now go from 6.5 visits per year to 7.4 visits a year. Again it doesn't sound like much, but what if you have 1,000 clients like most hair salons? You've just *added over 900 visits at about $50 each to your bottom line. That's another $45K just by getting clients to come back a little more often.*[33]

For seventeen years, Modern Salon Media of Illinois has produced Salon Today 200 (ST200) which features leading salon operators from across the US. In order to be considered for inclusion, Salon owners are judged according to ten industry KPIs.

In a January 3rd, 2014 article, Editor In Chief of Salon Today, Stacey Soble wrote:

We wanted to celebrate, recognize and honor the accomplishments of the salon and spa owner. We wanted to create a forum where owners could share best business practices with one another. And, we wanted to begin collecting the important data that both painted an accurate landscape of the salon business environment, but established important benchmarking goals against which owners across the country could measure themselves.[34]

I contacted Stacey and received permission to reproduce some of their benchmark data which is listed below. For those readers in this business category, you may want to visit salontoday.com and check out more of what the salon industry considers to be their important success factors.

• This year's class (2014) posted average gross sales of $1.823 million for 2012.

---

[33] Michael Lejeune, "What are KPIs and Why Are They Important?" accessed May 8, 2014, http://michaellejeune.wordpress.com/category/accounting.

[34] Stacey Stoble, "Defining Success for Salon and Spa Business," accessed May 8, 2014, http://www.salontoday.com/news/salon-business/2014-SALON-TODAY-200- Defining-Success-for-Salon-and-Spa-Business-238615791.html.

- The average sales increase over the previous year was 19%.

- The average charge for shampoo, cut, and style was $49.36.

- The average ST200 salon boasts 5,200 square-feet of space. In addition 79% of the majority of honorees lease their space.

- Seventy-five percent of honorees belong to one or more professional associations and more than half of the honorees have hired a professional salon coach or consultant in the past three years.

- The average sales ticket came in at $70.45.

- Salons charge an average of $49 for a shampoo, cut and style, and $67 for a single-process color.

- ST200 salons employ an average of thirty-seven employees.

- The average ST200 salon receives the largest portion of its gross revenues from hair color service sales and hair cutting service sales, which at 34% and 31% respectively, each represents about a third of gross revenues.

- Most of the honorees (73%) have one location. Of those companies who have more than one location, the average operated is four.

- Among the ST200, 66% of salon owners still perform client services. Of the owners who do, they report spending an average of twenty-five hours per week performing services.

- On average, owners of ST200 salons/spas look to three key performance indicators for assessing the health of their businesses: Productivity, Average Ticket and Client Retention.

- Over half (56%) maintain an annual budget for salon improvements.

SALON TODAY 200
Economic Trends
Percent of Gross Revenue by Category

Hair Color Service Sales	34%
Hair Cutting Service Sales	31%
Retail Sales	17%
Skin Care, Body Care, Spa-type Service Sales	8%
Nail Service Sales	4%
Chemical Service Sales	3%
Other	3%

SALON TODAY 200

Economic Trends

Controlling expenditures is one of the biggest management roles of a salon or spa owner. Knowing industry averages helps owners zone in on areas that need attention. Here's how the 2014 Salon Today 200 break down their costs:

Labor	48%
Supply Costs	11%
Rent/Mortgage	8%
Profit	6%
Taxes	5%
Owner Compensation	5%
Marketing/Advertising	3%
Education/Training	2%
Conventional Employee Benefits	2%
Professional Services	2%
Utilities	2%
Insurance	1%
Telecommunications	1%
Other	4%

I don't know about you, but this kind of information just blows me away in terms of its value to an aspiring SBO in this industry. This is decisive evidence that industry leaders become industry leaders by knowing their numbers, and striving to achieve preset goals.

I realize that I have mentioned this numerous times before, but it bears repeating. If you feel overwhelmed by all this KPI talk, I urge you to start with just one or two key measurements, and grow from there. I guarantee, you won't be disappointed.

Sample Financial KPIs

Please recall that our target group refers to businesses with gross annual revenues between $30,000 and $5 million.

1. ***Gross Profit Margin (GPM):*** This is the difference between your total revenue and the direct cost to produce that revenue. If you sell a widget for $1.00 and it costs $.50 to produce it, your gross profit margin is 50% ($.50/$1.00). It shocked me to learn how many SBOs in the pool industry did not know the answer to this most basic question. Most were simply concerned with their bottom lines (net income).

   Next you want to look at the top line (revenue). Are you charging enough? Check out the competition. Perhaps you can boost your selling price a bit? Perhaps you can train staff to sell more of the higher margin items, and offer them an incentive to do so.

   As an SBO, it is critical to get your gross profit metric in line, or you may not survive. It's just that simple.

   As outlined in Appendix 12, the average GPM in Canada in 2011 for incorporated businesses in our target group was 56.2%. While a national average may be interesting to know, it is not very useful in managing your specific type of business. You need to dig much deeper to find relevant comparisons to your enterprise, as you will see in Chapter 45.

2. *Labour as a Percent of Revenue*: Most SBOs seem to think they never have enough people, until they compare themselves to the leaders in their field. If you find the amount you allocate to this critical expense is comparable to similar businesses in your industry, and you still can't get all the work done on time, it must be a matter of productivity. Do you have the right people in the right positions? Are you tracking what they do? Have you given them targets to strive for? This is an important metric to keep in mind as it is one of the most difficult and stressful to change once it is out of whack.

3. *Advertising and Promotion Expense as a Percent of Revenue*: It seems that whatever amount you spend here, it's never enough. As you may recall from my earlier discussion on marketing, I mentioned that I have researched various sources and it looks like a general rule of thumb for an SBO to consider is 5% to 8% of projected annual revenue.

   I was surprised to see that the overall average in Canada at 1.4% of revenue. I guess our SBOs don't necessarily practice what is preached to them, myself included at times. In my pool business, I spent only 2.8% on advertising and promotion; however, this business was very well established.

   Again, averages may be interesting, but not very helpful, until you focus on finding comparable data that is specific to your business.

4. *Rent as a Percent of Revenue*: Comparing your rent to that of your peers is an excellent way to see if your digs are worth it? The Canadian average of all businesses in our target group was 3.6% of revenues.

5. *Net Income (Loss)*: Ah, net income, the bottom line! We are all anxious to get to this telling little number. The problem with focusing on this number is that it is like looking

through your rear view mirror while driving. You get to see where you've been, but you can't see where you are going.

Certainly every business owner knows this number like they know the back of their hand, right? Unfortunately, this is very often not the case. I know many SBOs who don't know until year end, how much money they are making (or losing). This is shocking I know, but true! These types of SBOs are, hopefully, a minority in our country.

The best operators do all they can to drive sales up, maximize gross profit by keeping cost of goods in line, and manage daily operating expenses by overseeing all spending; when the bottom line is determined, it is usually no surprise.

Appendix 12 shows that the average net profit in Canada for our target group in 2011 was 12.6% of revenue or $46,700. The average net profit of the top 25% of these businesses was 9.4% or $108,700. I will explain in Chapter 44 why these numbers, particularly the profit percentages, are misleading and not relevant for a comparison to the specific business you own, or the one you may be thinking of starting.

6. *Financial Ratios:* There are many standard ratios used to try to evaluate the overall financial condition of a business. These are usually calculated for larger enterprises and, if applicable, you should discuss these with your accountant on a regular basis. A few examples of these ratios are debt to equity ratio, current ratio, quick ratio, return on equity, return on assets, and return on capital.

In the swimming pool business, we developed a few indicators that were unique to our own business, and I was excited to share them with my peers at a national convention. Unfortunately, I was unable to find any other owners who were using KPIs to help manage their operations. I was truly stunned to find such a mature industry without any kind of KPI tracking and sharing initiatives.

KPIs are also of prime importance to enterprises operating under the franchise umbrella. Franchisors are masters at measuring, comparing, and sharing data that they believe will help drive sales.

Of the two franchises we owned, one was a more developed American organization, Mail Boxes Etc. (MBE) now called The UPS Store, and the other was a much newer Canadian owned franchise, Alarmforce. MBE tracked numerous results and compared them monthly to all franchisees in the network. With MBE it was easy to see how you were doing, and where you might improve. AlarmForce, on the other hand, wasn't nearly as developed in this regard.

Unfortunately, when it comes to implementing KPIs, much of the small business world in Canada is like the pool industry. It doesn't have to be this way for you. For most SBOs, the big question is, "Where the heck do you find the data to compare to in the first place?" I have outlined some sources below, and if none is readily available for your business type, I suggest some ways to build your own set of KPIs.

1. *Join Your Industry Association:* This is a definite must, and "the" most important source of KPI data you may ever find. There is usually a cost for such data, but it can be a great investment. You will also meet other members and share KPI data that may not be in the Association research reports.

2. *Ask Suppliers:* Believe it or not, this can be an excellent source of KPI data. Savvy suppliers often make it their business to know your business as well as you. They want to sell you products or services and the more they know about your customers, and how your business operates, the more products they are likely to sell you.

For example, I received some very helpful information from our Canon photocopier representative when we owned Mail Boxes Etc.

In the pool business, the chemical suppliers were a wealth of knowledge about what the industry leaders were doing.

There was a time when I didn't want to hear how others ran their businesses, thank you very much! I quickly realized, however, that I had to check my ego at the door and listen to what the industry-leading SBOs were doing to grow their businesses. It works, and it's free!

3. *Check the Financial Results in Part Six:* As a starting point, your business may fall into one of the 100 categories outlined in Chapter 45. If not, you can access Industry Canada's Financial Performance Data service to find a better comparable. I will explain how to do this in Chapter 45.

4. *Network:* If need be, set up your own network of contacts from your industry, and share information via regular conference calls or email. Also, attend all available regional and/or national conferences where you can exchange information with your peers from other markets.

5. *Start Your Own Association:* It's difficult to imagine a business type that isn't represented by an association of some description, but if your business category is just developing, it isn't that difficult to start your own. It only takes a half dozen or so participants, and communication is much easier these days with the help of the internet.

6. *Bizstats.com:* This site offers American KPI data for a fee.

7. *US Census Bureau:* This information is available by visiting *www.census.gov.* If you dig deep enough, you may find something useful here. In my opinion, however, it is nowhere

near as helpful as Industry Canada's benchmarking data located at *www.ic.gc.ca/eic/site/pp-pp.nsf/%20eng/home.*

I first learned about the value of KPIs from my mentor Keith Critchley. As mentioned earlier, Keith owned a commercial printing company in Regina for twenty years. He introduced me to the CPIA (Canadian Printing Industries Association) which he felt offered great value to his organization.

Each year, Keith sent his closely held financial and operating results to the CPIA so they could compile his data along with that of many other printers across Canada. This was done on a strictly confidential basis. In fact, I believe they used an independent accounting firm to compile and report on the data. The end result was a report that compared each participating firm with the average of all participating firms.

Interestingly, this report also included a comparison to the top 10% of participants. In addition to the standard metrics of sales growth, profitability, etc., "wastage", "paper costs", and "value added revenue" were also important metrics in the commercial printing industry.

Since then, my business goals have always been set to reach this top 10% category. In fact, I was able to transfer this management technique to our Yellow Pages company and started tracking our own KPIs soon thereafter. Within two years, our team became one of the top performing Yellow Pages organizations in Canada.

I know what you're thinking, "Tim, get real! I have no time for all this tracking! There's only me and a couple of staff!"

My answer to you is that, if you truly want to be at the top of your industry, you must start with at least one simple-to-track measurement, and build from there. For example, today most cash registers are computers that are capable of tracking a lot of important data like customer counts per hour, sales by product, average revenue per transaction, etc. This is important information that you can use to compare yourself to the best operators; it will help you know where you should be focusing your efforts.

When we were in retail, I found our average sale per customer was much lower than my peers in Ontario. What's up with that, I wondered? It was simple, I just had to be sure that my staff were well trained on the products, and that they were attempting to up-sell when a customer's need was apparent. If you don't have time for such a simple initiative I don't know what to say, except good luck.

The point here is that tracking came first (average revenue per customer), followed by the comparison to my best peers, which led me to the realization that we weren't up-selling. Tracking and comparing KPIs points out strengths, weaknesses, and opportunities in your business. It empowers you, and your people, to focus on the important issues that need attention which then leads to the attainment of your broader goal, such as improving the bottom line.

It's like wearing a pair of very dirty eyeglasses, taking them off, cleaning them, and when you put them back on everything looks so much clearer. That's what KPI tracking can do for your business; it allows you to better see where you are going, and focus on what is most important.

If you still believe that you don't have the time or resources to start a KPI program, let's look at one simple indicator that I once tracked in the past which took absolutely no time or additional resources. Yes, you heard me. It took no additional time from my normal working day.

At Sunshine Pools, I spent much of my day in my centrally located office. This office had a large glass window facing part of the customer area and my door was open at least 90% of the time. We had a chime on the entrance door and, although I could not see, I could hear customers entering at all times. I implemented a customer service initiative to have my retail staff greet "every" customer who entered that door, no matter how busy we were. If staff were busy, they were required to say, "Hello, we'll be with you in a moment."

I could then work in my office, listen while I worked, and measure how we were doing on this simple, yet important metric. Later, during the slow winter season, we conducted telephone surveys where we asked our customers how we were doing on various aspects of our customer service. The results were positive, and customer greetings always ranked high.

The KPI tracking was by no means the best it could have been at Sunshine. We did, however, develop a few key indicators which helped us better focus on what was important to our success. These examples include:

1. *New Pool Construction Gross Profit:* I didn't know how to build a pool, but it didn't take me long to figure out that this was a critically important profit center. I made it my job to control costs and improve efficiencies wherever I could. I reviewed and approved each and every invoice that came into this business. Pool construction along with pool liners and other renovations, made up about half of our business each year. We began tracking every cost by job name in order to target a 35% gross profit per pool.

2. *Pool Liner Installs per Week:* This was a high margin area which needed a great deal of organization. I managed this area personally, and we went from an average of two installs per week to just over three per week by the end of our first season.

3. *Retail Gross Margin:* A standard retail gross margin is about 50%. Our goal was to achieve only 45%. Due to the seasonality of this business, we purchased our goods

from wholesale distributors who offered a lower margin opportunity.

4. ***Number of Service Calls per Day:*** Our service department became much more efficient once we started tracking this simple indicator.

5. ***Service Call Profitability:*** We changed this department from a "service at all cost" center to a "profit" center. Terri, my Service Manager, began tracking and setting hourly, daily, and weekly targets for our service technicians. Terri made this area profitable within a year.

A common objection to the notion of comparing performance metrics is that they aren't comparable in the first place. Some SBOs will argue that their business is unique and not comparable. They might argue that the results for a car wash in Vancouver aren't comparable to a car wash in Toronto, or a restaurant in Calgary can't be compared to one in Montreal, for goodness sake!

Well, I beg to differ. Yes, every business has its own unique aspects, but there are always some common success factors that can be shared to the benefit of all involved. You may have to qualify the results a bit, but this won't detract from the huge benefits to be gained by those who make the effort to participate.

Another big benefit of tracking KPIs is that it creates great confidence on the part of the owner and staff. Such confidence stems from knowing ones numbers (KPI data) and how to use them to profitably grow the business.

I have saved one of the greatest benefits of tracking KPIs as my last. Effective KPI management will greatly help the owner to maximize his or her return when they decide to sell their business. This is because a well organized business is much more valuable to a buyer than one that is disorganized.

Think about it. Business Owner "A" who uses KPIs can quantifiably explain why her business has grown and how it will continue to grow in the future, while Business Owner "B" who lacks KPIs talks in generalities about past performance and offers little insight as to what the future may look like. Owner "A" is calm and confident because she and her people are organized and have a plan, while Owner "B" is tense and unsure because he was too busy to plan for this very day.

Which business would you rather buy, and how much more would you be willing to pay?

The number one fear of all business buyers is the risk of losing their money.

The number two fear of potential buyers is losing employees, especially key employees. I believe that good employees like to be challenged, they need to be recognized for their good work, and they enjoy working in an organized environment. Utilizing KPIs satisfies these needs; therefore, the best people are much more likely to stay with the new owner, which is what everybody wants.

So indirectly, an effective KPI program can improve job security for staff, maximize returns to you as a seller, and reduce risk for the new owner by securing key staff members. A win, win, and win situation!

Chapter Takeaway

Consistent tracking of key performance indicators is what differentiates a well-managed business from a poorly managed one.

CHAPTER 39

Find Your Edge

I N STOCK MARKET TRADING, anything that helps you attain results that are greater than a coin toss is called an "edge".

In small business, an edge is something that is found in businesses that consistently achieve above-average results in their industry. Offering quality products, great customer service, and a good price are no longer enough to differentiate yourself from the competition. Yes, you can still be a successful and profitable SBO without a clearly defined edge, but it is less likely that you will be in the top 25% of your peers.

Developing a competitive edge can take years. It can be created slowly as part of a maturing business practice, or it can be one of those "aha" moments when you realize that "my customers will love this," or "this is why my customers come back."

As mentioned earlier, our very first edge was developed by JoAnn in her secretarial business. JoAnn added value to her service by editing documents, in addition to typing them. The competing secretarial services didn't understand that customers would be willing to pay a significant premium for the extra service.

We were at least a year into our Mail Boxes Etc. franchise before I thought of packing and shipping wine. It also took about that long to discover how and why insurance companies appreciated monitored security systems. These "edges" made all the difference to our success in these two ventures.

In our swimming pool business, I believe we had three important edges. One was our longevity in the marketplace; the name, Sunshine Pools And Spas Ltd. had become the most established and trusted in the region. Much of our competition was comprised of numerous small operators working out of their trucks. Having a bricks and mortar presence gave comfort to customers showing them that we would be around the following season to service what we sold. Second, we became organized and reliable in an industry that was generally poorly managed. Lastly, becoming an "award winning pool builder" became our edge for growth.

During my stint as a realtor, I didn't develop an edge which is probably one of the reasons I didn't do very well. If I did develop an edge . . . it was the wrong one! I loved small business, but few real estate customers were interested in my business acumen; they just wanted to buy a home. Go figure.

We had two key edges when we owned the Yellow Pages company, DirectWest Publishers Ltd. First, we had the exclusive right to the Yellow Pages trademark which was a very strong brand at the time. It gave us instant credibility and fortified our barriers to entry. In addition, we started out with the exclusive right to consumer and business telephone number data. These two powerful edges were significant as we grew the business by stealing market share from newspapers, radio, and television.

Prior to publishing this book I asked my son, Matt, to critique it for me. After reading this chapter, this is what Matt had to say: "I was a little underwhelmed by this chapter, primarily because it lists all the 'edges' you developed throughout your career, yet does not offer any possible ways or ideas to help your readers develop one of their own."

I would hate to leave my offspring underwhelmed; unfortunately, I know of no quick and easy answer to this question. Developing a competitive edge is not a science. It's more of a process of developing a curious and open-minded approach to doing business. One needs to avoid tunnel vision, and never think or utter the words, "But that's the way we've always done it." Having said this, here are a few suggestions that may help you develop an edge.

- *Listen Closely to Customers:* This is probably the most direct way to discover missed opportunities. If people are asking for things that you don't currently offer, don't react negatively. Their request could be an "edge" in disguise.

- *Listen Closely to Suppliers:* For many years, I felt that sales reps were only interested in selling me something, not in helping me grow my business. A great supplier does both, and he can tip you off to a new opportunity that may be selling well in another market. This may help you to gain exclusivity on a hot item for your own market.

- *Monitor Your Competition:* Call them, visit them, and ask others what they think of your most fierce competitors. Emulate what they do well, and avoid their shortcomings.

- *Be Well Read:* Top SBOs know what's going on in their industry from coast to coast. Read trade magazines and join industry associations. I subscribe to business magazines such as *Canadian Business* and *Bloomberg Business Week* which keep me abreast of market trends. These magazines also offer inspiring entrepreneurial stories, and they are great sources for discovering a competitive edge.

- *Ask Successful Peers:* Your competitors obviously won't be too eager to share their edge with you, but your peers in other markets just might.

- *Attend Industry Trade Shows:* I have attended many trade shows over the years and I never come back thinking it was a waste of time or money. Events showcasing new products or services are great sources for learning how to create a competitive edge.

- *Think Vertically:* The farmer grows the grain; the mill produces the flour; the baker bakes the bread; and the restaurant sells the bread to the consumer. I am not suggesting the restaurateur grow his own grain, but he might consider baking his own bread to create a competitive edge.

Perhaps a better analogy is salon owners developing their own brand of skin or hair care products, thus eliminating the middleperson, and creating a valuable edge.

Chapter Takeaway

Find something that makes you unique and superior to your competition, and you will have discovered your edge.

CHAPTER 40

The Power of Networking

W E'RE NOT TALKING ABOUT connecting computers or job searching here, so let's define what we mean by business networking.

Webster.com: *The exchange of information or services among individuals, groups, or institutions; specifically, the cultivation of productive relationships for employment or business.*

Entrepreneur.com: *Developing and using contacts made in business for purposes beyond the reason for the initial contact.*

Author's Definition: *Meeting new people and building long-term relationships that will help each other's business grow.*

Networking is easier said than done. It is difficult for me to think of a task that is so easy to define and comprehend, yet so darn hard to accomplish. This important initiative was a challenge for me throughout my business career. I was active with my industry peers, but I didn't do as well when it came to networking at a local level.

Below are examples of various networking opportunities you may want to consider:

1. *Service Clubs:* Rotary International, Kiwanis International, Canadian Progress Club, Optimist International, Lions Club, etc. These are just a few great ways to meet new people, build strong and lasting relationships, and help worthy causes at the same time. What a triple play!

2. *Chambers of Commerce:* Being a member is not enough; attending events is even better; and serving as an executive member or Chairperson may be very beneficial to the health of your business.

3. *Industry Associations:* Most mature industries have numerous associations. For example, at Sunshine Pools we could choose from the Pool & Hot Tub Council of Canada, the Association of Pool and Spa Professionals, or the Independent Pool and Spa Service Association. Again, simply paying annual dues and reading their monthly publication is not enough. Taking the time to travel to and participate in meetings can pay big dividends in terms of learning what successful people in your industry are doing to be competitive.

4. *Breakfast Clubs:* These are specifically created as a networking opportunity, as opposed to service clubs whose primary goal is to serve the community. This is a great way to meet people without the much larger time commitment required by a service club. The opportunity to become recognized is greater because a club like this generally allows only one business from each category.

5. *Leverage Leadership Talent:* If you have an area of expertise outside of business, like a knack for coaching kids' baseball

or organizing curling championships, then you can multiply your contacts while enjoying your personal interests. A realtor in our city is often featured with his team in the local newspaper. Think of the leverage here. Each player has parents, friends, and relatives who can't wait to see media coverage of their child's activities, and their realtor coach gets some very targeted, subtle, and free advertising. This type of exposure builds credibility and trust.

6. *Sponsorships:* These might include a one-time special event sponsorship like a national hockey tournament, or longer term commitments to organizations like the United Way. In either case, it is crucial to not only provide funds, but to participate in the event itself so that you are able to meet new people and establish personal contacts. Event organizers and the public may then put a face to the name of the person who supported their cause.

I'll never forget how I first learned about the concept of networking. I was in an annual management meeting with my partner Keith Critchley. Keith, myself, and about ten of my management team were working together to define the elements of our first business plan as a new Yellow Pages Publishing company called DirectWest. As mentioned earlier, Keith had honed his networking skills for over twenty years as a highly successful commercial printer.

All was going well at our meeting until Keith asked when networking would be covered on the agenda. I was quick to respond by saying, "Oh, that's easy," and proceeded to disregard the comment. When I looked at Keith and saw his expression, I realized I may have been a bit hasty in dismissing the importance of his suggestion. I don't think Keith ever really corrected me on this point, at least not directly. What he did manage to do over the next while was educate me about networking in a very practical way.

The truth is, I was ignorant on this subject. I remember wondering what could be so difficult about going out for drinks and appetizers once in awhile? In fact, I would look forward to it, or so I thought.

It wasn't long before my phone started to ring with invitations to events all over town. You see, Keith had become well "connected" in the community as he built his commercial printing operations. He was President, Saskatchewan Roughriders; President, Regina Chamber of Commerce; President, Regina United Way; President, Saskatchewan Standardbred Association; President, Saskatchewan Graphic Arts Association; VP, Regina Exhibition Association; member of various service clubs; founding member of the Regina Breakfast Club, and so on.

Keith would ask me to join him at one or two events a week! Some of these events included Chamber of Commerce events, fundraisers, golf tournaments, retirement dinners, tours, political events, and presentations of all types. At first it was exciting because Keith introduced me to many interesting people. I didn't realize it then, but he was educating me on how "easy" it was to network. Yes, it didn't take long for me to become exhausted. I'd work a ten hour day, and then my secretary would remind me of a retirement dinner in an hour. My head would drop; I just wanted to go home and rest! Then I would hear Keith coming down the hall . . . "Hey Tim, ready to go?"

Networking can take up a lot of what otherwise might be free personal time. That is one important reason business networking can be challenging. Another reason is that it takes a lot of effort to be effective; you must be proactive. Standing in a corner with people you already know, just doesn't cut it.

Walking into a room full of people can make anyone feel awkward as the fear of rejection rises. Confidently introducing yourself and your business is much, much easier said than done; it can be quite uncomfortable, especially for shy types like me. However, the more you do it, the more comfortable and confident you will become. In addition, it is important to keep things "fresh" by trying new ways of networking that will help keep you motivated while broadening your base of connections.

An example of proactive networking is an initiative JoAnn and I undertook when we owned our MBE franchise. I was not the best networker, to say the least, but we had to do something to get the word out without breaking the bank.

As members of the local Chamber of Commerce (which is a must for all SBOs), I would attend "Business After Hours" functions from time to time. To be honest, I hated going, but you do what you have to do. These events were held weekly at the premises of the host business. The most well-attended functions were those of the wineries. Who could pass up a free glass of wine and appetizers? Unfortunately, many of the others were often poorly attended which is why we never thought of hosting our own until, well, we had to. We added our business to the schedule and set out a plan.

The standard way that people were informed about this event was through a flyer inserted in the Chamber newsletter which was then mailed out to all members. It occurred to me that this could be one of the reasons why the events were so poorly attended. We decided to do things differently.

In addition to the Chamber flyer, we decided to personally call each and every member a few days before we hosted the event. We spent days calling and suggesting that it would be a unique experience, and well worth their time. I thought we might as well make the calls since customers were staying away in droves; we obviously had some time on our hands.

Interestingly, while speaking to the Chamber members we discovered that only 10% to 20% were aware that there was an upcoming event, let alone know who was hosting it. As it turns out, SBOs are often too busy to read Chamber newsletters. Who would have thought?

The day of our event arrived, and people started to show up just after we closed the store at 5:30; and, they kept coming, and coming, and coming! Our store was soon so packed with people that they could barely move about to find the wine and appetizers that we had laid out.

Our plan was to meet each person and tell them about the services we offered, but it was just too crowded. Jo and I then decided to get behind the counters, and call everybody to attention. I made a brief presentation explaining the benefits of our services, and the group responded positively.

We then proceeded to collect a business card from each guest and put them in a hat. We drew one card at a time, and presented each winner with a gift that pertained to each of our profit centers. For example, to make everyone aware that that we rented business addresses, we gave a year's free mail box rental; and to highlight the fact that we provided courier service, we offered a free overnight document delivery; and so on. They listened intently because there were prizes to be won and, as a result, they learned about all of our service offerings. This was very important because the majority of the people in attendance were in our "business to business" target market.

We were pleased with the response that we received from our Chamber event, and it went a long way in helping us grow our business. The day following our event, I received a call from one of the Chamber Directors. He told me that he had attended many Business After Hours events, and ours was one of the best he had ever experienced.

My point in telling you this is to try to reinforce the idea that effective networking can make all the difference for SBOs.

Another challenge of networking is that the rewards are rarely immediate. It is likely that the connections you made last night may not become fruitful for weeks, months, or even years to come. This is where persistence pays off. If you think of it as building long-term relationships, instead of what is often referred to as "glad-handing," it will eventually pay handsome dividends.

As a commercial printer, Keith Critchley estimates that his networking efforts resulted in about 20% to 25% of his entire revenues each year! This is incredible. I suggest that this type of effective networking could be an "edge" in and of itself, which could propel you into the top of your industry. I have seen first-hand what effective networking can do; I witnessed Keith maintain a top 10% position in his industry for many years.

If helping to grow your business revenues isn't enough, there are other important benefits which may accrue to those who undertake effective networking. For example, it might help increase your gross margins. Generally, business derived from people who know and trust you is high-margin business. Your friends and associates are less likely to grind you on price because they don't want you to grind their pricing when you patronize their business.

Also, successful networking may reduce the amount you need to spend on your advertising and promotion expenses. Please don't misunderstand. Networking can't and shouldn't replace your advertising budget, but for those start-ups with limited funds (which is almost all of them), networking can be a prudent investment. Realizing a decent return on advertising dollars can be hit and miss, even for those with large budgets, so consider starting a networking initiative right out of the gate.

Another benefit of effective networking is that it can provide access to mentors, supporters, and advocates who can help the SBO better manage his or her business. My narrow, and perhaps selfish, understanding of networking was focused on getting more people to patronize my business. Yes, I would try to patronize them in return, but I didn't realize how much I could learn at the same time. SBOs don't have a large pool of employees to draw on for expertise in different management disciplines. Just think how much you might be able to learn from a network full of marketers, human resource specialists, accountants, lawyers, financial advisors, media types, and yes, even government officials.

Another thing I learned while managing our Yellow Pages business is that effective networking can provide an inside track to various business activities and opportunities in the community. If you are in the position of being one of the first to know, it could easily provide an edge over your competition.

I believe that there are few things in managing a business that cannot be delegated; however, networking, especially for start-ups, may be one of them. It is primarily the owner's responsibility to network. I say this because most salaried employees just don't have the same motivation and enthusiasm as those who have "skin in the game", or those who are paid a commission on the sales they bring in.

Below are more networking tips that I have found to be effective.

1. ***Start with a Networking Plan:*** I know, just what every SBO craves . . . more planning. The fact is that few things in business get accomplished without at least a basic plan of attack. Joining even one service club and participating in your own industry association can be a suitable plan for many SBOs. "Participating", is the operative word. We're all very busy; perhaps a target of attending 80% of meetings,

serving on one committee, and attending one annual conference will help grow your business faster than your competition.

2. ***Quality not Quantity:*** Successful business people believe that networking success is measured by the number of long term relationships you build, not by the number of business cards you collect. So stop counting cards, and start building trust in the people you meet.

3. ***Be Persistent:*** It can take months or years of networking on a regular basis to achieve positive, long-term results. This is all about the journey; it's not a race to a destination.

4. ***Be Proactive:*** People don't always come to you so, without being aggressive, overbearing, or phony, you must take the initiative to meet people. A little eye contact and sincerity will go a long way in building a positive relationship. Try to limit your talking time to 50% or less of any conversation.

5. ***Be Selective:*** We network in order to help build our businesses. The same goes for the person to whom you are introducing yourself. If it becomes clear that neither of you has any potential benefit for the other, politely move on. Spending time with someone who is unlikely to need your products or services, or someone who doesn't have the authority to make that decision, is not a productive use of your networking time.

6. ***Incorporate Social Media:*** Although last on this list, it is becoming increasingly important to add social media initiatives to your networking plan. Depending on your target market, an active LinkedIn, Facebook, and/or Twitter account can be very helpful. Try to keep the first five principals in mind when implementing your social media strategy. You are trying to build relationships as well as build followers. Social media should not replace face-to-face

networking; however, it is a tool that can be used to make connections that might someday lead to a face-to-face meeting.

In an op-ed for *The New York Times*, Sherry Turkle, a professor at M.I.T., echoed this sentiment when she wrote, "We have sacrificed conversation for mere connection."[35]

I couldn't agree more. A connection, while important as a means of introduction, is not a relationship. SBOs need to understand that long term relationship building is the goal of successful business networking, and social media is but one of many instruments to be used to initiate, nurture, and stay connected to that relationship.

Chapter Takeaway

Effective networking is an invaluable investment in your business, and it could become a primary "edge" over your competition.

---

[35] Sherry Turkle, S. "The Flight From Conversation," accessed May 8, 2014, http://www.nytimes.com/2012/04/22/opinion/sunday/the-flight-from-conversation.html?pagewanted=all&_r=0.

CHAPTER 41

Work "In" and "On" Your Business

FIRST, LET'S DEFINE WHAT is meant by working in and on your business. Basically, working in your business means the owner is physically completing the day to day tasks necessary to meet business and customer needs. Working on the business means the owner is completing big picture tasks which will help grow the business over the long-term.

Examples of the latter include: company vision; annual business plan; KPIs; marketing strategies; networking plans, etc. It is the transition from "doing" to "leading".

Michael Gerber's book, *E-Myth: Why Most Small Businesses Don't Work and What to Do About It,* and his follow up book *The E-Myth Revisited,* first suggested that entrepreneurs need to work "on" their businesses, not "in" their businesses, in order to grow.

I believe Michael was referring to larger enterprises than those we are focused on here. It's one thing for a mature company with many employees to hire extra resources so that the Chief Executive Officer (CEO) has more time for growth strategies. It's an entirely different proposition for the SBO just starting out, or for one with a very small staff complement. Nonetheless, the SBO must somehow focus on growing the business. This is why I have titled this chapter, *Work "In* **and** *"On" Your Business.* It is important to emphasize that for the SBO, it is a **balance** of doing both at the same time in order to fast track their growth. Doing one "or" the other is simply not a winning strategy.

I can empathize with SBOs who are so busy that they develop a kind of tunnel vision where they have enough trouble planning for tomorrow, let alone next year. It just doesn't seem like there is any time for "planning" type work when there are so many tasks that should have been completed yesterday.

This can be especially true if you are a task-driven person like me. I am the type of individual who creates a list of things to do, and I get great satisfaction from ticking each task off, one by one; and, no rest until all tasks are all completed. This was in fact, one of the business curses I had to eventually overcome. Like many SBOs, I focused too much on ringing that cash register to reach break-even as quickly as possible. My mantra was, "Don't bother me now, I've got a customer!"

It wasn't until the end of our first year as owners of Mail Boxes Etc. that I took a step back to reflect on what was a very slow start to our first business together. In order to avoid the distraction of my "to do" list, I forced myself to take time outside the business to think about our goals, and set strategies to achieve them. We were strong on goals; however, we were weak on strategies.

In order to explain what we did to balance working "in" our business with working "on" it, I have prepared a list of some of our initiatives.

- *Started Monthly Tracking:* We began taking about a half day per month to compare our numbers with the top franchisees in the network. As it turned out, our margins were okay, but our volume was weak in two key areas: copies and mail box rentals. The result of our renewed focus was that by the end of our second year we won an award for highest copy sales in the country.

- *Called the Top Two Franchisees:* I asked both franchisees what they were doing in the above-mentioned profit centers that set them apart. They were happy to be of assistance and offered some insight that proved to be very beneficial to our growth.

- *Hosted Chamber Business After Hours:* This was a big success because we really worked it by calling other SBOs to personally invite them to attend.

- *Attended Our First National and Regional Conferences:* The franchisor hosted these conferences and, although the expense of attending was high, we felt it was worth it.

- *Developed An Edge:* We successfully presented a wine shipping program to local wineries which made us one of the top shippers in the Canadian MBE franchise network.

- *Hired Staff:* There were certainly months where we paid our staff and not ourselves, but it allowed us time to plan for growth. I know how difficult this can be for an SBO, but if you commit to using your time on ways to grow the business, hiring can be a wise investment with acceptable risk.

We need to understand that transitioning from working solely "in" your business to also working "on" your business is exactly that; it is a transition into a balance of both. This transition happens over years, not weeks or months. The key is to start somewhere, and that somewhere is different for each business. You might begin a simple program once you reach break-even, or when cash flow will support your first hire.

The amount of time allocated will depend on the business and the people involved, but a couple of hours each week for the first six months is a good starting point. After six months, this can be increased to a committed half day. Ideally, mature businesses (over five years old) might devote one day per week to working "on" their businesses, but my guess is that very few actually do. By this time, the SBO should be delegating more, and spending much less time performing day-to-day tasks. We will be discussing more on the art of delegating in the next chapter.

Before I close this chapter, I would like to end with a quote from Michael E. Gerber's book, *The E-Myth Revisited*: "If your business depends on you, you don't own a business—you have a job. And it's the worst job in the world because you're working for a lunatic!"

Chapter Takeaway

*SBOs who wish to grow must balance working "in"
their businesses with working "on" their businesses.
They must balance "doing" with "leading".*

CHAPTER 42

Managing Your Most Important Asset

ARLIER I SUGGESTED THAT "It's All About Marketing" when it comes to growing a business. Now, I am going to suggest that in order to successfully manage a small business, "It's All About People!" Management includes overseeing all types of assets (equipment, real estate, inventory, money, etc.), but people are by far the most important asset of any business enterprise. No other asset can help propel your business into profitability like the human kind. Alternatively, unless managed properly, no other asset can cause as much stress and anxiety.

The management of human resources is a very broad topic due in part to its relative complexity among asset classes. My goal for this chapter is to merely highlight areas of weakness that I have witnessed in small enterprises, and offer some guidance on how to manage this valuable resource. This is an area where SBOs are most in need of assistance as they balance day to day tasks with trying to grow their businesses.

If effective people management skills are good for big business, then they are certainly good for small business. The only difference is that the SBO needs to scale things down to fit the available resources. The SBO must start with simple common sense initiatives and build her team thoughtfully.

After researching how management is defined these days, I think I am going to stick with a definition that has worked well for me as a small business owner. I believe management is simply *getting things done through other people.* This may sound insensitive, like I am suggesting that people be "used" in some nefarious fashion, however, nothing could be farther from the truth.

A talented manager has the ability to get a task completed by others, where they are pleased and motivated to do so. This happens when the manager creates an environment where job satisfaction can thrive. Getting things done through others is a way to leverage activities which leads to business growth. Used in this context, to leverage is just another way of saying to "multiply" the collective efforts of a group of people.

Lee Iacocca, the colorful leader of the Chrysler Corporation during the 1980's, once defined management as, "Nothing more than motivating other people." I hate to disagree with such an iconic business person, but I don't believe one person can directly motivate another unless that person wants to be motivated. The best that a good manager can do is to create an atmosphere where motivation can flourish.

Many SBOs have very little, if any, formal training or experience in the management of human resources. Many, however, have some type of experience managing other types of assets. For example, a plumber may know a lot about plumbing, but he is unlikely to possess much experience in managing people. It is far more complex and challenging to manage people than it is to fix a leaky pipe. Another classic example is that of star salespeople who decide to go out on their own. They may be able to sell sawdust to a lumber mill, but managing others to do the same can sometimes feel like herding cats into a swimming pool.

Personally, I believe a skilled manager can manage almost any type of business, up to that manager's level of competence. In other words, the SBO doesn't need to know everything about every detail of a business, he just has to hire and properly manage those that do.

As an example, I knew absolutely nothing about swimming pools when I purchased Sunshine Pools & Spas. I was, however, fairly confident I could manage the assets in such a way that would result in a good return on my investment and, as it turned out, that is exactly what happened. It's never easy, and the learning curve is always steep on new ventures, but managing is managing.

But what about that plumber or super salesperson without any experience managing people? What do they need to know about managing their human resources? The next few pages will cover, what I believe, are some key elements to successful people management, specifically for the small business owner.

The consistent integration of these principals into the workplace will create an environment where people can be empowered, and thus motivated, if they choose to be.

1. ***Choose Your People Carefully***: In his book, *Good to Great: Why Some Companies Make the Leap . . . and Others Don't*, James C. Collins explains how important it is to "Get the right people on the bus and then figure out where to go." This can be particularly important when you buy a business with existing employees. The new leader must clearly outline her plans and what she expects from the existing staff. The staff must then decide if they want to stay on the bus and the new owner must decide, over time, if they are qualified. If the new vision and qualifications don't match, the bus may have to pull over to let someone off. It's just business, and the sooner the better for all concerned.

   In terms of new hires, I can't stress enough how important it is to take whatever time is necessary to choose the very best people for every position. All too often SBOs make the mistake of hiring too quickly. They feel pressured to make a decision because the work is piling up fast, so they rush the process and as a result, decrease their chances of choosing the best candidate.

SBOs often don't understand the total cost of a bad hire. The first type of cost is direct costs. This category includes:

- Separation costs such as exit interviews and severance pay;
- Cost to temporarily cover an employee's duties such as overtime for other staff or temporary staffing;
- Replacement costs such as advertising, screening applicants, interviewing and selecting candidates, reference checks, hiring bonuses, and applicant travel and relocation costs;
- Training costs such as orientation, classroom training, certifications, on-the-job training, uniforms, and informational literature.

The second category of turnover costs is indirect costs. These include:

- Lost productivity from the departing employee who may spend the last days on the job with less motivation or reduced morale;
- Lost productivity due to the need to hire temporary employees;
- Added stress to existing employees who must take up the slack of the departing person;
- Costs incurred as the new employee learns his or her job, including reduced quality, increased errors, and additional waste;
- Reduced overall employee morale;
- Potential loss of customers resulting in lost future revenues.

In terms of dollars and cents, the following research may shock you.

According to the Compensation Planning Outlook 2002[36] published by the Conference Board of Canada, the average cost-per-hire is as follows:

Executive	$ 43,000
Management/Professional	$ 17,000
Technical	$ 13,300
Clerical/Support	$ 3,300

The Compensation Outlook 2002[37] reveals that the average time-to-hire has been calculated as:

Executive	15 weeks
Management/Professional	9 weeks
Technical	7 weeks
Clerical Support	4 weeks

The US Department of Labor estimates that, in addition to their salary, the average cost of a hiring mistake is 30% of their first year earning potential, and that's if the mistake is recognized and corrected within the first six months.

Upon further investigation, I discovered some very interesting research prepared for the Center For American Progress. This work is based on the most relevant research papers outlining the costs of employee turnover.

---

[36] "Calculating Cost vs. Time vs. Loss," Compensation Planning Outlook 2002, Conference Board of Canada, accessed May 8, 2014, http://www.canadahrcentre.com/solutions/calculating-cost/.

[37] "Calculating Cost vs. Time vs. Loss."

Our analysis reviews 30 case studies in 11 research papers published between 1992 and 2007 that provide estimates of the cost of turnover, finding that businesses spend about one-fifth of an employee's annual salary to replace that worker. Specifically, the economic studies we examined reveal a number of patterns about the cost of turnover:

- *For all positions except executives and physicians — jobs that require very specific skills — across the remaining 27 case studies, the typical (median) cost of turnover was 21 percent of an employee's annual salary.*

- *For workers earning less than $50,000 annually — which covers three-quarters of all workers in the United States — the 22 case studies show a typical cost of turnover of 20 percent of salary, the same as across positions earning $75,000 a year or less, which includes 9 in 10 U.S. workers.*

- *Among positions earning $30,000 or less, which includes more than half of all U.S. workers, the cost of replacing an employee is slightly less than among positions earning less than $75,000 annually. The typical cost of turnover for positions earning less than $30,000 annually is 16 percent of an employee's annual salary.*

Because some jobs have very high costs of turnover and others are less significant, there is a wide range of estimates across all types of employment. Above, we reported the "typical" cost of turnover using the median among the case studies. This means that half of the case studies had a cost above what is "typical" and half had a cost below. The estimates of the cost of turnover in the 30 case studies analyzed here range from 5.8 percent up to 213 percent, depending on the job and employee skills. But the estimates are clustered around the "typical" (median) values. Looking only at estimates of the cost of turnover for workers earning, on average, $75,000 per year or less,

> *17 case studies find a cost of turnover in the range of 10 percent to 30 percent.*"[38]

The Boushey and Glynn study reveals that turnover costs are a little lower than the above-mentioned Department of Labour results of 30%. Most likely, this difference is due to the overall average used by the Department of Labour.

If we assume that most (median) small business employees in Canada earn between $20,000 and $50,000 per year, then the cost of turnover is likely somewhere between $2,000 (10% of $20,000) and $10,000 (20% of $50,000) per employee. The determining factor of where one lies in this range is largely a function of levels of education and specialized skills required for the position.

As pointed out in the "Lies, Damned Lies, and Statistics" section of this book, in 2011, small business employees in Canada earned an average of $39,676. If we round this up to $40,000, it seems reasonable to estimate that SBOs should budget about **18%** of that $40,000 or about **$7,000** per employee turnover. This figure could be a little less for lower paid positions, and a little more for higher paid positions. The point is that this is a great deal of money for almost all small business owners! It is essential that the SBO take time and care when hiring.

So how can the SBO improve his or her chances of choosing great employees and avoid these high costs? Here are a few tips.

---

[38] Heather Boushey, and Sarah Jane Glynn, "There are Significant Business Costs to Replacing Employees," Center for American Progress, accessed April 25, 2014, https://cdn.americanprogress.org/wp-content/uploads/2012/11/CostofTurnover.pdf.

a) *Do it Yourself:* This is one function the SBO cannot delegate to anyone else, period. It's a good idea to have another person sit in on the interviews, like a foreman or a sales manager, but that's it.

b) *Hire for Attitude and Train for Skill:* If you don't have a good feeling the about the attitude of a candidate, take a pass. In most cases, it is much easier to train someone who gets along well with others than it is to deal with an overbearing or arrogant attitude.

c) *Prepare a Brief Job Description:* Most SBOs don't bother preparing job descriptions, and what a shame that is. The process is already prone to error as the candidates are unclear about what the job entails. It takes little time or effort to jot down the top three to five duties and how they will be monitored.

d) *Check References:* I never hire without positive work-related references and, in order to save time, I request that interested applicants include them with their resumes. My goal is to hire "problem solvers" who are also "team players". If there is only one question I am able to ask the person giving a reference, it is, "Would you hire this person again?"

e) *Conduct Formal Interviews:* Don't be too concerned about the word "formal". I recommend that the interview be conducted in private, and not in a mall food court. Treat each candidate with respect by coming prepared with a job description and a list of interview questions. Interview questions should be tailored to a specific job; however, I have attached some generic questions as a guide in Appendix 13. Try to limit your talk time to 20% of the conversation, allowing the candidate to speak 80% of the time. Remember, you are trying to discern whether this person is going to be solving or creating problems, so listen closely for clues.

I realize that all of this may sound quite formal, and perhaps onerous for an SBO; however, I can't stress the importance of this process enough. I can tell you from first-hand experience that you will feel pure elation if you choose wisely and put someone on your team that is helping you push that bus forward, instead of riding it for all it's worth.

2. *Pay More and Expect More:* While I don't subscribe to the theory that the more you pay your staff, the more motivated they will be, I have always tried to pay more than market rates. My reasoning is that I want to attract the best candidates to any job that I have available, and I want to keep those employees. In addition, I generally expected more from my people than most SBOs and, for that reason, I felt they deserved higher compensation.

This philosophy worked well in the Yellow Pages business where we attracted the most talented sales people from other media organizations. It also worked well in the swimming pool business where paying more ensured that seasonal workers returned after a winter layoff.

3. *Offer Employee Benefits Package:* One of the best "employment edges" we had at Sunshine Pools was that, in addition to paying more than the competition, we were the first and only pool company in our region to offer an employee benefits package. I was always concerned about losing staff over the winter months and having to re-train, so the added cost of benefits seemed prudent. A survey commissioned in 2013 by Sun Life Financial Inc. found that only 40% of small businesses with between five and forty-nine employees offered a group benefits plan.

Even though my staff at Sunshine had to pay half the cost of the package, they were extremely pleased and sincerely appreciative. According to a 2011 survey[39] commissioned by Sanofi Canada, people prefer extended health benefits to higher salaries. When offered a choice between $10,000 and their health benefits, 59% of the survey participants said they would rather keep their benefits, up from 56% in 2009.

In addition to our benefits package, I instituted pay for performance initiatives which included annual cash bonuses for those employees that reached their agreed upon targets. Once these were added to base wages and salaries, my people were paid noticeably more than our competition.

I can't tell you how my wages and benefits expense compared to our industry peers across Canada because such data was not available . . . quite sad, really. What I can tell you is that if you pay a little extra to attract great employees, the added productivity of those employees will more than offset the additional expense. I guesstimate that if you pay 10% or 15% more for highly productive staff, you are likely to receive 20% or 30% more productivity . . . definitely a win-win situation.

4. *Provide Adequate Training:* Adequate training is the first step in creating an environment where your new staff member can be successful. In addition to the specific task training, it is critical to clearly define the expectations for each position.

5. *Have Faith in Your Employees:* I believe that the vast majority of people want to do well and be successful at what they do. Employees, just like the SBO want to be happy in

---

[39] The Sanofi-aventis Healthcare Survey 2011, pp. 8-9, accessed September 24, 2014, http://www.sanofi.ca/l/ca/en/layout.jsp?cnt=65B67ABD-BEF6-487B-8FC1-5D06FF8568ED.

their workplace. This doesn't necessarily mean that they will automatically be motivated to work hard and solve all of your problems, but it is beneficial for the SBO to have a conscious awareness that people generally want to do a good job.

6. ***Monitor Performance and Provide Regular Feedback:*** Employees generally desire recognition and praise for a job well done. Work environments where this happens on a regular basis are generally more positive and productive.

   The SBO must regularly monitor how each employee is doing according to their predetermined goals. Employees should be praised and/or rewarded for good performance **and** corrected for poor performance.

   My experience in managing hundreds of staff has taught me that the vast majority of employees "want" to be properly managed. Employees may not come out and say it, but I believe they want to be told what to do, how to do it, how they will be measured, and what will happen if they do well, or if they do poorly.

   Some management gurus suggest that this thinking is archaic, that people thrive on autonomy and don't need management . . . just let them be free to work on their own, and all will be fine.

   Well, I don't think so! Such a management style might work in the new product division of Google or Apple, but not in most small business enterprises. Having said this, once an employee is properly trained, given clear objectives, and a performance monitoring system is in place, then by all means, a good manager gets out of the way. The employee should then be given as much autonomy as he or she can reasonably handle.

There are a great number of ways that an SBO can recognize and reward superior performance. It doesn't have to be complicated, and it can range from a genuine pat on the back to a glowing written performance review. It might be individual or group rewards. It might mean small gifts or larger annual cash bonuses if the business meets its financial goals. Just keep things simple and consistent, and ensure that all staff members are treated fairly. A good manager plays no favorites. This will go a long way in building a "team" atmosphere.

Earlier, I made reference to employee performance reviews. I should take a moment to discuss this more fully. Most SBOs do **not** prepare annual, much less quarterly, written performance reviews on their employees. Frankly, I consider this disrespectful to one's staff.

The performance review function is standard practice in big business, yet it is virtually absent in small business. I wonder why that is? Yes, reviews can take time to prepare and they are sometimes uncomfortable to deliver, but don't you think that employees deserve to hear how they are doing? Do you think they would be more, or less, productive if they were to receive thoughtful reviews? These are questions you should ask yourself if you want your business to grow, and be the best that it can be. I have included a performance evaluation form in Appendix 14 that I have used in the past. Perhaps it will prove useful one day when you develop your own performance appraisal program.

The most effective and successful leaders I know are decisive, yet humble, people who always give credit where credit is due. If you have trouble making decisions, don't be afraid to ask your staff for input. For example, I always made a point of asking my staff not to bring me problems without bringing possible solutions. This approach improved their problem solving abilities, and it helped me make better and more timely decisions. It is much easier and far more efficient to choose from two or three options presented by an employee than to start from square one. I didn't always choose from proposed solutions but, when I did, the team member beamed with pride as their recommendation was put into action, particularly if it solved the initial problem.

Before long your staff will get the feel of how you manage and how you want things done. They will begin to become more confident and proactive, leaving more time for you to work "on" the business rather than "in" the business.

Working people of all descriptions require a certain amount of order, clarity, and direction in their work environment. They expect and deserve consistent, fair, and expedient decision-making. They desire recognition and reward for a job well done. If you, the SBO, can create an environment where these things exist, then you have done about as much as you can to maximize morale and motivation levels. The only other thing you might add to this mix is a healthy dose of fun and laughter from time to time.

7. *Delegate Like Goldilocks:* For our purposes, delegating is the act of transferring responsibility for the completion of a task from the small business owner to an employee. Delegating is the process of letting go of progressively more important tasks, and allowing staff to make increasingly more important decisions. Ah, it sounds so simple, yet it can be surprisingly difficult to master.

Delegating is akin to sending your child off to university . . . you know it's for the best, but at the same time you fear for what might go wrong. Delegating in business is a bit like the Goldilocks story because it can't be served too hot or too cold; it must be served just right. In other words, delegate too much and the SBO may lose control, and delegate too little and there is no time to grow the business.

Why is it that most managers have such difficulty delegating? The answer boils down to having the wrong people on your team. Any other reasons are just excuses. You'll often hear managers say, "It's easier to do it myself," or "I don't want to lose control."

The fact is that they didn't take the time to hire and train the right people in the first place, and/or they failed to remove those who weren't contributing to company goals. I can tell you with a great deal of confidence that if you choose your people wisely, with a goal of selecting problem solvers to whom you can delegate, you will be able to grow your business much faster than your competition who do not delegate.

If you delegate effectively you will experience less stress and anxiety because delegating allows you a little extra time to think and plan instead of constantly putting out fires. I have experienced some of the most rewarding and satisfying moments as an SBO when I have left my business in the hands of staff, only to return, find all is well, and we made money, to boot!

If you currently work in the big corporate world managing a large staff, you may think that you know a lot about delegating, and that it will be a snap when you start your own business. In reality, it is far more difficult to delegate when you own your own enterprise.

When you manage staff in a large corporation and a costly mistake is made, it is certainly unfortunate; but when a mistake is made in a small business, the money to pay for that mistake comes directly out of the SBO's pocket.

There are few employees who understand the importance of controlling costs in a small business. Unfortunately, many employees believe that all SBOs make a ton of money; they must, or they wouldn't be self-employed. The reality is that most SBOs I know do it for the independence first, and the money second. Let's again put things in perspective: the average income in 2011 for Canadian small businesses was $46,700. That's hardly a ton of money.

Now, let's get back to delegating. Below are a few lessons I learned that helped me delegate with some success over the years, both in the corporate world and in the small business world.

a) *My "80% is Okay" Rule*: There was a time in my career when I would get upset if things weren't done perfectly, or exactly as I would have done them myself. In most cases, I have found that 80% results from employees are pretty darn good, and that not everyone is a high achiever.

b) *Understand That Employees Will Never Fully Relate, So Get Over It!* The first time I hired staff as an SBO I became frustrated by the lack of respect some employees had regarding the control of expenses. They just didn't seem to understand or care that I had to open my wallet every time a tool went missing, or when equipment wasn't properly maintained and needed to be repaired. It wasn't until I realized that, without "skin in the game," staff are unlikely to fully appreciate the consequences of wasteful activity. Accepting these occurrences for what they were, "costs of doing business", helped me de-stress and do a better job of delegating.

Offering annual bonuses based on profitability will contribute substantially to reduce unnecessary expenses.

c) *Delegate or Die:* Without being too dramatic, I believe that the SBO must realize they just can't do it all themselves. An attempt to "do it all" is dangerous to one's health and no amount of freedom or money is worth that. Additionally, running around like a chicken with its head cut off is bad for business, whether witnessed by your customers or your employees.

d) *Hire People Unlike You:* In order to broaden the knowledge base of the entire team, the SBO should hire people who have skills they do not possess. In a way, the SBO is forced to delegate because she does not have the skill set to do the job herself. For example, I managed a large number of engineers at one point in my career and thus I had no choice but to delegate. My management style was to be clear on the end results I expected. How the staff achieved those results was largely up to them.

e) *Offer Support and Remove Roadblocks:* I don't subscribe to the adage of supplying enough rope for employees to hang themselves. While I have seen this "do or die" approach work on occasion, the odds of your staff achieving success are much better if you offer your support throughout the project.

It is every manager's responsibility to remove as many roadblocks as possible that might hinder the progress of employees. For example, ensure that all staff have adequate resources (training, supplies, tools, equipment, software, funds, permits, travel, contacts, etc.) available so they are able to complete the task at hand. The SBO must also be available to answer questions and make timely decisions so that the efficiency of the team's efforts are not impeded.

8. *Hire Like a Turtle; Fire Like a Hare:* There will be times when it will be necessary to pull the bus over and help someone get off. This can be a very traumatic experience for all involved.

I have made mistakes in hiring as well as a few mistakes in firing. I caution SBOs to think long and hard before pulling the trigger on someone. It can be a potentially life-changing and traumatic experience for the employee. The employee is entitled to know when there is an issue with their performance, and they must then be given an opportunity to improve. If after making a sincere effort to correct the situation, and there is still no improvement, release the employee quickly and without fanfare.

There are two main reasons why you should promptly release poor performers. The first and most obvious reason is that continuing to pay a non-producing asset is an unnecessary cost to the business. Further, the longer you procrastinate, the higher the likelihood that your customers will be negatively impacted.

The second reason why an owner should release poor performers quickly is because it can negatively impact the morale of the productive staff, particularly if staff witness a problem going unnoticed by management. Employees expect and deserve fairness, and if they see no action being taken in the case of a poor performer, or a disrupter, or a non-team player, they may gravitate to that person's level of performance until the situation is rectified. If a situation like this goes on for too long, the SBO may lose the respect of the team. On occasion, I have seen good performers leave an organization because of the failure of the leader to remove a problem employee.

It should go without saying, but SBOs must be certain they understand all the labour laws in their province before they let someone go. Wrongful dismissal cases can be costly and time consuming, so be sure to follow every letter of employment law.

9. *First In - Last Out:* Setting a good example, particularly during the early years of your venture, should be a no-brainer for any SBO. There's a lot to be said for being the first to show up for work and the last to leave. Some may consider this an "old school" management approach, but don't underestimate the positive impacts it can have. I have never expected an employee of mine to work the hours that I have worked, and that is not the objective of this management practice. The objective is to instill in your team that you, the SBO, are 100% committed to the success of the business.

10. *Remember That Money Can be Replaced But Time Cannot:* Small business owners are people too. I offer this tip to help owners manage themselves. I have, from time to time, experienced considerable anguish over spending decisions. Perhaps this is just a personality thing, but my experience interacting with other SBOs suggests otherwise. For example, I have always had a tough time spending personal funds on advertising or similar 'difficult to quantify' initiatives. Another area which caused me pause was putting additional personal capital into expansion plans, such as increasing staff levels or lease space.

It can become increasingly more difficult to risk the capital that you have worked so hard to earn, particularly as you get older. While I understood that marketing was the key to business growth, I was still afraid of the monetary and emotional (fear of failure) risk.

If you encounter such fears, try to remember that money can be replaced, but time cannot. To help explain this statement I have included an article written by Janna Hoiberg of jannahoiberg.com. Janna is a Business Coach and her article, *What Would You Rather Spend Time or Money?* does a fine job of clarifying why it is often so difficult for small business people to reach into their own pockets and spend money on new and sometimes risky initiatives.

For many people the concept of losing money is understandably scary. There's a simple reason for this. They have a mindset of scarcity rather than one of abundance.

In this mindset, losing money becomes a fear, but you must remember, you can always make more money, but that simply isn't true of time. The reality is you can never get back time, once an hour, day, year has been wasted, you can never get it back. Money can be leveraged, earned back, replaced and grown to a point that you may not ever remember the loss, but time is finite. In life, you only get so many minutes.

The fear of losing money is a major factor in keeping many business owners from moving forward, but when you understand that time is your only finite asset, you can put this fear into perspective. A business owner is much more likely to take intelligent risks if they don't have that fear.

Questions like what if this idea doesn't work, what if this is the wrong decision, what if, what if become much easier to answer when you know you can always make what you invested into that decision back. Yes, we must evaluate our decisions; we must test and measure but we must also be decisive, take risks and move on or fear of losing money can keep us from being decisive.

But, you may ask, isn't time equal to money?

It is, therefore you must spend it wisely. Is your time being spent moving your business forward, or making you feel good since you checked off a bunch of "to do's" that weren't vital to your business' success. Is your time focused on profitable activities, business growth, business opportunity, or are you in reactive mode?

Reactive mode usually wastes time, while proactive mode provides you the choice as to how and when you will spend your time and understanding what is more important, time or money, can help you ultimately make your choice on how you spend your time.

Ask yourself the question for each task that you do: Is this activity moving me closer to increased revenue or profitability? If not, then either STOP IT, or delegate the task. And remember, time is irreplaceable – treasure it, spend it wisely and make sure you get a return on your investment.[40]

You may be thinking, "Where the heck am I going to get the time to track performance, do employee appraisals, and all those other non-revenue producing tasks?" You're probably also thinking that managing employees is not all peaches and cream, and that they can be a really big pain in the ass!

---

[40] Janna Hoiberg, "What Would You Rather Spend Time or Money?" accessed July 24, 2013, http://www.actioncoach.com/What-would-you-rather-spend-time-or-money?pressid=1311.

These are legitimate objections, and I admit that I have felt exactly the same way on more than one occasion. I never much enjoyed working nights and weekends doing performance reviews or planning the next day's activities for my staff, but one has to ask him or herself a simple question: "How badly do I want my business to succeed," or better yet, "How badly do I want my business to be in the top 10% to 25% of my industry?" You may be satisfied with mediocrity, but your chances of survival in the business world will be extremely limited, in my opinion.

As for employee issues, I would have to agree that, along with cash flow concerns, this is an area where the small business owner can lose a lot of sleep. I know that I have. Yes, employees can be a huge challenge at times, but if they are selected and managed properly, they can also be saviors. Staff issues are a transitional problem; you help some staff get off the bus, but you invite others to take a seat. Once you have everyone in their proper seats and all are contributing to moving the bus forward, the feeling can be enormously satisfying and the results hugely rewarding!

Chapter Takeaway

People are the most important asset of any business. Learning how to manage them effectively requires patience and experience. If you treat your staff as you would like to be treated, your business will have a much greater chance of success.

CHAPTER 43

The Future for SBOs

I F SOMEONE WERE TO ask me what has changed the most for the small business owner over the last thirty five years, I would have to say it's how the SBO acquires new customers. It is almost mandatory today for the SBO to embrace advancements in technology, particularly those involving e-commerce and social media advertising campaigns.

I suggest that existing SBOs need to increase their spending on advertising by 25% or more if they wish to grow and beat their competition. They need to continue spending on traditional media such as newspaper, television and radio, while at the same time adding robust social media campaigns. Straddling both the old and the new will undoubtedly be more time consuming, challenging, and costly for the SBO going forward.

Here are some additional changes and trends that new and existing SBOs may wish to contemplate:

1. *Retail Opportunities:* If you have or are considering a bricks and mortar storefront, try to focus on unique products that may be difficult to compare and buy online. The last thing you want is to provide a showroom for people to come in and try out a product, and have them go home and order it online at a lower price. This has become a common practice.

   In early 2013 this happened to the big box store, Best Buy, and it hurt their business a great deal. Best Buy responded by improving their online business and drastically reducing their prices to better compete with the likes of Amazon. Their new strategy worked, and the company began to turn around.

Whatever you are selling retail, try to leverage your product knowledge, pricing power, supplier contacts, and existing infrastructure to sell current and new products online. Pick a product line subset that lends itself well to e-commerce. For example, if you own a tea shop, perhaps you could sell your special blends online? Why not retail by the cup and e-tail by the ounce?

2. ***Poor Customer Service Will be Quickly Punished:*** More and more people, including me, are doing online research before patronizing almost any kind of business. I recently did a Google search on specific businesses in these areas: landscapers, tree planters, dog kennels, and even my doctor. I was looking for general information about these businesses, but I was more interested in the references and/or reviews of the products or services they offered. If people are having issues with a business, they will often post their concerns to alert other consumers.

As a business owner, you must monitor the internet to see what people are saying about your products and service. If it's negative, quickly make the necessary changes to rectify the problem. If it's positive, try to use it to your advantage in your marketing initiatives.

TripAdvisor.ca is a great example of the power of reviews and ratings at work. I will not travel anywhere without first checking the ratings on the destination. To further prove my point, just look at the growth of a site like angieslist.com. Here consumers actually pay a fee to become an angieslist member so that they can look up ratings on businesses in their area. There will be more and more services like this available and, therefore, SBOs must monitor what consumers are saying about their business online, and use this information to improve their operations..

3. *Offer More to Attract Top Employees and Deliver Better Management to Keep Them:* Not everyone is completely motivated by money. In fact, after the hiring is done, it's amazing how other needs ascend to the top of the priority list. Providing proper training, dealing fairly with employees, treating people with respect, setting clear goals, and providing an opportunity for advancement are just some of the things that will help you keep your best employees and have them remain loyal to you for a long time.

   I also urge SBOs to investigate ways to enhance employee loyalty, especially in key employees. Offering benefit plans, performance bonuses, off-site training, and ownership opportunities will encourage key employees to stay with you.

4. *Use Advances in Technology to Increase Productivity:* A quick cost benefit analysis will reveal the positive return that can be attained by having field staff wirelessly "connected". Whether it is a traveling sales person, a service technician, an insurance agent, a tree planter, or anyone else doing work outside the office, great productivity gains can be attained by being in constant communication with all staff. This will also lead to better customer service, as you are able to respond more quickly to customer enquiries.

   Today employees can visit a customer site, complete a job, create an invoice, collect payment, and print or email a receipt, all without even leaving their vehicle; now that's efficiency.

I took some time to research what people are saying about "the" growth industries for small business over the next decade. Not surprisingly, almost all trend experts have technology-related opportunities at the top of their lists, which is where they should be of course.

Following is a list of suggested business growth areas that may appeal to the typical SBO.

- *Computer, TV, and Home Theatre Installations:* Many baby boomers are easily frustrated by advancements in technology. They will gladly pay for someone to come to their home and do it for them.

- *3D Printer Sales and Service:* The rapid production of any type of prototype is an exciting and fast growing area. It does, however, require a good working knowledge of auto-cad types of software programs in order to tell the printer what to do.

- *Smartphone Repair:* The high cost and hassle of sending your Smartphone away for repair is alarming. If you have the expertise, you may wish to consider this service which caters to one of the fastest growing industries in the world.

- *Pilates and Yoga Studios:* The health and fitness industry continues to grow and this segment, in particular, is showing some "core" interest.

- *Social Network Game Development:* Design a successful game for Facebook, and you may be set for life.

- *Employment Services:* According to a Washington Post article this category grew by 21.4% in 2012.[41]

- *Information Technology Security Consulting:* Security of information that travels over the Internet is on everyone's mind these days. This may be too high tech and specialized

---

[41] J. D. Harrison, "The Best and Worst Small Businesses to Start in 2013," Washington Post, December 26, 2012.

for many SBOs, however, there may be opportunities around this broad theme?

- *Safe Self-Tanning Product Manufacturing:* Tanning beds are out, tanning sprays and lotions are in.

- *Flip Homes That You Live In:* This is a personal favorite as it is a low risk way to become a millionaire. If you are ambitious and handy with a hammer, the tax benefits of this option far outweigh the inconvenience of living in a construction zone.

- *Home Renovators:* Reliability and quality of workmanship can provide great opportunity for the handy SBO. This market is quite fragmented and ripe for competition.

- *Health Services:* Taking care of the health needs of baby boomers is big business.

- *Gourmet Food Trucks:* These trucks are popping up everywhere, and the owners utilize social media to drive traffic to changing locations.

- *Green Construction:* Contractors offering environmentally friendly construction methods and materials have an edge over their competition, and they have the potential for higher gross margins.

- *Child Care:* In order to pay for their lifestyle choices, most families experience the need for both parents to work.

- *Pet Care:* No matter the health of the economy, people continue to spend increasing amounts on their pets.

- *Online Travel Agencies:* Storefront locations are becoming less and less necessary, and cruise specialists are in demand.

- *Traditional and Gourmet Popcorn:* I have always been a fan of the popcorn industry, possibly because I eat a lot of popcorn. It is certainly time-tested. Popcorn is recession proof, has low barriers to entry, high profit margins, and relatively low competition in many markets. A well-run operation could also be franchised.

- *Ice Cream:* This market is much like the popcorn market, and baby boomers love this treat.

- *Artisanal Alcohol and Beer:* Check your provincial regulations on this one, but demand for new and unique recipes, especially in beer, are on the rise.

- *Medical Marijuana:* New Canadian regulations are allowing more commercial producers to service the needs of individuals. If you lack the capital to become a manufacturer, perhaps you can develop something related to this "growing" market.

Let's look at a few areas that aspiring SBOs may wish to avoid:

- *Mom and Pop Restaurants:* The big regional and national chains make for some tough competition. In addition, the relatively high fixed costs make it difficult to compete with mobile gourmet food services. Unless you have a great deal of practical experience in managing a restaurant, it could be a recipe for disaster.

- *Independent Retail Stores:* Big box stores, mass market retail chains, and e-tailers are making it tough for the independent operator to compete. Unless you have a real and lasting edge, please consider this option very carefully.

- *Wholesale Distributors:* Almost anything can be purchased directly from manufacturers these days which puts pressure on wholesale distribution companies. Exceptions may include those who supply seasonal operations, like our swimming pool business.

- *Lawn and Garden Equipment and Supply Stores:* Commercial customers still require products and services from this type of specialty retailer. Unfortunately, many consumers are buying their snowblowers and lawnmowers from Rona, Lowe's and Home Depot.

- *Dry Cleaning and Laundry Services:* The "business casual" and "re-wearing" trends have led to a slowdown in growth for this service. If the home dry cleaning machine catches on, it will add further challenges for this industry.

- *Office Supplies, Stationary, and Gift Stores:* Industry Canada has reported that from 2002 to 2011, operating revenues have decreased -0.9% per year, on average, for this industry. Businesses are spending less on office stationary and supplies than they once did.

- *Printing and Related Support Activities:* The need for "ink on paper" is facing continued pressure. Even personal diaries are being stored on a cloud somewhere in cyberspace. Statistics Canada reports that, between 2007 and 2012, this industry shrank by a compound annual rate of -3.6%.

Chapter Takeaway

Always choose an opportunity in a growing industry, and embrace technology in order to attract and keep new customers.

PART SIX

HOW MUCH MONEY DO SMALL BUSINESSES ACTUALLY MAKE?

CHAPTER 44

Canadian National Averages

I SERIOUSLY CONSIDERED NOT including this chapter. The reason: how helpful would it be for SBOs to learn about average results when the intent of this book is to offer advice on how not to be average.

The data in this chapter is offered primarily for interest sake. The next chapter provides more valuable industry specific financial reports.

The following data is based on Revenue Canada tax returns (T1; T2) for both incorporated and unincorporated businesses reporting between $30,000 and $5 million in total revenues. These are 2011 results accumulated by Stats Canada and published by Industry Canada through their Financial Performance Data online service, *www.ic.gc.ca/eic/site/pp-pp.nsf/eng/home*. It bears repeating that because these results are based on tax returns, I believe their accuracy to be the best available in North America.

The data on the next page is a condensed summary of the Canadian averages. A more detailed report is included in Appendix 12.

All Businesses - 1,843,457		
	$000's	%
Total Revenue	370.9	100.0
Gross Profit	241.0	65.0
Net Profit	46.7	12.6

Incorporated Businesses - 965,526 (52.4%)		
	$000's	%
Total Revenue	595.4	100.0
Gross Profit	334.6	56.2
Net Profit	$50.0	8.4

Unincorporated Businesses - 877,931 (47.6%)		
	$000's	%
Total Revenue	124.0	100.0
Gross Profit	99.4	80.2
Net Profit (Salary)	43.0	34.7

One can put almost any "spin" they want on such high level statistical data; thus, I feel compelled to offer some cautionary comments.

As you can see, these results show that the 2011 average net profit in Canada for all businesses (incorporated and unincorporated) was 12.6% of revenue or $46,700. Again, although this is nice to know, it is not really relevant information for comparison to the specific business you own, or the one you may be thinking of starting.

I really need to **caution** readers on my next point. As mentioned earlier, statistics can be misleading. For example, I can assure you that most small businesses in Canada do not have a bottom line of 12.6%, after paying the owner a market rate salary. In addition, small unincorporated businesses do not have an average net profit anywhere near 34.7%. This is because all labour and salaries have yet to be deducted. I am confident that your accountant will agree.

There are a couple of reasons why this average profit statistic is misleading. Firstly, it is an average and not the median which would be a much better indicator of what most SBOs experience. Mathematical averages are very often heavily skewed by large outlier data points. Unfortunately, median results are not available. Personally, I would be more comfortable knowing what "most" businesses earn rather than the mean average. Perhaps our friends at Industry Canada might one day provide median results.

Secondly, and most importantly, this overall average includes both incorporated and unincorporated businesses. Each of these groups report income differently for tax purposes, and when results are combined, they are much less useful. For example, a sole proprietor shows his or her compensation as net income, while a corporation typically reports net income after all wages and salaries are expensed; therefore, the unincorporated results do not coincide with our definition of business profitability. Remember, a business is really only profitable if there is money left over after the owner is paid a market rate salary to manage the business; thus, the only useful results shown here are those for the incorporated small enterprises that deduct all salaries to produce a net income.

As an example, let's say you are a painting contractor. On average, you are likely to have gross sales of $90,700 (see page 394) and show a net income of $30,000 after all expenses, not including the cost of your labour. Our statistics report a 33% bottom line when, in fact, there may not be a real bottom line at all after the owner is paid a market rate salary. Do you see how statistics can be misleading and why one must use caution when interpreting them?

The average net income of unincorporated businesses in Canada is shown as 34.7%, and the average for incorporated businesses (which report after all salaries are paid) is only 8.4%. The overall average of 12.6% referred to above is, therefore, skewed to the high side, making it much less useful to SBOs. This is further evidence that one must drill down as much as possible to compare apples to apples in terms of both comparable industries and business reporting structures.

This average data may, however, be somewhat relevant to someone comparing their current employment income to the idea of becoming self-employed. If you consider that you have average skill and ambition, does an average income of $46,700 interest you? This is the average of the averages, if you will. It represents an average of both the incorporated and unincorporated businesses. The data above shows that the average company owner nets about $50,000 plus a market rate salary. On the other hand, the average sole proprietor/partnership earns about $43,000 in total taxable income.

It is also important to keep in mind that it could take five years to reach this level of income, and you are not likely to have been paid in the first six months to a year. One must also take into account the capital investment required in order to get started. This capital demands a return greater than that which might have been available to you had you invested it elsewhere.

In other words, if you spent $200,000 to start a business and earned a net profit of $46,700, that's a return of about 23% per year; that is, if the $46,700 is after you have paid yourself a market rate salary for managing the business.

Even though it could take a while to attain this average profit level, such a return may well be worth the risks inherent to being self-employed.

For me, these numbers support my belief that for SBOs it's often more about the independence and self satisfaction than it is about the money. Are the extra hours, added stress, and higher risk really worth an average of $46,700 per year? I think it's more than just the money.

Perhaps this sounds a bit negative . . . like there isn't any money to be made running a small business in Canada. I hope you don't get that impression. The goal here is to present the facts so that potential SBOs can make informed decisions based on realistic expectations. For example, of the top 25% of incorporated businesses, the "average" net income is $211,500. Keep in mind that this is after the owner is paid, and it is the average of the top 25% of small corporations. The very best operators can therefore make much more than this; proving that there are great earnings opportunities for SBOs in Canada.

Many of these average results are more useful in providing dinner party discussion points, rather than making educated business decisions. There are, however, a few areas which may offer some useful insights.

1. *Total Annual Revenue:* For me, this information was enlightening. Frankly, I was a little surprised to see that in Canada, the overall average of small businesses gross only $370,900. We must keep in mind that these results include "all" businesses under $5,000,000 in sales, including those businesses just starting out.

2. *Big Picture View of "Is it Worth it?"* This data can assist those deciding on a career as an SBO. Do these types of dollars get you excited, or is independence your number one ambition? You must also keep in mind that all business owners want to make that bottom line as small as possible, in order to minimize their tax burden. Might one, therefore, infer that there can be more financial benefit to business owners than these results imply?

3. *Expenses as a Percent of Revenue:* Such broad averages can be helpful when you just can't find anything more directly comparable. These can be used for planning and budgeting

purposes. I was surprised by how low advertising and promotion was at only 1.4% of revenue. See Appendix 12.

4. ***International Comparisons:*** Neither the US Small Business Administration, nor any other US government organization publicly reports the type of tax return based data reproduced in this book; as such, I can't offer a direct and accurate comparison. If you require more dinner party discussion points, you may be interested in comparing the data in Appendix 7 to the averages in Appendix 12. This gives some insight into how Canadian SBOs compare to those south of the border. Keep in mind that Appendix 7 presents businesses that were **sold;** therefore, what is represented is above-average enterprises with real profits. If this weren't the case, these businesses most likely wouldn't have attracted a buyer.

Let us now move on from the interesting information to the more important and useful information. We will have to dig deeper to find information that is more relevant to our existing business, or the one we are thinking of starting or buying. The information in the next chapter will provide what we are looking for.

Chapter Takeaway

High level averages, while interesting, are not very useful to those considering a small business.

CHAPTER 45

Canadian Financial Benchmarks

WELL, WE HAVE FINALLY made it to the point where we try to answer the question posed in the title of this book. How much money do these risk-taking, self-starting headstrong, entrepreneurial people actually make? This reference section will give you a realistic picture of the financial results one might expect from 100 Canadian small business categories. I will also explain how to find similar data for approximately 950 more business types.

The comparison of Key Performance Indicators (KPIs) from one organization to a larger group in the same industry is called "benchmarking your business". Benchmarking is certainly not a new practice; in fact, it has been around for many years. However, the practice is used most often in larger organizations. Unfortunately, when it comes to smaller enterprises, I have found few that compare their financial results. This is clearly a missed opportunity as those who do manage by utilizing benchmark comparisons are almost always more profitable and faster growing operations.

A study in 2002 by PricewaterhouseCoopers (PwC)[42] determined that companies that benchmark achieve 69% faster growth, and 45% greater productivity than those that don't. This is powerful and

---

[42] Pete Collins, (2002 May). "Fast-Growth Companies That Benchmark Grow Faster, Are More Productive Than Their Peers", PricewaterhouseCoopers, accessed May 25, 2013, http://www.barometersurveys.com/vwAllNewsByDoc ID/86BFC1C668BDD72285256BAB006B1B28/index.html.

convincing research. It included larger companies (those with sales between $5 million and $10 million), but it can work for much smaller enterprises, too. SBOs just need to benchmark on a much smaller scale using comparisons that are simple to implement. Starting with only one important benchmark can make all the difference.

Further research support for benchmarking comes from the Global Benchmarking Network (GBN). This organization is an alliance of worldwide leading benchmarking centres. Current membership comprises twenty benchmarking centres in twenty countries which represent more than 30,000 businesses and government agencies. The GBN conducted a survey in 2008 which concluded:

> It is clear that if organisations perform benchmarking projects in a professional manner the gains from both the financial and non-financial perspective can be large (20% of respondents stated an average financial return of over US$250,000 per best practice benchmarking project).[43]

This study further concluded that, "Over 60% of organizations that are not currently using these (benchmarking) tools indicated they are likely to use them in the next three years."

We are fortunate in Canada to have free access to accurate financial benchmark data through the Financial Performance Data service (*www.ic.gc.ca/eic/site/pp-pp.nsf/eng/home*). I strongly encourage readers to use this tool to strengthen their operations.

Once again, the Financial Performance Data in these 100 reports are based on Revenue Canada tax returns (T1; T2) for both incorporated and unincorporated businesses earning between $30,000 and $5 million in total revenues. These are 2011 results

---

[43] Dr. Robin S. Mann, "*Global Survey on Business Improvement and Benchmarking*", Global Benchmarking Network, accessed March 11, 2014, http://www.excellence.ca/assets/files/legacy/GBN_Report_2008.pdf.

accumulated by Statistics Canada and published by Industry Canada through their Financial Performance Data service (*www.ic.gc.ca/ eic/site/pp-pp.nsf/eng/home*). This information is reproduced with the permission of the Minister of Public Works and Government Services, 2013 and was last updated in July of 2014.

For those concerned that this data may become less relevant as time passes, I reviewed changes to the prior year's results. It is interesting that the data has changed very little, especially in relative terms. This is most likely due to the fact that inflation in our country has been relatively tame over the last ten years at an average of approximately 1.8%. Unless there are drastic changes to the Canadian economy, adding this average inflation factor to subsequent years should provide readers with a reasonably up-to-date picture of current results.

The Financial Performance Data service provides approximately 1,000 reports to the public. It includes national results, as well as results by province. The data provided in this book is the same as that provided on-line; however, I have changed the presentation format in order to be more book-friendly and reader-friendly. It compares only income statement data. Balance sheet information is available online.

I have provided two business structures for each business category. One covers unincorporated businesses (sole proprietorships & partnerships), and the other includes incorporated businesses. These are on the same page for one reason only, and that is to conserve paper. Please remember that these two business structures are **not** at all comparable from a profitability or net income perspective. As mentioned earlier, the net income for the unincorporated business is essentially the salary of the owner(s). The net profit of the incorporated businesses is after all salaries are deducted.

In order to better explain this point, take a look at page 333. In 2011, the average unincorporated home builder/contractor had a

Net "Income" of $30,100. This is the income of the sole proprietor. I have referred to this amount as income rather than profit because, after the owner(s) are paid a market rate salary for managing the business, there is little (if any) left over that represents profit.

In the case of the incorporated home builder/contractor, some or all of the owner's salary is included in "Labour and Commissions". The actual amount of salary is determined according to the owner's personal needs, income tax implications, and capital requirements of the company. In this example, although we don't know the average salary of the owners, we can assume that they were paid something to manage the business and still have an average of $46,500 left over as "profit".

In order to help differentiate between Net "Income" and Net "Profit", all 100 reports show the former in regular text and the latter in bold text.

The incorporated structure is a more accurate representation of our definition of a "profitable" and, therefore, "investable" business. This structure may have a profit remaining after all wages and salaries are paid, thus facilitating a return on investment calculation which is needed to properly value a business and compare it to other investment opportunities.

Each line item in these reports is defined in the Glossary of Financial Terms in Appendix 15.

These 100 reports represent approximately 913,000 businesses, or one half of the 1.8 million small businesses in Canada, who had annual gross revenues between $30,000 and $5 million in 2011. The only qualification applied when preparing the data was that the category must have had at least 1,000 participants in order to be included.

These reports are relatively easy to follow and compare to your existing business results, assuming that you fall into one of the 100 categories. If your business is not covered here, the process you need to follow is:

1. ***Determine Your NAICS Code:*** This is a classification code from the North American Industry Classification System, and you can locate your businesses code at *http://www23.statcan.gc.ca/imdb/p3VD.pl?Function= getVDPage1&TVD=118464*. The pronunciation of the NAICS acronym rhymes with "takes". NAICS is Statistics Canada's standardized coding system for grouping businesses engaged in similar types of activity into non-overlapping industry categories. The first two digits designate the sector, the third digit designates the subsector, the fourth digit designates the industry group, and the fifth digit designates industries.

2. ***Create a Report:*** To generate a report, visit *www.ic.gc.ca/eic/ site/pp-pp.nsf/eng/home*. The process is straight forward, but if you have any issues you can contact Industry Canada for assistance. Be sure to select the correct status (unincorporated or incorporated) that pertains to your situation.

3. ***Compare Results:*** Do a line-by-line comparison to determine how your business compares. Take note of where you may be weak, and pat yourself on the back for the areas where you appear to be strong.

4. ***Take Action:*** Top SBOs don't just read these types of results; they take action by improving operations where necessary.

In addition to helping existing SBOs better manage their enterprises, there are other benefits to using the Financial Performance Data service. If you are considering starting a new venture, this information can provide a great starting point to determine how much money you might actually make. Keep in mind, however, that the data does not reflect how long it takes to achieve these results. I requested information pertaining to average number of years in business, unfortunately the information was unavailable. This data would also be useful for creating a start-up budget and cash flow projections for a business plan.

Another key application is to use this database to compare financial results to a business you are interested in purchasing. You would be well-served to use this information to help determine if fair value exists. In addition, one of these reports could be used as support documentation during a business purchase or sale negotiation.

I don't often go out of my way to praise government initiatives, and I am often critical of wasteful government spending. Having said this, I haven't come across anything from a government organization that is as valuable to Canadian small business as this Financial Performance Data service.

Studying reports like these is comparable to studying a treasure map. When one uncovers even a tiny nugget of useful information, it can lead to actions which improve efficiencies and lead one closer to a larger treasure or, in our case, a larger bottom line.

Most small business owners are independent types, forging their own way with little input from outsiders. They have no Board of Directors to provide feedback, governance, or direction. Benchmark reports are one important type of feedback that SBOs can use to evaluate their personal performance. In fact, such data can be a jolt of harsh reality, and quickly discern if one is a "hero" or a "zero" in their industry. Fortunately, benchmark reports can also be inspiring and provide clues on how to get closer to the hero zone, for those willing to take action.

Chapter Takeaway

Empirical evidence supports the premise that benchmarking works for big business. I can't think of a rational reason why such a practice won't benefit smaller enterprises as well.

Offices of Accountants
NAICS 541212
(17,578 Reporting)

	Unincorporated		Incorporated	
No. of Businesses Reporting	9,885 (56.2%)		7,693 (43.8%)	
REVENUES AND EXPENSES	$000's	%	$000's	%
Total Revenue	190.6	100.0	305.7	100.0
Sales of goods & services	0.0	0.0	290.4	95.0
All other revenues	0.0	0.0	15.2	5.0
Cost of Sales (direct expenses)	2.5	1.3	15.7	5.2
Wages and benefits	0.3	0.2	7.3	2.4
Purchases, materials & sub-contracts	2.0	1.1	13.0	4.3
Opening inventory	0.2	0.1	6.6	2.2
Closing inventory	0.1	0.0	11.2	3.7
Operating expenses (indirect expenses)	93.4	49.0	208.4	68.2
Labour and commissions	30.1	15.8	122.9	40.2
Amortization and depletion	2.5	1.3	5.3	1.7
Repairs and maintenance	0.9	0.5	2.3	0.8
Utilities and telecommunication	2.4	1.3	5.0	1.6
Rent	6.1	3.2	13.9	4.5
Interest and bank charges	1.5	0.8	1.8	0.6
Professional and business fees	14.2	7.4	21.1	6.9
Advertising and promotion	1.2	0.6	5.8	1.9
Delivery, shipping and warehouse	0.2	0.1	0.2	0.1
Insurance	1.7	0.9	3.1	1.0
Other expenses	32.5	17.1	27.0	8.8
Total Expenses	95.9	50.3	224.2	73.3
Net Income / **Net Profit**	94.7	49.7	**81.5**	**26.7**
Gross Profit Margin (%)		98.7		94.6

This Canadian industry comprises establishments primarily engaged in providing a range of accounting services, such as the preparation of financial statements, the preparation of management accounting reports, the review and auditing of accounting records, the development of budgets, the design of accounting systems, and the provision of advice on matters related to accounting. These establishments may also provide related services, such as bookkeeping services, tax return preparation services, payroll services, management consulting services and insolvency services.

Advertising Agencies
NAICS 541810
(3,413 Reporting)

	Unincorporated		Incorporated	
No. of Businesses Reporting	832 (24.4%)		2,581 (76.6%)	
REVENUES AND EXPENSES	$000's	%	$000's	%
Total Revenue	96.0	100.0	564.9	100.0
Sales of goods & services	0.0	0.0	541.6	95.9
All other revenues	0.0	0.0	23.3	4.1
Cost of Sales (direct expenses)	27.6	28.8	236.3	41.8
Wages and benefits	1.0	1.0	30.4	5.4
Purchases, materials & sub-contracts	26.6	27.7	207.6	36.8
Opening inventory	0.2	0.2	8.4	1.5
Closing inventory	0.2	0.2	10.1	1.8
Operating expenses (indirect expenses)	25.5	26.5	277.2	49.1
Labour and commissions	1.6	1.6	137.5	24.3
Amortization and depletion	1.6	1.7	7.4	1.3
Repairs and maintenance	0.3	0.3	2.7	0.5
Utilities and telecommunication	1.9	2.0	7.6	1.3
Rent	1.2	1.3	19.4	3.4
Interest and bank charges	0.5	0.5	1.6	0.3
Professional and business fees	1.1	1.1	22.0	3.9
Advertising and promotion	1.3	1.3	17.9	3.2
Delivery, shipping and warehouse	0.4	0.4	1.2	0.2
Insurance	0.3	0.3	3.1	0.6
Other expenses	15.3	16.0	56.7	10.0
Total Expenses	53.1	55.3	513.4	90.9
Net Income / **Net Profit**	42.9	44.7	**51.5**	**9.1**
Gross Profit Margin (%)		71.2		56.4

This Canadian industry comprises establishments primarily engaged in creating advertising campaigns and placing such advertising in periodicals and newspapers, on radio and television, on the Internet, or with other media. These establishments are organized to provide a full range of services (through in-house capabilities or subcontracting), including advice, creative services, account management, production of advertising material, media planning, and buying (i.e., placing advertising).

Automotive Body, Paint and Interior Repair and Maintenance
NAICS 811121
(7,947 Reporting)

	Unincorporated		Incorporated	
No. of Businesses Reporting	3,514 (44.2%)		4,433 (55.8%)	
REVENUES AND EXPENSES	$000's	%	$000's	%
Total Revenue	119.4	100.0	725.0	100.0
Sales of goods & services	0.0	0.0	713.0	98.3
All other revenues	0.0	0.0	12.1	1.7
Cost of Sales (direct expenses)	50.0	41.9	408.2	56.3
Wages and benefits	4.3	3.6	102.3	14.1
Purchases, materials & sub-contracts	45.8	38.4	307.5	42.4
Opening inventory	5.4	4.5	34.8	4.8
Closing inventory	5.5	4.6	36.3	5.0
Operating expenses (indirect expenses)	43.4	36.3	273.9	37.8
Labour and commissions	7.8	6.5	117.1	16.2
Amortization and depletion	3.1	2.6	14.7	2.0
Repairs and maintenance	1.5	1.3	9.2	1.3
Utilities and telecommunication	4.2	3.5	15.7	2.2
Rent	5.0	4.2	31.8	4.4
Interest and bank charges	1.7	1.4	3.9	0.5
Professional and business fees	1.3	1.1	11.0	1.5
Advertising and promotion	0.9	0.8	9.9	1.4
Delivery, shipping and warehouse	0.2	0.2	0.5	0.1
Insurance	2.2	1.8	9.2	1.3
Other expenses	15.4	12.9	50.8	7.0
Total Expenses	93.4	78.2	682.1	94.1
Net Income / **Net Profit**	26.0	21.8	**42.9**	**5.9**
Gross Profit Margin (%)		58.1		42.7

This Canadian industry comprises establishments primarily engaged in repairing, customizing and painting motor vehicle bodies, and repairing and customizing motor vehicle interiors.

Automotive Glass Replacement Shops
NAICS 811122
(1,126 Reporting)

	Unincorporated		Incorporated	
No. of Businesses Reporting	349 (31.0%)		777 (69.0%)	
REVENUES AND EXPENSES	$000's	%	$000's	%
Total Revenue	135.0	100.0	506.9	100.0
Sales of goods & services	0.0	0.0	501.0	98.9
All other revenues	0.0	0.0	5.8	1.1
Cost of Sales (direct expenses)	60.9	45.1	250.8	49.5
Wages and benefits	2.4	1.8	44.8	8.8
Purchases, materials & sub-contracts	58.0	43.0	206.5	40.7
Opening inventory	2.2	1.6	26.7	5.3
Closing inventory	1.8	1.3	27.2	5.4
Operating expenses (indirect expenses)	43.3	32.1	217.6	42.9
Labour and commissions	8.6	6.4	96.6	19.1
Amortization and depletion	2.5	1.8	9.8	1.9
Repairs and maintenance	1.1	0.8	6.1	1.2
Utilities and telecommunication	3.8	2.8	10.0	2.0
Rent	4.6	3.4	21.2	4.2
Interest and bank charges	1.6	1.2	2.6	0.5
Professional and business fees	1.2	0.9	8.6	1.7
Advertising and promotion	2.6	1.9	15.2	3.0
Delivery, shipping and warehouse	0.2	0.1	0.6	0.1
Insurance	1.7	1.3	5.9	1.2
Other expenses	15.5	11.5	41.0	8.1
Total Expenses	104.2	77.2	468.4	92.4
Net Income / **Net Profit**	30.8	22.8	**38.4**	**7.6**
Gross Profit Margin (%)		54.9		49.9

This Canadian industry comprises establishments primarily engaged in replacing and repairing motor vehicle glass.

Automotive Parts and Accessories Stores
NAICS 441310
(3,336 Reporting)

	Unincorporated		Incorporated	
No. of Businesses Reporting	1,310 (39.3%)		2,026 (60.7%)	
REVENUES AND EXPENSES	$000's	%	$000's	%
Total Revenue	187.8	100.0	901.4	100.0
Sales of goods & services	0.0	0.0	888.4	98.5
All other revenues	0.0	0.0	13.1	1.5
Cost of Sales (direct expenses)	113.2	60.3	570.1	63.2
Wages and benefits	2.6	1.4	31.7	3.5
Purchases, materials & sub-contracts	111.2	59.2	550.5	61.1
Opening inventory	23.3	12.4	197.2	21.9
Closing inventory	23.8	12.7	209.3	23.2
Operating expenses (indirect expenses)	50.7	27.0	292.7	32.5
Labour and commissions	9.9	5.3	143.7	15.9
Amortization and depletion	3.4	1.8	13.4	1.5
Repairs and maintenance	1.5	0.8	8.0	0.9
Utilities and telecommunication	4.1	2.2	13.3	1.5
Rent	4.8	2.6	27.2	3.0
Interest and bank charges	2.3	1.2	6.8	0.8
Professional and business fees	1.4	0.7	10.1	1.1
Advertising and promotion	1.8	0.9	11.6	1.3
Delivery, shipping and warehouse	1.3	0.7	2.8	0.3
Insurance	1.9	1.0	7.4	0.8
Other expenses	18.4	9.8	48.3	5.4
Total Expenses	164.0	87.3	862.7	95.7
Net Income / **Net Profit**	23.8	12.7	**38.7**	**4.3**
Gross Profit Margin (%)		39.7		35.8

This Canadian industry comprises establishments primarily engaged in retailing new, rebuilt and used automotive parts and accessories; both retailing automotive parts and accessories and repairing automobiles; and retailing automotive accessories that generally require installation.

Automotive Repair (General)
NAICS 811111
(18,884 Reporting)

	Unincorporated		Incorporated	
No. of Businesses Reporting	8,096 (42.9%)		10,788 (57.1%)	
REVENUES AND EXPENSES	$000's	%	$000's	%
Total Revenue	158.0	100.0	527.8	100.0
Sales of goods & services	0.0	0.0	520.7	98.6
All other revenues	0.0	0.0	7.2	1.4
Cost of Sales (direct expenses)	80.5	51.0	300.2	56.9
Wages and benefits	5.8	3.7	60.1	11.4
Purchases, materials & sub-contracts	74.6	47.2	241.2	45.7
Opening inventory	8.7	5.5	36.3	6.9
Closing inventory	8.6	5.4	37.5	7.1
Operating expenses (indirect expenses)	51.2	32.4	203.4	38.5
Labour and commissions	11.0	7.0	88.0	16.7
Amortization and depletion	4.0	2.5	11.0	2.1
Repairs and maintenance	1.9	1.2	7.2	1.4
Utilities and telecommunication	4.5	2.8	10.3	2.0
Rent	5.2	3.3	24.5	4.7
Interest and bank charges	2.4	1.5	3.5	0.7
Professional and business fees	1.6	1.0	6.4	1.2
Advertising and promotion	1.0	0.6	6.2	1.2
Delivery, shipping and warehouse	0.3	0.2	0.3	0.1
Insurance	2.6	1.6	7.5	1.4
Other expenses	16.7	10.6	38.3	7.3
Total Expenses	131.8	83.4	503.6	95.4
Net Income / **Net Profit**	26.3	16.6	**24.3**	**4.6**
Gross Profit Margin (%)		49.0		42.4

This Canadian industry comprises establishments primarily engaged in providing a range of mechanical and electrical repair and maintenance services for motor vehicles, such as engine repair and maintenance, exhaust system replacement, transmission repair and electrical system repair. Establishments specializing in engine repair and replacement are also included.

Bakeries (Retail) NAICS 311811 (1,129 Reporting)				
	Unincorporated		Incorporated	
No. of Businesses Reporting	286 (25.3%)		843 (74.7%)	
REVENUES AND EXPENSES	$000's	%	$000's	%
Total Revenue	175.4	100.0	636.9	100.0
Sales of goods & services	0.0	0.0	628.7	98.7
All other revenues	0.0	0.0	8.2	1.3
Cost of Sales (direct expenses)	80.3	45.80	342.4	53.8
Wages and benefits	9.6	5.50	91.4	14.4
Purchases, materials & sub-contracts	70.5	40.20	251.5	39.5
Opening inventory	3.2	1.80	20.7	3.2
Closing inventory	3.1	1.70	21.2	3.3
Operating expenses (indirect expenses)	73.4	41.80	275.6	43.3
Labour and commissions	25.2	14.40	127.0	19.9
Amortization and depletion	4.8	2.80	16.5	2.6
Repairs and maintenance	2.9	1.60	11.5	1.8
Utilities and telecommunication	6.8	3.90	18.4	2.9
Rent	10.7	6.10	39.1	6.1
Interest and bank charges	2.5	1.40	3.9	0.6
Professional and business fees	1.8	1.10	8.2	1.3
Advertising and promotion	1.7	0.90	6.5	1.0
Delivery, shipping and warehouse	0.9	0.50	3.7	0.6
Insurance	1.9	1.10	5.1	0.8
Other expenses	14.2	8.10	35.6	5.6
Total Expenses	153.7	87.60	618.0	97.0
Net Income / **Net Profit**	21.7	12.40	**18.9**	**3.0**
Gross Profit Margin (%)		54.2		45.5

This Canadian industry comprises establishments primarily engaged in manufacturing bakery products, for retail sale, but not for immediate consumption. Establishments in this industry make bakery products from flour, not from prepared dough's.

Barber Shops NAICS 812114 (2,023 Reporting)				
	Unincorporated		Incorporated	
No. of Businesses Reporting	1,787 (88.3%)		236 (11.7%)	
REVENUES AND EXPENSES	$000's	%	$000's	%
Total Revenue	77.0	100.0	213.3	100.0
Sales of goods & services	0.0	0.0	207.2	97.2
All other revenues	0.0	0.0	6.1	2.8
Cost of Sales (direct expenses)	13.3	17.3	36.8	17.2
Wages and benefits	4.1	5.3	20.6	9.6
Purchases, materials & sub-contracts	9.0	11.7	17.0	8.0
Opening inventory	1.2	1.6	3.4	1.6
Closing inventory	1.0	1.2	4.2	2.0
Operating expenses (indirect expenses)	38.6	50.1	164.4	77.1
Labour and commissions	11.4	14.7	92.5	43.4
Amortization and depletion	1.2	1.6	4.3	2.0
Repairs and maintenance	0.8	1.0	1.5	0.7
Utilities and telecommunication	2.5	3.2	4.1	1.9
Rent	11.2	14.6	33.7	15.8
Interest and bank charges	0.8	1.0	1.1	0.5
Professional and business fees	0.9	1.1	6.2	2.9
Advertising and promotion	0.7	1.0	2.6	1.2
Delivery, shipping and warehouse	0.0	0.0	0.0	0.0
Insurance	0.7	0.9	1.5	0.7
Other expenses	8.3	10.8	16.9	7.9
Total Expenses	51.9	67.4	201.2	94.3
Net Income / **Net Profit**	25.1	32.6	**12.1**	**5.7**
Gross Profit Margin (%)		82.7		82.2

This Canadian industry comprises establishments primarily engaged in providing hair care services to men, including hair cutting and styling, and the trimming or shaving of beards and moustaches.

Beauty Salons NAICS 812115 (14,349 Reporting)				
	Unincorporated		**Incorporated**	
No. of Businesses Reporting	9,497 (66.2%)		4,852 (33.8%)	
REVENUES AND EXPENSES	$000's	%	$000's	%
Total Revenue	85.2	100.0	284.4	100.0
Sales of goods & services	0.0	0.0	279.3	98.2
All other revenues	0.0	0.0	5.1	1.8
Cost of Sales (direct expenses)	19.5	22.9	83.8	29.5
Wages and benefits	4.6	5.4	39.7	13.9
Purchases, materials & sub-contracts	15.1	17.7	45.7	16.1
Opening inventory	2.4	2.8	11.6	4.1
Closing inventory	2.6	3.1	13.1	4.6
Operating expenses (indirect expenses)	43.1	50.6	191.1	67.2
Labour and commissions	12.3	14.4	96.0	33.7
Amortization and depletion	2.0	2.3	7.8	2.8
Repairs and maintenance	1.2	1.4	3.4	1.2
Utilities and telecommunication	2.8	3.3	6.2	2.2
Rent	10.3	12.1	35.3	12.4
Interest and bank charges	1.3	1.5	1.7	0.6
Professional and business fees	1.1	1.3	6.4	2.2
Advertising and promotion	1.3	1.5	6.0	2.1
Delivery, shipping and warehouse	0.1	0.1	0.2	0.1
Insurance	0.8	1.0	2.4	0.9
Other expenses	10.0	11.8	25.7	9.0
Total Expenses	62.6	73.5	274.9	96.7
Net Income / **Net Profit**	22.6	26.5	**9.5**	**3.3**
Gross Profit Margin (%)		77.1		70.0

This Canadian industry comprises establishments primarily engaged in providing hair care services to women, providing esthetic services such as manicures and pedicures, or a combination of these services.

Beer, Wine and Liquor Stores
NAICS 445310
(1,426 Reporting)

	Unincorporated		Incorporated	
No. of Businesses Reporting	420 (29.5%)		1,006 (70.5%)	
REVENUES AND EXPENSES	$000's	%	$000's	%
Total Revenue	180.3	100.0	1314.2	100.0
Sales of goods & services	0.0	0.0	1297.7	98.7
All other revenues	0.0	0.0	16.5	1.3
Cost of Sales (direct expenses)	103.5	57.4	987.9	75.2
Wages and benefits	2.6	1.4	9.0	0.7
Purchases, materials & sub-contracts	99.8	55.3	993.0	75.6
Opening inventory	19.2	10.6	149.6	11.4
Closing inventory	18.1	10.0	163.7	12.5
Operating expenses (indirect expenses)	60.2	33.4	282.7	21.5
Labour and commissions	13.0	7.2	119.9	9.1
Amortization and depletion	3.6	2.0	16.7	1.3
Repairs and maintenance	2.5	1.4	7.1	0.5
Utilities and telecommunication	5.3	2.9	13.2	1.0
Rent	10.2	5.6	43.2	3.3
Interest and bank charges	3.0	1.6	8.8	0.7
Professional and business fees	1.9	1.0	21.6	1.6
Advertising and promotion	2.7	1.5	10.1	0.8
Delivery, shipping and warehouse	0.6	0.3	1.1	0.1
Insurance	1.6	0.9	4.8	0.4
Other expenses	15.9	8.8	36.2	2.8
Total Expenses	163.7	90.8	1270.5	96.7
Net Income / **Net Profit**	16.6	9.2	**43.7**	**3.3**
Gross Profit Margin (%)		42.6		23.9

This Canadian industry comprises establishments primarily engaged in retailing packaged alcoholic beverages, such as beer, wine and liquor.

Bookkeeping, Payroll and Related Services
NAICS 541215
(14,839 Reporting)

	Unincorporated		Incorporated	
No. of Businesses Reporting	11,638 (78.4%)		3,201 (21.6%)	
REVENUES AND EXPENSES	$000's	%	$000's	%
Total Revenue	75.3	100.0	253.5	100.0
Sales of goods & services	0.0	0.0	231.9	91.5
All other revenues	0.0	0.0	21.6	8.5
Cost of Sales (direct expenses)	7.0	9.3	25.9	10.2
Wages and benefits	0.9	1.2	15.8	6.2
Purchases, materials & sub-contracts	6.0	8.0	11.4	4.5
Opening inventory	0.5	0.7	2.8	1.1
Closing inventory	0.4	0.6	4.1	1.6
Operating expenses (indirect expenses)	26.0	34.5	183.6	72.4
Labour and commissions	5.3	7.1	112.8	44.5
Amortization and depletion	1.8	2.4	5.8	2.3
Repairs and maintenance	0.5	0.6	3.3	1.3
Utilities and telecommunication	1.8	2.4	4.8	1.9
Rent	1.5	2.0	10.4	4.1
Interest and bank charges	0.6	0.8	1.9	0.8
Professional and business fees	1.1	1.4	11.7	4.6
Advertising and promotion	0.7	1.0	4.4	1.7
Delivery, shipping and warehouse	0.1	0.2	0.4	0.2
Insurance	0.4	0.5	2.0	0.8
Other expenses	12.1	16.1	26.1	10.3
Total Expenses	33.0	43.8	209.5	82.6
Net Income / **Net Profit**	42.3	56.2	**44.0**	**17.4**
Gross Profit Margin (%)		90.7		88.8

This Canadian industry comprises establishments primarily engaged in providing bookkeeping, billing or payroll processing services. These establishments do not provide accounting services, such as the preparation of financial statements, the preparation of management accounting reports, and the review and auditing of accounting records.

Building Construction (Residential)
NAICS 236110
(61,490 Reporting)

	Unincorporated		Incorporated	
No. of Businesses Reporting	29,106 (47.3%)		32,384 (52.7%)	
REVENUES AND EXPENSES	$000's	%	$000's	%
Total Revenue	124.3	100.0	656.5	100.0
Sales of goods & services	0.0	0.0	627.4	95.6
All other revenues	0.0	0.0	29.0	4.4
Cost of Sales (direct expenses)	59.1	47.6	431.8	95.6
Wages and benefits	5.3	4.3	64.7	4.4
Purchases, materials & sub-contracts	52.4	42.1	402.0	65.8
Opening inventory	3.4	2.7	226.8	9.9
Closing inventory	2.0	1.6	261.7	61.2
Operating expenses (indirect expenses)	35.1	28.2	178.2	34.5
Labour and commissions	6.8	5.5	67.0	39.9
Amortization and depletion	3.4	2.7	13.8	27.1
Repairs and maintenance	0.6	0.5	6.0	10.2
Utilities and telecommunication	1.9	1.6	6.7	2.1
Rent	0.7	0.5	7.8	0.9
Interest and bank charges	1.0	0.8	7.3	1.0
Professional and business fees	1.2	1.0	15.3	1.2
Advertising and promotion	0.5	0.4	5.5	1.1
Delivery, shipping and warehouse	0.1	0.1	0.3	2.3
Insurance	0.9	0.8	5.8	0.8
Other expenses	18.0	14.5	42.7	0.0
Total Expenses	94.2	75.8	610.0	0.9
Net Income / **Net Profit**	30.1	24.2	**46.5**	**6.5**
Gross Profit Margin (%)		52.4		31.2

This Canadian industry comprises establishments primarily engaged in the construction or remodeling and renovation of single-family and multi-family residential buildings. These establishments include residential housing general contractors, operative builders and remodelers of residential structures, residential project construction management firms, and residential design-build firms.

Building Inspection Services NAICS 541350 (1,289 Reporting)				
	Unincorporated		Incorporated	
No. of Businesses Reporting	306 (23.7%)		983 (76.3%)	
REVENUES AND EXPENSES	$000's	%	$000's	%
Total Revenue	75.8	100.0	253.3	100.0
Sales of goods & services	0.0	0.0	244.8	96.6
All other revenues	0.0	0.0	8.5	3.4
Cost of Sales (direct expenses)	5.5	7.2	51.6	20.4
Wages and benefits	0.3	0.5	16.3	6.4
Purchases, materials & sub-contracts	5.1	6.8	39.4	15.6
Opening inventory	0.1	0.1	3.5	1.4
Closing inventory	0.0	0.0	7.6	3.0
Operating expenses (indirect expenses)	29.3	38.6	154.6	61.0
Labour and commissions	4.0	5.3	73.4	29.0
Amortization and depletion	3.0	4.0	7.1	2.8
Repairs and maintenance	0.3	0.4	2.1	0.8
Utilities and telecommunication	1.9	2.5	5.0	2.0
Rent	0.7	0.9	5.5	2.2
Interest and bank charges	0.7	0.9	1.6	0.6
Professional and business fees	1.4	1.9	9.7	3.8
Advertising and promotion	1.4	1.8	6.5	2.6
Delivery, shipping and warehouse	0.2	0.2	0.7	0.3
Insurance	1.9	2.5	5.0	2.0
Other expenses	13.7	18.1	38.0	15.0
Total Expenses	34.8	45.9	206.2	81.4
Net Income / **Net Profit**	41.0	54.1	**47.1**	**18.6**
Gross Profit Margin (%)		92.8		78.9

This Canadian industry comprises establishments primarily engaged in providing building inspection services. These establishments typically evaluate all aspects of the building structure and component systems and prepare a report on the physical condition of the property, generally for buyers or others involved in real estate transactions.

Car Dealers (Used)
NAICS 441120
(5,253 Reporting)

	Unincorporated		Incorporated	
No. of Businesses Reporting	1,703 (32.4%)		3,550 (67.6%)	
REVENUES AND EXPENSES	$000's	%	$000's	%
Total Revenue	282.0	100.0	916.0	100.0
Sales of goods & services	0.0	0.0	899.0	98.1
All other revenues	0.0	0.0	17.1	1.9
Cost of Sales (direct expenses)	231.0	81.9	747.8	81.6
Wages and benefits	1.0	0.4	12.7	1.4
Purchases, materials & sub-contracts	231.1	82.0	741.4	80.9
Opening inventory	38.9	13.8	179.4	19.6
Closing inventory	40.1	14.2	185.8	20.3
Operating expenses (indirect expenses)	38.0	13.5	152.8	16.7
Labour and commissions	3.4	1.2	55.1	6.0
Amortization and depletion	1.1	0.4	6.9	0.8
Repairs and maintenance	3.1	1.1	6.6	0.7
Utilities and telecommunication	3.1	1.1	8.1	0.9
Rent	3.8	1.4	15.9	1.7
Interest and bank charges	2.2	0.8	4.7	0.5
Professional and business fees	1.5	0.5	6.6	0.7
Advertising and promotion	1.8	0.7	10.7	1.2
Delivery, shipping and warehouse	1.1	0.4	1.0	0.1
Insurance	2.4	0.8	6.5	0.7
Other expenses	14.5	5.1	30.7	3.4
Total Expenses	269.0	95.4	900.6	98.3
Net Income / **Net Profit**	13.0	4.6	**15.4**	**1.7**
Gross Profit Margin (%)		18.1		16.8

This Canadian industry comprises establishments primarily engaged in retailing used automobiles, sport utility vehicles, and light-duty trucks and vans, including mini-vans.

Car Washes NAICS 811192 (2,238 Reporting)				
	Unincorporated		Incorporated	
No. of Businesses Reporting	770 (34.4%)		1,468 (65.6%)	
REVENUES AND EXPENSES	$000's	%	$000's	%
Total Revenue	103.1	100.0	319.8	100.0
Sales of goods & services	0.0	0.0	306.1	95.7
All other revenues	0.0	0.0	13.7	4.3
Cost of Sales (direct expenses)	25.5	24.8	73.4	22.9
Wages and benefits	2.8	2.7	23.0	7.2
Purchases, materials & sub-contracts	22.9	22.2	52.5	16.4
Opening inventory	1.7	1.6	10.1	3.1
Closing inventory	1.8	1.8	12.2	3.8
Operating expenses (indirect expenses)	55.8	54.1	219.5	68.6
Labour and commissions	10.3	10.0	74.6	23.3
Amortization and depletion	3.9	3.8	19.0	5.9
Repairs and maintenance	2.7	2.6	13.6	4.3
Utilities and telecommunication	5.2	5.1	19.5	6.1
Rent	6.7	6.5	23.8	7.4
Interest and bank charges	1.9	1.9	8.9	2.8
Professional and business fees	1.2	1.1	8.8	2.7
Advertising and promotion	1.2	1.1	4.9	1.5
Delivery, shipping and warehouse	0.2	0.2	0.4	0.1
Insurance	1.7	1.6	5.1	1.6
Other expenses	20.9	20.3	41.0	12.8
Total Expenses	81.3	78.9	292.9	91.6
Net Income / **Net Profit**	21.8	21.1	**26.9**	**8.4**
Gross Profit Margin (%)		74.8		76.0

This Canadian industry comprises establishments primarily engaged in washing and cleaning motor vehicles.

Carpet and Upholstery Cleaning Services
NAICS 561740
(1,838 Reporting)

	Unincorporated		Incorporated	
No. of Businesses Reporting	1,174 (63.9%)		664 (36.1%)	
REVENUES AND EXPENSES	$000's	%	$000's	%
Total Revenue	90.3	100.0	435.5	100.0
Sales of goods & services	0.0	0.0	430.9	98.9
All other revenues	0.0	0.0	4.6	1.1
Cost of Sales (direct expenses)	19.4	21.5	152.6	35.0
Wages and benefits	0.9	1.0	46.9	10.8
Purchases, materials & sub-contracts	18.6	20.6	107.0	24.6
Opening inventory	1.0	1.1	14.3	3.3
Closing inventory	1.0	1.1	15.6	3.6
Operating expenses (indirect expenses)	42.9	47.6	245.3	56.3
Labour and commissions	8.2	9.0	107.1	24.6
Amortization and depletion	3.0	3.4	11.9	2.7
Repairs and maintenance	1.2	1.3	5.6	1.3
Utilities and telecommunication	3.3	3.6	10.2	2.3
Rent	2.8	3.1	16.1	3.7
Interest and bank charges	1.0	1.1	2.5	0.6
Professional and business fees	1.2	1.3	7.8	1.8
Advertising and promotion	2.3	2.5	18.4	4.2
Delivery, shipping and warehouse	0.1	0.2	0.7	0.2
Insurance	1.1	1.2	6.2	1.4
Other expenses	18.8	20.8	58.7	13.5
Total Expenses	62.4	69.1	397.8	91.4
Net Income / **Net Profit**	27.9	30.9	**37.6**	**8.6**
Gross Profit Margin (%)		78.5		64.6

This Canadian industry comprises establishments primarily engaged in cleaning and dyeing rugs, carpets, and upholstery.

Caterers NAICS 722320 (3,373 Reporting)				
	Unincorporated		Incorporated	
No. of Businesses Reporting	1,968 (58.3%)		1,405 (41.7%)	
REVENUES AND EXPENSES	$000's	%	$000's	%
Total Revenue	111.9	100.0	559.7	100.0
Sales of goods & services	0.0	0.0	545.9	97.5
All other revenues	0.0	0.0	13.8	2.5
Cost of Sales (direct expenses)	51.6	46.1	278.3	49.7
Wages and benefits	4.8	4.3	65.4	11.7
Purchases, materials & sub-contracts	46.7	41.8	213.0	38.1
Opening inventory	1.3	1.1	9.9	1.8
Closing inventory	1.3	1.1	9.9	1.8
Operating expenses (indirect expenses)	41.1	36.7	265.9	47.5
Labour and commissions	9.3	8.3	111.5	19.9
Amortization and depletion	2.6	2.3	15.6	2.8
Repairs and maintenance	1.2	1.1	11.1	2.0
Utilities and telecommunication	3.0	2.7	14.2	2.5
Rent	4.8	4.3	38.0	6.8
Interest and bank charges	1.1	1.0	4.4	0.8
Professional and business fees	1.2	1.1	12.8	2.3
Advertising and promotion	1.2	1.1	8.6	1.5
Delivery, shipping and warehouse	0.3	0.2	0.7	0.1
Insurance	1.0	0.9	5.8	1.0
Other expenses	15.4	13.7	43.2	7.7
Total Expenses	92.7	82.9	544.3	97.2
Net Income / **Net Profit**	19.2	17.1	**15.5**	**2.8**
Gross Profit Margin (%)		53.9		49.0

This Canadian industry comprises establishments primarily engaged in providing food services for events, such as graduation parties, wedding receptions and trade shows. These establishments generally have equipment and vehicles to transport meals and snacks to events and to prepare food at the event site. Caterers who own or manage permanent facilities in which they provide event-based food services are also included.

Chiropractors NAICS 621310 (2,784 Reporting)				
	Unincorporated		Incorporated	
No. of Businesses Reporting	1,257 (45.2%)		1,527 (54.8%)	
REVENUES AND EXPENSES	$000's	%	$000's	%
Total Revenue	139.8	100.0	350.3	100.0
Sales of goods & services	0.0	0.0	341.3	97.4
All other revenues	0.0	0.0	9.0	2.6
Cost of Sales (direct expenses)	3.2	2.3	20.3	5.8
Wages and benefits	0.3	0.2	4.0	1.1
Purchases, materials & sub-contracts	2.9	2.1	17.7	5.0
Opening inventory	0.0	0.0	1.5	0.4
Closing inventory	0.0	0.0	2.9	0.8
Operating expenses (indirect expenses)	79.5	56.9	247.8	70.7
Labour and commissions	18.9	13.5	107.5	30.7
Amortization and depletion	2.9	2.1	8.5	2.4
Repairs and maintenance	1.4	1.0	4.1	1.2
Utilities and telecommunication	3.4	2.5	6.6	1.9
Rent	13.5	9.7	30.7	8.8
Interest and bank charges	2.3	1.7	2.7	0.8
Professional and business fees	3.5	2.5	23.7	6.8
Advertising and promotion	2.7	1.9	10.7	3.0
Delivery, shipping and warehouse	0.1	0.0	0.1	0.0
Insurance	1.9	1.4	4.1	1.2
Other expenses	28.7	20.5	49.2	14.1
Total Expenses	82.7	59.2	268.1	76.5
Net Income / **Net Profit**	57.1	40.8	**82.2**	**23.5**
Gross Profit Margin (%)		97.7		94.1

This Canadian industry comprises establishments primarily engaged in the private or group practice of chiropractic medicine. These practitioners provide diagnostic and therapeutic treatment of neuro-musculoskeletal and related disorders through the manipulation and adjustment of the spinal column and extremities.

Clothing Stores – Women's NAICS 448120 (2,430 Reporting)				
	Unincorporated		Incorporated	
No. of Businesses Reporting	687 (28.3%)		1,743 (71.7%)	
REVENUES AND EXPENSES	$000's	%	$000's	%
Total Revenue	194.3	100.0	528.0	100.0
Sales of goods & services	0.0	0.0	518.3	98.2
All other revenues	0.0	0.0	9.7	1.8
Cost of Sales (direct expenses)	116.7	60.1	288.4	54.6
Wages and benefits	1.3	0.7	8.0	1.5
Purchases, materials & sub-contracts	115.4	59.4	281.6	53.3
Opening inventory	41.2	21.2	121.3	23.0
Closing inventory	41.3	21.3	122.5	23.2
Operating expenses (indirect expenses)	66.1	34.0	230.8	43.7
Labour and commissions	17.3	8.9	97.7	18.5
Amortization and depletion	1.6	0.8	7.5	1.4
Repairs and maintenance	1.5	0.8	3.5	0.7
Utilities and telecommunication	3.6	1.9	6.4	1.2
Rent	17.1	8.8	59.7	11.3
Interest and bank charges	4.4	2.3	2.8	0.5
Professional and business fees	2.2	1.1	7.3	1.4
Advertising and promotion	4.2	2.2	9.8	1.9
Delivery, shipping and warehouse	1.1	0.6	0.8	0.2
Insurance	1.5	0.8	3.3	0.6
Other expenses	11.5	5.9	32.0	6.1
Total Expenses	182.8	94.1	519.3	98.3
Net Income / **Net Profit**	11.4	5.9	**8.8**	**1.7**
Gross Profit Margin (%)		39.9		44.4

This Canadian industry comprises establishments primarily engaged in retailing a general line of new, women's, ready-to-wear clothing, including maternity wear.

Convenience Stores
NAICS 445120
(10,332 Reporting)

	Unincorporated		Incorporated	
No. of Businesses Reporting	5,087 (49.2%)		5,245 (50.8%)	
REVENUES AND EXPENSES	$000's	%	$000's	%
Total Revenue	390.2	100.0	734.3	100.0
Sales of goods & services	0.0	0.0	718.0	97.8
All other revenues	0.0	0.0	16.3	2.2
Cost of Sales (direct expenses)	313.9	80.4	574.2	78.2
Wages and benefits	1.2	0.3	6.3	0.9
Purchases, materials & sub-contracts	311.2	79.8	568.7	77.4
Opening inventory	32.1	8.2	49.4	6.7
Closing inventory	30.6	7.8	50.2	6.8
Operating expenses (indirect expenses)	56.9	14.6	150.9	20.5
Labour and commissions	12.9	3.3	71.5	9.7
Amortization and depletion	3.2	0.8	8.0	1.1
Repairs and maintenance	1.8	0.5	5.3	0.7
Utilities and telecommunication	6.2	1.6	10.6	1.4
Rent	13.8	3.5	22.5	3.1
Interest and bank charges	2.5	0.6	3.5	0.5
Professional and business fees	1.9	0.5	4.2	0.6
Advertising and promotion	0.3	0.1	1.7	0.2
Delivery, shipping and warehouse	0.3	0.1	0.4	0.1
Insurance	1.7	0.4	3.0	0.4
Other expenses	12.3	3.1	20.1	2.7
Total Expenses	370.8	95.0	725.0	98.7
Net Income / **Net Profit**	19.4	5.0	**9.3**	**1.3**
Gross Profit Margin (%)		19.6		20.0

This Canadian industry comprises establishments, known as convenience stores, primarily engaged in retailing a limited line of convenience items that generally includes milk, bread, soft drinks, snacks, tobacco products, newspapers and magazines.

Couriers NAICS 492110 (8,278 Reporting)				
	Unincorporated		Incorporated	
No. of Businesses Reporting	6,697 (80.9%)		1,581 (19.1%)	
REVENUES AND EXPENSES	$000's	%	$000's	%
Total Revenue	75.7	100.0	400.4	100.0
Sales of goods & services	0.0	0.0	389.0	97.1
All other revenues	0.0	0.0	11.4	2.9
Cost of Sales (direct expenses)	9.1	12.0	128.5	32.1
Wages and benefits	0.9	1.1	20.6	5.1
Purchases, materials & sub-contracts	8.3	10.9	107.6	26.9
Opening inventory	0.3	0.3	3.5	0.9
Closing inventory	0.3	0.4	3.0	0.8
Operating expenses (indirect expenses)	37.3	49.3	209.4	52.3
Labour and commissions	2.5	3.3	85.5	21.3
Amortization and depletion	2.9	3.8	9.7	2.4
Repairs and maintenance	1.0	1.3	8.8	2.2
Utilities and telecommunication	3.3	4.3	14.7	3.7
Rent	0.7	1.0	15.5	3.9
Interest and bank charges	0.5	0.7	5.2	1.3
Professional and business fees	0.8	1.1	8.7	2.2
Advertising and promotion	0.3	0.4	4.5	1.1
Delivery, shipping and warehouse	0.2	0.3	5.5	1.4
Insurance	0.8	1.0	6.2	1.5
Other expenses	24.3	32.1	45.3	11.3
Total Expenses	46.4	61.3	338.0	84.4
Net Income / **Net Profit**	29.3	38.7	**62.4**	**15.6**
Gross Profit Margin (%)		88.0		67.0

This Canadian industry comprises establishments primarily engaged in providing air, surface or combined courier delivery services. Courier establishments of the Post Office are included. **Illustrative example(s):** courier service; parcel delivery, private. **Exclusion(s):** providing local messenger and delivery services, including bicycle couriers (See 492210 Local messengers and local delivery).

Data Processing, Hosting, and Related Services
NAICS 518210
(2,526 Reporting)

	Unincorporated		Incorporated	
No. of Businesses Reporting	1,804 (71.4%)		722 (28.6%)	
REVENUES AND EXPENSES	$000's	%	$000's	%
Total Revenue	81.1	100.0	538.5	100.0
Sales of goods & services	0.0	0.0	508.5	94.4
All other revenues	0.0	0.0	30.0	5.6
Cost of Sales (direct expenses)	12.7	15.7	134.9	25.1
Wages and benefits	0.8	1.0	35.4	6.6
Purchases, materials & sub-contracts	11.9	14.7	100.4	18.6
Opening inventory	0.3	0.4	5.4	1.0
Closing inventory	0.3	0.4	6.2	1.2
Operating expenses (indirect expenses)	21.7	26.8	371.8	69.0
Labour and commissions	3.2	3.9	181.4	33.7
Amortization and depletion	1.4	1.8	17.3	3.2
Repairs and maintenance	0.3	0.4	2.6	0.5
Utilities and telecommunication	1.8	2.2	10.7	2.0
Rent	1.1	1.4	20.8	3.9
Interest and bank charges	0.6	0.7	5.5	1.0
Professional and business fees	0.9	1.1	32.0	5.9
Advertising and promotion	0.9	1.1	17.4	3.2
Delivery, shipping and warehouse	0.2	0.2	1.0	0.2
Insurance	0.4	0.5	2.9	0.5
Other expenses	11.0	13.5	80.3	14.9
Total Expenses	34.5	42.5	506.8	94.1
Net Income / **Net Profit**	46.6	57.5	**31.8**	**5.9**
Gross Profit Margin (%)		84.3		73.5

This Canadian industry comprises establishments primarily engaged in providing hosting or data processing services. Hosting establishments may provide specialized hosting activities, such as web hosting, video and audio streaming services, application hosting, application service provisioning, or may provide general time-share mainframe facilities to clients. Data processing establishments may provide complete processing and preparation of reports from data supplied by the customer; specialized services, such as automated data entry; or they may make data processing resources available to clients on an hourly or time-sharing basis.

Day-Care Services (Child) NAICS 624410 (33,838 Reporting)				
	Unincorporated		Incorporated	
No. of Businesses Reporting	28,867 (85.3%)		4,971 (14.7%)	
REVENUES AND EXPENSES	$000's	%	$000's	%
Total Revenue	59.4	100.0	722.0	100.0
Sales of goods & services	0.0	0.0	319.4	44.2
All other revenues	0.0	0.0	402.6	55.8
Cost of Sales (direct expenses)	7.4	12.5	38.7	5.4
Wages and benefits	1.2	2.0	27.8	3.9
Purchases, materials & sub-contracts	6.1	10.2	11.1	1.5
Opening inventory	0.6	0.9	0.6	0.1
Closing inventory	0.4	0.6	0.8	0.1
Operating expenses (indirect expenses)	23.9	40.3	650.4	90.1
Labour and commissions	5.0	8.5	447.4	62.0
Amortization and depletion	1.1	1.8	14.3	2.0
Repairs and maintenance	1.0	1.7	11.2	1.6
Utilities and telecommunication	1.0	1.8	6.9	1.0
Rent	1.4	2.4	40.1	5.6
Interest and bank charges	0.3	0.6	4.0	0.6
Professional and business fees	0.6	1.0	15.0	2.1
Advertising and promotion	0.2	0.4	3.6	0.5
Delivery, shipping and warehouse	0.1	0.1	0.9	0.1
Insurance	0.3	0.6	3.3	0.5
Other expenses	12.7	21.5	103.6	14.4
Total Expenses	31.3	52.8	689.1	95.4
Net Income / **Net Profit**	28.0	47.2	**32.9**	**4.6**
Gross Profit Margin (%)		87.5		87.9

This Canadian industry comprises establishments primarily engaged in providing day-care services for infants or children. These establishments may care for older children when they are not in school and may also offer pre-kindergarten educational programs.

Delivery and Messengers
NAICS 492210
(2,427 Reporting)

	Unincorporated		Incorporated	
No. of Businesses Reporting	1,458 (60.0%)		969 (40%)	
REVENUES AND EXPENSES	$000's	%	$000's	%
Total Revenue	70.8	100.0	521.9	100.0
Sales of goods & services	0.0	0.0	513.2	98.3
All other revenues	0.0	0.0	8.7	1.7
Cost of Sales (direct expenses)	13.9	19.7	186.0	35.6
Wages and benefits	0.4	0.6	24.8	4.7
Purchases, materials & sub-contracts	13.5	19.1	161.4	30.9
Opening inventory	0.1	0.2	2.7	0.5
Closing inventory	0.1	0.2	2.9	0.5
Operating expenses (indirect expenses)	30.3	42.9	255.6	49.0
Labour and commissions	1.5	2.2	109.8	21.0
Amortization and depletion	2.6	3.6	10.2	1.9
Repairs and maintenance	0.7	1.0	12.0	2.3
Utilities and telecommunication	2.4	3.4	15.7	3.0
Rent	0.5	0.7	15.6	3.0
Interest and bank charges	0.4	0.6	2.8	0.5
Professional and business fees	0.6	0.9	17.8	3.4
Advertising and promotion	0.3	0.4	5.5	1.0
Delivery, shipping and warehouse	0.4	0.6	7.1	1.4
Insurance	0.6	0.8	6.4	1.2
Other expenses	20.3	28.7	52.6	10.1
Total Expenses	44.3	62.6	441.6	84.6
Net Income / **Net Profit**	26.5	37.4	**80.4**	**15.4**
Gross Profit Margin (%)		80.3		63.8

This Canadian industry comprises establishments primarily engaged in providing messenger and delivery services of small parcels within a single urban area. Establishments engaged in the delivery of letters and documents, such as legal documents, often by bicycle or on foot; and the delivery of small parcels, such as take-out restaurant meals, alcoholic beverages and groceries, on a fee basis, usually by small truck or van, are included.

Dentists NAICS 621210 (18,688 Reporting)				
	Unincorporated		Incorporated	
No. of Businesses Reporting	9,074 (48.6%)		9,614 (51.4%)	
REVENUES AND EXPENSES	$000's	%	$000's	%
Total Revenue	303.6	100.0	865.7	100.0
Sales of goods & services	0.0	0.0	844.0	97.5
All other revenues	0.0	0.0	21.6	2.5
Cost of Sales (direct expenses)	3.7	1.2	48.0	5.5
Wages and benefits	1.0	0.3	20.8	2.4
Purchases, materials & sub-contracts	2.6	0.9	28.9	3.3
Opening inventory	0.1	0.0	4.5	0.5
Closing inventory	0.1	0.0	6.1	0.7
Operating expenses (indirect expenses)	178.0	58.6	590.2	68.2
Labour and commissions	58.9	19.4	296.5	34.2
Amortization and depletion	5.4	1.8	26.7	3.1
Repairs and maintenance	3.0	1.0	9.0	1.0
Utilities and telecommunication	3.4	1.1	8.5	1.0
Rent	12.4	4.1	43.4	5.0
Interest and bank charges	3.7	1.2	5.6	0.6
Professional and business fees	8.8	2.9	63.9	7.4
Advertising and promotion	2.4	0.8	12.5	1.4
Delivery, shipping and warehouse	0.1	0.0	0.2	0.0
Insurance	2.5	0.8	8.7	1.0
Other expenses	77.4	25.5	115.2	13.3
Total Expenses	181.6	59.8	638.3	73.7
Net Income / **Net Profit**	122.0	40.2	**227.4**	**26.3**
Gross Profit Margin (%)		98.8		94.3

This Canadian industry comprises establishments of licensed dentists primarily engaged in the private or group practice of general or specialized dentistry or dental surgery. Offices of dentists, especially walk-in centres that accept patients without appointment and that often have extended office hours, are sometimes called clinics or dental centres.

Drafting Services
NAICS 541340
(1,925 Reporting)

REVENUES AND EXPENSES	Unincorporated		Incorporated	
No. of Businesses Reporting	677 (35.2%)		1,248 (64.8%)	
REVENUES AND EXPENSES	$000's	%	$000's	%
Total Revenue	70.7	100.0	265.1	100.0
Sales of goods & services	0.0	0.0	260.1	98.1
All other revenues	0.0	0.0	5.1	1.9
Cost of Sales (direct expenses)	4.9	6.9	57.3	21.6
Wages and benefits	0.1	0.1	24.5	9.2
Purchases, materials & sub-contracts	4.8	6.7	34.0	12.8
Opening inventory	0.1	0.1	5.3	2.0
Closing inventory	0.1	0.1	6.5	2.4
Operating expenses (indirect expenses)	19.2	27.2	146.9	55.4
Labour and commissions	3.7	5.2	89.2	33.6
Amortization and depletion	1.9	2.7	4.6	1.7
Repairs and maintenance	0.3	0.4	1.3	0.5
Utilities and telecommunication	1.5	2.1	3.4	1.3
Rent	0.7	1.0	7.7	2.9
Interest and bank charges	0.3	0.5	1.1	0.4
Professional and business fees	0.8	1.1	11.9	4.5
Advertising and promotion	0.4	0.5	3.7	1.4
Delivery, shipping and warehouse	0.1	0.1	0.2	0.1
Insurance	0.4	0.6	2.2	0.8
Other expenses	9.1	12.9	21.6	8.1
Total Expenses	24.1	34.0	204.2	77.0
Net Income / **Net Profit**	46.6	66.0	**61.0**	**23.0**
Gross Profit Margin (%)		93.1		78.0

This Canadian industry comprises establishments primarily engaged in drawing detailed layouts, plans and illustrations of buildings, structures, systems or components from engineering and architectural specifications.

Drinking Places (Alcoholic Beverages) NAICS 722410 (4,361 Reporting)				
	Unincorporated		Incorporated	
No. of Businesses Reporting	606 (13.9%)		3,755 (86.1%)	
REVENUES AND EXPENSES	$000's	%	$000's	%
Total Revenue	184.8	100.0	713.5	100.0
Sales of goods & services	0.0	0.0	683.7	95.8
All other revenues	0.0	0.0	29.8	4.2
Cost of Sales (direct expenses)	92.6	50.1	322.5	45.2
Wages and benefits	5.5	3.0	32.9	4.6
Purchases, materials & sub-contracts	87.7	47.4	290.1	40.7
Opening inventory	4.8	2.6	19.9	2.8
Closing inventory	5.4	2.9	20.4	2.9
Operating expenses (indirect expenses)	79.1	42.8	362.5	50.8
Labour and commissions	25.1	13.6	147.8	20.7
Amortization and depletion	3.2	1.8	18.9	2.7
Repairs and maintenance	4.8	2.6	21.6	3.0
Utilities and telecommunication	8.0	4.3	19.7	2.8
Rent	9.2	5.0	51.6	7.2
Interest and bank charges	2.6	1.4	5.5	0.8
Professional and business fees	2.0	1.1	15.5	2.2
Advertising and promotion	2.2	1.2	20.9	2.9
Delivery, shipping and warehouse	0.2	0.1	0.2	0.0
Insurance	2.9	1.6	9.0	1.3
Other expenses	18.8	10.2	51.7	7.2
Total Expenses	171.7	92.9	685.1	96.0
Net Income / **Net Profit**	13.1	7.1	**28.5**	**4.0**
Gross Profit Margin (%)		49.9		52.8

This Canadian industry comprises establishments, known as bars, taverns or drinking places, primarily engaged in preparing and serving alcoholic beverages for immediate consumption. These establishments may also provide limited food services.

Dry Cleaning and Laundry Services (Except Coin-Operated)
NAICS 812320
(2,514 Reporting)

	Unincorporated		Incorporated	
No. of Businesses Reporting	859 (34.2%)		1,655 (65.8%)	
REVENUES AND EXPENSES	$000's	%	$000's	%
Total Revenue	95.3	100.0	329.9	100.0
Sales of goods & services	0.0	0.0	320.8	97.2
All other revenues	0.0	0.0	9.1	2.8
Cost of Sales (direct expenses)	19.2	20.2	83.3	25.3
Wages and benefits	0.6	0.6	41.4	12.5
Purchases, materials & sub-contracts	18.7	19.6	42.9	13.0
Opening inventory	0.9	0.9	7.8	2.4
Closing inventory	0.9	0.9	8.7	2.6
Operating expenses (indirect expenses)	58.2	61.1	229.1	69.4
Labour and commissions	9.5	10.0	94.7	28.7
Amortization and depletion	4.0	4.2	13.3	4.0
Repairs and maintenance	1.4	1.5	9.0	2.7
Utilities and telecommunication	5.6	5.9	17.4	5.3
Rent	20.9	21.9	35.7	10.8
Interest and bank charges	1.4	1.5	4.2	1.3
Professional and business fees	1.4	1.5	6.5	2.0
Advertising and promotion	0.5	0.5	4.2	1.3
Delivery, shipping and warehouse	0.3	0.3	1.7	0.5
Insurance	1.3	1.4	4.8	1.5
Other expenses	11.9	12.5	37.4	11.3
Total Expenses	77.4	81.2	312.4	94.7
Net Income / **Net Profit**	17.9	18.8	**17.5**	**5.3**
Gross Profit Margin (%)		79.8		74.0

This Canadian industry comprises establishments primarily engaged in laundering, dry cleaning, and pressing apparel and linens of all types, including leather. These establishments may also provide clothing repair and alteration services. Laundry pick-up and delivery stations, operated independently from power laundries and dry-cleaning plants, and establishments primarily engaged in cleaning, repairing and storing fur garments are also included.

Drywall and Insulation Contractors
NAICS 238310
(9,893 Reporting)

	Unincorporated		Incorporated	
No. of Businesses Reporting	6,218 (62.9%)		3,675 (37.1%)	
REVENUES AND EXPENSES	$000's	%	$000's	%
Total Revenue	91.3	100.0	649.1	100.0
Sales of goods & services	0.0	0.0	641.1	98.8
All other revenues	0.0	0.0	7.9	1.2
Cost of Sales (direct expenses)	28.4	31.1	418.9	64.5
Wages and benefits	2.5	2.8	122.6	18.9
Purchases, materials & sub-contracts	25.8	28.3	297.4	45.8
Opening inventory	0.3	0.3	15.8	2.4
Closing inventory	0.2	0.3	16.9	2.6
Operating expenses (indirect expenses)	28.5	31.2	178.7	27.5
Labour and commissions	5.0	5.5	84.1	13.0
Amortization and depletion	2.8	3.1	10.8	1.7
Repairs and maintenance	0.3	0.3	4.9	0.8
Utilities and telecommunication	1.7	1.9	6.3	1.0
Rent	0.5	0.5	8.1	1.3
Interest and bank charges	0.5	0.6	1.8	0.3
Professional and business fees	1.0	1.1	9.0	1.4
Advertising and promotion	0.4	0.4	5.4	0.8
Delivery, shipping and warehouse	0.1	0.1	0.3	0.0
Insurance	0.6	0.6	5.6	0.9
Other expenses	15.8	17.3	42.3	6.5
Total Expenses	57.0	62.4	597.6	92.1
Net Income / **Net Profit**	34.4	37.6	**51.4**	**7.9**
Gross Profit Margin (%)		68.9		34.7

This Canadian industry comprises establishments primarily engaged in drywall, plaster work, and building insulation work. Plaster work includes applying plain or ornamental plaster, and installation of lath to receive plaster. The work performed may include new work, additions, alterations, maintenance, and repairs.

Employment Placement Agencies and Executive Search Services
NAICS 561310
(2,666 Reporting)

	Unincorporated		Incorporated	
No. of Businesses Reporting	638 (23.9%)		2,028 (76.1%)	
REVENUES AND EXPENSES	$000's	%	$000's	%
Total Revenue	102.8	100.0	560.5	100.0
Sales of goods & services	0.0	0.0	511.1	91.2
All other revenues	0.0	0.0	49.4	8.8
Cost of Sales (direct expenses)	28.2	27.4	122.1	21.8
Wages and benefits	0.7	0.7	63.5	11.3
Purchases, materials & sub-contracts	27.7	26.9	58.8	10.5
Opening inventory	1.0	1.0	1.2	0.2
Closing inventory	1.3	1.2	1.3	0.2
Operating expenses (indirect expenses)	27.4	26.7	343.6	61.3
Labour and commissions	4.3	4.2	230.4	41.1
Amortization and depletion	1.8	1.7	4.7	0.8
Repairs and maintenance	0.8	0.8	1.9	0.3
Utilities and telecommunication	2.5	2.4	6.3	1.1
Rent	1.9	1.8	16.2	2.9
Interest and bank charges	0.7	0.6	1.3	0.2
Professional and business fees	1.3	1.3	27.0	4.8
Advertising and promotion	1.2	1.2	11.2	2.0
Delivery, shipping and warehouse	0.1	0.1	0.3	0.0
Insurance	0.6	0.6	3.6	0.6
Other expenses	12.3	12.0	40.6	7.3
Total Expenses	55.6	54.1	465.7	83.1
Net Income / **Net Profit**	47.2	45.9	**94.8**	**16.9**
Gross Profit Margin (%)		72.6		76.1

This Canadian industry comprises establishments primarily engaged in listing employment vacancies and selecting, referring and placing applicants in employment, either on a permanent or temporary basis. The individuals placed are not employees of the placement agencies.

Engineering Services NAICS 541330 (17,906 Reporting)				
	Unincorporated		Incorporated	
No. of Businesses Reporting	4,921 (27.5%)		12,985 (72.5%)	
REVENUES AND EXPENSES	$000's	%	$000's	%
Total Revenue	100.8	100.0	433.5	100.0
Sales of goods & services	0.0	0.0	414.5	95.6
All other revenues	0.0	0.0	19.0	4.4
Cost of Sales (direct expenses)	6.0	6.0	87.0	20.1
Wages and benefits	0.3	0.3	28.8	6.6
Purchases, materials & sub-contracts	5.8	5.7	62.0	14.3
Opening inventory	0.5	0.5	8.7	2.0
Closing inventory	0.5	0.5	12.5	2.9
Operating expenses (indirect expenses)	25.0	24.8	251.0	57.9
Labour and commissions	3.6	3.5	143.6	33.1
Amortization and depletion	1.7	1.7	8.4	1.9
Repairs and maintenance	0.3	0.2	2.6	0.6
Utilities and telecommunication	1.3	1.3	5.4	1.2
Rent	0.8	0.8	12.7	2.9
Interest and bank charges	0.4	0.4	1.9	0.4
Professional and business fees	2.0	2.0	20.8	4.8
Advertising and promotion	0.3	0.3	5.8	1.3
Delivery, shipping and warehouse	0.1	0.1	0.4	0.1
Insurance	0.8	0.8	6.5	1.5
Other expenses	13.9	13.8	42.8	9.9
Total Expenses	31.1	30.8	338.0	78.0
Net Income / **Net Profit**	69.8	69.2	**95.5**	**22.0**
Gross Profit Margin (%)		94.0		79.0

This Canadian industry comprises establishments primarily engaged in applying principles of engineering in the design, development and utilization of machines, materials, instruments, structures, processes and systems. The assignments undertaken by these establishments may involve any of the following activities: the provision of advice, the preparation of feasibility studies, the preparation of preliminary and final plans and designs, the provision of technical services during the construction or installation phase, the inspection and evaluation of engineer projects, and related services.

Environmental Consulting
NAICS 541620
(3,682 Reporting)

	Unincorporated		Incorporated	
No. of Businesses Reporting	1,683 (45.7%)		1,999 (54.3%)	
REVENUES AND EXPENSES	$000's	%	$000's	%
Total Revenue	85.7	100.0	405.6	100.0
Sales of goods & services	0.0	0.0	386.1	95.2
All other revenues	0.0	0.0	19.5	4.8
Cost of Sales (direct expenses)	9.9	11.50	77.9	19.2
Wages and benefits	0.6	0.70	24.9	6.1
Purchases, materials & sub-contracts	9.3	10.90	55.0	13.6
Opening inventory	0.2	0.20	3.1	0.8
Closing inventory	0.2	0.20	5.1	1.3
Operating expenses (indirect expenses)	25.5	29.70	237.5	58.5
Labour and commissions	3.2	3.70	118.6	29.2
Amortization and depletion	2.3	2.60	10.3	2.5
Repairs and maintenance	0.4	0.50	4.2	1.0
Utilities and telecommunication	1.8	2.10	6.0	1.5
Rent	0.7	0.80	11.6	2.8
Interest and bank charges	0.4	0.50	2.2	0.6
Professional and business fees	1.4	1.70	22.8	5.6
Advertising and promotion	0.5	0.60	5.7	1.4
Delivery, shipping and warehouse	0.1	0.20	0.6	0.1
Insurance	0.7	0.80	5.3	1.3
Other expenses	13.9	16.20	50.2	12.4
Total Expenses	35.3	41.20	315.3	77.7
Net Income / **Net Profit**	50.4	58.80	**90.3**	**22.3**
Gross Profit Margin (%)		88.5		79.8

This Canadian industry comprises establishments primarily engaged in providing advice and assistance to other organizations on environmental issues, such as the control of environmental contamination from pollutants, toxic substances and hazardous materials. These establishments identify problems, measure and evaluate risks, and recommend solutions. They employ a multi-disciplined staff of scientists, engineers and other technicians, with expertise in areas such as air and water quality, asbestos contamination, remediation and environmental law.

Farming - Beef Cattle Ranching and Farming, Including Feedlots
NAICS 112110
(2,563 Reporting)

	Unincorporated		Incorporated	
No. of Businesses Reporting	0		2,563 (100.0%)	
REVENUES AND EXPENSES	$000's	%	$000's	%
Total Revenue	0.0	0.0	601.3	100.0
Sales of goods & services	0.0	0.0	523.7	87.1
All other revenues	0.0	0.0	77.5	12.9
Cost of Sales (direct expenses)	0.0	0.0	23.5	3.9
Wages and benefits	0.0	0.0	1.0	0.2
Purchases, materials & sub-contracts	0.0	0.0	24.1	4.0
Opening inventory	0.0	0.0	13.0	2.2
Closing inventory	0.0	0.0	14.7	2.4
Operating expenses (indirect expenses)	0.0	0.0	720.7	119.9
Labour and commissions	0.0	0.0	41.7	6.9
Amortization and depletion	0.0	0.0	49.4	8.2
Repairs and maintenance	0.0	0.0	26.6	4.4
Utilities and telecommunication	0.0	0.0	30.6	5.1
Rent	0.0	0.0	21.2	3.5
Interest and bank charges	0.0	0.0	20.2	3.4
Professional and business fees	0.0	0.0	8.0	1.3
Advertising and promotion	0.0	0.0	3.2	0.5
Delivery, shipping and warehouse	0.0	0.0	6.0	1.0
Insurance	0.0	0.0	9.5	1.6
Other expenses	0.0	0.0	504.3	83.9
Total Expenses	0.0	0.0	744.2	123.8
Net Income (Loss) / **Net Profit (Loss)**	0.0	0.0	(143.0)	(23.8)
Gross Profit Margin (%)	0.0	0.0		95.5

This Canadian industry comprises establishments primarily engaged in raising and fattening cattle. The raising of cattle for dairy herd replacements is also included in this industry.

Farming - Dairy Cattle and Milk Production
NAICS 112120
(6,647 Reporting)

	Unincorporated		Incorporated	
No. of Businesses Reporting	0		6,647 (100.0%)	
REVENUES AND EXPENSES	$000's	%	$000's	%
Total Revenue	0.0	0.0	677.2	100.0
Sales of goods & services	0.0	0.0	632.1	93.3
All other revenues	0.0	0.0	45.2	6.7
Cost of Sales (direct expenses)	0.0	0.0	11.1	1.6
Wages and benefits	0.0	0.0	1.7	0.3
Purchases, materials & sub-contracts	0.0	0.0	9.5	1.4
Opening inventory	0.0	0.0	5.1	0.8
Closing inventory	0.0	0.0	5.3	0.8
Operating expenses (indirect expenses)	0.0	0.0	724.5	107.0
Labour and commissions	0.0	0.0	68.3	10.1
Amortization and depletion	0.0	0.0	72.7	10.7
Repairs and maintenance	0.0	0.0	36.0	5.3
Utilities and telecommunication	0.0	0.0	34.9	5.1
Rent	0.0	0.0	19.2	2.8
Interest and bank charges	0.0	0.0	40.7	6.0
Professional and business fees	0.0	0.0	7.1	1.1
Advertising and promotion	0.0	0.0	12.4	1.8
Delivery, shipping and warehouse	0.0	0.0	7.3	1.1
Insurance	0.0	0.0	14.1	2.1
Other expenses	0.0	0.0	411.7	60.8
Total Expenses	0.0	0.0	735.6	108.6
Net Income (Loss) / **Net Profit (Loss)**	0.0	0.0	**(58.4)**	**(8.6)**
Gross Profit Margin (%)	0.0	0.0		98.2

This Canadian industry comprises establishments primarily engaged in milking dairy cattle.

Farming - Other Grain
NAICS 111190
(5,933 Reporting)

	Unincorporated		Incorporated	
No. of Businesses Reporting	0		5,933 (100.0%)	
REVENUES AND EXPENSES	$000's	%	$000's	%
Total Revenue	0.0	0.0	729.9	100.0
Sales of goods & services	0.0	0.0	633.6	86.8
All other revenues	0.0	0.0	96.4	13.2
Cost of Sales (direct expenses)	0.0	0.0	11.3	1.5
Wages and benefits	0.0	0.0	1.0	0.1
Purchases, materials & sub-contracts	0.0	0.0	10.4	1.4
Opening inventory	0.0	0.0	4.6	0.6
Closing inventory	0.0	0.0	4.7	0.6
Operating expenses (indirect expenses)	0.0	0.0	755.3	103.5
Labour and commissions	0.0	0.0	43.1	5.9
Amortization and depletion	0.0	0.0	95.7	13.1
Repairs and maintenance	0.0	0.0	34.9	4.8
Utilities and telecommunication	0.0	0.0	41.3	5.7
Rent	0.0	0.0	51.5	7.1
Interest and bank charges	0.0	0.0	22.6	3.1
Professional and business fees	0.0	0.0	8.2	1.1
Advertising and promotion	0.0	0.0	1.9	0.3
Delivery, shipping and warehouse	0.0	0.0	10.0	1.4
Insurance	0.0	0.0	10.8	1.5
Other expenses	0.0	0.0	435.2	59.6
Total Expenses	0.0	0.0	766.6	105.0
Net Income (Loss) / **Net Profit (Loss)**	0.0	0.0	**(36.7)**	**(5.0)**
Gross Profit Margin (%)	0.0	0.0		98.2

This Canadian industry comprises establishments, not classified to any other Canadian industry, primarily engaged in growing grains. Farms primarily engaged in growing a combination of oilseeds and grains are also included. Illustrative example(s): buckwheat farming; grain growing (except rice, wheat and corn) oil seed and grain farming; combination; wild rice, farming.

Farming - Wheat NAICS 111140 (1,856 Reporting)				
	Unincorporated		Incorporated	
No. of Businesses Reporting	0 (0%)		1,856 (100%)	
REVENUES AND EXPENSES	$000's	%	$000's	%
Total Revenue	0.0	0.0	695.4	100.0
Sales of goods & services	0.0	0.0	597.8	86.0
All other revenues	0.0	0.0	97.6	14.0
Cost of Sales (direct expenses)	0.0	0.0	10.8	1.6
Wages and benefits	0.0	0.0	0.4	0.1
Purchases, materials & sub-contracts	0.0	0.0	11.5	1.6
Opening inventory	0.0	0.0	6.4	0.9
Closing inventory	0.0	0.0	7.4	1.1
Operating expenses (indirect expenses)	0.0	0.0	688.9	99.1
Labour and commissions	0.0	0.0	38.5	5.5
Amortization and depletion	0.0	0.0	90.8	13.1
Repairs and maintenance	0.0	0.0	32.4	4.7
Utilities and telecommunication	0.0	0.0	38.1	5.5
Rent	0.0	0.0	42.7	6.1
Interest and bank charges	0.0	0.0	20.2	2.9
Professional and business fees	0.0	0.0	10.1	1.4
Advertising and promotion	0.0	0.0	2.0	0.3
Delivery, shipping and warehouse	0.0	0.0	10.1	1.5
Insurance	0.0	0.0	10.6	1.5
Other expenses	0.0	0.0	393.6	56.6
Total Expenses	0.0	0.0	699.7	100.6
Net Income (Loss) / **Net Profit (Loss)**	0.0	0.0	**(4.3)**	**(0.6)**
Gross Profit Margin (%)		0.0		98.2

This Canadian industry comprises establishments primarily engaged in growing wheat.

Finish Carpentry Contractors
NAICS 238350
(13,349 Reporting)

	Unincorporated		Incorporated	
No. of Businesses Reporting	7,510 (56.3%)		5,839 (43.7%)	
REVENUES AND EXPENSES	$000's	%	$000's	%
Total Revenue	97.3	100.0	457.1	100.0
Sales of goods & services	0.0	0.0	451.9	98.9
All other revenues	0.0	0.0	5.2	1.1
Cost of Sales (direct expenses)	35.9	36.9	269.7	59.0
Wages and benefits	3.3	3.4	63.8	14.0
Purchases, materials & sub-contracts	32.6	33.5	210.8	46.1
Opening inventory	0.8	0.8	25.4	5.6
Closing inventory	0.8	0.8	30.2	6.6
Operating expenses (indirect expenses)	30.6	31.4	155.4	34.0
Labour and commissions	5.7	5.8	71.1	15.5
Amortization and depletion	3.4	3.4	9.7	2.1
Repairs and maintenance	0.5	0.5	4.0	0.9
Utilities and telecommunication	1.9	1.9	6.1	1.3
Rent	1.0	1.0	11.1	2.4
Interest and bank charges	0.7	0.8	2.1	0.5
Professional and business fees	1.0	1.0	6.6	1.4
Advertising and promotion	0.4	0.4	5.6	1.2
Delivery, shipping and warehouse	0.1	0.1	0.4	0.1
Insurance	0.9	0.9	4.5	1.0
Other expenses	15.2	15.6	34.2	7.5
Total Expenses	66.5	68.3	425.1	93.0
Net Income / **Net Profit**	30.8	31.7	**31.9**	**7.0**
Gross Profit Margin (%)		63.1		40.3

This Canadian industry comprises establishments primarily engaged in finish carpentry work. The work performed may include new work, additions, alterations, maintenance, and repairs. Carpentry work (except framing).

Fishing (Salt Water)
NAICS 114113
(13,176 Reporting)

	Unincorporated		Incorporated	
No. of Businesses Reporting	10,489 (79.6%)		2,687 (20.4%)	
REVENUES AND EXPENSES	$000's	%	$000's	%
Total Revenue	83.1	100.0	396.2	100.0
Sales of goods & services	0.0	0.0	372.3	94.0
All other revenues	0.0	0.0	24.0	6.0
Cost of Sales (direct expenses)	0.0	0.0	49.6	12.5
Wages and benefits	0.0	0.0	11.7	2.9
Purchases, materials & sub-contracts	0.0	0.0	39.4	9.9
Opening inventory	0.0	0.0	5.9	1.5
Closing inventory	0.0	0.0	7.4	1.9
Operating expenses (indirect expenses)	53.6	64.5	283.8	71.6
Labour and commissions	18.5	22.3	121.1	30.6
Amortization and depletion	6.9	8.4	27.9	7.0
Repairs and maintenance	3.2	3.8	19.7	5.0
Utilities and telecommunication	5.0	6.0	24.0	6.1
Rent	0.0	0.0	12.0	3.0
Interest and bank charges	2.1	2.5	7.1	1.8
Professional and business fees	0.4	0.5	8.5	2.1
Advertising and promotion	0.0	0.0	1.1	0.3
Delivery, shipping and warehouse	0.0	0.0	0.8	0.2
Insurance	1.0	1.2	6.8	1.7
Other expenses	16.6	20.0	54.7	13.8
Total Expenses	53.6	64.5	333.4	84.1
Net Income / **Net Profit**	29.5	35.5	**62.9**	**15.9**
Gross Profit Margin (%)		100.0		86.7

This Canadian industry comprises establishments primarily engaged in catching all types of finfish, shellfish and other marine animals, and harvesting other sea products.

Fitness and Recreational Sports Centres
NAICS 713940
(3,535 Reporting)

	Unincorporated		Incorporated	
No. of Businesses Reporting	798 (22.6%)		2,737 (77.4%)	
REVENUES AND EXPENSES	$000's	%	$000's	%
Total Revenue	80.4	100.0	406.5	100.0
Sales of goods & services	0.0	0.0	350.5	86.2
All other revenues	0.0	0.0	56.0	13.8
Cost of Sales (direct expenses)	10.3	12.8	44.1	10.8
Wages and benefits	1.7	2.1	15.1	3.7
Purchases, materials & sub-contracts	8.7	10.8	29.3	7.2
Opening inventory	0.7	0.9	4.1	1.0
Closing inventory	0.8	1.0	4.3	1.1
Operating expenses (indirect expenses)	54.8	68.2	341.8	84.1
Labour and commissions	10.0	12.5	122.6	30.2
Amortization and depletion	3.9	4.8	25.0	6.1
Repairs and maintenance	1.7	2.2	16.4	4.0
Utilities and telecommunication	3.5	4.4	16.3	4.0
Rent	13.1	16.2	62.4	15.3
Interest and bank charges	2.2	2.8	7.2	1.8
Professional and business fees	1.3	1.6	15.2	3.7
Advertising and promotion	2.7	3.3	12.7	3.1
Delivery, shipping and warehouse	0.1	0.1	0.7	0.2
Insurance	1.1	1.4	4.5	1.1
Other expenses	15.2	18.9	58.9	14.5
Total Expenses	65.1	81.0	385.9	94.9
Net Income / **Net Profit**	15.3	19.0	**20.6**	**5.1**
Gross Profit Margin (%)		87.2		87.4

This Canadian industry comprises establishments primarily engaged in operating health clubs and similar facilities featuring exercise and other active physical fitness conditioning, or recreational sports activities, such as swimming, skating or racquet sports.

Floor Covering Stores
NAICS 442210
(1,462 Reporting)

REVENUES AND EXPENSES	Unincorporated		Incorporated	
No. of Businesses Reporting	133 (9.1%)		1,329 (90.9%)	
REVENUES AND EXPENSES	$000's	%	$000's	%
Total Revenue	200.1	100.0	1102.6	100.0
Sales of goods & services	0.0	0.0	1082.9	98.2
All other revenues	0.0	0.0	19.7	1.8
Cost of Sales (direct expenses)	111.7	55.8	714.4	64.8
Wages and benefits	2.5	1.2	48.7	4.4
Purchases, materials & sub-contracts	103.6	51.8	673.2	61.1
Opening inventory	23.7	11.8	153.9	14.0
Closing inventory	18.0	9.0	161.4	14.6
Operating expenses (indirect expenses)	53.0	26.5	338.9	30.7
Labour and commissions	9.1	4.5	155.7	14.1
Amortization and depletion	2.8	1.4	12.7	1.2
Repairs and maintenance	1.0	0.5	8.7	0.8
Utilities and telecommunication	3.6	1.8	13.5	1.2
Rent	6.9	3.5	42.0	3.8
Interest and bank charges	2.3	1.1	5.7	0.5
Professional and business fees	2.4	1.2	10.1	0.9
Advertising and promotion	4.5	2.2	24.3	2.2
Delivery, shipping and warehouse	0.7	0.4	1.6	0.1
Insurance	1.2	0.6	6.7	0.6
Other expenses	18.5	9.3	57.9	5.3
Total Expenses	164.7	82.3	1053.3	95.5
Net Income / **Net Profit**	35.4	17.7	**49.3**	**4.5**
Gross Profit Margin (%)		44.2		34.0

This Canadian industry comprises establishments primarily engaged in retailing new floor coverings, such as rugs and carpets, vinyl floor coverings, wood floor coverings, and floor tiles, except ceramic. These establishments also typically provide installation and repair services.

Flooring Contractors NAICS 238330 (6,955 Reporting)				
	Unincorporated		Incorporated	
No. of Businesses Reporting	4,614 (65.5%)		2,341 (34.5%)	
REVENUES AND EXPENSES	$000's	%	$000's	%
Total Revenue	95.5	100.0	479.5	100.0
Sales of goods & services	0.0	0.0	475.5	99.2
All other revenues	0.0	0.0	4.0	0.8
Cost of Sales (direct expenses)	29.8	31.2	294.7	61.5
Wages and benefits	2.8	2.9	58.0	12.1
Purchases, materials & sub-contracts	26.9	28.2	240.1	50.1
Opening inventory	0.6	0.6	27.2	5.7
Closing inventory	0.5	0.5	30.5	6.4
Operating expenses (indirect expenses)	31.3	32.8	153.2	31.9
Labour and commissions	5.3	5.5	69.4	14.5
Amortization and depletion	2.8	2.9	8.7	1.8
Repairs and maintenance	0.3	0.4	3.7	0.8
Utilities and telecommunication	1.9	2.0	6.0	1.3
Rent	0.6	0.6	10.8	2.3
Interest and bank charges	0.6	0.6	2.0	0.4
Professional and business fees	1.0	1.1	6.7	1.4
Advertising and promotion	0.5	0.5	6.3	1.3
Delivery, shipping and warehouse	0.1	0.1	0.3	0.1
Insurance	0.7	0.7	4.3	0.9
Other expenses	17.5	18.4	35.0	7.3
Total Expenses	61.1	64.0	447.9	93.4
Net Income / **Net Profit**	34.4	36.0	**31.6**	**6.6**
Gross Profit Margin (%)		68.8		38.0

This Canadian industry comprises establishments primarily engaged in the installation of resilient floor tile, carpeting, linoleum, and hardwood flooring. The work performed may include new work, additions, alterations, maintenance, and repairs.

Florists NAICS 453110 (2,711 Reporting)				
	Unincorporated		Incorporated	
No. of Businesses Reporting	1,302 (48.0%)		1409 (52.0%)	
REVENUES AND EXPENSES	$000's	%	$000's	%
Total Revenue	140.2	100.0	369.5	100.0
Sales of goods & services	0.0	0.0	364.6	98.7
All other revenues	0.0	0.0	4.8	1.3
Cost of Sales (direct expenses)	71.3	50.9	178.8	48.4
Wages and benefits	2.6	1.8	15.2	4.1
Purchases, materials & sub-contracts	68.1	48.5	163.5	44.3
Opening inventory	13.3	9.4	30.0	8.1
Closing inventory	12.6	9.0	30.0	8.1
Operating expenses (indirect expenses)	56.8	40.5	185.3	50.1
Labour and commissions	13.1	9.3	81.0	21.9
Amortization and depletion	2.7	2.0	6.6	1.8
Repairs and maintenance	1.4	1.0	3.7	1.0
Utilities and telecommunication	5.1	3.7	9.8	2.7
Rent	10.6	7.6	25.3	6.8
Interest and bank charges	3.0	2.2	2.5	0.7
Professional and business fees	1.8	1.3	4.7	1.3
Advertising and promotion	2.8	2.0	9.3	2.5
Delivery, shipping and warehouse	2.0	1.4	5.1	1.4
Insurance	1.3	0.9	3.3	0.9
Other expenses	12.9	9.2	33.8	9.1
Total Expenses	128.1	91.4	364.0	98.5
Net Income / **Net Profit**	12.1	8.6	**5.4**	**1.5**
Gross Profit Margin (%)		49.1		51.0

This Canadian industry comprises establishments primarily engaged in retailing cut flowers, floral arrangements, and potted plants grown elsewhere. These establishments typically prepare the arrangements they sell.

Framing Contractors
NAICS 238130
(3,526 Reporting)

	Unincorporated		Incorporated	
No. of Businesses Reporting	1,159 (32.9%)		2,367 (67.1%)	
REVENUES AND EXPENSES	$000's	%	$000's	%
Total Revenue	114.5	100.0	417.5	100.0
Sales of goods & services	0.0	0.0	412.5	98.8
All other revenues	0.0	0.0	5.1	1.2
Cost of Sales (direct expenses)	40.5	35.4	231.0	55.3
Wages and benefits	8.3	7.3	63.5	15.2
Purchases, materials & sub-contracts	32.1	28.0	173.4	41.5
Opening inventory	0.6	0.5	29.2	7.0
Closing inventory	0.5	0.4	35.2	8.4
Operating expenses (indirect expenses)	36.8	32.1	141.5	33.9
Labour and commissions	11.3	9.8	71.6	17.1
Amortization and depletion	3.4	2.9	9.5	2.3
Repairs and maintenance	0.6	0.5	3.5	0.8
Utilities and telecommunication	1.8	1.5	4.2	1.0
Rent	0.7	0.6	6.5	1.6
Interest and bank charges	0.7	0.6	1.6	0.4
Professional and business fees	1.1	1.0	7.2	1.7
Advertising and promotion	0.3	0.3	3.3	0.8
Delivery, shipping and warehouse	0.1	0.0	0.1	0.0
Insurance	0.9	0.8	4.3	1.0
Other expenses	16.1	14.0	29.8	7.1
Total Expenses	77.3	67.5	372.5	89.2
Net Income / **Net Profit**	37.2	32.5	**45.0**	**10.8**
Gross Profit Margin (%)		64.6		44.0

This Canadian industry comprises establishments primarily engaged in structural framing and sheathing using materials other than structural steel or concrete. The work performed may include new work, additions, alterations, maintenance, and repairs.

Funeral Homes
NAICS 812210
(1,137 Reporting)

	Unincorporated		Incorporated	
No. of Businesses Reporting	100 (8.8%)		1,037 (91.2%)	
REVENUES AND EXPENSES	$000's	%	$000's	%
Total Revenue	119.9	100.0	783.2	100.0
Sales of goods & services	0.0	0.0	748.6	95.6
All other revenues	0.0	0.0	34.6	4.4
Cost of Sales (direct expenses)	23.8	19.8	224.7	28.7
Wages and benefits	1.2	1.0	29.5	3.8
Purchases, materials & sub-contracts	23.4	19.5	196.5	25.1
Opening inventory	3.6	3.0	38.0	4.9
Closing inventory	4.4	3.7	39.3	5.0
Operating expenses (indirect expenses)	66.2	55.2	471.4	60.2
Labour and commissions	12.2	10.2	187.8	24.0
Amortization and depletion	4.6	3.8	37.0	4.7
Repairs and maintenance	3.5	2.9	25.5	3.3
Utilities and telecommunication	5.3	4.4	24.2	3.1
Rent	4.6	3.9	20.7	2.6
Interest and bank charges	1.5	1.2	16.9	2.2
Professional and business fees	1.8	1.5	22.1	2.8
Advertising and promotion	2.3	1.9	25.0	3.2
Delivery, shipping and warehouse	0.2	0.2	1.6	0.2
Insurance	1.4	1.1	11.0	1.4
Other expenses	28.9	24.1	99.7	12.7
Total Expenses	90.0	75.0	696.1	88.9
Net Income / **Net Profit**	29.9	25.0	**87.1**	**11.1**
Gross Profit Margin (%)		80.2		70.0

This Canadian industry comprises establishments primarily engaged in preparing the dead for burial or interment and conducting funerals.

Furniture Stores NAICS 442110 (2,829 Reporting)				
	Unincorporated		Incorporated	
No. of Businesses Reporting	674 (23.8%)		2,155 (76.2%)	
REVENUES AND EXPENSES	$000's	%	$000's	%
Total Revenue	156.2	100.0	1051.6	100.0
Sales of goods & services	0.0	0.0	1029.9	97.9
All other revenues	0.0	0.0	21.7	2.1
Cost of Sales (direct expenses)	82.9	53.1	619.8	58.9
Wages and benefits	1.5	1.0	13.3	1.3
Purchases, materials & sub-contracts	79.4	50.8	612.6	58.3
Opening inventory	28.8	18.5	221.9	21.1
Closing inventory	26.8	17.2	228.0	21.7
Operating expenses (indirect expenses)	53.8	34.5	410.6	39.0
Labour and commissions	7.9	5.0	167.8	16.0
Amortization and depletion	2.9	1.9	12.8	1.2
Repairs and maintenance	1.5	0.9	10.3	1.0
Utilities and telecommunication	4.4	2.8	16.4	1.6
Rent	11.7	7.5	73.2	7.0
Interest and bank charges	2.7	1.7	6.6	0.6
Professional and business fees	1.6	1.0	12.0	1.1
Advertising and promotion	3.4	2.2	37.8	3.6
Delivery, shipping and warehouse	1.8	1.1	6.2	0.6
Insurance	1.5	0.9	6.9	0.7
Other expenses	14.5	9.3	60.5	5.8
Total Expenses	136.7	87.6	1030.4	98.0
Net Income / **Net Profit**	19.4	12.4	**21.2**	**2.0**
Gross Profit Margin (%)		46.9		39.8

This Canadian industry comprises establishments primarily engaged in retailing new household and office furniture. These establishments may also retail major appliances, home electronics, home furnishings and floor coverings, and may provide interior decorating services.

Gasoline Stations with Convenience Stores
NAICS 447110
(3,446 Reporting)

	Unincorporated		Incorporated	
No. of Businesses Reporting	537 (15.6%)		2,909 (84.4%)	
REVENUES AND EXPENSES	$000's	%	$000's	%
Total Revenue	838.7	100.0	1726.7	100.0
Sales of goods & services	0.0	0.0	1692.2	98.0
All other revenues	0.0	0.0	34.5	2.0
Cost of Sales (direct expenses)	722.2	86.1	1416.3	82.0
Wages and benefits	5.0	0.6	15.8	0.9
Purchases, materials & sub-contracts	715.7	85.3	1501.0	86.9
Opening inventory	28.5	3.4	63.2	3.7
Closing inventory	27.0	3.2	163.7	9.5
Operating expenses (indirect expenses)	91.8	10.9	290.1	16.8
Labour and commissions	39.6	4.7	135.6	7.9
Amortization and depletion	3.9	0.5	12.8	0.7
Repairs and maintenance	4.3	0.5	12.4	0.7
Utilities and telecommunication	7.3	0.9	14.7	0.8
Rent	8.9	1.1	42.9	2.5
Interest and bank charges	5.4	0.6	7.4	0.4
Professional and business fees	2.6	0.3	8.4	0.5
Advertising and promotion	1.0	0.1	3.3	0.2
Delivery, shipping and warehouse	0.3	0.0	0.4	0.0
Insurance	2.9	0.4	5.1	0.3
Other expenses	15.4	1.8	47.1	2.7
Total Expenses	813.9	97.0	1706.4	98.8
Net Income / **Net Profit**	24.8	3.0	**20.3**	**1.2**
Gross Profit Margin (%)		13.9		16.3

This Canadian industry comprises establishments primarily engaged in retailing automotive fuels combined with the retail sale of a limited line of merchandise, such as milk, bread, soft drinks and snacks in a convenience store setting. Establishments that operate such establishments on behalf of their owners are also included.

Gift, Novelty and Souvenir Stores
NAICS 453220
(3,868 Reporting)

	Unincorporated		Incorporated	
No. of Businesses Reporting	1,984 (51.3%)		1,884 (48.7%)	
REVENUES AND EXPENSES	$000's	%	$000's	%
Total Revenue	122.2	100.0	438.7	100.0
Sales of goods & services	0.0	0.0	414.7	94.5
All other revenues	0.0	0.0	24.1	5.5
Cost of Sales (direct expenses)	62.0	50.7	224.1	51.1
Wages and benefits	1.3	1.1	6.9	1.6
Purchases, materials & sub-contracts	59.7	48.8	217.4	49.6
Opening inventory	26.3	21.5	104.8	23.9
Closing inventory	25.3	20.7	105.1	24.0
Operating expenses (indirect expenses)	46.8	38.3	205.1	46.7
Labour and commissions	9.2	7.6	86.4	19.7
Amortization and depletion	2.0	1.6	7.7	1.8
Repairs and maintenance	1.0	0.8	3.7	0.8
Utilities and telecommunication	3.2	2.6	7.2	1.6
Rent	11.3	9.2	44.8	10.2
Interest and bank charges	2.7	2.2	2.8	0.6
Professional and business fees	1.4	1.2	6.4	1.5
Advertising and promotion	2.1	1.7	7.5	1.7
Delivery, shipping and warehouse	1.3	1.0	1.5	0.3
Insurance	1.1	0.9	3.3	0.8
Other expenses	11.5	9.4	33.8	7.7
Total Expenses	108.7	89.0	429.2	97.8
Net Income / **Net Profit**	13.5	11.0	**9.6**	**2.2**
Gross Profit Margin (%)		49.3		46.0

This Canadian industry comprises establishments primarily engaged in retailing new gifts, novelty merchandise, souvenirs, greeting cards, seasonal and holiday decorations, and curios. These establishments may also retail stationery.

Golf Courses and Country Clubs
NAICS 713910
(1,806 Reporting)

	Unincorporated		Incorporated	
No. of Businesses Reporting	148 (8.2%)		1,658 (91.8%)	
REVENUES AND EXPENSES	$000's	%	$000's	%
Total Revenue	136.0	100.0	922.4	100.0
Sales of goods & services	0.0	0.0	787.0	85.3
All other revenues	0.0	0.0	135.4	14.7
Cost of Sales (direct expenses)	29.5	21.7	225.9	24.5
Wages and benefits	5.6	4.1	59.9	6.5
Purchases, materials & sub-contracts	23.6	17.4	168.0	18.2
Opening inventory	3.8	2.8	37.7	4.1
Closing inventory	3.5	2.6	39.7	4.3
Operating expenses (indirect expenses)	76.2	56.0	708.4	76.8
Labour and commissions	20.7	15.2	261.2	28.3
Amortization and depletion	7.0	5.1	80.8	8.8
Repairs and maintenance	5.2	3.8	68.5	7.4
Utilities and telecommunication	5.5	4.1	28.6	3.1
Rent	5.4	3.9	32.7	3.5
Interest and bank charges	3.5	2.5	31.4	3.4
Professional and business fees	1.4	1.0	27.6	3.0
Advertising and promotion	2.0	1.5	13.2	1.4
Delivery, shipping and warehouse	0.2	0.2	1.0	0.1
Insurance	2.0	1.5	12.8	1.4
Other expenses	23.3	17.1	150.6	16.3
Total Expenses	105.7	77.7	934.3	101.3
Net Income / **Net Profit**	30.3	22.3	**11.9**	**1.3**
Gross Profit Margin (%)		78.3		71.3

This Canadian industry comprises establishments primarily engaged in operating golf courses and country clubs that operate golf courses along with dining facilities and other recreational facilities. These establishments often provide food and beverage services, equipment rental services and golf instruction services.

Graphic Design Services NAICS 541430 (5,368 Reporting)				
	Unincorporated		Incorporated	
No. of Businesses Reporting	2,711 (50.5%)		2,657 (49.5%)	
REVENUES AND EXPENSES	$000's	%	$000's	%
Total Revenue	70.2	100.0	348.8	100.0
Sales of goods & services	0.0	0.0	343.3	98.4
All other revenues	0.0	0.0	5.6	1.6
Cost of Sales (direct expenses)	12.0	17.10	132.5	38.0
Wages and benefits	0.6	0.90	32.4	9.3
Purchases, materials & sub-contracts	11.4	16.30	100.5	28.8
Opening inventory	0.2	0.30	5.4	1.6
Closing inventory	0.2	0.30	5.8	1.7
Operating expenses (indirect expenses)	19.9	28.30	176.1	50.5
Labour and commissions	1.7	2.40	92.6	26.5
Amortization and depletion	1.8	2.60	7.4	2.1
Repairs and maintenance	0.3	0.40	2.2	0.6
Utilities and telecommunication	1.7	2.40	5.9	1.7
Rent	1.2	1.80	16.1	4.6
Interest and bank charges	0.4	0.60	1.2	0.3
Professional and business fees	1.1	1.50	10.8	3.1
Advertising and promotion	0.6	0.80	6.7	1.9
Delivery, shipping and warehouse	0.2	0.30	0.7	0.2
Insurance	0.2	0.40	2.6	0.8
Other expenses	10.7	15.20	30.0	8.6
Total Expenses	31.9	45.40	308.6	88.5
Net Income / **Net Profit**	38.3	54.60	**40.2**	**11.5**
Gross Profit Margin (%)		82.9		61.4

This Canadian industry comprises establishments primarily engaged in planning, designing and managing the production of visual communication, so as to convey specific messages or concepts, clarify complex information or project visual identities. These services include designing the visual layout of printed materials, web pages, packaging labels and graphics, advertising, signage systems, logos and corporate identification. This Canadian industry also includes commercial artists engaged exclusively in generating drawings and illustrations requiring technical accuracy or interpretative skills.

Health Care Services (Home)
NAICS 621610
(1,203 Reporting)

	Unincorporated		Incorporated	
No. of Businesses Reporting	716 (59.5%)		487 (40.5%)	
REVENUES AND EXPENSES	$000's	%	$000's	%
Total Revenue	63.9	100.0	861.0	100.0
Sales of goods & services	0.0	0.0	725.4	84.3
All other revenues	0.0	0.0	135.6	15.7
Cost of Sales (direct expenses)	4.9	7.7	159.8	18.6
Wages and benefits	0.2	0.3	98.0	11.4
Purchases, materials & sub-contracts	4.7	7.3	64.3	7.5
Opening inventory	0.2	0.3	8.4	1.0
Closing inventory	0.1	0.2	10.9	1.3
Operating expenses (indirect expenses)	24.6	38.6	625.1	72.6
Labour and commissions	6.3	9.8	421.6	49.0
Amortization and depletion	1.7	2.6	16.2	1.9
Repairs and maintenance	0.6	0.9	4.1	0.5
Utilities and telecommunication	1.5	2.4	8.6	1.0
Rent	1.4	2.2	24.6	2.9
Interest and bank charges	0.5	0.8	5.1	0.6
Professional and business fees	0.8	1.2	40.0	4.6
Advertising and promotion	0.6	0.9	11.3	1.3
Delivery, shipping and warehouse	0.1	0.1	0.3	0.0
Insurance	0.6	0.9	4.8	0.6
Other expenses	10.7	16.8	88.3	10.3
Total Expenses	29.6	46.3	784.8	91.2
Net Income / **Net Profit**	34.3	53.7	**76.2**	**8.8**
Gross Profit Margin (%)		92.3		78.0

This Canadian industry comprises establishments primarily engaged in providing skilled nursing services in the home, combined with a range of other home services, such as personal care services, homemaker and companion services, physical therapy, medical social services, counseling, occupational and vocational therapy, dietary and nutritional services, speech therapy, audiology, medical equipment and supplies, medications and intravenous therapy. Only establishments that provide nursing services in combination with the other services listed are included.

Hobby, Toy and Game Stores
NAICS 451120
(1,329 Reporting)

	Unincorporated		Incorporated	
No. of Businesses Reporting	709 (53.3%)		620 (46.7%)	
REVENUES AND EXPENSES	$000's	%	$000's	%
Total Revenue	142.9	100.0	545.0	100.0
Sales of goods & services	0.0	0.0	538.9	98.9
All other revenues	0.0	0.0	6.1	1.1
Cost of Sales (direct expenses)	83.8	58.6	313.2	57.5
Wages and benefits	1.5	1.1	9.4	1.7
Purchases, materials & sub-contracts	81.9	57.3	302.9	55.6
Opening inventory	39.3	27.5	122.5	22.5
Closing inventory	39.0	27.3	121.6	22.3
Operating expenses (indirect expenses)	47.6	33.3	222.2	40.8
Labour and commissions	8.1	5.7	97.3	17.9
Amortization and depletion	1.8	1.3	8.3	1.5
Repairs and maintenance	1.0	0.7	3.1	0.6
Utilities and telecommunication	3.4	2.4	7.6	1.4
Rent	11.6	8.1	47.0	8.6
Interest and bank charges	2.8	2.0	2.9	0.5
Professional and business fees	1.5	1.1	7.4	1.4
Advertising and promotion	2.3	1.6	10.5	1.9
Delivery, shipping and warehouse	2.3	1.6	1.7	0.3
Insurance	1.1	0.8	3.4	0.6
Other expenses	11.6	8.1	33.0	6.1
Total Expenses	131.4	92.0	535.4	98.2
Net Income / **Net Profit**	11.5	8.0	**9.6**	**1.8**
Gross Profit Margin (%)		41.4		41.9

This Canadian industry comprises establishments primarily engaged in retailing new toys, games, and hobby and craft supplies.

Human Resources Consulting Services
NAICS 541612
(3,298 Reporting)

	Unincorporated		Incorporated	
No. of Businesses Reporting	1,522 (46.1%)		1,776 (53.9%)	
REVENUES AND EXPENSES	$000's	%	$000's	%
Total Revenue	88.9	100.0	342.0	100.0
Sales of goods & services	0.0	0.0	308.0	90.1
All other revenues	0.0	0.0	34.0	9.9
Cost of Sales (direct expenses)	7.6	8.5	35.7	10.4
Wages and benefits	0.2	0.2	11.0	3.2
Purchases, materials & sub-contracts	7.3	8.2	25.7	7.5
Opening inventory	0.1	0.1	2.5	0.7
Closing inventory	0.1	0.1	3.6	1.0
Operating expenses (indirect expenses)	23.8	26.8	235.7	68.9
Labour and commissions	2.8	3.2	128.7	37.6
Amortization and depletion	1.4	1.6	5.3	1.5
Repairs and maintenance	0.3	0.3	1.7	0.5
Utilities and telecommunication	1.8	2.0	5.4	1.6
Rent	0.9	1.0	13.8	4.0
Interest and bank charges	0.3	0.4	1.2	0.4
Professional and business fees	2.2	2.4	29.7	8.7
Advertising and promotion	0.7	0.8	9.1	2.7
Delivery, shipping and warehouse	0.1	0.1	0.3	0.1
Insurance	0.3	0.3	2.9	0.8
Other expenses	13.0	14.6	37.5	11.0
Total Expenses	31.4	35.3	271.4	79.3
Net Income / **Net Profit**	57.5	64.7	**70.6**	**20.7**
Gross Profit Margin (%)		91.5		88.4

This Canadian industry comprises establishments primarily engaged in providing advice and assistance to other organizations on human resources management issues, such as human resource and personnel policies, practices and procedures; employee benefits planning, communication, and administration; compensation systems planning; wage and salary administration; and executive search and recruitment.

Hunting and Fishing Camps NAICS 721212 (1,285 Reporting)				
	Unincorporated		Incorporated	
No. of Businesses Reporting	298 (23.2%)		987 (76.8%)	
REVENUES AND EXPENSES	$000's	%	$000's	%
Total Revenue	104.3	100.0	341.6	100.0
Sales of goods & services	0.0	0.0	322.6	94.4
All other revenues	0.0	0.0	19.0	5.6
Cost of Sales (direct expenses)	19.1	18.3	66.7	19.5
Wages and benefits	1.2	1.1	9.3	2.7
Purchases, materials & sub-contracts	17.9	17.1	58.1	17.0
Opening inventory	1.4	1.4	10.5	3.1
Closing inventory	1.4	1.3	11.2	3.3
Operating expenses (indirect expenses)	77.5	74.3	275.4	80.6
Labour and commissions	6.2	5.9	74.7	21.9
Amortization and depletion	10.7	10.2	32.2	9.4
Repairs and maintenance	8.3	8.0	17.5	5.1
Utilities and telecommunication	10.4	10.0	19.4	5.7
Rent	1.4	1.3	10.8	3.2
Interest and bank charges	5.4	5.2	8.4	2.5
Professional and business fees	1.8	1.7	11.3	3.3
Advertising and promotion	2.8	2.7	10.7	3.1
Delivery, shipping and warehouse	0.1	0.1	6.0	1.8
Insurance	4.5	4.4	10.6	3.1
Other expenses	25.9	24.8	73.7	21.6
Total Expenses	96.6	92.6	342.1	100.2
Net Income / **Net Profit**	7.7	7.4	**0.5**	**0.2**
Gross Profit Margin (%)		81.7		79.3

This Canadian industry comprises establishments primarily engaged in operating hunting and fishing camps. These establishments provide a range of services, such as access to outpost camps or housekeeping cabins, meals and guides, and they may also provide transportation to the facility, and sale of food, beverages, and hunting and fishing supplies.

Interior Design Services
NAICS 541410
(3,371 Reporting)

	Unincorporated		Incorporated	
No. of Businesses Reporting	1,449 (43.0%)		1,922 (57.0%)	
REVENUES AND EXPENSES	$000's	%	$000's	%
Total Revenue	97.3	100.0	390.8	100.0
Sales of goods & services	0.0	0.0	381.8	97.7
All other revenues	0.0	0.0	9.0	2.3
Cost of Sales (direct expenses)	40.4	41.5	165.2	42.3
Wages and benefits	0.5	0.5	20.8	5.3
Purchases, materials & sub-contracts	39.9	41.0	147.4	37.7
Opening inventory	0.8	0.8	13.9	3.6
Closing inventory	0.8	0.8	16.8	4.3
Operating expenses (indirect expenses)	24.6	25.2	180.0	46.1
Labour and commissions	1.8	1.9	87.8	22.5
Amortization and depletion	1.8	1.8	6.1	1.6
Repairs and maintenance	0.4	0.4	2.0	0.5
Utilities and telecommunication	1.8	1.9	5.1	1.3
Rent	1.3	1.4	15.5	4.0
Interest and bank charges	0.6	0.6	1.1	0.3
Professional and business fees	1.2	1.3	13.4	3.4
Advertising and promotion	1.2	1.3	7.5	1.9
Delivery, shipping and warehouse	0.2	0.2	0.8	0.2
Insurance	0.4	0.4	3.1	0.8
Other expenses	13.8	14.1	37.4	9.6
Total Expenses	64.9	66.8	345.3	88.3
Net Income / **Net Profit**	32.3	33.2	**45.5**	**11.7**
Gross Profit Margin (%)		58.5		56.7

This Canadian industry comprises establishments primarily engaged in planning, designing and administering projects in interior spaces to meet the physical and aesthetic needs of people, taking into consideration building codes, health and safety regulations, traffic patterns and floor planning, mechanical and electrical needs, and interior fittings and furniture. Interior designers and interior design consultants work in areas such as hospitality design, health care design, institutional design, commercial and corporate design and residential design. This Canadian industry also includes interior decorating consultants engaged exclusively in providing aesthetic services associated with interior spaces.

Internet Publishing and Broadcasting, and Web Search Portals
NAICS 519130
(1,196 Reporting)

	Unincorporated		Incorporated	
No. of Businesses Reporting	639 (53.4%)		557 (46.6%)	
REVENUES AND EXPENSES	$000's	%	$000's	%
Total Revenue	78.2	100.0	586.6	100.0
Sales of goods & services	0.0	0.0	549.8	93.7
All other revenues	0.0	0.0	36.8	6.3
Cost of Sales (direct expenses)	11.3	14.4	138.2	23.6
Wages and benefits	0.6	0.8	25.3	4.3
Purchases, materials & sub-contracts	10.7	13.6	112.9	19.2
Opening inventory	0.1	0.2	11.8	2.0
Closing inventory	0.2	0.2	11.7	2.0
Operating expenses (indirect expenses)	20.1	25.7	466.7	79.6
Labour and commissions	1.4	1.8	204.6	34.9
Amortization and depletion	1.4	1.8	25.1	4.3
Repairs and maintenance	0.2	0.2	1.3	0.2
Utilities and telecommunication	1.6	2.0	14.2	2.4
Rent	0.9	1.1	21.7	3.7
Interest and bank charges	0.6	0.8	13.3	2.3
Professional and business fees	1.2	1.6	45.4	7.7
Advertising and promotion	1.1	1.5	29.8	5.1
Delivery, shipping and warehouse	0.1	0.2	1.9	0.3
Insurance	0.1	0.1	2.3	0.4
Other expenses	11.4	14.6	107.1	18.3
Total Expenses	31.4	40.1	605.0	103.1
Net Income (Loss) / **Net Profit (Loss)**	46.8	59.9	**18.4**	**3.1**
Gross Profit Margin (%)		85.6		74.9

This Canadian industry comprises establishments exclusively engaged in publishing and/or broadcasting content on the Internet or operating web sites, known as web search portals, that use a search engine to generate and maintain extensive databases of Internet addresses and content in an easily searchable format. The Internet publishing and broadcasting establishments in this industry provide textual, audio, and/or video content of general or specific interest. These establishments do not provide traditional (non-Internet) versions of the content that they publish or broadcast. Establishments known as web search portals often provide additional Internet services, such as e-mail, connections to other web sites, auctions, news, and other limited content, and serve as a home base for Internet users.

Janitorial Services (Except Window Cleaning)
NAICS 561722
(27,469 Reporting)

	Unincorporated		Incorporated	
No. of Businesses Reporting	21,372 (77.8%)		6,097 (22.2%)	
REVENUES AND EXPENSES	$000's	%	$000's	%
Total Revenue	96.6	100.0	433.2	100.0
Sales of goods & services	0.0	0.0	413.9	95.5
All other revenues	0.0	0.0	19.4	4.5
Cost of Sales (direct expenses)	29.2	30.2	154.7	35.7
Wages and benefits	3.9	4.0	63.7	14.7
Purchases, materials & sub-contracts	25.3	26.2	92.1	21.3
Opening inventory	1.2	1.3	5.4	1.2
Closing inventory	1.2	1.2	6.5	1.5
Operating expenses (indirect expenses)	35.8	37.0	218.2	50.4
Labour and commissions	8.6	8.9	122.0	28.2
Amortization and depletion	2.5	2.6	8.9	2.1
Repairs and maintenance	0.7	0.7	7.1	1.6
Utilities and telecommunication	2.2	2.3	7.7	1.8
Rent	1.7	1.7	8.7	2.0
Interest and bank charges	0.7	0.8	1.9	0.4
Professional and business fees	1.4	1.4	9.8	2.3
Advertising and promotion	0.8	0.8	5.7	1.3
Delivery, shipping and warehouse	0.1	0.2	0.3	0.1
Insurance	0.8	0.8	5.1	1.2
Other expenses	16.2	16.8	41.0	9.5
Total Expenses	65.0	67.3	372.9	86.1
Net Income / **Net Profit**	31.6	32.7	**60.4**	**13.9**
Gross Profit Margin (%)		69.8		62.6

This Canadian industry comprises establishments primarily engaged in cleaning building interiors, and/or transportation equipment (aircraft, ships, rail cars) interiors.

Jewelry Stores NAICS 448310 (4,168 Reporting)				
	Unincorporated		Incorporated	
No. of Businesses Reporting	2,154 (51.7%)		2,014 (48.3%)	
REVENUES AND EXPENSES	$000's	%	$000's	%
Total Revenue	118.3	100.0	583.0	100.0
Sales of goods & services	0.0	0.0	573.1	98.3
All other revenues	0.0	0.0	9.9	1.7
Cost of Sales (direct expenses)	53.0	44.8	312.0	53.5
Wages and benefits	1.0	0.8	7.0	1.2
Purchases, materials & sub-contracts	52.5	44.4	325.4	55.8
Opening inventory	34.8	29.4	282.3	48.4
Closing inventory	35.3	29.9	302.7	51.9
Operating expenses (indirect expenses)	40.6	34.4	236.9	40.6
Labour and commissions	7.1	6.0	109.6	18.8
Amortization and depletion	1.6	1.4	8.0	1.4
Repairs and maintenance	0.8	0.7	3.6	0.6
Utilities and telecommunication	2.6	2.2	6.6	1.1
Rent	9.0	7.6	44.7	7.7
Interest and bank charges	1.8	1.5	3.9	0.7
Professional and business fees	1.5	1.3	8.3	1.4
Advertising and promotion	2.1	1.8	16.2	2.8
Delivery, shipping and warehouse	0.7	0.6	1.3	0.2
Insurance	1.0	0.9	5.3	0.9
Other expenses	12.5	10.5	29.3	5.0
Total Expenses	93.6	79.1	548.8	94.1
Net Income / **Net Profit**	24.7	20.9	**34.2**	**5.9**
Gross Profit Margin (%)		55.1		45.6

This Canadian industry comprises establishments primarily engaged in retailing jewelry, sterling and plated silverware, and watches and clocks. These establishments may provide services such as cutting and mounting stones and jewelry repair.

Landlords of Residential Buildings and Dwellings
NAICS 531111
(163,765 Reporting)

	Unincorporated		Incorporated	
No. of Businesses Reporting	149,591 (91.3%)		14,174 (8.7%)	
REVENUES AND EXPENSES	$000's	%	$000's	%
Total Revenue	113.0	100.0	369.3	100.0
Sales of goods & Services	0.0	0.0	23.1	6.3
All other revenue	0.0	0.0	346.2	93.7
Cost of Sales (direct expenses)	0.0	0.0	17.6	4.8
Wages and benefits	0.0	0.0	1.3	0.3
Purchases, materials & sub-contracts	0.0	0.0	21.4	5.8
Opening inventory	0.0	0.0	20.2	5.5
Closing inventory	0.0	0.0	25.3	6.9
Operating expenses (indirect expenses)	94.6	83.7	315.5	85.4
Labour and commissions	1.8	1.6	44.0	11.9
Amortization and depletion	3.8	3.3	40.0	10.8
Repairs and maintenance	17.0	15.0	42.9	11.6
Utilities and telecommunication	8.4	7.4	28.9	7.8
Rent	0.0	0.0	9.7	2.6
Interest and bank charges	20.4	18.1	45.0	12.2
Professional and business fees	5.6	4.9	20.4	5.5
Advertising and promotion	0.3	0.3	1.8	0.5
Delivery, shipping and warehouse	0.0	0.0	0.1	0.0
Insurance	3.3	2.9	7.4	2.0
Other expenses	34.0	30.1	75.3	20.4
Total Expenses	94.6	83.7	333.1	90.2
Net Income / **Net Profit**	18.4	16.3	**36.3**	**9.8**
Gross Profit Margin (%)		N/A		24.0

This Canadian industry comprises establishments primarily engaged in renting and leasing residential buildings and dwellings, except social housing project. These establishments may operate (lease, administer and maintain) their properties on own account, or they may subcontract the operation to a third party, and they may provide additional services, such as security, maintenance, parking, and snow and trash removal.

Landscape Architectural Services
NAICS 541320
(1,773 Reporting)

	Unincorporated		Incorporated	
No. of Businesses Reporting	1,238 (69.8%)		535 (30.2%)	
REVENUES AND EXPENSES	$000's	%	$000's	%
Total Revenue	113.3	100.0	478.2	100.0
Sales of goods & services	0.0	0.0	464.1	97.1
All other revenues	0.0	0.0	14.1	2.9
Cost of Sales (direct expenses)	34.6	30.6	105.3	22.0
Wages and benefits	5.3	4.7	48.0	10.0
Purchases, materials & sub-contracts	29.3	25.9	60.5	12.7
Opening inventory	0.4	0.4	6.9	1.4
Closing inventory	0.4	0.3	10.2	2.1
Operating expenses (indirect expenses)	49.3	43.5	300.3	62.8
Labour and commissions	10.1	8.9	168.2	35.2
Amortization and depletion	5.3	4.7	10.3	2.2
Repairs and maintenance	1.9	1.7	4.3	0.9
Utilities and telecommunication	3.2	2.8	6.8	1.4
Rent	1.2	1.0	20.2	4.2
Interest and bank charges	1.1	1.0	2.2	0.5
Professional and business fees	1.3	1.1	23.9	5.0
Advertising and promotion	1.1	0.9	7.7	1.6
Delivery, shipping and warehouse	0.1	0.1	0.2	0.0
Insurance	1.6	1.4	6.6	1.4
Other expenses	22.5	19.8	50.0	10.4
Total Expenses	84.0	74.1	405.7	84.8
Net Income / **Net Profit**	29.3	25.9	**72.5**	**15.2**
Gross Profit Margin (%)		69.4		77.3

This Canadian industry comprises establishments primarily engaged in planning, designing and administering the development of land areas for projects such as parks and other recreational areas, airports, highways, hospitals, schools, land subdivisions, and commercial, industrial and residential areas by applying knowledge of land characteristics, location of buildings and structures, use of land areas, and design of landscape projects.

Landscaping Services NAICS 561730 (12,111 Reporting)				
	Unincorporated		Incorporated	
No. of Businesses Reporting	4,329 (35.7%)		7,782 (64.3%)	
REVENUES AND EXPENSES	$000's	%	$000's	%
Total Revenue	112.1	100.0	533.7	100.0
Sales of goods & services	0.0	0.0	525.8	98.5
All other revenues	0.0	0.0	7.9	1.5
Cost of Sales (direct expenses)	33.4	29.8	235.6	44.1
Wages and benefits	6.7	6.0	73.2	13.7
Purchases, materials & sub-contracts	26.7	23.8	163.2	30.6
Opening inventory	0.4	0.3	12.1	2.3
Closing inventory	0.4	0.4	12.8	2.4
Operating expenses (indirect expenses)	53.4	47.6	257.6	48.3
Labour and commissions	10.8	9.7	95.6	17.9
Amortization and depletion	7.4	6.6	26.2	4.9
Repairs and maintenance	2.9	2.6	15.3	2.9
Utilities and telecommunication	3.8	3.4	10.9	2.0
Rent	1.3	1.2	16.8	3.2
Interest and bank charges	1.4	1.2	4.1	0.8
Professional and business fees	1.1	1.0	9.0	1.7
Advertising and promotion	1.1	0.9	7.2	1.4
Delivery, shipping and warehouse	0.1	0.1	0.9	0.2
Insurance	2.0	1.8	10.0	1.9
Other expenses	21.6	19.3	61.5	11.5
Total Expenses	86.8	77.4	493.2	92.4
Net Income / **Net Profit**	25.3	22.6	**40.5**	**7.6**
Gross Profit Margin (%)		70.2		55.2

This Canadian industry comprises establishments primarily engaged in providing landscape care and maintenance services and/or installing trees, shrubs, plants, lawns or gardens, and establishments engaged in these activities.

Lawyers NAICS 541110 (24,140 Reporting)				
	Unincorporated		Incorporated	
No. of Businesses Reporting	16,851 (69.8%)		7,289 (30.2%)	
REVENUES AND EXPENSES	$000's	%	$000's	%
Total Revenue	267.9	100.0	479.2	100.0
Sales of goods & services	0.0	0.0	444.3	92.7
All other revenues	0.0	0.0	35.0	7.3
Cost of Sales (direct expenses)	1.1	0.4	12.3	2.6
Wages and benefits	0.1	0.0	3.1	0.7
Purchases, materials & sub-contracts	1.0	0.4	17.6	3.7
Opening inventory	0.0	0.0	13.1	2.7
Closing inventory	0.0	0.0	21.5	4.5
Operating expenses (indirect expenses)	125.5	46.9	328.7	68.6
Labour and commissions	39.9	14.9	182.9	38.2
Amortization and depletion	2.2	0.8	6.1	1.3
Repairs and maintenance	1.1	0.4	2.5	0.5
Utilities and telecommunication	3.7	1.4	6.2	1.3
Rent	11.1	4.1	26.5	5.5
Interest and bank charges	1.9	0.7	2.7	0.6
Professional and business fees	14.5	5.4	37.7	7.9
Advertising and promotion	3.1	1.2	11.2	2.3
Delivery, shipping and warehouse	0.3	0.1	0.5	0.1
Insurance	3.1	1.1	5.0	1.0
Other expenses	44.6	16.6	47.3	9.9
Total Expenses	126.6	47.3	341.0	71.2
Net Income / **Net Profit**	141.3	52.7	**138.3**	**28.8**
Gross Profit Margin (%)		99.6		97.2

This Canadian industry comprises offices of legal practitioners, known as lawyers, barristers and solicitors, primarily engaged in the practice of law. These establishments may provide expertise in a range of, or specific area of law, such as criminal law, corporate law, real estate law, family and estate law, and intellectual property law.

Logging (Contract)
NAICS 113312
(4,271 Reporting)

	Unincorporated		Incorporated	
No. of Businesses Reporting	1,027 (24.1%)		3,244 (75.9%)	
REVENUES AND EXPENSES	$000's	%	$000's	%
Total Revenue	146.3	100.0	669.5	100.0
Sales of goods & services	0.0	0.0	652.7	97.5
All other revenues	0.0	0.0	16.8	2.5
Cost of Sales (direct expenses)	31.1	21.2	166.6	24.9
Wages and benefits	2.9	2.0	44.0	6.6
Purchases, materials & sub-contracts	28.3	19.4	126.4	18.9
Opening inventory	1.1	0.8	17.2	2.6
Closing inventory	1.3	0.9	21.1	3.1
Operating expenses (indirect expenses)	85.4	58.3	437.5	65.4
Labour and commissions	12.3	8.4	134.5	20.1
Amortization and depletion	10.4	7.1	53.6	8.0
Repairs and maintenance	12.7	8.7	66.3	9.9
Utilities and telecommunication	14.8	10.1	40.6	6.1
Rent	1.7	1.2	14.0	2.1
Interest and bank charges	2.5	1.7	23.3	3.5
Professional and business fees	1.7	1.2	10.2	1.5
Advertising and promotion	0.5	0.3	2.6	0.4
Delivery, shipping and warehouse	0.7	0.5	3.9	0.6
Insurance	3.0	2.0	13.8	2.1
Other expenses	25.2	17.2	74.8	11.2
Total Expenses	116.5	79.6	604.1	90.2
Net Income / **Net Profit**	29.9	20.4	**65.3**	**9.8**
Gross Profit Margin (%)		78.8		74.5

This Canadian industry comprises establishments primarily engaged in cutting timber, producing rough, round, hewn, or riven primary wood, and producing wood chips in the forest, on a fee or contract basis. Establishments primarily engaged in cutting and transporting timber are also included.

Machine Shops NAICS 332710 (3,147 Reporting)				
	Unincorporated		Incorporated	
No. of Businesses Reporting	624 (19.8%)		2,523 (80.2%)	
REVENUES AND EXPENSES	$000's	%	$000's	%
Total Revenue	128.1	100.0	853.0	100.0
Sales of goods & services	0.0	0.0	836.4	98.1
All other revenues	0.0	0.0	16.6	1.9
Cost of Sales (direct expenses)	48.8	38.1	477.5	56.0
Wages and benefits	6.0	4.7	196.4	23.0
Purchases, materials & sub-contracts	42.8	33.4	289.3	33.9
Opening inventory	4.7	3.7	62.8	7.4
Closing inventory	4.6	3.6	71.1	8.3
Operating expenses (indirect expenses)	47.3	36.9	301.9	35.4
Labour and commissions	7.9	6.1	119.0	14.0
Amortization and depletion	6.7	5.2	30.9	3.6
Repairs and maintenance	2.2	1.8	10.5	1.2
Utilities and telecommunication	4.7	3.6	13.7	1.6
Rent	3.7	2.9	28.9	3.4
Interest and bank charges	2.0	1.6	7.0	0.8
Professional and business fees	1.2	0.9	14.8	1.7
Advertising and promotion	0.5	0.4	6.5	0.8
Delivery, shipping and warehouse	0.6	0.5	1.7	0.2
Insurance	1.6	1.3	8.0	0.9
Other expenses	16.2	12.6	61.0	7.1
Total Expenses	96.1	75.0	779.4	91.4
Net Income / **Net Profit**	32.0	25.0	**73.6**	**8.6**
Gross Profit Margin (%)		61.9		42.9

This Canadian industry comprises establishments primarily engaged in operating machine tools, such as lathes (including computer numerically controlled), automatic screw machines, and machines for boring, grinding, milling and otherwise working metal, to produce machine parts and equipment, other than complete machines, for the trade. Machine shops providing custom and repair services are included.

Management Consulting Services (Administrative Management and General Management)
NAICS 541611
(34,364 Reporting)

	Unincorporated		Incorporated	
No. of Businesses Reporting	13,342 (38.8%)		21,022 (61.2%)	
REVENUES AND EXPENSES	$000's	%	$000's	%
Total Revenue	89.1	100.0	268.5	100.0
Sales of goods & services	0.0	0.0	221.4	82.5
All other revenues	0.0	0.0	47.1	17.5
Cost of Sales (direct expenses)	9.0	10.1	27.8	10.3
Wages and benefits	0.3	0.3	5.1	1.9
Purchases, materials & sub-contracts	8.0	9.0	24.6	9.2
Opening inventory	1.2	1.3	5.6	2.1
Closing inventory	0.5	0.6	7.4	2.8
Operating expenses (indirect expenses)	20.6	23.2	155.7	58.0
Labour and commissions	2.4	2.6	75.3	28.1
Amortization and depletion	1.4	1.6	5.4	2.0
Repairs and maintenance	0.2	0.3	1.7	0.6
Utilities and telecommunication	1.5	1.6	3.6	1.3
Rent	1.0	1.1	7.7	2.9
Interest and bank charges	0.4	0.4	2.7	1.0
Professional and business fees	2.2	2.5	21.6	8.1
Advertising and promotion	0.5	0.6	5.4	2.0
Delivery, shipping and warehouse	0.1	0.1	0.5	0.2
Insurance	0.3	0.3	2.4	0.9
Other expenses	10.7	12.0	29.4	11.0
Total Expenses	29.6	33.2	183.5	68.3
Net Income / **Net Profit**	59.5	66.8	**85.0**	**31.7**
Gross Profit Margin (%)		89.9		87.4

This Canadian industry comprises establishments primarily engaged in providing advice and assistance to other organizations on administrative management issues, such as financial planning and budgeting; equity and asset management; records management; office planning; strategic and organizational planning; site selection; new business start-up; and business process improvement. This Canadian industry also includes general management consultants that provide a full range of administrative; human resource; marketing; process, physical distribution and logistics; or other management consulting services to clients.

Meat Markets NAICS 445210 (1,990 Reporting)				
	Unincorporated		Incorporated	
No. of Businesses Reporting	406 (20.4%)		1,584 (79.6%)	
REVENUES AND EXPENSES	$000's	%	$000's	%
Total Revenue	272.2	100.0	957.6	100.0
Sales of goods & services	0.0	0.0	948.4	99.0
All other revenues	0.0	0.0	9.2	1.0
Cost of Sales (direct expenses)	189.4	69.6	675.6	70.6
Wages and benefits	6.3	2.3	27.9	2.9
Purchases, materials & sub-contracts	182.5	67.1	647.8	67.6
Opening inventory	8.5	3.1	35.7	3.7
Closing inventory	8.0	2.9	35.8	3.7
Operating expenses (indirect expenses)	65.8	24.2	266.1	27.8
Labour and commissions	17.5	6.4	120.5	12.6
Amortization and depletion	4.6	1.7	14.9	1.6
Repairs and maintenance	3.8	1.4	10.0	1.0
Utilities and telecommunication	7.1	2.6	16.6	1.7
Rent	9.6	3.5	30.5	3.2
Interest and bank charges	3.3	1.2	4.1	0.4
Professional and business fees	1.7	0.6	7.4	0.8
Advertising and promotion	1.7	0.6	18.1	1.9
Delivery, shipping and warehouse	0.3	0.1	1.1	0.1
Insurance	1.7	0.6	4.0	0.4
Other expenses	14.4	5.3	39.0	4.1
Total Expenses	255.1	93.7	941.7	98.3
Net Income / **Net Profit**	17.1	6.3	**15.9**	**1.7**
Gross Profit Margin (%)		30.4		28.8

This Canadian industry comprises establishments primarily engaged in retailing fresh, frozen, or cured meats and poultry. Delicatessens primarily engaged in retailing fresh meat are included.

Mobile Food Services
NAICS 722330
(1,505 Reporting)

	Unincorporated		Incorporated	
No. of Businesses Reporting	1,358 (90.2%)		147 (9.8%)	
REVENUES AND EXPENSES	$000's	%	$000's	%
Total Revenue	106.9	100.0	279.0	100.0
Sales of goods & services	0.0	0.0	268.9	96.4
All other revenues	0.0	0.0	10.2	3.6
Cost of Sales (direct expenses)	53.9	50.4	130.3	46.7
Wages and benefits	2.2	2.1	15.6	5.6
Purchases, materials & sub-contracts	51.6	48.3	115.6	41.4
Opening inventory	1.3	1.2	4.7	1.7
Closing inventory	1.2	1.2	5.6	2.0
Operating expenses (indirect expenses)	38.8	36.3	129.6	46.5
Labour and commissions	10.8	10.1	55.4	19.9
Amortization and depletion	3.1	2.9	10.2	3.7
Repairs and maintenance	1.5	1.4	7.8	2.8
Utilities and telecommunication	2.7	2.6	7.5	2.7
Rent	3.5	3.2	12.8	4.6
Interest and bank charges	1.1	1.0	1.6	0.6
Professional and business fees	0.9	0.8	5.4	1.9
Advertising and promotion	0.5	0.5	2.9	1.0
Delivery, shipping and warehouse	0.3	0.3	0.3	0.1
Insurance	1.0	1.0	4.8	1.7
Other expenses	13.3	12.4	20.8	7.5
Total Expenses	92.6	86.7	259.9	93.2
Net Income / **Net Profit**	14.3	13.3	**19.1**	**6.8**
Gross Profit Margin (%)		49.6		51.5

This Canadian industry comprises establishments primarily engaged in preparing and serving meals and snacks for immediate consumption from motorized vehicles or non-motorized carts.

Motels NAICS 721114 (2,117 Reporting)				
	Unincorporated		Incorporated	
No. of Businesses Reporting	401 (18.9%)		1716 (81.1%)	
REVENUES AND EXPENSES	$000's	%	$000's	%
Total Revenue	109.1	100.0	440.1	100.0
Sales of goods & services	0.0	0.0	398.8	90.6
All other revenues	0.0	0.0	41.3	9.4
Cost of Sales (direct expenses)	10.9	10.0	75.5	17.1
Wages and benefits	1.4	1.2	11.4	2.6
Purchases, materials & sub-contracts	9.7	8.8	64.3	14.6
Opening inventory	0.6	0.6	6.3	1.4
Closing inventory	0.7	0.7	6.5	1.5
Operating expenses (indirect expenses)	78.7	72.1	329.5	74.9
Labour and commissions	11.0	10.0	108.7	24.7
Amortization and depletion	7.7	7.1	32.0	7.3
Repairs and maintenance	8.7	7.9	25.0	5.7
Utilities and telecommunication	14.5	13.3	37.3	8.5
Rent	0.6	0.5	7.4	1.7
Interest and bank charges	6.7	6.2	22.8	5.2
Professional and business fees	2.1	1.9	14.4	3.3
Advertising and promotion	1.6	1.4	6.9	1.6
Delivery, shipping and warehouse	0.0	0.0	0.6	0.1
Insurance	4.0	3.6	8.1	1.8
Other expenses	21.9	20.1	66.3	15.1
Total Expenses	89.6	82.1	405.0	92.0
Net Income / **Net Profit**	19.5	17.9	**35.1**	**8.0**
Gross Profit Margin (%)		90.0		81.1

This Canadian industry comprises establishments primarily engaged in providing short-term lodging in facilities known as motels. These establishments are designed to accommodate clients travelling by motor vehicle, and provide short-stay suites or guest rooms, within a one or two-storey structure, characterized by exterior access to rooms and ample parking areas adjacent to the room entrances. Limited complementary services and amenities may also be provided.

Motor Vehicle Towing
NAICS 488410
(1,627 Reporting)

	Unincorporated		Incorporated	
No. of Businesses Reporting	526 (32.3%)		1,101 (67.7%)	
REVENUES AND EXPENSES	$000's	%	$000's	%
Total Revenue	101.3	100.0	566.9	100.0
Sales of goods & services	0.0	0.0	557.7	98.4
All other revenues	0.0	0.0	9.2	1.6
Cost of Sales (direct expenses)	12.5	12.3	149.1	26.3
Wages and benefits	1.1	1.1	45.8	8.1
Purchases, materials & sub-contracts	11.9	11.8	104.7	18.5
Opening inventory	0.7	0.6	9.0	1.6
Closing inventory	1.2	1.2	10.4	1.8
Operating expenses (indirect expenses)	68.3	67.5	368.2	65.0
Labour and commissions	5.9	5.9	131.3	23.2
Amortization and depletion	6.2	6.1	32.3	5.7
Repairs and maintenance	3.9	3.9	30.3	5.3
Utilities and telecommunication	8.9	8.8	29.4	5.2
Rent	2.1	2.1	23.5	4.2
Interest and bank charges	1.6	1.6	7.4	1.3
Professional and business fees	1.3	1.2	9.5	1.7
Advertising and promotion	1.2	1.2	6.9	1.2
Delivery, shipping and warehouse	0.1	0.1	1.4	0.2
Insurance	2.8	2.8	16.1	2.8
Other expenses	34.2	33.7	80.2	14.1
Total Expenses	80.8	79.8	517.3	91.3
Net Income / **Net Profit**	20.5	20.2	**49.6**	**8.7**
Gross Profit Margin (%)		87.7		73.3

This Canadian industry comprises establishments primarily engaged in towing motor vehicles. Establishments engaged in providing light and heavy towing services, both local and long distance, to the general public, commercial, transportation and other sectors, are included. These establishments may offer incidental services, such as tire repair, battery boosting and other emergency road services.

Motorcycle, Boat and Other Motor Vehicle Dealers
NAICS 441220
(1,604 Reporting)

	Unincorporated		Incorporated	
No. of Businesses Reporting	175 (10.9%)		1,429 (89.1%)	
REVENUES AND EXPENSES	$000's	%	$000's	%
Total Revenue	195.6	100.0	1321.1	100.0
Sales of goods & services	0.0	0.0	1300.4	98.4
All other revenues	0.0	0.0	20.8	1.6
Cost of Sales (direct expenses)	143.7	73.5	993.3	75.2
Wages and benefits	0.3	0.1	28.5	2.2
Purchases, materials & sub-contracts	143.2	73.2	973.6	73.7
Opening inventory	36.9	18.9	544.1	41.2
Closing inventory	36.7	18.8	552.9	41.9
Operating expenses (indirect expenses)	39.9	20.4	307.6	23.3
Labour and commissions	4.2	2.1	135.1	10.2
Amortization and depletion	2.6	1.3	17.7	1.3
Repairs and maintenance	1.5	0.8	10.3	0.8
Utilities and telecommunication	3.6	1.9	13.2	1.0
Rent	4.0	2.0	22.5	1.7
Interest and bank charges	3.0	1.5	13.0	1.0
Professional and business fees	1.7	0.9	10.7	0.8
Advertising and promotion	1.6	0.8	17.8	1.3
Delivery, shipping and warehouse	1.0	0.5	1.6	0.1
Insurance	1.9	1.0	11.1	0.8
Other expenses	14.9	7.6	54.7	4.1
Total Expenses	183.6	93.8	1300.9	98.5
Net Income / **Net Profit**	12.0	6.2	**20.2**	**1.5**
Gross Profit Margin (%)		26.5		23.6

This Canadian industry comprises establishments primarily engaged in retailing new and used motorcycles, watercraft and other vehicles, such as snowmobiles, off-road all-terrain vehicles, utility trailers, and aircraft. These establishments also typically retail replacement parts and accessories, and provide repair services.

Nursery Stores and Garden Centres
NAICS 444220
(2,021 Reporting)

	Unincorporated		Incorporated	
No. of Businesses Reporting	1,161 (57.5%)		860 (42.5%)	
REVENUES AND EXPENSES	$000's	%	$000's	%
Total Revenue	148.7	100.0	894.9	100.0
Sales of goods & services	0.0	0.0	877.0	98.0
All other revenues	0.0	0.0	17.9	2.0
Cost of Sales (direct expenses)	65.3	44.0	502.1	56.1
Wages and benefits	8.9	6.0	36.9	4.1
Purchases, materials & sub-contracts	56.0	37.7	469.8	52.5
Opening inventory	8.0	5.4	137.7	15.4
Closing inventory	7.5	5.1	142.2	15.9
Operating expenses (indirect expenses)	61.9	41.6	377.2	42.1
Labour and commissions	16.5	11.1	149.1	16.7
Amortization and depletion	6.1	4.1	24.1	2.7
Repairs and maintenance	3.2	2.1	15.3	1.7
Utilities and telecommunication	4.6	3.1	18.5	2.1
Rent	3.2	2.1	26.9	3.0
Interest and bank charges	2.4	1.6	9.1	1.0
Professional and business fees	1.5	1.0	12.0	1.3
Advertising and promotion	2.0	1.4	16.4	1.8
Delivery, shipping and warehouse	0.5	0.4	2.4	0.3
Insurance	2.1	1.4	8.2	0.9
Other expenses	19.9	13.4	95.1	10.6
Total Expenses	127.2	85.6	879.3	98.3
Net Income / **Net Profit**	21.4	14.4	**15.6**	**1.7**
Gross Profit Margin (%)		56.0		42.7

This Canadian industry comprises establishments primarily engaged in retailing nursery and garden products, such as trees, shrubs, plants, seeds, bulbs and sod that are predominantly grown elsewhere. These establishments may provide landscaping services.

Optometrists NAICS 621320 (2,201 Reporting)				
	Unincorporated		Incorporated	
No. of Businesses Reporting	885 (40.2%)		1,316 (59.8%)	
REVENUES AND EXPENSES	$000's	%	$000's	%
Total Revenue	173.6	100.0	654.3	100.0
Sales of goods & services	0.0	0.0	632.0	96.6
All other revenues	0.0	0.0	22.3	3.4
Cost of Sales (direct expenses)	10.7	6.1	182.3	27.9
Wages and benefits	0.2	0.1	9.8	1.5
Purchases, materials & sub-contracts	10.6	6.1	177.6	27.1
Opening inventory	2.2	1.3	45.0	6.9
Closing inventory	2.3	1.3	50.2	7.7
Operating expenses (indirect expenses)	74.9	43.1	350.3	53.5
Labour and commissions	19.7	11.4	181.9	27.8
Amortization and depletion	2.7	1.6	19.8	3.0
Repairs and maintenance	0.8	0.5	5.1	0.8
Utilities and telecommunication	1.8	1.0	7.2	1.1
Rent	6.1	3.5	35.3	5.4
Interest and bank charges	1.5	0.9	3.6	0.5
Professional and business fees	4.2	2.4	26.4	4.0
Advertising and promotion	1.0	0.6	10.6	1.6
Delivery, shipping and warehouse	0.1	0.1	0.6	0.1
Insurance	1.2	0.7	4.8	0.7
Other expenses	35.7	20.6	55.2	8.4
Total Expenses	85.6	49.3	532.6	81.4
Net Income / **Net Profit**	88.1	50.7	**121.7**	**18.6**
Gross Profit Margin (%)		93.9		71.2

This Canadian industry comprises establishments primarily engaged in the private or group practice of optometry. These practitioners provide eye examinations to determine visual acuity or the presence of vision problems and to prescribe eyeglasses, contact lenses and eye exercises. They may also perform those services provided by an optician, such as selling and fitting prescription eyeglasses and contact lenses.

Paint and Wallpaper Stores
NAICS 444120
(1,449 Reporting)

	Unincorporated		Incorporated	
No. of Businesses Reporting	914 (63.1%)		535 (36.9%)	
REVENUES AND EXPENSES	$000's	%	$000's	%
Total Revenue	103.0	100.0	779.6	100.0
Sales of goods & services	0.0	0.0	767.6	98.5
All other revenues	0.0	0.0	12.0	1.5
Cost of Sales (direct expenses)	43.7	42.4	484.9	62.2
Wages and benefits	2.3	2.2	21.2	2.7
Purchases, materials & sub-contracts	41.2	40.0	464.9	59.6
Opening inventory	4.0	3.9	115.1	14.8
Closing inventory	3.9	3.8	116.3	14.9
Operating expenses (indirect expenses)	31.7	30.7	273.5	35.1
Labour and commissions	5.4	5.2	135.1	17.3
Amortization and depletion	2.4	2.4	10.5	1.3
Repairs and maintenance	0.5	0.5	6.7	0.9
Utilities and telecommunication	2.2	2.1	11.0	1.4
Rent	1.6	1.5	35.1	4.5
Interest and bank charges	1.0	0.9	4.3	0.6
Professional and business fees	1.3	1.3	8.4	1.1
Advertising and promotion	0.8	0.8	15.4	2.0
Delivery, shipping and warehouse	0.2	0.2	1.2	0.2
Insurance	0.7	0.7	4.6	0.6
Other expenses	15.6	15.2	41.1	5.3
Total Expenses	75.3	73.1	758.3	97.3
Net Income / **Net Profit**	27.7	26.9	**21.2**	**2.7**
Gross Profit Margin (%)		57.6		36.8

This Canadian industry comprises establishments primarily engaged in retailing paint, wall-paper and related supplies.

Painting and Wall Covering Contractors
NAICS 238320
(12,840 Reporting)

	Unincorporated		Incorporated	
No. of Businesses Reporting	8,643 (67.3%)		4,197 (32.7%)	
REVENUES AND EXPENSES	$000's	%	$000's	%
Total Revenue	90.7	100.0	440.3	100.0
Sales of goods & services	0.0	0.0	436.1	99.0
All other revenues	0.0	0.0	4.2	1.0
Cost of Sales (direct expenses)	31.8	35.0	232.4	52.8
Wages and benefits	4.5	4.9	86.4	19.6
Purchases, materials & sub-contracts	27.3	30.1	146.9	33.4
Opening inventory	0.5	0.5	9.4	2.1
Closing inventory	0.5	0.5	10.3	2.3
Operating expenses (indirect expenses)	28.9	31.8	160.0	36.3
Labour and commissions	5.7	6.3	76.0	17.3
Amortization and depletion	2.1	2.4	7.9	1.8
Repairs and maintenance	0.3	0.3	3.3	0.8
Utilities and telecommunication	1.7	1.8	6.2	1.4
Rent	0.6	0.7	9.0	2.0
Interest and bank charges	0.5	0.6	1.6	0.4
Professional and business fees	1.0	1.1	7.6	1.7
Advertising and promotion	0.7	0.8	5.6	1.3
Delivery, shipping and warehouse	0.0	0.1	0.3	0.1
Insurance	0.7	0.7	4.8	1.1
Other expenses	15.5	17.1	37.6	8.5
Total Expenses	60.7	66.9	392.4	89.1
Net Income / **Net Profit**	30.0	33.1	**48.0**	**10.9**
Gross Profit Margin (%)		65.0		46.7

This Canadian industry comprises establishments primarily engaged in painting, paperhanging and decorating in buildings and painting heavy (engineering) structures. Paint or paper stripping, including sandblasting when it is an incidental part of surface preparation by paint and wall covering contractors, is included in this industry. The work performed may include new work, additions, alterations, maintenance, and repairs.

Pet and Pet Supplies Stores
NAICS 453910
(1,357 Reporting)

	Unincorporated		Incorporated	
No. of Businesses Reporting	364 (26.8%)		993 (73.2%)	
REVENUES AND EXPENSES	$000's	%	$000's	%
Total Revenue	181.5	100.0	718.3	100.0
Sales of goods & services	0.0	0.0	710.8	99.0
All other revenues	0.0	0.0	7.5	1.0
Cost of Sales (direct expenses)	107.8	59.4	421.4	58.7
Wages and benefits	2.1	1.1	9.9	1.4
Purchases, materials & sub-contracts	106.3	58.6	416.4	58.0
Opening inventory	23.5	13.0	87.5	12.2
Closing inventory	24.1	13.3	92.5	12.9
Operating expenses (indirect expenses)	61.1	33.7	277.0	38.6
Labour and commissions	16.3	9.0	119.2	16.6
Amortization and depletion	2.3	1.3	10.8	1.5
Repairs and maintenance	1.9	1.0	5.4	0.8
Utilities and telecommunication	4.6	2.5	11.0	1.5
Rent	15.2	8.4	59.3	8.3
Interest and bank charges	3.4	1.9	3.4	0.5
Professional and business fees	1.6	0.9	6.5	0.9
Advertising and promotion	2.9	1.6	13.1	1.8
Delivery, shipping and warehouse	0.5	0.3	1.0	0.1
Insurance	1.3	0.7	3.2	0.4
Other expenses	11.1	6.1	44.2	6.1
Total Expenses	168.9	93.1	698.4	97.2
Net Income / **Net Profit**	12.6	6.9	**20.0**	**2.8**
Gross Profit Margin (%)		40.6		40.7

This Canadian industry comprises establishments primarily engaged in retailing pets, pet food and pet supplies. These establishments may also provide pet grooming services.

Pet Care (Except Veterinary) Services
NAICS 812910
(1,556 Reporting)

	Unincorporated		Incorporated	
No. of Businesses Reporting	900 (57.8%)		656 (42.2%)	
REVENUES AND EXPENSES	$000's	%	$000's	%
Total Revenue	74.6	100.0	244.6	100.0
Sales of goods & services	0.0	0.0	220.0	89.9
All other revenues	0.0	0.0	24.6	10.1
Cost of Sales (direct expenses)	11.5	15.4	42.1	17.2
Wages and benefits	1.6	2.1	12.2	5.0
Purchases, materials & sub-contracts	9.9	13.3	29.9	12.2
Opening inventory	1.3	1.7	7.9	3.2
Closing inventory	1.2	1.7	7.9	3.2
Operating expenses (indirect expenses)	40.6	54.4	180.5	73.8
Labour and commissions	9.4	12.6	81.2	33.2
Amortization and depletion	2.7	3.6	8.6	3.5
Repairs and maintenance	1.7	2.2	5.5	2.2
Utilities and telecommunication	3.3	4.4	7.7	3.2
Rent	5.3	7.1	20.1	8.2
Interest and bank charges	1.3	1.8	2.4	1.0
Professional and business fees	1.0	1.3	10.0	4.1
Advertising and promotion	1.9	2.5	6.7	2.7
Delivery, shipping and warehouse	0.1	0.1	0.1	0.0
Insurance	1.0	1.3	2.6	1.1
Other expenses	12.9	17.3	35.6	14.6
Total Expenses	52.1	69.9	222.6	91.0
Net Income / **Net Profit**	22.5	30.1	**22.0**	**9.0**
Gross Profit Margin (%)		84.6		80.9

This Canadian industry comprises establishments primarily engaged in grooming, boarding and training pet animals.

Pharmacies and Drug Stores
NAICS 446110
(5,181 Reporting)

	Unincorporated		Incorporated	
No. of Businesses Reporting	940 (18.1%)		4,241 (81.9%)	
REVENUES AND EXPENSES	$000's	%	$000's	%
Total Revenue	772.9	100.0	1798.7	100.00
Sales of goods & services	0.0	0.0	1743.8	96.90
All other revenues	0.0	0.0	54.9	3.10
Cost of Sales (direct expenses)	428.8	55.5	1135.1	63.10
Wages and benefits	0.1	0.0	10.9	0.60
Purchases, materials & sub-contracts	431.0	55.8	1135.8	63.10
Opening inventory	39.8	5.1	194.6	10.80
Closing inventory	42.1	5.4	206.2	11.50
Operating expenses (indirect expenses)	193.8	25.1	538.9	30.00
Labour and commissions	39.5	5.1	289.6	16.10
Amortization and depletion	5.8	0.8	19.1	1.10
Repairs and maintenance	1.7	0.2	10.2	0.60
Utilities and telecommunication	2.1	0.3	13.0	0.70
Rent	9.0	1.2	59.7	3.30
Interest and bank charges	6.0	0.8	11.7	0.60
Professional and business fees	74.2	9.6	34.4	1.90
Advertising and promotion	2.8	0.4	17.0	0.90
Delivery, shipping and warehouse	0.9	0.1	5.8	0.30
Insurance	1.1	0.1	6.1	0.30
Other expenses	50.7	6.6	72.3	4.00
Total Expenses	622.6	80.6	1674.0	93.10
Net Income / **Net Profit**	150.3	19.4	**124.7**	**6.90**
Gross Profit Margin (%)		44.5		34.9

This Canadian industry comprises establishments, known as pharmacies and drug stores, primarily engaged in retailing prescription or non-prescription drugs and medicines. These establishments also typically retail snacks, cosmetics, personal hygiene products, greeting cards and stationery, and health aids, and may also retail confectionery, tobacco products, novelties and giftware, and cameras and photographic supplies.

Photographic Services
NAICS 541920
(4,893 Reporting)

	Unincorporated		Incorporated	
No. of Businesses Reporting	3,627 (74.1%)		1,266 (25.9%)	
REVENUES AND EXPENSES	$000's	%	$000's	%
Total Revenue	81.7	100.0	266.3	100.0
Sales of goods & services	0.0	0.0	261.3	98.1
All other revenues	0.0	0.0	5.0	1.9
Cost of Sales (direct expenses)	16.8	20.6	81.6	30.6
Wages and benefits	0.7	0.9	16.9	6.3
Purchases, materials & sub-contracts	16.1	19.7	65.0	24.4
Opening inventory	0.9	1.1	7.0	2.6
Closing inventory	0.9	1.1	7.3	2.7
Operating expenses (indirect expenses)	34.8	42.6	161.0	60.5
Labour and commissions	2.8	3.4	65.0	24.4
Amortization and depletion	3.9	4.8	11.0	4.1
Repairs and maintenance	0.7	0.9	3.0	1.1
Utilities and telecommunication	2.2	2.7	5.7	2.1
Rent	3.2	4.0	18.1	6.8
Interest and bank charges	1.0	1.2	1.6	0.6
Professional and business fees	1.1	1.4	10.9	4.1
Advertising and promotion	1.7	2.1	7.5	2.8
Delivery, shipping and warehouse	0.3	0.4	1.1	0.4
Insurance	0.7	0.8	3.3	1.2
Other expenses	17.1	20.9	33.9	12.7
Total Expenses	51.7	63.2	242.6	91.1
Net Income / **Net Profit**	30.1	36.8	**23.7**	**8.9**
Gross Profit Margin (%)		79.4		68.8

This Canadian industry comprises establishments primarily engaged in providing still, video or computer photography services, including the video taping of special events. These establishments may specialize in a particular field of photography, such as aerial photography, commercial and industrial photography, portrait photography and special event photography.

Plumbing, Heating and Air-Conditioning Contractors
NAICS 238220
(19,119 Reporting)

	Unincorporated		Incorporated	
No. of Businesses Reporting	6,862 (35.9%)		12,257 (64.1%)	
REVENUES AND EXPENSES	$000's	%	$000's	%
Total Revenue	135.0	100.0	735.5	100.0
Sales of goods & services	0.0	0.0	726.9	98.8
All other revenues	0.0	0.0	8.6	1.2
Cost of Sales (direct expenses)	57.9	42.9	446.3	60.7
Wages and benefits	4.1	3.1	137.1	18.6
Purchases, materials & sub-contracts	53.6	39.7	313.2	42.6
Opening inventory	2.5	1.8	29.4	4.0
Closing inventory	2.3	1.7	33.5	4.6
Operating expenses (indirect expenses)	44.2	32.7	237.4	32.3
Labour and commissions	9.5	7.0	112.6	15.3
Amortization and depletion	3.7	2.8	13.6	1.9
Repairs and maintenance	0.7	0.5	5.3	0.7
Utilities and telecommunication	2.9	2.1	9.3	1.3
Rent	1.1	0.8	11.0	1.5
Interest and bank charges	1.2	0.9	2.6	0.3
Professional and business fees	1.4	1.0	9.9	1.4
Advertising and promotion	1.2	0.9	9.4	1.3
Delivery, shipping and warehouse	0.2	0.1	0.4	0.0
Insurance	1.6	1.2	8.8	1.2
Other expenses	20.7	15.4	54.4	7.4
Total Expenses	102.0	75.6	683.7	93.0
Net Income / **Net Profit**	32.9	24.4	**51.8**	**7.0**
Gross Profit Margin (%)		57.1		38.6

This Canadian industry comprises establishments primarily engaged in installing or servicing plumbing, heating, and air-conditioning equipment. Contractors in this industry may provide both parts and labour when performing work. The work performed may include new work, additions, alterations, maintenance, and repairs.

Printing NAICS 32311 (4,602 Reporting)				
	Unincorporated		Incorporated	
No. of Businesses Reporting	1,149 (25.0%)		3,453 (75.0%)	
REVENUES AND EXPENSES	$000's	%	$000's	%
Total Revenue	124.4	100.0	705.4	100.0
Sales of goods & services	0.0	0.0	694.8	98.5
All other revenues	0.0	0.0	10.6	1.5
Cost of Sales (direct expenses)	54.4	43.7	388.9	55.1
Wages and benefits	3.4	2.8	104.1	14.8
Purchases, materials & sub-contracts	50.7	40.8	286.2	40.6
Opening inventory	3.2	2.6	36.8	5.2
Closing inventory	3.0	2.4	38.2	5.4
Operating expenses (indirect expenses)	42.2	33.9	291.0	41.3
Labour and commissions	6.3	5.0	124.9	17.7
Amortization and depletion	3.6	2.9	22.5	3.2
Repairs and maintenance	1.4	1.1	8.0	1.1
Utilities and telecommunication	3.1	2.5	11.4	1.6
Rent	5.1	4.1	32.5	4.6
Interest and bank charges	1.8	1.4	6.2	0.9
Professional and business fees	1.3	1.1	12.6	1.8
Advertising and promotion	1.4	1.1	9.4	1.3
Delivery, shipping and warehouse	0.9	0.8	3.8	0.5
Insurance	1.0	0.8	5.2	0.7
Other expenses	16.4	13.2	54.5	7.7
Total Expenses	96.6	77.7	679.9	96.4
Net Income / **Net Profit**	27.8	22.3	**25.5**	**3.6**
Gross Profit Margin (%)		56.3		44.0

This industry comprises establishments primarily engaged in printing. This industry includes commercial screen printing; quick printing; digital printing; manifold business forms printing and other printing.

Property Managers (Real Estate)
NAICS 531310
(14,017 Reporting)

	Unincorporated		Incorporated	
No. of Businesses Reporting	2,816 (20.1%)		11,201 (79.9%)	
REVENUES AND EXPENSES	$000's	%	$000's	%
Total Revenue	110.6	100.0	386.3	100.0
Sales of goods & services	0.0	0.0	212.6	55.0
All other revenues	0.0	0.0	173.7	45.0
Cost of Sales (direct expenses)	17.1	15.4	36.2	9.4
Wages and benefits	0.7	0.6	4.9	1.3
Purchases, materials & sub-contracts	15.4	13.9	49.5	12.8
Opening inventory	2.2	2.0	28.9	7.5
Closing inventory	1.2	1.1	47.1	12.2
Operating expenses (indirect expenses)	41.6	37.6	293.1	75.9
Labour and commissions	3.4	3.0	83.1	21.5
Amortization and depletion	3.0	2.7	30.1	7.8
Repairs and maintenance	2.2	2.0	22.5	5.8
Utilities and telecommunication	2.9	2.6	14.5	3.8
Rent	1.6	1.4	14.3	3.7
Interest and bank charges	2.3	2.1	30.7	8.0
Professional and business fees	4.1	3.7	29.9	7.7
Advertising and promotion	2.9	2.6	4.0	1.0
Delivery, shipping and warehouse	0.1	0.1	0.2	0.0
Insurance	0.8	0.7	5.9	1.5
Other expenses	18.4	16.7	58.0	15.0
Total Expenses	58.7	53.0	329.3	85.3
Net Income / **Net Profit**	52.0	47.0	**57.0**	**14.7**
Gross Profit Margin (%)		84.6		83.0

This Canadian industry comprises establishments primarily engaged in managing real estate properties on behalf of property owners (on a contract or fee basis). These establishments are engaged in administrative and co-ordination activities, such as the negotiation and approval of lease agreements, the collection of rental payments, the administration of contracts for property services (for example, cleaning, maintenance and security) and the preparation of accounting statements.

Real Estate Agents NAICS 531211 (36,670 Reporting)				
	Unincorporated		Incorporated	
No. of Businesses Reporting	34,689 (94.6%)		1,981 (5.4%)	
REVENUES AND EXPENSES	$000's	%	$000's	%
Total Revenue	106.8	100.0	301.5	100.0
Sales of goods & services	0.0	0.0	198.6	65.9
All other revenues	0.0	0.0	102.9	34.1
Cost of Sales (direct expenses)	4.5	4.2	42.0	13.9
Wages and benefits	0.2	0.2	3.4	1.1
Purchases, materials & sub-contracts	4.1	3.8	47.8	15.8
Opening inventory	0.5	0.5	29.3	9.7
Closing inventory	0.3	0.3	38.4	12.7
Operating expenses (indirect expenses)	47.7	44.7	191.7	63.6
Labour and commissions	3.0	2.8	76.8	25.5
Amortization and depletion	2.2	2.1	9.9	3.3
Repairs and maintenance	0.3	0.3	5.5	1.8
Utilities and telecommunication	2.3	2.1	6.2	2.1
Rent	1.2	1.1	9.2	3.0
Interest and bank charges	0.6	0.6	9.0	3.0
Professional and business fees	5.0	4.7	16.8	5.6
Advertising and promotion	7.5	7.0	17.1	5.7
Delivery, shipping and warehouse	0.1	0.1	0.2	0.1
Insurance	0.3	0.3	2.7	0.9
Other expenses	25.3	23.7	38.3	12.7
Total Expenses	52.2	48.9	233.7	77.5
Net Income / **Net Profit**	54.6	51.1	**67.8**	**22.5**
Gross Profit Margin (%)		95.8		78.9

This Canadian industry comprises establishments, known as independent real estate sales persons that are licensed to participate in the activities of buying and selling real estate for others, on a fee or commission basis. These establishments assist vendors by advertising and listing properties and conducting open houses for prospective buyers, assist prospective buyers by selecting, visiting and making purchase offers. They may also rent or lease properties on behalf of clients. Real estate agents are obligated by contract to represent real estate brokers and can be identified by various names such as sales representatives, sales associates and associate brokers. This category also includes brokers that are acting in the capacity of independent real estate sales persons.

Real Estate Appraisers
NAICS 531320
(1,868 Reporting)

	Unincorporated		Incorporated	
No. of Businesses Reporting	813 (43.5%)		1,055 (56.5%)	
REVENUES AND EXPENSES	$000's	%	$000's	%
Total Revenue	89.1	100.0	366.5	100.0
Sales of goods & services	0.0	0.0	345.4	94.2
All other revenues	0.0	0.0	21.1	5.8
Cost of Sales (direct expenses)	4.1	4.6	27.3	7.4
Wages and benefits	0.1	0.2	10.4	2.8
Purchases, materials & sub-contracts	3.8	4.3	20.9	5.7
Opening inventory	0.2	0.2	5.5	1.5
Closing inventory	0.1	0.1	9.6	2.6
Operating expenses (indirect expenses)	35.2	39.5	260.5	71.1
Labour and commissions	5.3	5.9	146.7	40.0
Amortization and depletion	2.7	3.0	7.5	2.0
Repairs and maintenance	0.2	0.3	3.2	0.9
Utilities and telecommunication	2.4	2.7	7.0	1.9
Rent	1.3	1.5	12.8	3.5
Interest and bank charges	0.5	0.6	2.6	0.7
Professional and business fees	1.4	1.6	24.9	6.8
Advertising and promotion	1.3	1.4	6.8	1.8
Delivery, shipping and warehouse	0.1	0.1	0.1	0.0
Insurance	1.6	1.8	6.2	1.7
Other expenses	18.5	20.7	42.7	11.7
Total Expenses	39.3	44.1	287.8	78.5
Net Income / **Net Profit**	49.8	55.9	**78.7**	**21.5**
Gross Profit Margin (%)		95.4		92.1

This Canadian industry comprises establishments primarily engaged in appraising the value of real estate and preparing appraisal reports for creditors, insurance companies, courts, buyers, sellers or auctioneers.

Real Estate Brokers NAICS 531212 (9,742 Reporting)				
	Unincorporated		Incorporated	
No. of Businesses Reporting	2,227 (22.9%)		7,515 (77.1%)	
REVENUES AND EXPENSES	$000's	%	$000's	%
Total Revenue	112.3	100.0	463.5	100.0
Sales of goods & services	0.0	0.0	281.4	60.7
All other revenues	0.0	0.0	182.1	39.3
Cost of Sales (direct expenses)	5.1	4.5	78.0	16.8
Wages and benefits	0.3	0.2	14.1	3.0
Purchases, materials & sub-contracts	4.8	4.2	69.7	15.0
Opening inventory	0.3	0.3	25.0	5.4
Closing inventory	0.3	0.3	30.8	6.7
Operating expenses (indirect expenses)	50.0	44.5	324.4	70.0
Labour and commissions	3.3	3.0	179.0	38.6
Amortization and depletion	2.3	2.0	13.3	2.9
Repairs and maintenance	0.3	0.2	7.4	1.6
Utilities and telecommunication	2.2	2.0	8.1	1.7
Rent	1.4	1.2	16.1	3.5
Interest and bank charges	0.5	0.5	10.8	2.3
Professional and business fees	5.1	4.5	23.0	5.0
Advertising and promotion	7.9	7.0	16.0	3.5
Delivery, shipping and warehouse	0.1	0.1	1.0	0.2
Insurance	0.4	0.4	3.1	0.7
Other expenses	26.5	23.6	46.6	10.1
Total Expenses	55.1	49.0	402.4	86.8
Net Income / **Net Profit**	57.2	51.0	**61.1**	**13.2**
Gross Profit Margin (%)		95.5		72.3

This Canadian industry comprises establishments that are licensed or registered as real estate brokers where the primary activity is renting, buying and selling real estate for others, on a fee or commission basis. Brokers may also assist vendors by advertising and listing properties, conducting open houses for prospective buyers, assist prospective buyers by selecting, visiting and making purchase offers. *Note: This definition sounds very much like that used for realtors as one must be a licensed real estate agent before one can become a broker. A broker typically rents office space and offers services to realtors for a fee, and may also sell properties.*

Restaurants (Full-Service)
NAICS 7221
(27,691 Reporting)

	Unincorporated		Incorporated	
No. of Businesses Reporting	5,075 (18.3%)		22,616 (81.6%)	
REVENUES AND EXPENSES	$000's	%	$000's	%
Total Revenue	198.6	100.0	767.8	100.0
Sales of goods & services	0.0	0.0	754.5	98.3
All other revenues	0.0	0.0	13.3	1.7
Cost of Sales (direct expenses)	90.3	45.5	339.0	44.2
Wages and benefits	11.2	5.6	63.6	8.3
Purchases, materials & sub-contracts	79.1	39.8	275.9	35.9
Opening inventory	3.2	1.6	15.7	2.0
Closing inventory	3.2	1.6	16.2	2.1
Operating expenses (indirect expenses)	94.7	47.7	412.3	53.7
Labour and commissions	37.9	19.1	182.4	23.8
Amortization and depletion	3.9	2.0	20.9	2.7
Repairs and maintenance	4.0	2.0	17.7	2.3
Utilities and telecommunication	9.6	4.8	25.9	3.4
Rent	15.1	7.6	64.1	8.3
Interest and bank charges	3.1	1.5	5.5	0.7
Professional and business fees	2.1	1.1	11.5	1.5
Advertising and promotion	1.7	0.9	18.3	2.4
Delivery, shipping and warehouse	0.2	0.1	1.2	0.2
Insurance	2.1	1.1	5.7	0.7
Other expenses	15.0	7.6	59.1	7.7
Total Expenses	185.1	93.2	751.3	97.9
Net Income / **Net Profit**	13.6	6.8	**16.4**	**2.1**
Gross Profit Margin (%)		54.5		55.1

This Canadian industry comprises establishments primarily engaged in providing food services to patrons who order and are served while seated and pay after eating. These establishments may sell alcoholic beverages, provide take-out services, operate a bar or present live entertainment, in addition to serving food and beverages.

Restaurants (Limited Service Eating Places)
NAICS 722512
(20,699 Reporting)

	Unincorporated		Incorporated	
No. of Businesses Reporting	3,323 (16.1%)		17,376 (83.9%)	
REVENUES AND EXPENSES	$000's	%	$000's	%
Total Revenue	144.2	100.0	648.7	100.0
Sales of goods & services	0.0	0.0	639.0	98.5
All other revenues	0.0	0.0	9.7	1.5
Cost of Sales (direct expenses)	66.0	45.8	289.4	44.6
Wages and benefits	5.7	4.0	53.4	8.2
Purchases, materials & sub-contracts	60.2	41.8	236.4	36.4
Opening inventory	2.5	1.7	9.2	1.4
Closing inventory	2.5	1.7	9.6	1.5
Operating expenses (indirect expenses)	65.3	45.3	335.9	51.8
Labour and commissions	21.7	15.0	135.1	20.8
Amortization and depletion	3.1	2.2	18.1	2.8
Repairs and maintenance	2.3	1.6	11.1	1.7
Utilities and telecommunication	6.0	4.2	17.2	2.6
Rent	13.0	9.0	60.2	9.3
Interest and bank charges	1.9	1.3	3.6	0.6
Professional and business fees	1.7	1.2	9.6	1.5
Advertising and promotion	1.4	1.0	19.3	3.0
Delivery, shipping and warehouse	0.5	0.3	2.5	0.4
Insurance	1.4	1.0	3.6	0.5
Other expenses	12.3	8.5	55.8	8.6
Total Expenses	131.3	91.0	625.3	96.4
Net Income / **Net Profit**	12.9	9.0	**23.4**	**3.6**
Gross Profit Margin (%)		54.2		54.7

This Canadian industry comprises establishments primarily engaged in providing food services to patrons who order or select items at a counter, food bar or cafeteria line (or order by telephone) and pay before eating. Food and drink are picked up for consumption on the premises or for take-out, or delivered to the customer's location. These establishments may offer a variety of food items or they may offer specialty snacks or non-alcoholic beverages.

Roofing Contractors
NAICS 238160
(5,136 Reporting)

REVENUES AND EXPENSES	Unincorporated		Incorporated	
No. of Businesses Reporting	2,253 (43.9%)		2,883 (56.1%)	
REVENUES AND EXPENSES	$000's	%	$000's	%
Total Revenue	154.3	100.0	741.1	100.0
Sales of goods & services	0.0	0.0	734.8	99.2
All other revenues	0.0	0.0	6.3	0.8
Cost of Sales (direct expenses)	72.7	47.1	462.4	62.4
Wages and benefits	8.3	5.3	136.7	18.4
Purchases, materials & sub-contracts	64.3	41.7	327.9	44.2
Opening inventory	0.7	0.5	22.7	3.1
Closing inventory	0.6	0.4	24.8	3.3
Operating expenses (indirect expenses)	50.5	32.7	231.5	31.2
Labour and commissions	13.2	8.6	97.8	13.2
Amortization and depletion	3.5	2.3	13.6	1.8
Repairs and maintenance	0.8	0.5	7.3	1.0
Utilities and telecommunication	2.4	1.5	8.5	1.1
Rent	0.9	0.6	11.6	1.6
Interest and bank charges	0.8	0.5	2.9	0.4
Professional and business fees	1.3	0.8	11.7	1.6
Advertising and promotion	1.5	1.0	10.8	1.5
Delivery, shipping and warehouse	0.2	0.1	0.3	0.0
Insurance	1.5	1.0	11.9	1.6
Other expenses	24.5	15.9	55.2	7.4
Total Expenses	123.1	79.8	694.0	93.6
Net Income / **Net Profit**	31.2	20.2	**47.1**	**6.4**
Gross Profit Margin (%)		52.9		37.1

This Canadian industry comprises establishments primarily engaged in roofing. This industry also includes establishments treating roofs (i.e., spraying, painting, or coating) and installing skylights. The work performed may include new work, additions, alterations, maintenance, and repairs.

RV (Recreational Vehicle) Parks and Campgrounds
NAICS 721211
(1,729 Reporting)

	Unincorporated		Incorporated	
No. of Businesses Reporting	466 (27.0%)		1,263 (73%)	
REVENUES AND EXPENSES	$000's	%	$000's	%
Total Revenue	109.0	100.0	373.3	100.0
Sales of goods & services	0.0	0.0	326.5	87.5
All other revenues	0.0	0.0	46.8	12.5
Cost of Sales (direct expenses)	11.1	10.2	59.3	15.9
Wages and benefits	1.0	0.9	7.5	2.0
Purchases, materials & sub-contracts	10.2	9.3	53.1	14.2
Opening inventory	1.1	1.0	20.8	5.6
Closing inventory	1.2	1.1	22.2	5.9
Operating expenses (indirect expenses)	76.6	70.3	269.2	72.1
Labour and commissions	9.3	8.5	78.0	20.9
Amortization and depletion	9.6	8.8	31.4	8.4
Repairs and maintenance	11.0	10.0	30.9	8.3
Utilities and telecommunication	12.8	11.7	30.7	8.2
Rent	1.5	1.3	7.4	2.0
Interest and bank charges	6.3	5.8	14.0	3.8
Professional and business fees	2.9	2.7	11.2	3.0
Advertising and promotion	2.1	1.9	7.2	1.9
Delivery, shipping and warehouse	0.1	0.1	0.4	0.1
Insurance	3.5	3.2	7.8	2.1
Other expenses	17.7	16.3	50.1	13.4
Total Expenses	87.7	80.5	328.5	88.0
Net Income -- **Net Profit**	21.2	19.5	**44.8**	**12.0**
Gross Profit Margin (%)		89.8		81.8

This Canadian industry comprises establishments primarily engaged in operating serviced or non-serviced sites to accommodate campers and their equipment, including tents, tent trailers, travel trailers and recreational vehicles (RVs). These establishments may provide access to facilities, such as washrooms, laundry rooms, recreation halls and facilities, and stores and snack bars.

Security Systems Services (Except Locksmiths)
NAICS 561621
(1,423 Reporting)

	Unincorporated		Incorporated	
No. of Businesses Reporting	311 (21.9%)		1,112 (78.1%)	
REVENUES AND EXPENSES	$000's	%	$000's	%
Total Revenue	106.5	100.0	607.0	100.0
Sales of goods & services	0.0	0.0	589.4	97.1
All other revenues	0.0	0.0	17.6	2.9
Cost of Sales (direct expenses)	36.1	33.9	272.2	44.8
Wages and benefits	1.6	1.5	62.4	10.3
Purchases, materials & sub-contracts	34.6	32.5	211.3	34.8
Opening inventory	1.1	1.1	27.4	4.5
Closing inventory	1.3	1.2	28.9	4.8
Operating expenses (indirect expenses)	36.6	34.4	293.8	48.4
Labour and commissions	5.1	4.8	148.4	24.4
Amortization and depletion	2.1	1.9	12.8	2.1
Repairs and maintenance	0.5	0.4	4.2	0.7
Utilities and telecommunication	2.7	2.5	13.3	2.2
Rent	1.2	1.1	13.6	2.2
Interest and bank charges	1.1	1.0	3.5	0.6
Professional and business fees	1.4	1.3	20.1	3.3
Advertising and promotion	1.4	1.3	12.5	2.1
Delivery, shipping and warehouse	0.2	0.1	0.7	0.1
Insurance	1.3	1.3	7.2	1.2
Other expenses	19.7	18.5	57.5	9.5
Total Expenses	72.6	68.2	566.0	93.2
Net Income / **Net Profit**	33.8	31.8	**41.1**	**6.8**
Gross Profit Margin (%)		66.1		53.8

This Canadian industry comprises establishments primarily engaged in remote monitoring of electronic security alarm systems, such as burglar and fire alarms; and selling security systems, along with installation, maintenance or monitoring services.

Services for the Elderly and Persons with Disabilities
NAICS 624120
(1,954 Reporting)

	Unincorporated		Incorporated	
No. of Businesses Reporting	956 (48.9%)		998 (51.1%)	
REVENUES AND EXPENSES	$000's	%	$000's	%
Total Revenue	86.0	100.0	712.8	100.0
Sales of goods & services	0.0	0.0	318.5	44.7
All other revenues	0.0	0.0	394.3	55.3
Cost of Sales (direct expenses)	13.8	16.1	59.3	8.3
Wages and benefits	1.5	1.7	42.3	5.9
Purchases, materials & sub-contracts	12.3	14.3	18.0	2.5
Opening inventory	0.7	0.8	2.5	0.3
Closing inventory	0.7	0.8	3.4	0.5
Operating expenses (indirect expenses)	41.8	48.7	626.7	87.9
Labour and commissions	13.8	16.0	389.3	54.6
Amortization and depletion	2.6	3.1	20.9	2.9
Repairs and maintenance	1.3	1.5	8.9	1.3
Utilities and telecommunication	2.5	2.9	9.8	1.4
Rent	1.7	2.0	33.9	4.8
Interest and bank charges	1.3	1.5	12.7	1.8
Professional and business fees	1.0	1.2	20.4	2.9
Advertising and promotion	0.7	0.8	8.3	1.2
Delivery, shipping and warehouse	0.1	0.1	0.5	0.1
Insurance	0.8	1.0	2.7	0.4
Other expenses	16.0	18.6	119.2	16.7
Total Expenses	55.6	64.7	685.9	96.2
Net Income / **Net Profit**	30.3	35.3	**26.9**	**3.8**
Gross Profit Margin (%)		83.9		81.4

This Canadian industry comprises establishments primarily engaged in providing non-residential social assistance services to improve the quality of life for the elderly, the developmentally handicapped or persons with disabilities. These establishments provide for the welfare of these individuals in such areas as day-care, non-medical home care, social activities, group support and companionship. Illustrative example(s): adult day-care centres; home-maker services; senior citizen centres.

Sewing, Needlework and Piece Goods Stores
NAICS 451130
(1,500 Reporting)

	Unincorporated		Incorporated	
No. of Businesses Reporting	1,109 (73.9%)		391 (26.1%)	
REVENUES AND EXPENSES	$000's	%	$000's	%
Total Revenue	99.9	100.0	455.7	100.0
Sales of goods & services	0.0	0.0	446.4	98.0
All other revenues	0.0	0.0	9.3	2.0
Cost of Sales (direct expenses)	43.6	43.7	236.5	51.9
Wages and benefits	1.7	1.7	13.2	2.9
Purchases, materials & sub-contracts	41.3	41.4	220.7	48.4
Opening inventory	21.3	21.3	154.4	33.9
Closing inventory	20.7	20.7	151.7	33.3
Operating expenses (indirect expenses)	38.7	38.8	196.2	43.1
Labour and commissions	8.4	8.4	87.2	19.1
Amortization and depletion	2.0	2.0	7.0	1.5
Repairs and maintenance	1.0	1.0	4.2	0.9
Utilities and telecommunication	2.8	2.8	8.5	1.9
Rent	7.7	7.7	32.4	7.1
Interest and bank charges	2.0	2.0	4.0	0.9
Professional and business fees	1.0	1.0	7.5	1.7
Advertising and promotion	1.7	1.7	9.6	2.1
Delivery, shipping and warehouse	0.7	0.7	1.8	0.4
Insurance	1.0	1.0	4.3	0.9
Other expenses	10.6	10.6	29.7	6.5
Total Expenses	82.4	82.5	432.8	95.0
Net Income / **Net Profit**	17.5	17.5	**22.9**	**5.0**
Gross Profit Margin (%)		56.3		47.0

This Canadian industry comprises establishments primarily engaged in retailing new sewing supplies, fabrics, patterns, yarns and other needlework accessories. These stores may also retail sewing machines.

Siding Contractors NAICS 238170 (3,018 Reporting)				
	Unincorporated		Incorporated	
No. of Businesses Reporting	1,583 (52.5%)		1,435 (47.5%)	
REVENUES AND EXPENSES	$000's	%	$000's	%
Total Revenue	111.1	100.0	616.5	100.0
Sales of goods & services	0.0	0.0	612.5	99.4
All other revenues	0.0	0.0	4.0	0.6
Cost of Sales (direct expenses)	42.9	38.6	382.1	62.0
Wages and benefits	3.7	3.3	87.5	14.2
Purchases, materials & sub-contracts	39.1	35.2	298.0	48.3
Opening inventory	0.8	0.7	22.5	3.7
Closing inventory	0.6	0.5	25.9	4.2
Operating expenses (indirect expenses)	34.3	30.9	188.0	30.5
Labour and commissions	6.2	5.6	86.5	14.0
Amortization and depletion	3.5	3.1	12.4	2.0
Repairs and maintenance	0.4	0.4	4.4	0.7
Utilities and telecommunication	2.1	1.9	6.8	1.1
Rent	0.7	0.7	10.5	1.7
Interest and bank charges	0.7	0.7	2.2	0.3
Professional and business fees	1.0	0.9	8.0	1.3
Advertising and promotion	0.6	0.6	8.3	1.3
Delivery, shipping and warehouse	0.1	0.1	0.3	0.0
Insurance	0.9	0.8	5.8	0.9
Other expenses	18.1	16.3	43.0	7.0
Total Expenses	77.2	69.5	570.2	92.5
Net Income / **Net Profit**	33.9	30.5	**46.3**	**7.5**
Gross Profit Margin (%)		61.4		37.6

This Canadian industry comprises establishments primarily engaged in installing siding of wood, aluminum, vinyl or other exterior finish material (except brick, stone, stucco, or curtain wall). This industry also includes establishments installing eaves troughs, gutters and down-spouts. The work performed may include new work, additions, alterations, maintenance, and repairs.

Sporting Goods Stores
NAICS 45111
(4,051 Reporting)

	Unincorporated		Incorporated	
No. of Businesses Reporting	1,138 (28.1%)		2,913 (71.9%)	
REVENUES AND EXPENSES	$000's	%	$000's	%
Total Revenue	168.8	100.0	879.6	100.0
Sales of goods & services	0.0	0.0	866.7	98.5
All other revenues	0.0	0.0	12.9	1.5
Cost of Sales (direct expenses)	98.1	58.1	552.6	62.8
Wages and benefits	2.3	1.3	10.1	1.2
Purchases, materials & sub-contracts	97.1	57.5	558.0	63.4
Opening inventory	39.7	23.5	262.8	29.9
Closing inventory	41.0	24.3	278.5	31.7
Operating expenses (indirect expenses)	48.5	28.7	302.9	34.4
Labour and commissions	8.7	5.2	143.4	16.3
Amortization and depletion	2.5	1.5	11.3	1.3
Repairs and maintenance	1.1	0.6	5.3	0.6
Utilities and telecommunication	3.3	1.9	10.2	1.2
Rent	6.9	4.1	43.9	5.0
Interest and bank charges	3.1	1.8	6.0	0.7
Professional and business fees	1.7	1.0	10.1	1.1
Advertising and promotion	2.8	1.6	20.3	2.3
Delivery, shipping and warehouse	1.2	0.7	1.8	0.2
Insurance	1.4	0.8	5.5	0.6
Other expenses	16.1	9.5	45.2	5.1
Total Expenses	146.6	86.8	855.5	97.3
Net Income / **Net Profit**	22.2	13.2	**24.1**	**2.7**
Gross Profit Margin (%)		41.9		36.2

This industry comprises establishments primarily engaged in retailing new sporting goods. These establishments may also retail used sporting goods, and provide repair services.

Supermarkets and Other Grocery (Except Convenience) Stores
NAICS 445110
(5,791 Reporting)

	Unincorporated		Incorporated	
No. of Businesses Reporting	1,849 (31.9%)		3,942 (68.1%)	
REVENUES AND EXPENSES	$000's	%	$000's	%
Total Revenue	370.0	100.0	1239.3	100.0
Sales of goods & services	0.0	0.0	1210.9	97.7
All other revenues	0.0	0.0	28.5	2.3
Cost of Sales (direct expenses)	288.6	78.0	933.0	75.3
Wages and benefits	2.0	0.5	15.3	1.2
Purchases, materials & sub-contracts	283.5	76.6	918.9	74.1
Opening inventory	32.6	8.8	90.5	7.3
Closing inventory	29.5	8.0	91.7	7.4
Operating expenses (indirect expenses)	61.8	16.7	286.7	23.1
Labour and commissions	14.6	4.0	134.8	10.9
Amortization and depletion	3.3	0.9	15.0	1.2
Repairs and maintenance	2.3	0.6	12.4	1.0
Utilities and telecommunication	7.3	2.0	21.0	1.7
Rent	12.3	3.3	34.0	2.7
Interest and bank charges	2.7	0.7	7.1	0.6
Professional and business fees	1.7	0.4	7.9	0.6
Advertising and promotion	1.2	0.3	8.6	0.7
Delivery, shipping and warehouse	0.8	0.2	1.4	0.1
Insurance	1.9	0.5	5.1	0.4
Other expenses	13.6	3.7	39.4	3.2
Total Expenses	350.4	94.7	1219.7	98.4
Net Income / **Net Profit**	19.6	5.3	**19.6**	**1.6**
Gross Profit Margin (%)		22.0		22.9

This Canadian industry comprises establishments, known as supermarkets and grocery stores, primarily engaged in retailing a general line of food, such as canned, dry and frozen foods; fresh fruits and vegetables; fresh and prepared meats, fish, poultry, dairy products, baked products and snack foods. These establishments also typically retail a range of non-food household products, such as household paper products, toiletries and non-prescription drugs.

Taxi Service NAICS 485310 (20,295 Reporting)				
	Unincorporated		Incorporated	
No. of Businesses Reporting	19,241 (94.8%)		1,054 (5.2%)	
REVENUES AND EXPENSES	$000's	%	$000's	%
Total Revenue	54.0	100.0	408.7	100.0
Sales of goods & services	0.0	0.0	383.6	93.9
All other revenues	0.0	0.0	25.1	6.1
Cost of Sales (direct expenses)	4.9	9.1	60.5	14.8
Wages and benefits	0.3	0.6	14.9	3.7
Purchases, materials & sub-contracts	4.6	8.5	45.9	11.2
Opening inventory	0.3	0.6	1.9	0.5
Closing inventory	0.3	0.6	2.2	0.5
Operating expenses (indirect expenses)	32.9	60.9	308.8	75.6
Labour and commissions	1.9	3.4	126.3	30.9
Amortization and depletion	1.9	3.4	17.3	4.2
Repairs and maintenance	1.1	2.0	19.3	4.7
Utilities and telecommunication	2.6	4.8	17.5	4.3
Rent	2.9	5.3	20.6	5.0
Interest and bank charges	0.7	1.4	3.9	1.0
Professional and business fees	1.3	2.4	11.6	2.8
Advertising and promotion	0.2	0.3	6.3	1.5
Delivery, shipping and warehouse	0.1	0.1	2.0	0.5
Insurance	1.2	2.2	22.1	5.4
Other expenses	19.2	35.6	62.0	15.2
Total Expenses	37.8	70.1	369.3	90.4
Net Income / **Net Profit**	16.2	29.9	**39.4**	**9.6**
Gross Profit Margin (%)		90.9		84.2

This Canadian industry comprises establishments primarily engaged in providing passenger transportation by taxi (that is, automobiles, except limousines), not operated on regular schedules or routes. Taxicab fleet owners and organizations that provide dispatch services are included, regardless of whether drivers are hired, rent their cabs or are otherwise compensated. Owner-operated taxicabs are included.

Tile and Terrazzo Contractors
NAICS 238340
(3,056 Reporting)

	Unincorporated		Incorporated	
No. of Businesses Reporting	1,866 (61.1%)		1,190 (38.9%)	
REVENUES AND EXPENSES	$000's	%	$000's	%
Total Revenue	95.7	100.0	462.1	100.0
Sales of goods & services	0.0	0.0	456.7	98.8
All other revenues	0.0	0.0	5.4	1.2
Cost of Sales (direct expenses)	31.4	32.8	281.2	60.9
Wages and benefits	2.2	2.3	83.8	18.1
Purchases, materials & sub-contracts	29.5	30.8	200.5	43.4
Opening inventory	1.3	1.4	23.3	5.0
Closing inventory	1.6	1.7	26.4	5.7
Operating expenses (indirect expenses)	30.9	32.3	144.5	31.3
Labour and commissions	4.5	4.7	66.5	14.4
Amortization and depletion	2.6	2.8	8.4	1.8
Repairs and maintenance	0.3	0.3	2.9	0.6
Utilities and telecommunication	2.0	2.0	5.5	1.2
Rent	1.1	1.2	11.2	2.4
Interest and bank charges	0.7	0.7	1.4	0.3
Professional and business fees	1.2	1.2	8.6	1.9
Advertising and promotion	0.4	0.4	5.0	1.1
Delivery, shipping and warehouse	0.1	0.1	0.5	0.1
Insurance	0.6	0.6	4.3	0.9
Other expenses	17.4	18.2	30.3	6.6
Total Expenses	62.3	65.1	425.7	92.1
Net Income / **Net Profit (Loss)**	33.5	34.9	**36.3**	**7.9**
Gross Profit Margin (%)		67.2		38.4

This Canadian industry comprises establishments primarily engaged in setting and installing ceramic tile, stone (interior only), and mosaic and/or mixing marble particles and cement to make terrazzo at the job site. The work performed may include new work, additions, alterations, maintenance, and repairs.

Tire Dealers NAICS 441320 (1,156 Reporting)				
	Unincorporated		Incorporated	
No. of Businesses Reporting	86 (7.4%)		1,070 (92.6%)	
REVENUES AND EXPENSES	$000's	%	$000's	%
Total Revenue	222.4	100.0	1327.4	100.0
Sales of goods & services	0.0	0.0	1313.1	98.9
All other revenues	0.0	0.0	14.3	1.1
Cost of Sales (direct expenses)	145.3	65.3	883.4	66.6
Wages and benefits	4.2	1.9	61.8	4.7
Purchases, materials & sub-contracts	143.2	64.4	831.6	62.6
Opening inventory	16.8	7.6	170.9	12.9
Closing inventory	19.0	8.5	180.9	13.6
Operating expenses (indirect expenses)	59.2	26.6	384.4	29.0
Labour and commissions	9.2	4.1	191.3	14.4
Amortization and depletion	5.0	2.3	20.7	1.6
Repairs and maintenance	1.7	0.8	13.5	1.0
Utilities and telecommunication	4.0	1.8	15.7	1.2
Rent	5.7	2.6	35.5	2.7
Interest and bank charges	3.0	1.3	6.8	0.5
Professional and business fees	1.4	0.6	12.1	0.9
Advertising and promotion	1.5	0.7	15.1	1.1
Delivery, shipping and warehouse	0.4	0.2	0.7	0.1
Insurance	2.3	1.1	10.7	0.8
Other expenses	24.9	11.2	62.5	4.7
Total Expenses	204.4	91.9	1267.9	95.5
Net Income / **Net Profit**	18.00	8.1	**59.6**	**4.5**
Gross Profit Margin (%)		34.7		32.7

This Canadian industry comprises establishments primarily engaged in retailing tires and tubes. These establishments also typically provide complementary services, such as tire mounting and wheel balancing and aligning.

Travel Agencies NAICS 561510 (5,021 Reporting)				
	Unincorporated		Incorporated	
No. of Businesses Reporting	2,498 (49.8%)		2,523 (50.2%)	
REVENUES AND EXPENSES	$000's	%	$000's	%
Total Revenue	119.7	100.0	958.5	100.0
Sales of goods & services	0.0	0.0	905.1	94.4
All other revenues	0.0	0.0	53.4	5.6
Cost of Sales (direct expenses)	43.8	36.5	711.3	74.2
Wages and benefits	0.7	0.6	17.7	1.8
Purchases, materials & sub-contracts	41.8	34.9	692.5	72.2
Opening inventory	2.0	1.7	5.7	0.6
Closing inventory	0.7	0.6	4.5	0.5
Operating expenses (indirect expenses)	33.6	28.0	227.3	23.7
Labour and commissions	4.1	3.5	123.1	12.8
Amortization and depletion	1.7	1.4	5.2	0.5
Repairs and maintenance	0.6	0.5	2.2	0.2
Utilities and telecommunication	2.4	2.0	8.1	0.8
Rent	2.1	1.8	19.3	2.0
Interest and bank charges	0.7	0.5	2.0	0.2
Professional and business fees	1.5	1.2	12.4	1.3
Advertising and promotion	2.3	1.9	14.3	1.5
Delivery, shipping and warehouse	0.2	0.2	0.6	0.1
Insurance	0.5	0.4	2.9	0.3
Other expenses	17.5	14.6	37.2	3.9
Total Expenses	77.3	64.6	938.6	97.9
Net Income / **Net Profit**	42.4	35.4	**20.0**	**2.1**
Gross Profit Margin (%)		63.5		21.4

This Canadian industry comprises establishments primarily engaged in acting as agents for tour operators, transportation companies and accommodation establishments in selling travel, tour and accommodation services to the general public and commercial clients.

Trucking - General Freight NAICS 484110 (21,313 Reporting)				
	Unincorporated		Incorporated	
No. of Businesses Reporting	8,653 (40.6%)		12,660 (59.4%)	
REVENUES AND EXPENSES	$000's	%	$000's	%
Total Revenue	126.1	100.0	353.2	100.0
Sales of goods & services	0.0	0.0	348.3	98.6
All other revenues	0.0	0.0	4.9	1.4
Cost of Sales (direct expenses)	14.9	11.8	78.1	22.1
Wages and benefits	1.9	1.5	14.5	4.1
Purchases, materials & sub-contracts	13.1	10.4	78.0	22.1
Opening inventory	0.3	0.2	4.3	1.2
Closing inventory	0.4	0.3	18.7	5.3
Operating expenses (indirect expenses)	79.6	63.1	230.4	65.2
Labour and commissions	5.9	4.7	63.1	17.9
Amortization and depletion	7.0	5.6	17.9	5.1
Repairs and maintenance	8.4	6.7	25.2	7.1
Utilities and telecommunication	17.5	13.9	35.4	10.0
Rent	1.4	1.1	12.5	3.5
Interest and bank charges	1.6	1.3	2.8	0.8
Professional and business fees	1.4	1.1	6.4	1.8
Advertising and promotion	0.3	0.2	3.5	1.0
Delivery, shipping and warehouse	0.4	0.3	2.2	0.6
Insurance	3.5	2.8	10.2	2.9
Other expenses	32.3	25.6	51.3	14.5
Total Expenses	94.5	74.9	308.6	87.4
Net Income / **Net Profit**	31.6	25.1	**44.6**	**12.6**
Gross Profit Margin (%)		88.2		77.6

This Canadian industry comprises establishments primarily engaged in local general freight trucking. These establishments primarily provide trucking services within a metropolitan area and its hinterland.

Wood Kitchen Cabinet and Counter Top Manufacturing
NAICS 337110
(1,987 Reporting)

	Unincorporated		Incorporated	
No. of Businesses Reporting	779 (39.2%)		1,208 (60.8%)	
REVENUES AND EXPENSES	$000's	%	$000's	%
Total Revenue	132.8	100.0	879.2	100.0
Sales of goods & services	0.0	0.0	863.9	98.3
All other revenues	0.0	0.0	15.3	1.7
Cost of Sales (direct expenses)	66.2	49.9	558.3	63.5
Wages and benefits	6.2	4.7	176.4	20.1
Purchases, materials & sub-contracts	60.0	45.2	386.7	44.0
Opening inventory	4.1	3.1	64.6	7.3
Closing inventory	4.1	3.1	69.4	7.9
Operating expenses (indirect expenses)	41.4	31.2	286.4	32.6
Labour and commissions	8.7	6.5	121.9	13.9
Amortization and depletion	4.4	3.3	23.6	2.7
Repairs and maintenance	1.0	0.8	9.9	1.1
Utilities and telecommunication	3.0	2.3	15.1	1.7
Rent	3.4	2.5	32.5	3.7
Interest and bank charges	1.5	1.1	5.9	0.7
Professional and business fees	1.0	0.7	10.7	1.2
Advertising and promotion	0.8	0.6	8.8	1.0
Delivery, shipping and warehouse	0.3	0.2	1.4	0.2
Insurance	1.4	1.0	7.8	0.9
Other expenses	16.1	12.1	48.9	5.6
Total Expenses	107.7	81.1	844.7	96.1
Net Income / **Net Profit**	25.1	18.9	**34.4**	**3.9**
Gross Profit Margin (%)		50.1		35.4

This Canadian industry comprises establishments primarily engaged in manufacturing wood kitchen cabinets, bathroom vanities, and counters, designed for permanent installation.

Writers & Authors (Independent) NAICS 711513 (3,381 Reporting)				
	Unincorporated		Incorporated	
No. of Businesses Reporting	2,423 (71.7%)		958 (28.3%)	
REVENUES AND EXPENSES	$000's	%	$000's	%
Total Revenue	85.7	100.0	179.9	100.0
Sales of goods & services	0.0	0.0	161.9	90.0
All other revenues	0.0	0.0	18.0	10.0
Cost of Sales (direct expenses)	13.7	16.0	14.4	8.0
Wages and benefits	.4	.5	2.5	1.4
Purchases, materials & sub-contracts	13.3	15.5	18.0	10.0
Opening inventory	1.7	2.0	3.9	2.2
Closing inventory	1.7	2.0	10.0	5.6
Operating expenses (indirect expenses)	29.6	34.5	109.2	60.7
Labour and commissions	2.1	2.5	51.8	28.8
Amortization and depletion	2.1	2.4	4.3	2.4
Repairs and maintenance	.5	.5	1.5	.9
Utilities and telecommunication	2.3	2.7	3.1	1.7
Rent	2.0	2.5	6.4	3.6
Interest and bank charges	.7	.8	.6	.4
Professional and business fees	2.8	3.3	10.4	5.8
Advertising and promotion	1.0	1.1	4.8	2.7
Delivery, shipping and warehouse	.2	.2	.1	.1
Insurance	.4	.4	1.6	.9
Other expenses	15.5	18.1	24.5	13.6
Total Expenses	43.3	5.5	123.5	68.7
Net Income (Loss) / **Net Profit (Loss)**	42.5	49.5	**56.4**	**31.3**
Gross Profit Margin (%)		84.0		91.1

This Canadian industry comprises independent individuals (freelance) primarily engaged in creating artistic and cultural literary works, technical writing or copywriting. Independent print journalists are included. **Illustrative examples:** freelance journalist, newspaper columnists, playwrights, reporters, song writers.

APPENDIX 1

Original Book Financial Projections

Quantity Sold	2,000		5,000		10,000	
	$	%	$	%	$	%
Retail Price $14.95						
Retail Revenue	30,000		75,000		150,000	
Less 50% Discount	15,000		37,500		75,000	
Gross Earnings	15,000		37,500		75,000	
Less Printing Cost	5,000	16.7	8,750	11.7	13,000	8.7
Less Pre-Press	500		500		500	
Less Shipping (To Toronto)	900		1,600		3,000	
GP Before G & A Expenses	8,600	28.7	26,650	35.5	58,500	39.0
Print Cost for 256 Pages	2.50		1.75		1.30	
Retail Price $15.95						
GP Before G & A Expenses	9,550	29.8	29,025	36.3	63,500	39.7
Retail Price $16.95						
GP Before G & A Expenses	10,550	31.0	31,525	37.0	68,500	40.3

APPENDIX 2

Book Start-up Cost Estimates

	Quantity	
	2,000	**5,000**
Print Cost Based on 256 Pages ($2.50 / $1.75)	$5,000	$8,750
Additional Pre-Press	500	500
Bulk Shipping Cost to Toronto	900	1,600
Miscellaneous (software; dotcom; name registration; etc.	500	600
Website Design and One-year Maintenance	800	800
Promotion and Mailings	1,000	2,000
Travel	1,000	2,000
Total Estimated Capital Investment	$9,700	$16,250

APPENDIX 3

Small Business Valuation - Rules of Thumb

Accounting Firms/CPAs (89,188[44])

100-125% of annual revenues
2-3 x SDE[45]
2 x EBIT[46]
2.2 x EBITDA[47]

Arcade, Food & Entertainment Complexes (N/A)

25% of annual sales (includes inventory)
3 x SDE (includes inventory)
3-3.5 x EBITDA

Auto Repair (Auto Service Centers)

30-40% of annual sales plus inventory
1-2.5 x SDE plus inventory ($75,000 to $100,000 SDE)
3 x SDE plus inventory ($150,000 + SDE)
3.25 x SDE
1.5-2 x EBIT
2.5-2.75 x EBITDA

---

[44] Number of businesses reporting. 2013 Business Reference Guide, 23rd Edition, with permission from Thomas L. West, editor.

[45] Seller's discretionary earnings.

[46] Earnings before interest + taxes.

[47] Earnings before interest + taxes + depreciation + amortization.

Beauty Salons, not including barber shops or men's-only hair cutting (1,078,141)

35% of annual revenues plus fixtures, equipment plus inventory
2x SDE plus inventory
2.5 x EBIT

Car Washes – Coin Operated/Self-Service (14,616)

Operations less than five years old generally sell for cost of original real estate, equipment, and improvement cost, plus negotiated figure 2-3 x EBIT
4 x annual gross sales –"A good place to start"

Car Washes – Full Service/Exterior (14,616)

.80-1 x annual sales plus inventory
3.75 to 4.75 x EBITDA

Coffee Shops (50,123)

3.5-4 x monthly sales plus inventory
35-40 % of annual sales plus inventory
2-2.2 x SDE plus inventory

Convenience Stores With Gas (67,921)

20–25% of annual sales plus inventory
2-2.5 x SDE plus inventory. 3.5 x SDE would be for SDE of $300,000+ on a consistent basis
1-2.5 x SDE (with service bays) plus inventory
2.25-3.75 x EBITDA (business only) higher multiples as EBITDA increases
5-6 x SDE includes real estate
5-7 x EBITDA includes real estate

Dental Practices (172,082)

50% of annual sales includes inventory
1.3-1.8 x SDE includes inventory
4 x EBIT
4-5 x EBITDA
50-70% of annual collections subject to how weighted practice is towards
managed care versus private fee for service (cash pay) and condition of
equipment

Dog Kennels (9,000)

1 x annual sales plus inventory
2-3 x SDE plus inventory
2.7 x EBIT

Dry Cleaners (41,454)

70-80% of sales plus inventory. Plants with on-site laundry equipment will get
a higher multiple. Plants with over-the-counter sales of $35,000 will receive
higher multiples
2.5-3 x SDE plus inventory
2-3 x EBIT
2.5-3 x EBITDA
2 x SDE for a poor unit, 2.5 x SDE for a "so-so" business, 3 x SDE for a good
store, 3.5 x SDE for a "hot" unit with a good lease & equipment, 4 x SDE for a
real "winner."

Fitness Centers (33,000)

70-100% of annual sales plus inventory
2 x SDE plus inventory
3 x EBITDA

Funeral Homes/Services (28,556)

200% of annual sales includes inventory and real estate
6 x SDE includes inventory and real estate; 4 x SDE without real estate
Under 75 funerals per year, 3-4.5 x EBITA; 75-150 funerals, 4-5 x EBITDA;
and 150+ funerals, 4.5-6 x EBITDA
6.5 x EBITDA if real estate is included. If real estate is not included, long-term
triple net lease is a must (8-10% of sales); purchase price would be 4 x EBITDA
or approx. 1 x trailing 12 months sales
6 x EBIT includes real estate

Ice Cream/Yogurt Shops (20,000)

60% of annual sales plus inventory
2.2 x SDE plus inventory (franchised only)
3 x EBITDA
15-20 x weekly sales (independent only)

Law Firms (434,500)

90-100% of annual fee revenue; firms specializing in estate work would
approach 100 percent; may require earn out
4 x SDE includes inventory
3.5 x EBIT
3.5 x EBITDA

Liquor Stores/Package Stores -- Beer, Wine & Liquor Stores (43,488)

40-45% of annual sales plus inventory
2-3 x SDE plus inventory
2.5-3.5 x EBITDA
3x EBIT

Motels (40,000)

2.25-3.5 x annual revenues; up to 5 x for resort properties
7-9 x SDE
$20,000 per room
2.5-3 x room revenues
7.5-8 x SDE
8-10 x EBIT
8-10 x EBITDA
10-12% cap rate

Pet Stores (17,247)

25-30% of annual sales plus inventory
2 x SDE plus inventory

Portable Toilet Companies (4,050)

$1,000 per unit
85-90% of annual revenues

Restaurants – Full Service (N/A)

20-30% of annual sales includes inventory
1.8-2.5 x SDE includes inventory
2-3 x EBIT
2.5-3 x EBITDA

Retail Stores – Small Specialty (117,832)

15-20% of annual sales plus inventory
1.8-2.2 x SDE plus inventory

Sporting Goods Stores (41,997)

25% of annual sales plus inventory
4 x EBIT

Elements of an Effective Business Plan For a Small Business Start-up

Product / Service

- Features & Benefits
- Unique Characteristics
- Proprietary Rights
- Barriers to Entry

Market Research

- Define Target Market
- Market Size & Growth Opportunity
- Trend & Demographic Analysis
- Competition Analysis
- Size of Opportunity
- Market Testing

Marketing Plan

- How to Reach Target Market?
- Pricing Strategy
- Sales Channel Definition & Strategy
- Advertising & Promotion Strategy
- E-commerce Strategy

Operating Plan

- Who Is Responsible For Doing What?
- Key Performance Indicators
- Key Success Factors
- Location & Equipment Needs

Financial Plan

- Key Financial Assumptions
- 3 Year Financial Statements
- 1 - 2 Year Cash Flow Statements

Funding Requirements

- How Much Money Do I Need?
- How Will Funds be Used?
- Terms - What Will I Offer In Return?

Support Documentation

- Sample Products/Prototypes
- Menus/Food Samples/Packaging Samples
- Survey Results
- Web Page Designs
- Resume of Each Principal (partner)

APPENDIX 5

Franchisee Interview Questions

1. How long have you owned this franchise?

2. Did it cost more or less than you expected to start this business? By how much?

3. How long did it take to become cash flow positive?

4. After you pay yourself for managing this franchise, about how much profit is left over?

5. On a scale of 1 to 10 (10 being excellent), how would you rate the franchisor on delivering what they promised?

6. How would you rate your entire franchise experience thus far?

7. What has been your biggest challenge so far?

8. Is there anything else you think I should know before I buy into this franchise?

9. With respect to your confidentiality, are there any financial results you are able to share with me?

10. May I visit your location to discuss this further?

Note: You may wish to check out some independent internet sites which support franchisee interests. *Blue Mau Mau* at www.bluemaumau.org is a good one, and if you want to learn which franchises are being complained about the most visit *The Unhappy Franchisee* at www.unhappyfranchisee.com.

APPENDIX 6

Letter of Understanding / Letter of Intent

THIS agreement is entered into today this _____ of _____ in the year _____. The parties understand that this is a non-binding agreement and that the intent of its execution is to facilitate a more formal and legally binding document of purchase and sale for the business assets (or shares) of the business commonly known as _____.

The parties agree as follows:

1. The purchase price is $_____ in total plus inventory to be valued upon closing of this transaction. The inventory will be counted by both parties and valued at cost minus 15% (to allow for unsalable merchandise).

2. A deposit of $_____ is attached, and made out to the Sellers Solicitors Trust account and is refundable in full (without interest) immediately upon demand by the Buyer if a formal agreement cannot be reached.

3. A list of all included and excluded assets of the business are attached and may become part of the formal agreement.

4. This agreement is subject to the following conditions only:

    (a) The Buyer having their legal and/or financial counsel review and approve all documentation as it pertains to this transaction.

(b) The Buyer interviewing the key employees of the Seller's business and approving the outcome of such interviews.

(c) The Buyer being approved as a suitable tenant by the landlord of the business premises.

(d) The Buyer may undertake financial holdbacks from the purchase price for taxation payments or other unforeseen circumstances which may arise.

5. The anticipated closing date for this transaction is _____.

SELLER: **BUYER:**

Name: _____   Name: _____

Address: _____   Address: _____

Signature: _____   Signature: _____

Business Sales Transaction Data for Businesses with Less than $5 mil in Annual Revenue

	Canada		USA	
Time Frame	6/15/1996 – 5/30/2013		1/16/1990 – 6/17/2013	
	Number Reporting	Median	Number Reporting	Median
Net Sales Revenue	184	$526,507	12,824	$425,560
Market Value of Invested Capital (MVIC*)	184	$242,875	12,824	$180,454
EBITDA	171	$58,027	9,861	$49,642
EBIT	184	$52,000	12,604	$43,712
Net Income	178	$40,000	12,156	$40,474
Gross Profit Margin	184	0.56	12,631	0.65
Operating Profit Margin	184	0.09	12,602	0.11
Net Profit Margin	178	0.07	12,154	0.10
MVIC/Net Sales	184	0.46	12,822	0.47
MVIC/Gross Profit	184	0.88	12,622	0.77
MVIC/EBIT	149	4.30	10,460	3.37
MVIC/EBITDA	149	3.75	8,560	3.46
MVIC/Disc Earnings	149	2.36	7,617	2.24
MVIC/Book Value of Invested Capital	116	1.48	2,428	2.10

---

* MVIC – Market Value of Invested Capital = Business Selling Price, *Pratt's Stats*, (A publication of Business Valuation Resources).

Sample FSBBO Valuation Range

	Year 3	Year 2	Year 1	Average
SAMPLE DATA				
Annual Sales	$2,054,823	$1,486,151	$1,709,546	
Income Before Income Taxes	175,078	(68,634)	181,048	
Add Back Amortization	59,427	52,194	42,484	
Earnings Before Interest/Taxes/ Depreciation/Amort. (EBITDA)	**234,505**	**(16,440)**	**223,532**	
Average EBITDA				**$147,199**
Add Back Owner's Salary	85,000	60,000	60,000	
Seller's Discretionary Earnings SDE)	**319,505**	**43,560**	**283,532**	**$215,532**

EBITDA APPROACH

4 x Average EBITDA	**$588,796**

SELLER'S DISCRETIONARY EARNINGS (SDE) APPROACH

3 x Average SDE	**$646,596**

RETURN ON INVESTMENT (ROI) APPROACH

Average EBITDA	147,199
Less est. tax @ 18%	26,495
	$120,704
Value at Anticipated 15% ROI ($120,704 / .15)	**$804,693**

Notice to Reader

We have compiled this Analysis of Estimated Value for ABC Ventures Ltd. as at these dates from information provided by Management. We have not audited, reviewed, or otherwise attempted to verify the accuracy or completeness of such information. Readers are cautioned that these financial statements may not be appropriate for their purposes.

XYZ Chartered Accountants

APPENDIX 9

Sample Confidentiality Agreement

Between
Numbered Company Ltd.
of Somewhere, ON
(hereinafter referred to as the "Company")
– and –

_____

Name (please print)

_____

Name of Corporation (if applicable)

_____

Address

_____

Telephone Number

(hereinafter referred to as the "Undersigned")

WHEREAS THE COMPANY IS interested in selling the whole of its undertaking by way of a sale of its shares, or by way of a sale of its assets, and the undersigned is interested in purchasing same.

AND WHEREAS the undersigned requires certain of the Company's material, including but without limitation, non-public financial and business information and documents of the company (hereinafter referred to as the **"confidential material"**), in order to evaluate the Company's business and market value.

AND WHEREAS the undersigned acknowledges and recognizes the competitive value and confidential nature of the confidential material.

NOW THEREFORE WITNESSETH that in consideration of the company releasing the confidential material to the undersigned for the aforesaid purposes, the undersigned hereby covenants, acknowledges and agrees as follows:

A. That the confidential material to be hereinafter furnished to the undersigned with respect to the business and affairs of the Company, have a competitive value and are very confidential in nature;

B. That the undersigned and its directors, officers, agents, representatives and employees will not disclose or release any of the confidential material, hereafter received or obtained by it, or any information derived therefrom, to any third party, except as required by law, without the prior written consent of the Company; provided however that any such information may be disclosed by the undersigned to its directors, officers, agents, representatives and employees who need to know such information for the purpose of evaluating the subject transaction;

C. That without the prior written consent of the Company, the undersigned will not allow its directors, officers, agents, representatives and employees to disclose to any third party anything whatsoever that a possible purchase and sale of the Company may occur;

D. That promptly on the request of the Company to return the confidential material to the Company, whether delivered to the undersigned by the Company, or whether copies thereof were made by the undersigned; provided however that the return of the confidential material shall in no way relieve the undersigned from any obligation of confidentiality as set out herein;

E. That in the event the transaction contemplated herein is not consummated, then neither the undersigned nor its directors, officers, agents, representatives or employees will use any of the confidential material or information derived there from in furtherance of its business, or the business of anyone else unless such information has become available to the public at large by a means other than as a result of the acts of the undersigned;

F. That without the prior written consent of the Company, the undersigned will not for a period two (2) years from the date hereof, directly or indirectly solicit for employment any person who is employed by the company who is identified by the undersigned as a result of its current investigation of the company;

G. In consideration of the confidential information provided by the Company the undersigned hereby agrees not to compete directly or indirectly with the Company in the Okanagan Valley of BC for a period of not less than two (2) years from the date hereof.

This agreement shall be binding up the successors and assigns, heirs, executors and administrators of the undersigned.

Dated this _____ day of _____, 20 _____.

_____

Signature of Undersigned

Business Sale Preliminary Information Sheet

Lower Mainland, BC
Business Opportunity
(Preliminary Information)

- 2025 Gross Annual Revenue $1.75 mil
- $100,000 EBITDA (Earnings Before Interest, Taxes, Depreciation and Amortization)
- Asking Price $500,000 Plus Inventory of Approx. $100,000 (Asset Sale)
- 20% ROI
- Sports & Leisure Industry
- Most Well Established Operation in the Region (18 Years)
- High Exposure Retail Space Approx. 2000 sq. ft. (Plus Storage)
- Recipient of Numerous National Awards
- Significant Barriers to Entry
- Staff Complement of 6 FT & 2 PT (During Peak Season)
- Main Profit Center Data:
    - 90% Residential / 10% Commercial
    - 40% Large Ticket Construction Jobs / 35% Retail Products / 25% Service
    - 400 Maintenance Contracts

Important Note

Our edge in this market is our long-term positive reputation and convenient central location.

Sample Business Sale Advertisement

VERIFIABLE 20% ROI
(AFTER MANAGEMENT SALARY)

Somewhere, ON

Sports & Leisure Wholesale Industry

Asking $795,000 plus Inventory

Contact Seller Direct For CA

businfo@shaw.ca

Note: If the person inquiring doesn't know the meaning of ROI or CA, you most likely won't want to deal with them.

APPENDIX 12

Canadian National Averages - 2011[49]

	All Businesses		Incorporated Businesses		Unincorporated Businesses	
No. of Businesses Reporting	1,843,457		965,526 (52.4%)		877,931 (47.6%)	
	($000)	%	($000)	%	($000)	%
Total Revenue	370.9	100.0	595.4	100.0	124.0	100.0
Cost of Sales (Direct)	129.9	35.0	225.6	37.9	24.6	19.8
Wages & Benefits	19.8	5.3	36.3	6.1	1.6	1.3
Purchases & Materials	113.2	30.5	195.3	32.8	22.9	18.4
Opening Inventory	25.38	6.8	46.1	7.7	2.5	2.0
Closing Inventory	28.4	7.6	52.1	8.7	2.3	1.9
Gross Profit	241.0	65.0	334.6	56.2	99.4	80.2
Operating Expenses	194.4	52.4	319.8	53.7	56.6	45.5
Labour & Commissions	66.9	18.0	120.4	20.2	8.0	6.4
Amortization	13.2	3.6	22.3	3.8	3.2	2.6
Repairs & Maintenance	8.9	2.4	13.1	2.2	4.2	3.4
Utilities & Telecom	9.4	2.5	13.9	2.3	4.5	3.7
Rent	13.2	3.6	22.5	3.8	3.0	2.4
Interest & Bank Fees	8.0	2.2	11.2	1.9	4.5	3.6
Professional Fees	11.2	3.0	18.4	3.1	3.3	2.7
Advertising & Promotion	5.1	1.4	8.7	1.5	1.2	1.0
Delivery & Shipping	1.0	.3	1.8	.3	.2	.2
Insurance	4.1	1.1	6.5	1.1	1.6	1.3
Other Expenses	53.3	14.4	81.1	13.6	22.8	18.4
Total Expenses	324.3	87.4	545.4	91.6	81.0	65.3
Net Profit/Loss	46.7	12.6	50.0	8.4	43.0	34.7

[49] Industry Canada, Financial Performance Data.

APPENDIX 13

Employee Interview Questions

1. Tell me about yourself outside of work and what you are passionate about?

2. Describe your work experience and skills and how they relate to this job opportunity.

3. What did you like most and worst about your previous jobs?

4. Do you prefer to work independently or on a team?

5. Why do you want to work here?

6. Once trained, we like to set goals, measure and reward performance. How would you function in such an environment?

7. What motivates you?

8. What do you expect from your supervisor?

9. What will you likely be doing five years from now?

10. What turns you "off" most about a job?

11. If your supervisor asked you to do something that you didn't think was right, what would you do?

12. Do you have any questions for me?

13. Please take a few moments and in your own handwriting compose a paragraph or two about any topic you wish.

APPENDIX 14

Performance Evaluation Form

Employee Name: _____ Date:_____

Position: _____

Date of Last Evaluation: _____

<u>Rating Structure</u>

5 = Outstanding Performance is exceptional, consistently exceeding expectations. Employee has made significant contributions to the goals of the company.

4 = Commendable Performance consistently meets and often exceeds position requirements. Employee is recognized as a definite asset to the company.

3 = Satisfactory Employee meets all job requirements in a competent manner. This is the expected minimum performance level for all employees.

2 = Improvement **Required** Employee meets some job requirements and minimally meets others.

1 = Unsatisfactory Employee does not meet position requirements. Immediate and significant improvement is required.

N/A = Not Applicable

1. Knowledge / Skills / Abilities..4
2. Quality Of Work 4

3. Quantity Of Work 3
4. Initiative / Problem Solving / Decision Making 3
5. Dependability / Punctuality / Attendance.........................4.5
6. Communication 3
7. Planning & Organizing..3.5
8. Leadership 2
9. Delegation ....N/A
10. Customer Service / Follow-Up 4
11. Team Player...4
12. Supervisory Skills...3
13. Sales Skills / Results 3.5
14. Time Management / Ability To Prioritize Workload...........3
15. Attitude...4

Goals / Objectives For: 20____

1. _____
2. _____
3. _____

Employee Feedback:

On a scale of 1 to 10 (10 = extremely satisfied), I rate my overall job satisfaction level at _____.

Comments: _____
_____

_____   _____
Employee Signature   Supervisor Signature

Glossary of Financial Terms for Benchmark Reports[50]

Advertising and promotion

Advertising and promotion covers all advertising expenses, such as promotions, signs, window dressings, catalogues, etc.

All other revenues

All other revenue includes revenue from interest, dividends, commissions, rent, and other sources of revenue.

Amortization and depletion

Amortization and depletion includes allocation of the cost of revenue producing assets (which are assumed to be around for more than a year) among the life of the asset. The items that correspond to this amortization and depletion definition are: declaration allowance on capital property amount, capital cost allowance amount.

Closing inventory

Closing inventory includes tangible assets held for sale in the ordinary course of business, or goods in the process of production for such sale, or materials to be consumed in the production of goods and services for sale. It excludes assets held for rental purposes.

---

[50] Industry Canada, Financial Performance Data.

Cost of sales (direct expenses)

Cost of sales (direct expenses) represents direct costs incurred by businesses from the process of selling goods. This item is calculated as wages and benefits + purchases, materials and sub-contracts + opening inventory - closing inventory.

Delivery, shipping and warehouse expenses

Delivery, shipping and warehouse expenses include expenses for delivery, shipping, courier and distribution services used by businesses, except for those in the transportation industry, which are contained in purchases and materials.

Efficiency ratios

Efficiency ratios measure the efficiency with which businesses utilize their assets.

Gross margin

Gross margin is calculated as (Sales of Goods and Services - Costs of sales X 100 / Sales of Goods and Services) . This percentage provides a relative measure of gross profitability or profit margin.

Insurance

Insurance includes all types of insurance such as bonding, car insurance, fire and liability insurance, premium expenses, etc.

Interest and bank charges

Interest and bank charges include all interest expense and discounts paid by the business, such as real estate mortgages, chattel mortgages, mortgage bonds, advances and demand loans, bank interest, etc.

Labour and commissions

Labour and commissions include remuneration paid to the employees of the business not shown in the cost of sales and includes: salaries and wages.

Net profit/loss

Net profit/loss is the profit or loss resulting from normal business operations, recorded before income taxes, extraordinary items and other income not related to normal operations. For unincorporated firms, the owners' or partners' salaries and withdrawals are included.

Opening Inventory

Opening inventory includes tangible assets held for sale in the ordinary course of business, or goods in the process of production for such sale, or materials to be consumed in the production of goods and services for sale. It excludes assets held for rental purposes.

Operating expenses (indirect expenses)

Operating expenses are all expenses incurred in the course of running the business or in the operation of the business. It includes labour and commissions + amortization and depletion + repairs and maintenance + utilities and telephone/ telecommunication + rent + interest and bank charges + professional and business fees + advertising and promotion + delivery, shipping and warehouse expenses + insurance + other indirect expenses.

Other indirect expenses

Other indirect expenses includes all other expenses such as bad debts, laundry and cleaning expenses, some taxes (such as beverage licences, business charges and taxes, interest on taxes, and fines and penalties), etc. This item is calculated as operating expenses;

labour and commissions; amortization and depletion; repairs and maintenance; utilities and telephone/tele-communication; rent; interest and bank charges - professional and business fees; advertising and promotion; delivery, shipping and warehouse expenses; insurance = other indirect expenses.

Professional and business fees

Professional and business fees include all expenditures on external professional advice or services, such as accounting fees, legal fees, management fees and incorporation fees.

Purchases, materials and sub-contracts

Purchases, materials and sub-contracts includes purchases used to produce revenue for product sales, land costs or land purchased for resale and other recorded direct costs including costs incurred by businesses that hire outside firms to perform special trade tasks.

Rent

Rent includes all rental expenditures paid to other companies or agencies for the use of land, offices, building, machinery and equipment, but excludes capital leases.

Repairs and maintenance

Repairs and maintenance includes costs related to new or replacement parts, or the restoration of plant and machinery to keep properties in efficient working condition.

Total expenses

Total expenses include all expenses incurred by firms in order to generate revenues in the normal operation of the business. This item comes directly from tax forms as: total expenses.

Total revenue

Total revenue includes revenue from the sale of goods and services, interest, dividends, commissions, rent and other sources of revenue. It excludes capital gains or losses, extraordinary gains or losses and equity in net income of related parties.

Utilities and telephone/telecommunication

Utilities includes expenses for heat, light, water and telephone / telecommunication expenses for the location in which the business operates, as well as the electricity or fuel used to power its factory or plant.

Wages and benefits

Wages and benefits include wages and benefits paid to employees that are shown in the cost of sales.

ABOUT THE AUTHOR

MANY SMALL BUSINESS AUTHORS talk the talk, but few have walked the walk like Tim Young. With more than twelve business ventures under his belt over the last thirty-five years, Tim has experienced firsthand the highs and lows of being a small business owner in Canada.

Armed with a business degree, Tim set out to climb the corporate ladder only to find his passion was small business. Tim's entrepreneurial spirit and profound desire for independence chronicles a journey worthy of note by all potential and current small business owners who strive to become above-average operators in their chosen field.

Born and educated in Regina, Saskatchewan, Tim and his wife, JoAnn, spent the first part of their business careers on the prairies. They have lived and worked in beautiful Kelowna, British Columbia for the past twenty-three years and counting.

Visit *howmuchmoneycanimake.com* for more information.

CPSIA information can be obtained
at www.ICGtesting.com
Printed in the USA
LVOW04s0435100116

469918LV00018BA/558/P

9 780993 982200